THE RICH GET RICHER
AND THE POOR GET PRISON

EIGHTH EDITION

THE RICH GET RICHER AND THE POOR GET PRISON

Ideology, Class, and Criminal Justice

JEFFREY REIMAN

American University

PEARSON

Boston ■ New York ■ San Francisco

New Mexico ■ Montreal ■ Toronto ■ London ■ Madrid ■ Munich ■ Paris

Hong Kong ■ Singapore ■ Tokyo ■ Cape Town ■ Sydney

Executive Editor: *Dave Repetto*
Editorial Assistant: *Liz DiMenno*
Marketing Manager: *Kelly May*
Production Supervisor: *Karen Mason*
Manufacturing Buyer: *Megan Cochran*
Cover Administrator: *Joel Gendron*
Editorial Production Service and Electronic Composition: *WestWords, Inc.*

For related titles and support materials, visit our online catalog at
www.ablongman.com.

Between the time website information is gathered and then published, some sites
may have closed. Also, the transcription of URLs can result in typographical errors.
The publishers would appreciate being notified of any problems with URLs so that
they may be corrected in subsequent editions.

Library of Congress Cataloging-in-Publication Data

Reiman, Jeffrey H.
    The rich get richer and the poor get prison : ideology, class, and criminal justice /
Jeffrey Reiman. -- 8th ed.
        p. cm.
    Includes bibliographical references and index.
    ISBN 0-205-46172-7
        1. Criminal justice, Administration of--United States. 2. Social classes--United
States. 3. United States--Social policy. I. Title.

HV9950.R46 2007
364.973--dc22   2006045718

Printed in the United States of America

10 9 8 7 6 5 4 3 2   11 10 09 08 07

For Sue

CONTENTS

FIGURES AND TABLES

PREFACE TO THE EIGHTH EDITION

Readers of *The Rich Get Richer* are invited to look at the American criminal justice system as if it were aimed, not at protecting us against crime, but at keeping before our eyes—in our courts and in our prisons, in our newspapers and on our TVs—a large criminal population consisting primarily of poor people. I argue that this occurs because it serves the interests of the rich and powerful by broadcasting the message that the real danger to most Americans comes from below them on the economic ladder, rather than from above. I contend that looking at the criminal justice system this way makes more sense out of criminal justice policy than accepting the idea that the system is really aiming at protecting our lives and limbs. All of this is summed up by saying that *the rich get richer and the poor get prison.*

Supporting the thesis that the criminal justice system is aimed at maintaining a large visible population of poor criminals requires defending two main claims: first, that the system could reduce our high crime rates, but fails to do so; and second, that the system is biased against the poor at every stage. This second claim means that *for the same crimes,* the poor are more likely than the well-off to get arrested and, if arrested, more likely to be charged and, if charged, more likely to be convicted and, if convicted, more likely to be sentenced to prison and, if sentenced to prison, more likely to receive a long sentence. But it means even more: The bias against the poor starts earlier, at the point at which legislators decide what is to be a crime in the first place. Many of the ways in which the well-off harm their fellows (deadly pollution, unsafe working conditions, and the like) are not even defined as crimes, *though they do more damage to life and limb than the acts that are treated as crimes.*

But what of the first claim, namely, that the system could reduce our high crime rates, but fails to do so? In recent years we have seen both an enormous increase in the number of Americans behind bars and significant drops in our crime rates. Surely this is evidence that the system is succeeding in reducing our high crime rates. But this fact does not undermine my claim about the system's failure; rather, it requires that the claim be stated more precisely.

When the first edition of *The Rich Get Richer* was being written, and continuing through the next several editions, crime was rising dramatically and it was easy to see that the system was failing. Now there has been some success in reducing crime. And, while I shall show that only a small fraction of this reduction is due to criminal justice policies, some of it undoubtedly is.

However, this doesn't undermine the thesis of the book because the thesis requires only that the criminal justice system maintain before our eyes a large population of poor criminals, and that is no less the case today than it was when the book was first written. Though crime is down these days, there is still plenty of it, and our citizens are still afraid of it. And our prisons are jammed full of people who are far poorer, and far more likely to have been unemployed or underemployed before entering prison, than their counter-parts in the larger population.

Moreover, the criminal justice system—by which I always mean the whole system from lawmakers to law enforcers—continues not to implement programs that could alleviate the disabilities of poverty and dramatically reduce our high crime rates. And, as I shall document in detail, little has been done to make the harmful noncriminal acts of the well-off into crimes, or to reduce the bias against poor people caught up in the system. In short, though the system has had some success in reducing crime, it is still failing in the way that the thesis of *The Rich Get Richer* asserts: We still face the specter of a large and scary population of poor criminals. For all the changes of recent years, *the rich are still getting richer and the poor are still getting prison.*

In revising the book for this eighth edition, I have mainly tried to show that this is true by bringing statistics on criminal and noncriminal harms up to date, and incorporating the results of the relevant research that has appeared since the last edition. As always, I have tried to introduce these updates with as little violation of the original edition's style and argument as possible.

This edition reports findings of studies published as recently as 2006. However, where I compare the relative danger of criminal versus noncrimi-nal harms (such as occupational and environmental hazards), I generally use figures for 2003, the latest year for which there are adequate statistics on both types of harm. When new statistics were not available, I have, where it seemed plausible, assumed that earlier statistics reflect continuing trends and enable projections from the past into the present. In all cases, I have kept my assumptions and estimates extremely conservative in order to keep the argument on the firmest ground. In addition to new studies and data, I also continue to report some of the most striking of the older studies. I think that this shows how deep-seated the bias in our system is, and that the recent studies are not of merely passing phenomena.

I mentioned the following in the preface to the sixth and seventh edi-tions, but it bears repeating: This is the eighth time that I have reviewed the scholarly sociology and criminology journals looking for studies on the rela-tionship between economic status and arrest, conviction, and sentencing. When the first edition of *The Rich Get Richer and the Poor Get Prison* appeared in 1979, there were many such studies, largely stimulated by President John-son's establishment in 1965 of the President's Commission on Law Enforce-ment and the Administration of Justice. These studies consistently showed the presence of significant bias against lower-class suspects at every stage of criminal justice processing from arrest on. With each subsequent edition of *The Rich Get Richer*, the number of new studies on this topic has decreased, so that now, having once again reviewed every major journal (and many not-so-major ones) in the field, I find that the number of new studies has dwindled to a trickle. Nonetheless, the studies that do exist show the bias to be alive and well. Furthermore, this is also the eighth time that I have tried to arrive at an estimate of the total amount and cost of white-collar crime in the United States. There are organizations that study one or another type of white-collar crime, such as insurance fraud; but, while we are literally inundated with statistics on "common" crimes, there is no public or private agency that regularly measures the full extent of white-collar crime in all its varieties. Social scientists who study the ways in which social problems are framed and addressed would do well to consider why we have so little research on economic bias in criminal justice and no measurement of the full extent of white-collar crime.

In preparation for this edition of *The Rich Get Richer*, as for earlier ones, the publishers sought the views of a number of instructors who use the book in their courses. The reviewers for this edition were Roland Chilton, University of Massachusetts at Amherst; Rodney L. Engen, North Carolina State University; Phoebe C. Godfrey, Texas A & M University; Tim Kubal, California State University, Fresno; Christine M. O'Neil, University of Montana Western; and Michael Polakowski, University of Arizona. I am indebted to these reviewers and thank them heartily.

From the reviewers' comments, I am happy to learn that the book continues to be used both by teachers who agree with its thesis and by those who do not. This is as it should be. *The Rich Get Richer* is meant to stimulate thought, pro and con, not to gather disciples. These reviewers were kind enough to make a large number of recommendations, many of which I have adopted, and which I believe have improved the book. For example, I have added a section on the work of Michel Foucault, whose thesis about prisons is similar in certain ways to my own, and yet different in other important ways. I have taken note of some of the interesting theoretical insights of David Garland. I have tried to include more statistics on the treatment of Hispanics in the criminal justice system. In other cases, I have added clarifications in the text where readers' comments indicated that they were needed.

Some of the recommendations—to discuss epistemology and scientific method, to present evidence conflicting with my theory alongside evidence that supports it, to provide detailed proposals for solving some of the problems I identify in the criminal justice system, to address the larger political questions raised by the Iraq war, to call for overthrow of the capitalist system, and so on—I have resisted. Though I am as grateful for these recommendations as for the ones I have accepted, I believe that following them would detract from the aim of the book. And this leads me to think that it is worth stating clearly what that aim is. *The Rich Get Richer* is not meant to be a complete survey of the criminal justice system, and certainly not a complete survey of American social problems, and it is not meant to be a complete recipe for fixing either. Nor is it meant to be a balanced presentation of conservative and progressive views. Its goal is more limited and more focused; namely, to show students that much that goes on in the criminal justice system violates their own sense of basic fairness, to present evidence that the system does not function in the way it says it does or in the way that students believe it should, and then to sketch a whole theoretical perspective from which they might understand these failures and evaluate them morally—and to do it all in a short and relatively inexpensive book, written in plain language.

For those who want a larger theoretical context in which to place the thesis of *The Rich Get Richer*, I have provided in the first appendix a short essay entitled "The Marxian Critique of Criminal Justice." The essay covers the ground from a general statement of Marxian theories of capitalism, ideology, and law, to a Marxian theory of criminal justice—and the ethical judgments to which that theory leads. Many instructors have found this a handy and economical way of introducing their students to Marxian theory and its relation to criminal law and criminology. The essay addresses some of the same issues discussed in the main text of *The Rich Get Richer* and thus offers an alternative theoretical framework for understanding those issues. Although this framework is compatible with that developed in the main text, the argument of *The Rich Get Richer* stands alone without it.

To this first appendix, I have, in this edition, added a second, entitled "Between Philosophy and Criminology." Like the first appendix, this second appendix is separate from the argument of the main text but extends it in ways that might interest some instructors and some students. Unlike the first appendix, however, "Between Philosophy and Criminology" is a very personal statement. It aims, you might say, to stitch together the disparate parts of my intellectual life as a professional philosopher interested in criminal justice. I argue in it that criminology has a special need for philosophical reflection that other social sciences may not have, and I go on to spell out the philosophical framework within which *The Rich Get Richer* stands. As with everything in this book, I will be as happy if this essay is used by those who criticize it as by those who agree with it.

One other change is noteworthy: I have added some discussion of the last published work of the late philosopher John Rawls, *Justice as Fairness: A Restatement*, that bears on the question of the relationship between poverty in a capitalist welfare state and the incidence of crime.

In the third edition, I introduced two changes aimed at making the book more useful for instructors and students. Summaries and study questions were added to the chapters after the Introduction. The study questions require the student both to recall what he or she has read and to think critically about it. The questions can be used by instructors for the purpose of testing and review, and by students as a way of making sure they have covered and thought about the most important issues in each chapter. I have continued these two changes in this edition. I have also continued a change that first appeared in the fourth edition, a list of additional readings at the end of each chapter so that students stimulated by the material in the chapter could read further on particular topics. Moreover, the additional readings should help instructors when they assign outside reading or research on the topics touched upon in the book.

To provide a forum for discussing criminal justice policy, a website accompanies this book. It is available at *www.ablongman.com/reiman* or "Rich Get Richer," *www.paulsjusticepage.com.* The website is managed by Paul Leighton. I hope that it will offer the possibility for teachers, students, and other readers of the book to delve deeper into the workings of the current criminal justice system and how it can be improved. The website includes concise chapter outlines and summaries with links to additional related resources, as well as Internet-based exercises for students. Several articles that I have written with Paul about corporate crime are available there, and he will be providing new links to keep readers abreast of new developments.

Because I have revised rather than rewritten *The Rich Get Richer,* I am still indebted to those who helped me with the original edition. They are thanked in the following section, "Acknowledgments for the First Edition." For this eighth edition, as for the fourth, fifth, sixth, and seventh, I have been assisted by Paul Leighton, now associate professor of sociology, anthropology, and criminology at Eastern Michigan University. With this edition, Paul's responsibilities have expanded significantly. In addition to assembling the data, statistics, and studies needed to update the book, Paul has written first drafts of revised language throughout the text, which I have in most cases accepted, sometimes with modifications, though more often without. It is a sign of the excellent collaboration that Paul and I have enjoyed for more than ten years now that I rarely find his writing to veer from the style that has characterized the book from the beginning, and we easily reach agreement on what additions or subtractions are appropriate. I thank Paul for his fine work and good judgment; for his excellent suggestions, many of which I have incorporated in the book in this and earlier editions, and that have made it a better book; and for the friendly and responsible way in which he has always participated in the project. I look forward to many more years of working with him. I am grateful also to Carrie Leigh Buist, a graduate student at Eastern Michigan University, for her energetic and responsive help in gathering much of the data used in this edition.

As before, I continue to be grateful to American University for providing me with a supportive and lively intellectual environment. I thank Jennifer Jacobson, my former editor at Allyn & Bacon, for her good counsel and hard work over the years; and I thank Dave Repetto, my new editor at

Allyn & Bacon, for accepting the baton from Jennifer without missing a step. I look forward to working with him on future editions. I am grateful to Cheryl Adam for her careful and sharp-sighted editing. And I thank Pat McCutcheon for coordinating the copyediting and review process.

I dedicate the book to my wife, friend, partner, and colleague, Sue Headlee, who has delighted, encouraged, inspired, and astonished me for more than 30 years.

Jeffrey Reiman

ACKNOWLEDGMENTS FOR THE FIRST EDITION

This book is the product of seven years of teaching in the School of Justice (formerly, the Center for the Administration of Justice), a multidisciplinary criminal justice education program at American University in Washington, D.C. I have had the benefit of the school's lively and diverse faculty and student body. And, although they will surely not agree with all that I have to say, I have drawn heavily on what I have learned from my colleagues over the years and stand in their debt. In addition, more than is ordinarily recognized, a teacher receives guidance from students as they test, confirm, reject, and expand what they learn in class in the light of their own experience. Here, too, I am deeply in debt. My thanks go to the hundreds of students who have shared some part of their world with me as they passed through American University, and in particular to three students whose encouragement, loyalty, and wisdom are very much a part of the development of the ideas in this book: Elizabeth Crimi, Bernard Demczuk, and Lloyd Raines.

I express my gratitude to American University for providing me with a summer research grant that enabled me to devote full time to the book in the summer of 1976, when most of the actual writing was done. I am also grateful to Bernard Demczuk, who was my research assistant during the academic year 1975 to 1976 and who gathered much of the research data. I owe thanks as well to Cathy Sacks for ably and carefully typing the final manuscript.

Drafts of the manuscript for this book were read in whole or in part by (or to) Bernard Demczuk, Sue Hollis, Richard Myren, Lloyd Raines, Phillip Scribner, I. F. Stone, and John Wildeman. I am grateful for their many comments and I incorporate many of their recommendations in the final version. I have made my mistakes in spite of them.

Finally, for teaching me about artichokes, the meaning of history, and countless other mysteries, this book is dedicated to Sue Headlee Hollis.

J. R.
1979

THE RICH GET RICHER
AND THE POOR GET PRISON

INTRODUCTION

Criminal Justice through the Looking Glass, or Winning by Losing

The inescapable conclusion is that society secretly wants crime, needs crime, and gains definite satisfactions from the present mishandling of it.
—Karl Menninger, *The Crime of Punishment*[1]

A criminal justice system is a mirror in which a whole society can see the darker outlines of its face. Our ideas of justice and evil take on visible form in it, and thus we see ourselves in deep relief. Step through this looking glass to view the American criminal justice system—and ultimately the whole society it reflects—from a radically different angle of vision.

In particular, entertain the idea that the goal of our criminal justice system is not to eliminate crime or to achieve justice, *but to project to the American public a visible image of the threat of crime as a threat from the poor.* To do this, the justice system must present us with a sizable population of poor criminals. To do that, it must fail in the struggle to eliminate the crimes that poor people commit, or even to reduce their number dramatically. Crime may, of course, occasionally decline, as it has recently—*but largely because of factors other than criminal justice policies.*

These last statements must be explained. The recent news of declines in the crime rate has been quickly snatched up by leaders at all levels from the White House to the local police station as an occasion to declare the success of their crime-reduction policies. Later, I shall point to a number of causes of the recent decline, for example, the stabilization of the illegal drug trade and thus the reduction in drug-related violence, which have nothing to do with the success of criminal justice policies. If anything, the stabilization of the illegal drug trade is a sign of the failure of a long-standing justice policy, namely, the so-called war on drugs: Rather than the drug trade ending, that trade has become "business as usual." Nonetheless, I do not go so far as to say that criminal justice policy has made *no* contribution to the drop in crime rates.

In recent years, we have quadrupled our prison population and, in cities such as New York, allowed the police new freedom to stop and search people they suspect. No one can deny that if you lock up enough people, and allow the police greater and greater power to interfere with the liberty and

1

privacy of citizens, you will eventually prevent some crime that might otherwise have taken place. Later, I shall point out just how costly and inefficient this means of reducing crime is, in money for new prisons, in its destructive effect on inner-city life, in reduced civil liberties, and in increased complaints of police brutality. I don't deny, however, that these costly means do contribute *in some small measure* to reducing crime. Thus, when I say in this book that criminal justice policy is failing, I mean that it is failing to eliminate our high crime rates. We continue to see a large population of poor criminals in our prisons and our courts, while our crime-reduction strategies do not touch on the social causes of crime. Moreover, our citizens remain fearful about criminal victimization, even after the recent declines. I will document this failure in Chapter 1, "Crime Control in America: Nothing Succeeds like Failure."

You will rightly demand to know how and why a society such as ours would tolerate a criminal justice system that fails in the fight against crime. A considerable portion of this book is devoted to answering this question. Right now, however, a short explanation of how this upside-down idea of criminal justice was born will best introduce it, and me.

Nearly 30 years ago, I taught a seminar for graduate students titled "The Philosophy of Punishment and Rehabilitation." Many of the students were already working in the field of corrections as probation officers, prison guards, or halfway-house counselors. Together we examined the various philosophical justifications for legal punishment, and then we directed our attention to the actual functioning of our correctional system. For much of the semester, we talked about the myriad inconsistencies and cruelties and the overall irrationality of the system. We discussed the arbitrariness with which offenders are sentenced to prison and the arbitrariness with which they are treated once there. We discussed the lack of privacy and the deprivation of sources of personal identity and dignity, the ever-present physical violence, as well as the lack of meaningful counseling or job training within prison walls. We discussed the harassment of parolees, the inescapability of the "ex-con" stigma, the refusal of society to let a person finish paying his or her "debt to society," and the absence of meaningful noncriminal opportunities for the ex-prisoner. We confronted time and again the bald irrationality of a society that builds prisons to prevent crime knowing full well that they do not, and one that does not seriously try to rid its prisons and postrelease practices of those features that guarantee a high rate of *recidivism*, the return to crime by prison alumni. How could we fail so miserably? We are neither an evil nor a stupid nor an impoverished people. How could we continue to bend our energies and spend our hard-earned tax dollars on cures we know are not working?

Toward the end of the semester, I asked the students to imagine that, instead of designing a criminal justice system to reduce and prevent crime, we designed one that would maintain a stable and visible "class" of criminals. What would it look like? The response was electrifying. Here is a sample of the proposals that emerged in our discussion.

First.   It would be helpful to have laws on the books against drug use, prostitution, and gambling—laws that prohibit acts that have no unwilling victim. This would make many people "criminals" for what they regard as normal behavior and would increase their need to engage in *secondary crime* (the drug addict's need to steal to pay for drugs, the prostitute's need for a pimp because police protection is unavailable, and so on).

Second.   It would be good to give police, prosecutors, and/or judges broad discretion to decide who got arrested, who got charged, and who got sentenced to prison. This would mean that almost anyone who got as far as prison would know of others who committed the same crime but were not arrested, were not charged, or were not sentenced to prison. This would assure us that a good portion of the prison population would experience their confinement as arbitrary and unjust and thus respond with rage, which would make them more antisocial, rather than respond with remorse, which would make them feel more bound by social norms.

Third.   The prison experience should be not only painful but also demeaning. The pain of loss of liberty might deter future crime. But demeaning and emasculating prisoners by placing them in an enforced childhood characterized by no privacy and no control over their time and actions, as well as by the constant threat of rape or assault, is sure to overcome any deterrent effect by weakening whatever capacities a prisoner had for self-control. Indeed, by humiliating and brutalizing prisoners, we can be sure to increase their potential for aggressive violence.[2]

Fourth.   Prisoners should neither be trained in a marketable skill nor provided with a job after release. Their prison records should stand as a perpetual stigma to discourage employers from hiring them. Otherwise, they might be tempted *not* to return to crime after release.

Fifth.   Ex-offenders' sense that they will always be different from "decent citizens," that they can never finally settle their debt to society, should be reinforced by the following means. They should be deprived for the rest of their lives of rights, such as the right to vote.[3] They should be harassed by police as "likely suspects" and be subject to the whims of parole officers who can at any time threaten to send them back to prison for things no ordinary citizens could be arrested for, such as going out of town, or drinking, or fraternizing with the "wrong people."

And so on.

In short, *when asked to design a system that would maintain and encourage the existence of a stable and visible "class of criminals," we "constructed" the American criminal justice system!*

What is to be made of this? First, it is, of course, only part of the truth. Some steps have been taken to reduce sentencing discretion. And some prison officials do try to treat their inmates with dignity and to respect their privacy and self-determination to the greatest extent possible within an institution dedicated to involuntary confinement. Minimum-security prisons and halfway houses are certainly moves in this direction. Some prisons do provide meaningful job training, and some parole officers not only are fair but also go out of their way to help their "clients" find jobs and make it legally. And plenty of people are arrested for doing things that no society ought to tolerate, such as rape, murder, assault, or armed robbery, and many are in prison who might be preying on their fellow citizens if they were not. *All of this is true.* Complex social practices are just that: *complex.* They are neither all good nor all bad. For all that, though, the "successes" of the system, the "good" prisons, and the halfway houses that really help offenders make it are still the exceptions. They are not even prevalent enough to be called the beginning of the trend of the future. *On the whole, most of the system's practices make more sense if we look at them as ingredients in an attempt to maintain rather than reduce crime!*

This statement calls for an explanation. The one I will offer is that the practices of the criminal justice system keep before the public the *real* threat of crime and the *distorted* image that crime is primarily the work of the poor. The value of this *to those in positions of power* is that it deflects the discontent and potential hostility of Middle America away from the classes above them and toward the classes below them. If this explanation is hard to swallow, it should be noted in its favor that it not only explains the dismal failure of criminal justice policy to protect us against crime but also explains why the criminal justice system functions in a way that is biased against the poor at every stage from arrest to conviction. Indeed, even at an earlier stage, when crimes are defined in law, the system concentrates primarily on the predatory acts of the poor and tends to exclude or deemphasize the equally or more dangerous predatory acts of those who are well off.

In sum, I will argue that *the criminal justice system fails in the fight against crime while making it look as if crime is the work of the poor.* This conveys the image that the real danger to decent, law-abiding Americans comes from below them, rather than from above them, on the economic ladder. This image sanctifies the status quo with its disparities of wealth, privilege, and opportunity, and thus serves the interests of the rich and powerful in America—the very ones who could change criminal justice policy if they were really unhappy with it.

Therefore, it seems appropriate to ask you to look at criminal justice "through the looking glass." On the one hand, this suggests a reversal of common expectations. Reverse your expectations about criminal justice and entertain the notion that the system's real goal is the very reverse of its announced goal. On the other hand, the figure of the looking glass suggests the prevalence of image over reality. My argument is that the system functions the way it does *because it maintains a particular image of crime: the image that it is a threat from the poor.* Of course, for this image to be believab must be a reality to back it up. The system must actually fight crim least some crime—but only enough to keep it from getting out of hand and to keep the struggle against crime vividly and dramatically in the public's view, never enough to substantially reduce or eliminate crime.

I call this outrageous way of looking at criminal justice policy the *Pyrrhic defeat* theory. A "Pyrrhic victory" is a military victory purchased at such a cost in troops and treasure that it amounts to a defeat. The Pyrrhic defeat theory argues that the failure of the criminal justice system yields such benefits to those in positions of power that it amounts to success. In what follows, I will try to explain the failure of the criminal justice system to reduce crime by showing the benefits that accrue to the powerful in America from this failure. I will argue that from the standpoint of those with the power to make criminal justice policy in America, *nothing succeeds like failure.* I challenge you to keep an open mind and determine for yourself whether the Pyrrhic defeat theory does not make more sense out of criminal justice policy and practice than the old-fashioned idea that the goal of the system is to reduce crime substantially.

The Pyrrhic defeat theory has several components. Above all, it must provide an explanation of *how* the failure to reduce crime substantially could benefit anyone—anyone other than criminals, that is. This is the task of Chapter 4, "To the Vanquished Belong the Spoils: Who Is Winning the Losing War against Crime?" I argue there that the failure to reduce crime substantially broadcasts a potent *ideological* message to the American people, a message that benefits and protects the powerful and privileged in our society by legitimating the present social order with its disparities of wealth and privilege, and by diverting public discontent and opposition away from the rich and powerful and onto the poor and powerless.

To provide this benefit, however, not just any failure will do. It is necessary that the failure of the criminal justice system take a particular shape. *It must fail in the fight against crime while making it look as if serious crime and thus the real danger to society are the work of the poor.* The system accomplishes this both by what it does and by what it refuses to do. In Chapter 2, "A Crime by Any Other Name . . . ," I argue that the criminal justice system refuses to label and treat as crime a large number of acts of the rich that produce as much or more damage to life and limb as the crimes of the poor. In Chapter 3, ". . . and the Poor Get Prison," I show how, even among the acts treated as crimes, the criminal justice system is biased from start to finish in a way that guarantees that, *for the same crimes,* members of the lower classes are much more likely than members of the middle and upper classes to be arrested, convicted, and imprisoned—thus providing living "proof" that crime is a threat from the poor. (A statement of the main propositions that form the core of the Pyrrhic defeat theory is found in Chapter 2 in the section titled "Criminal Justice as Creative Art.")

One caution is in order: The argument in Chapters 1 through 4 is not a "conspiracy theory." It is the task of social analysis to find patterns in social behavior and then explain them. Naturally, when we find patterns, particularly patterns that serve some people's interests, we are inclined to think of these patterns as *intended* by those whose interests are served, as somehow brought into being *because* they serve those interests. This way of thinking is generally called a *conspiracy theory*. Later I will say more about the shortcomings of this way of thinking, and I will explain in detail how the Pyrrhic defeat theory differs from it. For the present, however, note that although I speak of the criminal justice system as "not wanting" to reduce crime and of the failure to reduce crime significantly as resulting in benefits to the rich and powerful in our society, *I am not maintaining that the rich and powerful intentionally make the system fail to gather up the resulting benefits.* My view is rather that the system has grown up piecemeal over time and usually with the best of intentions. The unplanned and unintended overall result is a system that not only fails to really reduce crime but also does so in a way that serves the interests of the rich and powerful. One consequence of this fact is that those who could change the system feel no need to do so. And thus it keeps on rolling along.

Our criminal justice system is characterized by beliefs about what is criminal, and beliefs about how to deal with crime, that predate industrial society. Rather than being anyone's conscious plan, the system reflects attitudes so deeply embedded in tradition as to appear natural. To understand why it persists even though it fails to protect us, all that is necessary is to recognize that, on the one hand, those who are the most victimized by crime are not those in positions to make and implement policy. Crime falls more frequently and more harshly on the poor than on the better off. On the other hand, there are enough benefits to the wealthy from the identification of crime with the poor and the system's failure to reduce crime that those with the power to make profound changes in the system feel no compulsion nor see any incentive to make them. In short, the criminal justice system came into existence in an earlier epoch and persists in the present because, even though it is failing—indeed, because of the way it fails—it generates no effective demand for change. When I speak of the criminal justice system as "designed to fail," I mean no more than this. I call this explanation of the existence and persistence of our failing criminal justice system the *historical inertia* explanation. In Chapter 4, I shall spell out this explanation in greater detail.

In the concluding chapter, I present an argument that the conditions described in Chapters 1, 2, and 3 (whether or not one accepts my explanation for them in Chapter 4) undermine the essential moral difference between criminal justice and crime itself. In this chapter, called "Criminal *Justice* or *Criminal* Justice," I make some recommendations for reform of the system. These are not offered as ways to "improve" the system but as the minimal conditions necessary to establish the moral superiority of that system to crime itself.

It will prevent confusion later if the reader remembers that when I speak of the *criminal justice system*, I mean more than the familiar institutions of police, courts, and prisons. I mean the entire system that runs from the decisions of lawmakers about what acts are criminal all the way to the decisions of judges and parole boards about who will be in prison to pay for these acts.

The Pyrrhic defeat theory is a child of the marriage of several ideas from Western social theory. Although this is discussed at greater length in what follows, it will serve clarity to indicate from the start the parents and the grandparents of this child. The idea that crime serves important functions for a society comes from Émile Durkheim. The notion that public policy can be best understood as serving the interests of the rich and powerful in a society stems from Karl Marx. From Kai Erikson is derived the notion that the institutions designed to fight crime instead contribute to its existence. From Richard Quinney comes the concept of the "reality" of crime as *created* in the process that runs from the definition of some acts as "criminal" in the law to the treatment of some persons as "criminals" by the agents of the law. The Pyrrhic defeat theory combines these ideas into the view that the failure of criminal justice policy becomes intelligible when we see that it creates the "reality" of crime as the work of the poor and thus projects an image that serves the interests of the rich and powerful in American society.

Though the Pyrrhic defeat theory draws on the ideas just mentioned, it changes them in the process. For example, the theory veers away from traditional Marxist accounts of legal institutions insofar as such accounts generally emphasize the *repressive* function of the criminal justice system, whereas my view emphasizes its *ideological* function. Marxists tend to see the criminal justice system as serving the powerful by *successfully* repressing the poor. My view is that the system serves the powerful by its *failure* to reduce crime, not by its success. Needless to add, insofar as the system fails in some respects and succeeds in others, these approaches are not necessarily incompatible. Nevertheless, in looking at the ideological rather than the repressive function of criminal justice, I will focus primarily on the image its *failure* conveys rather than on what it actually *succeeds* in repressing.[4]

Having located the Pyrrhic defeat theory in its family tree, I wish to say a word about the relationship between crime and economics. It is my view that the social order (shaped decisively by the economic system) bears responsibility for most of the crime that troubles us. This is true for all classes in the society, because a competitive economy that refuses to guarantee its members a decent living places pressures on all members to enhance their economic position by whatever means available. It degrades and humiliates the poor while encouraging the greed of the well off.[5] Nevertheless, these economic pressures work with particular harshness on the poor because their condition of extreme need and their relative lack of access to opportunities for lawful economic advancement vastly intensify for them the pressures toward crime that exist at all levels of our society.

These views lead to others that, if not taken in their proper context, may strike you as paradoxical. Evidence will be presented showing that there is a considerable amount of crime in our society at all socioeconomic levels. At the same time, it will be argued that poverty is a *source* of crime—I say "source" rather than "cause," because the link between poverty and crime is not a simple relationship between cause and effect. Poverty doesn't force poor people to commit crimes. Rather it confronts them with needs that they are less able than well-off people to satisfy legally, and it offers them fewer rewards for staying straight. Thus they face pressures and incentives that make crime more tempting, and noncriminal avenues less appealing, than they are for better-off people. Consequently, while most poor people do not commit serious crimes, evidence suggests that the particular pressures of poverty lead poor people to commit a higher proportion (in relation to their number in the population) of the crimes that people fear, such as homicide, burglary, and assault. There is no contradiction between this and the recognition that those who are well off commit many more crimes than is generally acknowledged, both the crimes widely feared and those not widely feared (such as white-collar crimes). There is no contradiction here, because, as will be shown, the poor are arrested far more frequently than those who are well off when they have committed the same crimes, and the well-to-do are only rarely arrested for white-collar crimes. Thus, if arrest records were brought in line with the real incidence of crime, it is likely that those who are well off would appear in the records far more than they do at present, even though the poor would still probably appear in numbers greater than their proportion of the population in arrests for the crimes people fear. In addition to this, I will argue that those who are well off commit dangerous acts that are not defined as crimes and yet are as or more harmful than the crimes people fear. Thus, if we had an accurate picture of who is really dangerous to society, there is reason to believe that those who are well off would receive still greater representation. On this basis, the following propositions will be put forth, which may appear contradictory if these various levels of analysis are not kept distinct.

1. Society fails to protect people from the crimes they fear by, among other things, refusing to alleviate the poverty that breeds them (documented in Chapter 1).

2. The criminal justice system fails to protect people from the most serious dangers by failing to define the dangerous acts of those who are well off as crimes (documented in Chapter 2) and by failing to enforce the law vigorously against the well-to-do when they commit acts that are defined as crimes (documented in Chapter 3).

3. By virtue of these and other failures, the criminal justice system succeeds in creating the image that crime is almost exclusively the work of the poor, an image that serves the interests of the powerful (argued in Chapter 4).

The view that the social order is responsible for crime does not mean that individuals are wholly blameless for their criminal acts or that we ought not have a criminal justice system able to protect us against them. To borrow an analogy from Ernest van den Haag, it would be foolhardy to refuse to fight a fire because its causes were suspect. The fact that society produces criminals is no reason to avoid facing the realization that many of these criminals are dangerous and must be dealt with. Also, although blaming society for crime may require that we tone down our blame of individual criminals, it does not require that we eliminate blame entirely or deny that they are responsible for their crimes. This is particularly important to remember because so many of the victims of the crimes of the poor are poor themselves. To point to the unique social pressures that lead the poor to prey on one another is to point to a mitigating, not an excusing, factor. Even the victims of exploitation and oppression have moral obligations not to harm those who do not exploit them or who share their oppression.

ABBREVIATIONS USED IN THE NOTES

Challenge   *The Challenge of Crime in a Free Society: A Report by the President's Commission on Law Enforcement and Administration of Justice* (Washington, DC: U.S. Government Printing Office, February 1967).

Sourcebook—2003   Kathleen Maguire and Ann L. Pastore, eds., *Sourcebook of Criminal Justice Statistics—2003*, U.S. Department of Justice, Bureau of Justice Statistics (Washington, DC: U.S. Government Printing Office, 2003). References to other editions of this annual publication will be indicated by *Sourcebook*, followed by the year in the title. Other editions may have different editors. The *Sourcebook* can be accessed online at *www.albany.edu/sourcebook/*.

StatAbst—2004–5   U.S. Census Bureau, *Statistical Abstract of the United States: 2004–5*, 124th ed. (Washington, DC: U.S. Government Printing Office, 2004). References to other editions of this annual publication will be indicated by *StatAbst*, followed by the year in the title. *StatAbst—2004–5* is available online at *www.census.gov/prod/www/statistical-abstract.html*.

UCR–2004   U.S. Department of Justice, Federal Bureau of Investigation, *Uniform Crime Reports for the United States: 2004* (Washington, DC: U.S. Government Printing Office, 2005). References to other editions of this annual report will be indicated by *UCR*, followed by the year for which the statistics are reported. In general, these reports are published in the fall of the year following the year they cover. The Federal Bureau of Investigation can be accessed online at *www.fbi.gov*.

BJS   Bureau of Justice Statistics, a source of many reports cited in this book. The Bureau of Justice Statistics is an agency of the U.S. Department of Justice. It is part of the Justice Department's Office of Justice Programs, which also includes the Bureau of Justice Assistance, the National Institute of Justice, the Office of Juvenile Justice and Delinquency Prevention, and the Office for Victims of Crime. Reports of the Bureau of Justice Statistics are published by the U.S. Government Printing Office in Washington, DC, normally in the year following the year in the title of the report. The Bureau of Justice Statistics can be accessed online at *www.ojp.usdoj.gov/bjs*.

NCJRS   The National Criminal Justice Reference Service is a clearinghouse for government publications from several agencies dealing with crime and criminal justice. The National Criminal Justice Reference Service can be accessed online at *www.ncjrs.org*.

NOTES

1. Karl Menninger, *The Crime of Punishment* (New York: Viking, 1968).
2. Consider the following:

   Dr. Meredith Bombar, a social psychologist and associate professor of psychology at Elmira College, notes that it would be difficult intentionally to shape a more effective breeding ground for aggression than that which already exists in the average prison. In personal correspondence, Dr. Bombar writes, "When I teach Social Psychology class, I spend a week or so going over the social/learned causes of aggression (e.g., provocation, modeling, punishment, extreme frustration, roles and social norms calling for aggression, physical discomfort, crowding, presence of guns and other objects associated with aggression, etc.). After the students have digested that, I ask them to imagine a horrible fantasy world which would put together all of these known social/environmental causes of aggression. What would it be? A typical prison." (From Lee Griffith, The Fall of the Prison: Biblical Perspectives on Prison Abolition [Grand Rapids, MI: Eerdmans, 1993], p. 65 n.)

3. Almost 5 million American citizens are currently deprived of the right to vote because they have been convicted of a felony. See Jeffrey Reiman, "Liberal and Republican Arguments against the Disenfranchisement of Felons," *Criminal Justice Ethics* 24, no. 1 (Winter–Spring 2005): pp. 3–18.
4. To these remarks should be added the recognition that, since the 1960s, a new generation of Marxist theorists, primarily French, has begun to look specifically at the ideological functions performed by the institutions of the state. Most noteworthy in this respect is the work of Louis Althusser and Nicos Poulantzas. See, especially, Louis Althusser, "Ideology and Ideological State Apparatuses," in his *Lenin and Philosophy and Other Essays* (London: New Left Books, 1971), pp. 121–73; and Nicos Poulantzas, *Fascism and Dictatorship* (London: New Left Books, 1974), pp. 299–309. These writers refer to the pioneering insights of Antonio Gramsci into the ideological functions of state institutions. See Quintin Hoare and Geoffrey Nowell-Smith, eds., *Selections from the Prison Notebooks of Antonio Gramsci* (London: Lawrence and Wishart, 1971); and Carl Boggs, *Gramsci's Marxism* (London: Pluto Press, 1976). For other broadly Marxian analyses of the relationship between the state and ideology, see Ralph

Miliband, *The State in Capitalist Society* (New York: Basic Books, 1969), pp. 179–264; and Jürgen Habermas, *Legitimation Crisis* (Boston: Beacon Press, 1975). A contemporary writer who takes seriously the ideological message of criminal justice practices is David Garland. See his *Punishment and Modern Society* (Chicago: University of Chicago Press, 1990), esp. ch. 11, "Punishment as a Cultural Agent," pp. 249–76.

5. See, for example, John Braithwaite, "Poverty, Power, and White-Collar Crime: Sutherland and the Paradoxes of Criminological Theory," in *White-Collar Crime Revisited*, ed. Kip Schlegel and David Weisburd (Boston: Northeastern University Press, 1992), pp. 78–107.

■ ■ ■ ■ ■

CHAPTER 1

CRIME CONTROL IN AMERICA
Nothing Succeeds like Failure

My love she speaks softly
She knows there's no success like failure
And that failure's no success at all.
—Bob Dylan, "Love Minus Zero/No Limit"

DESIGNED TO FAIL

In the last 40 years, crime rates have gone up and down, although mostly up until the 1990s. When crime rates increase, politicians never take responsibility for it. They play to voters' fears by advocating "law and order" or the many varieties of "getting tough on crime": more police, harsher sentences, mandatory minimums, three-strikes-and-you're-out laws, or increased use of capital punishment. When crime rates start to come down, politicians jump to claim credit for the reductions. Franklin Zimring calls this "a version of 'heads I win, tails you lose,' in which decreases in crime are evidence that hard-line punishments work, whereas increases are evidence that they are needed."[1] For example, in his 1994 State of the Union Address, President Bill Clinton told us that

> while Americans are more secure from threats from abroad, I think we all know that in many ways we are less secure from threats here at home. . . . Violent crime and the fear it provokes are crippling our society, limiting personal freedom and fraying the ties that bind us.[2]

But then the good news began to arrive: A *New York Times* headline for September 18, 1996, announced, "A Large Drop in Violent Crime Is Reported."[3] The article said that President Clinton "asserted that his policies, including putting more police officers on the streets and regulating the sale of handguns and assault rifles, had helped contribute to the decline."

Less than two weeks later, *U.S. News & World Report* ran a cover article entitled "Popgun Politics," asserting that neither President Clinton nor his opponent in the race for the presidency, Senator Bob Dole, was telling the truth about the crime issue. For example, while Clinton claimed that his policy of putting 100,000 new police on the street "played a big role in [the] recent crime drop," the magazine reported that "Clinton has won funding for 44,000 officers; [of whom] 20,000 are on the beat so far. Experts say that number could not have reduced crime much."[4] With officers working on shifts, taking vacations, and so on, it requires at least five officers to provide one officer on the street, around the clock, for a whole year.[5] So those 20,000 probably amount to no more than 4,000 new police on the streets around the clock.

Untroubled by such facts, President Clinton reported, in his radio address to the nation of January 11, 1997,

> We had a comprehensive plan to fight crime—to put 100,000 new community police officers on the street and tough new penalties on the books. . . . This approach is working.
> This week the FBI reported that serious crime dropped another three percent last year, dropping for the fifth year in a row, the longest decline in more than 25 years. This is great news.

And how shall we respond to this news? Continues President Clinton,

> Now that we've finally turned crime on the run, we have to redouble our efforts. We have to drive the forces of violence further and further into retreat.[6]

Two years later, in his 1999 State of the Union Address, the president was singing the same tune:

> I propose a 21st Century Crime Bill to deploy the latest technologies and tactics to make our communities even safer. Our balanced budget will help put up to 50,000 more police on the street in the areas hardest hit by crime, and then to equip them with new tools from crime mapping computers to digital mug shots.[7]

Early in his first term, President George W. Bush noted the decline in crime and added, "[B]ut, unfortunately, American society is still far too violent. The violent crime rate in the United States remains among the highest in the industrialized world."[8] This speech was in the context of the president's *Blueprint for New Beginings*, which included $821 million for prison construction and private prison space, plus $140 million to support additional detention beds.[9] The declining crime rates coupled with the terrorist attacks of September 11, 2001, brought about the opposite situation described by President Clinton above: Americans became more concerned with threats from abroad, so crime has become a low-priority issue, with funding and initiatives headed now to homeland security. But a 2005 statement shows the administration's support for more of the same in its support for the Gang Deterrence and Community Protection Act: "Aggressive law enforcement and tougher sentencing laws bear a good deal of the responsibility for the precipitous reduction in crime rates, especially for violent crime, over the past decade."[10] The Department of Justice's 2006 budget notes the need for $1.2 billion to incarcerate larger numbers of prisoners because of "the aggressive enforcement of the Administration's law enforcement initiatives, and the resulting detainee population increase."[11] It's the same story: Whatever the news—whether crime goes up or down—we need more cops arresting more crooks and putting them behind bars for longer amounts of time.

The plain fact is that virtually no student of the crime problem believes we can arrest and imprison our way out of the crime problem. To be sure, we have seen an enormous increase in the number of Americans behind bars. Between 1980 and 2004, the number of persons incarcerated in state and federal prisons more than quadrupled, growing from 329,000 to nearly 1.5 million. If we add those who are locked up in jails, locked up in military or juvenile facilities, and being held by the Bureau of Immigration and Customs Enforcement (formerly the Immigration and Naturalization Service), there are currently more than 2.2 million people behind bars in the United States, a number equivalent to the entire population of states such as Utah or Nevada![12] The Bureau of Justice Statistics reports that, if current incarceration rates remain unchanged, 11.3 percent of men and 32 percent of black men can expect to serve time in prison during their lifetime![13]

And what are the results? Violent crimes have declined since 1992, but crime rates are still very high. For example, in its *Uniform Crime Reports* (*UCR*) for 1992, the FBI reported 1,932,270 crimes of violence and a violent crime rate of 758 per 100,000 persons in the population. In 2004 the FBI reported a decline in the number of violent crimes to 1,367,009 and in the violent crime rate to 465.5 per 100,000, about what it was in 1976, when the FBI reported a violent crime rate of 468 per 100,000 in the population.[14] Says criminologist Elliott Currie, "[T]he recent declines . . . mainly represent a falling-off from an extraordinary peak."[15] And they have come down to rates that existed when far fewer Americans were locked up. In short, the crime reductions for which our leaders are now claiming credit are actually reductions from *very, very high* crime rates to rates that are merely *very high*.

On October 18, 1999, *The Washington Post* reported more good news: "Crime Rates Down for the 7th Straight Year," said the headline, but the news was not all good. The homicide rate was down to 6 per 100,000 inhabitants, a rate comparable to that in 1967, when it was thought to be a high rate. Moreover, national rates conceal important geographic and demographic differences: "Large cities experienced declines in murder," says the article, "but small cities (those with populations between 10,000 and 24,999, a total of about 20 million people) experienced the *only* increase in murder volume— 4 percent." And while "[y]outh homicide rates are half of what they were five years ago," they are "twice as high as they were 15 years ago."[16]

An even less comforting view appeared in a December 5, 1999, article in *The Washington Post* under the headline "Despite Rhetoric, Violent Crime Climbs." The article begins,

> Rosy assessments of the nation's declining crime rate wrongly focus on the short-term drops from crime peaks early in the decade and ignore the overall rise of violence since the 1960s, according to a new report.
>
> The 30-year update of a landmark study by the National Commission on the Causes and Prevention of Violence found that violent crime in major cities reported to the FBI has risen by 40 percent since 1969.
>
> The new study is intended as a counterpoint to the drumbeat of optimistic reports describing the current drop in crime, and it offers a sober reminder that the United States still suffers from a historically high level of violence.[17]

This 1999 study was conducted by the Milton S. Eisenhower Foundation, an organization devoted to continuing the work of the original 1969 violence commission and the 1968 Kerner commission on race. The foundation study noted the strikingly higher rates of violent crime in the United States compared to other industrialized nations: "In 1995, handguns were used to kill 2 people in New Zealand, 15 in Japan, 30 in Great Britain, 106 in Canada, 213 in Germany, and 9,390 in the United States."[18] "The most optimistic view after looking at this," said foundation president Lynn A. Curtis, who also worked on the 1969 violence report, "is that we are in roughly the same ballpark now in the late 1990s as we were in the late 1960s, when everyone said crime is so bad we need a national commission to study it."[19] The difference is that in 1969, there were 197,136 individuals in state and federal prisons, but by 1999 that number had grown *over 700 percent* to 1,496,629— growth that has cost us billions of dollars, given prison records to huge numbers of nonviolent criminals, and torn up inner-city communities, but that has not made much of a difference in the amount of crime we have[20] (see Figure 1.1; note that this figure reflects only the number of people in prisons, jail inmates are not included).

In an article entitled "The Limited Importance of Prison Expansion," William Spelman concludes, "The crime drop would have been 27 percent smaller than it actually was, had the prison build-up never taken place."[21] In short, *quadrupling* the number of people in prison—most of them nonviolent offenders—may have been responsible for *one-quarter* of the crime drop. Jason Zeidenberg, a policy analyst at the Justice Policy Institute, adds,

> A number of jurisdictions—California, Texas and the federal government— have had huge increases in incarceration rates, but those are not necessarily the jurisdictions that have had the biggest drops in crime. New York and California both increased their prison and jail populations, but California did so at a much higher rate that helped to drive up the national total. New York, however, experienced a much, much deeper drop in crime. . . .[22]

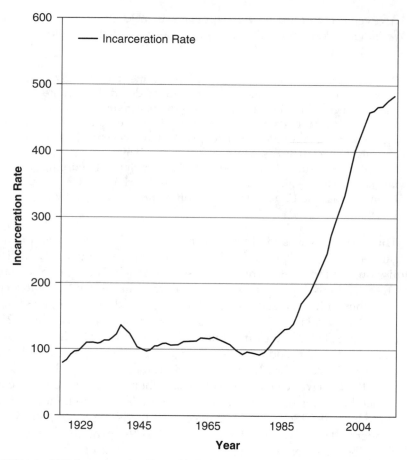

FIGURE 1.1 U.S. Incarceration Rate, 1929–2004: Number of Sentenced Individuals in State and Federal Prisons (per 100,000 residents) as of December 31

Source: Sourcebook 2003, Table 6.26, p. 500; and BJS, *Prisoners in 2004,* NCJ210677 (October 2005), p. 2.

According to Zeidenberg, New York's drop in crime was greatest between 1992 and 1997, a period during which it had the second-slowest-growing prison population in the country.

It's not hard to figure out why this unprecedented imprisonment binge has produced such meager effects. First of all, because American jurisdictions have always been highly likely to imprison violent offenders, an increase in the rate of imprisonment necessarily means that we are imprisoning more criminals who are less dangerous than the criminals already in prison. The result is that

> during the last two decades, the percentage of state prisoners incarcerated for violent offenses has actually declined from 57 percent to 48 percent. From 1980

to 1997, the number of violent offenders doubled, the number of nonviolent offenders tripled, and the number of drug offenders increased eleven-fold. At the end of 2001, there were an estimated 1.2 million nonviolent offenders locked up in America at a cost of more than $24 billion annually.[23]

Moreover, after a spate of bad publicity about crimes committed by individuals on parole, parole officers began revoking paroles at a very high rate. In 2000, state prisons admitted more than 200,000 parole violators, which amounted to one in every three prison admissions (up from 17 percent in 1980, and larger than the total number of prison admissions in 1980). About two-thirds of the revocations were for technical violations, not a new felony conviction.[24]

Alfred Blumstein argues, on the basis of careful analysis of arrest rates, that the extreme growth in violence during the late 1980s and early 1990s was driven by a "homicide epidemic" made up primarily of murders committed by young men using guns. This was the period in which crack cocaine was introduced into inner cities. Juveniles were recruited into the drug business in part because older drug dealers were being increasingly incarcerated, and the juveniles were "less vulnerable to the punishments imposed by the increasingly punitive adult criminal justice system."[25] At the same time there was a large influx of handguns into inner cities, often with higher power and faster action than traditional handguns. The mixture was highly volatile, because young men are not known for their peaceful dispute-resolution skills. Conflicts that previously would have been resolved by fists or knives were now increasingly solved with guns, indeed, often with extremely lethal semiautomatic pistols. During this period, homicide arrests for young men rose dramatically, while those for men 24 years old or older stayed relatively stable.

By 1993, murders started to decline, and so too did homicide arrests of young men. Though Blumstein acknowledges that the imprisonment binge played some role in this decline, he doubts that incarceration played more than a small role. First of all, crime was still rising in the 1980s when the prison population was already growing. Second, the juveniles recruited into the drug trade were, on the whole, less likely to face incarceration due to their youth (32 is the median age of state prisoners). And, because these juveniles were frequently replacing less violent, older drug dealers who were incarcerated, the growth in imprisonment actually contributed to the increase in violence.[26] Blumstein observes,

> It is somewhat ironic that the growth in violence with handguns was at least partly a consequence of the drug war's incarceration of many of the older drug sellers. . . . As older sellers were taken off the street, the drug market turned to younger individuals, particularly inner-city African-Americans. . . . The reduction in age of the workers in the crack trade entailed a predictable increase in violence, as the inclination to deliberate before acting is simply less developed in the young.[27]

For convicted drug dealers, there is a well-documented "replacement effect." That is, an imprisoned drug dealer is quickly replaced by another. Consequently, because drug offenders are the fastest-growing sector of the prison population, increased rates of imprisonment are not likely to pay off in substantial reductions in crime. Indeed, recent reports indicate that "Mexican traffickers are sending greater quantities and larger loads of drugs into the United States," and new statistics show "rising marijuana use among American teenagers."[28] Add to this the troubling fact that the money used to fund the imprisonment boom of the past decades has been taken from public programs that provide welfare, education, and medical treatment for the poor, thereby weakening programs that reduce crime in the long run. Criminologist William Chambliss writes that

> California, whose higher education system was once the envy of every other state, now is 'envied' by correctional officers and criminal justice employees, who saw an increase of more than 25,000 employees in the Department of Corrections workforce between 1984 and 1994; at the same time, there was a decline of more than 8,000 employees in higher education.[29]

A study by the Justice Policy Institute (JPI) and the Correctional Association of New York found that

> since 1988, spending for New York's public universities had dropped by 29 percent while funding for prisons increased by 76 percent; and the state's annual prison budget has increased by $761 million while funding for the New York City and state university systems has declined by $615 million.[30]

This is not to deny that we have recently seen some significant declines in crime rates. The point is that only a small fraction of these declines can be attributed to the enormous increase in our prison population. Even those who think that the growth in imprisonment is responsible for more of the reduction in crime than observers such as Blumberg believe are forced to concede that "the expansion of the inmate population certainly incurred exorbitant costs, both in terms of its disasterous impact on the lives of offenders and their families and in terms of the huge expenditure of tax revenue."[31] Thus, the overall "success" of this policy seems questionable even to those who believe it may have been effective.

Numerous students of the crime problem attribute the recent declines to factors other than criminal justice policies. For example, though we have seen some recent upturns, in the late 1990s, the United States had an unemployment rate of slightly above 4 percent, the lowest rate in over 30 years, but none of the officials in the criminal justice system who are claiming credit for reducing crime mentions this as a cause of lower crime rates. Moreover, the recent declines in crime come after a period in which much violent crime was attributed to turf wars between inner-city drug gangs. Now that the wars have been fought, more or less stable turf boundaries exist, and the rate of violence has subsided, not because the police have succeeded, but in fact because the (surviving) drug dealers have succeeded in turning their trade into a stable inner-city business. The late John Jay College of Criminal Justice Distinguished Professor of Criminology and former New York City Police Captain James Fyfe commented, "When a new illegal and profitable substance comes along, there is fighting and scratching for control. . . . Then dealers kill each other off, and the market stabilizes and the amount of violence decreases."[32] *U.S. News & World Report* points out that "contrary to popular impression, turf wars among [drug] gangs are increasingly rare. A staple of the late 1980s and early 1990s . . . such battles have now largely succumbed to what criminologist James Lynch [also of the John Jay College of Criminal Justice] terms the 'routinization of the drug trade.'"[33]

Blumstein credits the decline in crime to a number of factors. After giving very limited credit to the imprisonment binge, he points to the disaffection with crack cocaine that led to a drying up of many drug markets: "As recognition of its deleterious effects became widespread, word spread through the streets that crack was an undesirable drug . . . diminishing the number of new users"; the reduction in the use of handguns by juveniles, credited to a combination of police pressure and action by community groups trying to clean up their neighborhoods; and the robust economy that "has provided legitimate job opportunities for [many young people], which has created incentives to avoid illegal activities."[34]

One place where some experts are willing to credit police tactics with helping to reduce crime is New York City, where murder and felony rates have decreased dramatically in recent years. Some of the credit for this is said to go to the aggressive policing encouraged by former New York City Police Commissioner William Bratton. This aggressiveness may have helped reduce crime, but it brought with it a 62 percent increase in the number of citizen complaints between 1994 and 1997 to the Civilian Complaint Review Board about police abuse, excessive force, and discourtesy.[35] To "black and Latino leaders who say some of Bratton's cops carry his aggressive style too far—'that's too damn bad,' says Bratton."[36] But, against the thesis that such aggressive policing is necessary to reduce crime, Elliott Currie points out that many cities in California saw crime reductions when their police engaged in "more positive and community-oriented" activities, and that there are other "cities in which the police have done practically *nothing* that is new, and still the levels of violent crime have dropped strikingly."[37] John Conklin, in his book *Why Crime Rates Fell*, concurs that there is little to support a general link between policing and crime rates, and the research on

> zero-tolerance policing offers little support for the claim that the quality of life initiative reduced violent crime in New York City. There is also no reason to

think that this measure was implemented widely enough to account for the decline in national crime rates.[38]

So, while politicians claim credit for the recent declines in crime, the real story appears to be this: The enormous growth in our prison population over the last decade, coupled with questionable police tactics, may have contributed in some measure to the decline, but most of the decline can be attributed to factors beyond the criminal justice system: the reduction in unemployment, the stabilization of the drug trade, and the decline in the popularity of crack cocaine.

The recent decline in the crime rates does not represent dramatic success in dealing with the U.S. crime problem. As discussed above, it represents, rather, a reduction from extremely high crime rates to rates that are slightly less high, *but high nonetheless.* In short, crime is still rampant, and, for all their crowing and claiming credit, neither politicians nor criminal justice policy makers have come close to changing this fact. The criminal justice system may win the occasional skirmish, but it is still losing the war against crime.

In 1960, the average citizen had less than a 1-in-50 chance of being a victim of one of the crimes on the FBI Index (murder, forcible rape, robbery, aggravated assault, burglary, larceny, or auto theft—the most important crimes for which the FBI collects and publishes national statistics in its annual *Uniform Crime Reports*). In 1970, that chance grew to 1 in 25. In 1986, the FBI reported nearly 5,500 Index crimes per 100,000 citizens, a further increase in the likelihood of victimization to a 1-in-18 chance. By 1991, this had reached 5,898 per 100,000 citizens, a better than 1-in-17 chance. The FBI reported slight declines in 1992 and 1993, with the rate for 1993 at 5,483 per 100,000, roughly where it was in 1986. Most of the decline was accounted for by a drop in property crimes. Even with these declines, the FBI said in its 1993 report, "Every American now has a realistic chance of murder victimization in view of the random nature the crime has assumed."[39] For 2001, the FBI reports a further decline to 4,161 Index crimes per 100,000 in the U.S. population, a decrease in the chance of victimization to roughly 1 in 24, about what it was in the 1970s, and much higher than it was during the 1960s, before our enormous investment in prisons began and while a far smaller number of Americans were behind bars.[40] In 2004, the U.S. murder rate was down to 5.5 per 100,000 in the population, about what it was in 1966.[41] To keep these numbers in context, recall that crime was troublesome enough in the 1960s that then-President Lyndon Johnson established the President's Commission on Law Enforcement and Administration of Justice to study the problem.

Moreover, American violent crime rates are still far higher than those in other countries. Writes criminologist Elliot Currie,

By the mid-1990s . . . a young American male was 37 times as likely to die by deliberate violence as his English counterpart—and 12 times as likely as a

Canadian youth, 20 times as likely as a Swede, 26 times as likely as a young Frenchman, and over 60 times as likely as a Japanese.[42]

In sum, when we look behind the politicians' claims to have turned the tide against violence, the fact remains that criminal justice policy is failing to make our lives substantially safer. How are we to comprehend this failure? It appears that our government is failing to fulfill the most fundamental task of governance: keeping our streets and homes safe, assuring us of what the Founding Fathers called "domestic tranquility," and providing us with the minimum requirement of civilized society. It appears that our new centurions, with all their modern equipment and know-how, are no more able than the old Roman centurions to hold the line against the forces of barbarism and chaos. There are a number of ways in which to respond to this failure. One is to define it out of existence. So, for example, David Garland, responding to the claim that prisons have failed to reduce crime, contends that, if the prison is "evaluated in terms of its ability to deprive offenders of their liberty in accordance with a court order, to exclude them from society for a period of time, or to inflict mental suffering in ways which satisfy a punitive public . . . its only failures would be occasional escapes and unwanted leniencies."[43] To be sure, if all we ask of prisons is that they be prisons, that is, that they lock some people up for a while under unpleasant conditions, they succeed quite well. It should be clear, however, from the statements I have already cited from politicians defending increased imprisonment that our leaders assert that prisons will make our society safer by reducing crime. We should, then, hold prisons and the rest of the criminal justice system to this test. And when we do, they largely fail.

Another way to come to terms with this failure is to look at the *excuses* that are offered for it. This we will do—but mainly to show that they do not hold up!

One commonly heard excuse is that we can't reduce crime because our laws and our courts are too lenient. *Translation:* We are failing to reduce crime because we don't have the heart to do what has to be done.

Other excuses point to some feature of modern life, such as urbanization or population growth (particularly the increase in the number of individuals in the crime-prone ages of 15 to 24), and say that this feature is responsible for the growth in crime. This means that crime cannot be reduced unless we are prepared to return to horse-and-buggy days or to abolish adolescence. *Translation:* We are failing to reduce crime because it is impossible to reduce crime.

Soon, I shall look at these excuses in greater detail and show that they do not explain our failure to reduce crime, and I will present evidence to support my claim that we could reduce crime and the harm it causes if we wanted to. So the question "How are we to comprehend our failure to reduce crime?" still stares us in the face. Examination of the excuses and then of policies that could reduce crime suggest that our failure is avoidable. What has to be explained is not why *we cannot* reduce crime, but why *we will not!* Oddly enough, this paradoxical result points us in the direction of an answer to our question.

Failure is, after all, in the eye of the beholder. The last runner across the finish line has failed in the race only if he or she wanted to win. If the runner wanted to lose, the "failure" is, in fact, a success. Here, I think, lies the key to understanding our criminal justice system.

If we look at the system as "wanting" to reduce crime, it is an abysmal failure that we cannot understand. If we look at it as *not* wanting to reduce crime, it's a howling success, and all we need to understand is why the goal of the criminal justice system is to fail to reduce crime. If we can understand this, then the system's "failure," as well as its obstinate refusal to implement the policies that could remedy that "failure," become perfectly understandable. In other words, I propose that we can make more sense out of criminal justice policy by assuming that its goal is to maintain crime than by assuming that its goal is to reduce crime!

In the remainder of this chapter, I explore the excuses for the failure to reduce crime and offer evidence to back up my assertion that there are policies that could reduce crime that we refuse to implement. I then briefly outline the relationship between the Pyrrhic defeat theory and the criminological theory of Kai Erikson and Émile Durkheim, to which it is akin. I will close with a word on the work of Michel Foucault, whose views run parallel for a while to those that I shall defend in this book, before heading off in a different direction.

THREE EXCUSES THAT WILL NOT WASH, OR HOW WE COULD REDUCE CRIME IF WE WANTED TO

On July 23, 1965, President Lyndon Johnson signed an executive order establishing the President's Commission on Law Enforcement and Administration of Justice to investigate the causes and nature of crime, to collect existing knowledge about our criminal justice system, and to make recommendations about how that system might better meet "the challenge of crime in a free society." The commission presented its report to the president early in 1967, thick with data and recommendations. Because we are a nation higher on commissions than on commitments, it should come as no surprise that, for all the light cast on the crime problem by the President's Commission, little heat has been generated and—aside from the massive imprisonment binge— virtually no profound changes in criminal justice policy have taken place in the 39 years since the report was issued.

During this period, however, more and more money has been poured into crime control, with the bleak results I have already outlined. When the commission wrote, it estimated that more than $4 billion was being spent annually at the national, state, and local levels to pay for police, courts, and correctional facilities in the fight against crime.[44] Since that time, the violent crime rate climbed from 200 per 100,000 in the population in 1965 to 465 in 2004, and the property crime rate went from 2,249 to 3,517 per 100,000.[45] The annual cost to the public of this brand of domestic tranquility was more than $167 billion by 2001, with 2.3 million persons employed by the criminal justice system. Taking inflation into account, this represents real growth of more than 600 percent in criminal justice spending since 1965, and 165 percent since 1982.[46] And this doesn't even count the more than $100 billion spent each year on private security.[47] Dollar for dollar, crime control is hardly an impressive investment—that is, if you think you are investing in crime reduction. Later, when I comment on the burgeoning private corrections industry, touted by corporations to their stockholders, we shall see that, for those who think that high crime rates are here to stay, crime control is quite a good investment!

Multiplying almost as fast as crime and anticrime dollars are excuses for our failure to reduce crime significantly in the face of increased expenditure, personnel, research, and knowledge. Three excuses have sufficient currency to make them worthy of consideration as well as to set in relief the Pyrrhic defeat thesis, which I propose in their place.

First Excuse: We're Too Soft!

One excuse is that we are too soft on crime.[48] This view is widespread among laypersons (in 2002, 67 percent of people polled thought courts were not harsh enough) and conservative critics of criminal justice policy (the late Ernest van den Haag, for example, claimed that "non-punishment is the major 'social' cause of crime").[49] This view is hard to disprove because, no matter how harsh we are, one can always say we should have been harsher. Nonetheless, the evidence is that we are quite harsh, in general harsher than other modern industrial nations, and that we have gotten strikingly harsher in recent years, with relatively little effect on the crime rate.

Consider the situation in America and elsewhere, before the recent crime drop began. In 1988, the U.S. rate of incarceration (in jails and prisons) was 388 prisoners per 100,000 people in the national population. For the same year, the rate for the United Kingdom was 97 per 100,000, for West Germany it was 85, and for Belgium it was 65. The rate for Canada, which has a society in many ways much like our own, was about 110 persons for every 100,000 inhabitants.[50] In 2003, after the crime drop, the U.S. rate of incarceration (in jails and prisons) was 724 per 100,000 in the national population.[51] For the United Kingdom, it was 144, for Germany 96, for Belgium 88, and for Canada, it was 116 prisoners for every 100,000 persons in the national population.[52] Before and after the recent declines in crime, we had far greater percentages of our population under lock and key than comparably advanced European nations as well as our neighbor to the north.

Some have argued that our incarceration rates are not so different from those of other countries when compared with our higher crime rates. This finding is based on comparing our incarceration rates for serious crimes with those of other countries for those same crimes. We are still incarcerating more people than those other countries, because we criminalize acts, such as prostitution and other victimless crimes, that other countries do not.[53] In 2003, Canada decriminalized possession of small amounts of marijuana, and some Canadian cities are embracing "safe injection centers" for users of harder drugs.[54] But even if our incarceration rates stand in the same proportion to our crime rates as those of other countries, that still indicates that we are no more lenient than other modern nations. Nor, of course, should it be forgotten that we are the only Western industrialized nation that still has the death penalty, let alone (until 2005) the only such nation that executed people who had committed crimes while under the age of 18. In the 1990s, Congress approved a crime bill that expanded the federal death penalty to cover 52 offenses.[55] At the close of 2003, the state and federal prison systems held 3,374 prisoners under sentence of death. In 2003, 65 individuals were executed.[56] On December 2, 2005, North Carolina carried out the 1,000th execution in the United States since the reinstatement of the death penalty by the U.S. Supreme Court in 1976.

What's more, we have become markedly harsher during the last decade. Recall the dramatic increases in criminal justice personnel and expenditures mentioned above. Here's what we got for this investment: Where we used to have the third-highest rate of incarceration in the world, behind South Africa and the (now former) Soviet Union, we have now pulled ahead of these two paragons of justice to lead the world in the percentage of inhabitants behind bars.[57] Our incarceration rate of 724 prisoners per 100,000 people in the national population doesn't include those who are currently on probation and parole. When these are added to those in jail or prison, the number of *adults* under some form of correctional supervision in 2003 reached a new high of nearly 6.9 million; that is, one of every 32 American adults—3.2 percent of the U.S. adult population—was incarcerated or on probation or parole in 2003. This represents more than a tripling of the number since 1980, when 1.84 million persons were under correctional supervision.[58] Our high crime rates persist in the face of this toughening of sentencing and, thus, suggest that crime persists even though we have a harsh criminal justice system, leading one criminologist to characterize the get-tough approach to crime as a conservative social experiment that has been tested and shown to fail.[59]

Second Excuse: A Cost of Modern Life

Another excuse is that crime is an inescapable companion of any complex, populous, industrialized society. As we become more complex, more populous, more industrialized, and particularly more *urbanized*, we will have more crime as inevitably as we will have more ulcers and more traffic. These are costs of modern life, the benefits of which abound and clearly outweigh the costs. Crime, then, takes its place alongside death and taxes. We can fight, but we cannot win, and we should not tear our hair out about it.

It takes little reflection to see that this is less an explanation than a recipe for resignation. Furthermore, it does not account for the fact that other complex, populous, and highly industrialized nations such as Japan have crime rates that are considerably lower than ours. In 2002, the total number of violent offenses known to the police in Japan was 30,179, about 24 offenses for every 100,000 inhabitants, compared with 1.4 million violent offenses reported to the FBI for a U.S. violent crime rate of 495 for every 100,000 inhabitants.[60] In other words, with about half the population of the United States crowded onto a landmass less than 1/25 the size of the United States, Japan had about 2 *percent* the number of serious offenses known to the police in America that year.

Reporting the results of her study of the relationship between crime and modernization around the world, Louise Shelley writes,

> Although both societies have undergone urbanization and industrialization, Japan and Switzerland have been exempt from many of the crime problems that currently plague the other developed countries. Most other developed countries have considerably higher rates of crime commission than these two societies, but few developed countries have as high rates of crime commission as the United States.[61]

This generalization is borne out strikingly by comparing homicide rates in the United States with those in other modern nations. In 2000, Japan had about two-thirds as many homicides (1,391) as California (which had 2,079). That year, when the homicide rate in the United States was 5.5 per 100,000 inhabitants, Japan's rate was 1.1 per 100,000; Switzerland had a rate of 2.25; Denmark, 4; France, 3.7; and Canada, 4.25.[62]

The "costs of modern life," or urbanization, excuse also fails to account for the striking differences in the crime rates *within* our own modern, complex, populous, and urbanized nation. Within the United States in 2004, the homicide rate ranged from 1.4 per 100,000 inhabitants in North Dakota, Maine, and New Hampshire to 12.7 in Louisiana.[63] In 1968, *Time* magazine reported that

> Texas, home of the shoot-out and divorce-by-pistol, leads the U.S. with about 1000 homicides a year, more than 14 other states combined. Houston is the U.S. murder capital: 244 last year, more than in England, which has 45 million more people.[64]

By 2004, Texas (with 1,364 homicides) was in second place, ahead of Florida and New York (with 946 and 889, respectively), and behind California (with 2,392), and Houston's glory as murder capital had clearly faded.

Houston reported 272 homicides for 2004, roundly outdone by New York City (with 570), Los Angeles (518), and even Detroit (385).[65]

Such variations are not limited to murder. A comparison of crime rates (incidence of FBI Index crimes per 100,000 inhabitants) for Standard Metropolitan Statistical Areas (SMSAs, areas "made up of a core city with a population of 50,000 or more inhabitants and the surrounding county or counties which share certain metropolitan characteristics") reveals a striking *lack* of correlation between crime rate and population size (which we can take as a reasonable, though rough, index of urbanization and the other marks of modernity, such as complexity and industrialization, that are offered as explanations for the intractability of crime). See Table 1.1, in which metropolitan areas of different sizes and similar crime rates are ranked by population.

In other words, classifying crime with death and taxes and saying that it is an inevitable companion of modernity or urbanization just will not explain our failure to reduce it. Even if death and taxes are inevitable (unfortunately, not in that order), some die prematurely and some die suspiciously and some pay too much in taxes and some pay none at all. None of these variations is inevitable or unimportant. So too with crime. Even if crime is inevitable in modern societies, its rates and types vary extensively, and this is neither inevitable nor unimportant. Indeed, the variations in crime rates between modern cities and nations is proof that the *extent* of crime is not a simple consequence of urbanization. Other factors must explain the differences. It is these differences that suggest that although some crime may be

TABLE 1.1   Metropolitan Areas by Population and FBI Crime Rates, 2004

CITY	POPULATION	VIOLENT CRIME RATE (PER 100,000 PEOPLE)	PROPERTY CRIME RATE (PER 100,000 PEOPLE)
New York City	11,454,104	583	2,092
Atlanta, GA	4,686,829	522	4,224
Oakland, CA	2,490,569	528	4,323
Boston, MA	1,817,764	599	2,893
Birmingham, AL	1,079,659	578	4,434
Tacoma, WA	749,699	538	5,145
Wichita, KS	585,348	575	4,757
Pensacola, FL	438,508	564	3,048
Atlantic City, NJ	265,254	531	4,034
Houma, LA	198,242	549	4,346
Lima, OH	108,461	500	4,115
Carson City, NV	57,621	509	2,888

Source: UCR–2004, Table 6, pp. 97–134.

an unavoidable consequence of urbanization, this in no way excuses our failure to reduce crime at least to the lowest rates reported in modern cities and nations.

Third Excuse: Blame It on the Kids!

A third excuse takes the form of attributing crime to young people, particularly young men between the ages of 14 or 15 or 16 and 24 or 25. This explanation goes as follows: Young people in our society, especially males, find themselves emerging from the security of childhood into the frightening chaos of adult responsibility. Little is or can be done by the adult society to ease the transition by providing meaningful outlets for the newly bursting youthful energy aroused in still immature and irresponsible youngsters. Hence, these youngsters both mimic the power of manhood and attack the society that frightens and ignores them by resorting to violent crime. Add to this the rapid increase of people in this age group since the baby boom of the 1940s (only tapering off as we entered the 1980s), and we have another explanation that amounts to a recipe for resignation: We can no more expect to reduce crime than we can hope to eradicate adolescence. We can fight crime, but it will be with us until we figure out a way for people to get from childhood to adulthood without passing through their teens.

There can be no doubt that youngsters show up disproportionately in crime statistics. In 1975, *Time* reported that "forty-four percent of the nation's murderers are 25 or younger, and 10 percent are under 18. Of those arrested for street crimes, excluding murder, fully 75 percent are under 25 and 45 percent are under 18."[66] In 2003, persons between the ages of 15 and 24 constituted 14.2 percent of the nation's population. They represented, however, 41 percent of those arrested for all crimes.[67]

However, there are problems with attributing crime to youth. The most important is that crime rates have grown faster than either the absolute number of young people or their percentage of the population. See Table 1.2, comparing national crime rates over the past 40 years with the percentage of the population represented by people aged 14 to 24.

Notice that, while there is some correlation between the rise and fall of crime rates and percentage of young people in the population, there are also important divergences: The percentage of young people in the population in 2000 was about what it was in 1960, yet the crime rate in 2000 was almost *four times higher* than that of 1960. Obviously, this growth in crime cannot be attributed to youth. The same can be said of the years 1970 and 1975, when young people's percentage in the population grew slightly, and crime rates doubled. Or compare 1980 and 1990, when the youth percentage dropped almost 5 points and the crime rate dropped only slightly. In that same period, the number of 15 to 24 year olds decreased absolutely by 5,660,000, while the absolute number of Index crimes rose by over 1 million.[68]

TABLE 1.2   Crime Rates Compared with Youth Population, 1960–2003

YEAR	VIOLENT CRIME RATE (CRIMES PER 100,000 PERSONS)	PROPERTY CRIME RATE (CRIMES PER 100,000 PERSONS)	14–24 YEAR OLDS (% OF POPULATION)
1960	161	1,726	15.1
1970	364	3,621	19.9
1975	488	4,811	20.8
1980	597	5,353	20.4
1985	558	4,666	18.2
1990	730	5,073	16.2
1995	685	4,591	15.2
2000	507	3,618	15.4
2003	475	3,588	15.6

Source: Sourcebook 2003, Table 3.106, pp. 278–79; *UCR–2003,* pp. 11, 41; *StatAbst—2004–5,* Table 11, p. 12; *StatAbst—2001,* Table 11, p. 13; *StatAbst—1995,* p. 17; *StatAbst—1992,* pp. 14–15; and *StatAbst—1987,* p. 14.

Similar discrepancies show up when the National Crime Victimization Survey (NCVS) is used. Compare, for example, 1981 with 1973, the first year for which we have NCVS survey results. In 1973 the number of people aged 16 to 24 was 34,967,000, and in 1981 their number had increased 10 percent to 38,591,000. As a percentage of the national population, they went from 16.5 to 16.8—an increase of slightly under 2 percent in their percentage of the population (16.8 − 16.5 = 0.3; 0.3 is 1.8 percent of 16.5). During that same period, the NCVS shows an increase in reported violent victimizations of *23 percent,* from 5,351,000 to 6,582,000, more than twice the increase in the absolute number of 16 to 24 year olds, more than ten times the increase in their fraction of the population. Or compare 1975 and 1997, years in which the number of 16 to 24 year olds is nearly the same (36,544,000 and 36,580,000, respectively). The NCVS reports an increase in violent victimizations of *55 percent* from 1975 (5,573,000 victimizations) to 1997 (8,614,000). In 1997 there were 36,000 more 16 to 24 year olds than there were in 1975, but over 3,000,000 more violent victimizations.[69]

What's more, the period of decline in the youth population coincided with an increase in serious crime in New York City; and even when crime rates went down recently, they never returned to the levels of the 1940s, when the percentage of young people 16 to 24 years old was about 14, roughly comparable to what it is now.[70]

I am not denying that a large number of crimes are committed by young people. The facts suggest that, although the number of youngsters in the populace has an important effect on crime rates, it cannot fully explain them or explain them away. That young people have higher rates of crime than older folks does not mean that young people always have the same rate of crime. When this group declined, crime went down, but not in proportion to the decline in the youth population. When this group was growing, the crime rates were growing faster. If crime increases faster (or decreases more slowly) than the youth population, that increase (or decrease) cannot be explained by the increase (or decrease) in youths. If crime *among* these youngsters increases, then this certainly is not explained by their youth. Something other than their youth or their numbers must explain why they are committing more crimes than people their age did in other periods.[71]

In any case, the greater likelihood of young people committing crime provides no excuse for failing to reduce the growth of crime at least to the rate at which the number of young people is growing (or shrinking). So another excuse for our failure fails to excuse. To get an idea of what criminal justice policy truly aimed at reducing crime might look like, let's look at the known sources of crime and the promising crime-prevention programs.

KNOWN SOURCES OF CRIME

There are many things that we do know about the sources of crime. Note that I have said *sources* rather than *causes* because the kind of knowledge we have is far from the precise knowledge that a physicist has about how some event *causes* another. We know that poverty, slums, and unemployment are *sources* of street crime. We know that they breed alienation from social institutions, and that they reduce the likely rewards of going straight. But, we do not fully understand how they *cause* crime, because we know as well that many, if not most, poor, unemployed slum dwellers do not engage in street crime. Yet, to say that this means we do not know that poverty and the other conditions discussed below are sources of violent crime is like saying that we do not know that a bullet in the head is deadly because some people survive or because we do not fully understand the physiological process that links the wound with the termination of life.

Poverty

Those youngsters who figure so prominently in arrest statistics are not drawn equally from all economic strata. Although there is much reported and even more unreported crime among middle-class youngsters, the street crime attributed to this age group that makes our city streets a perpetual war zone is largely the work of poor inner-city youth. This is the group at the lowest end of the economic spectrum. This is a group among whom unemployment hovers around 25 percent, with *under*employment (the percentage of persons either jobless or with part-time, low-wage jobs) still higher. This is a group with no realistic chance (for any but a rare individual) to enter college or amass sufficient capital (legally) to start a business or to get into the high-wage, skilled job markets. We know that poverty is a *source* of crime, and yet we do virtually nothing to improve the life chances of the vast majority of the inner-city poor. They are as poor as ever and are facing cuts in welfare and other services.

That poverty is a source of crime is not refuted by the large and growing amount of white-collar crime that I shall document later. In fact, poverty contributes to crime by creating need, while, at the other end of the spectrum, wealth can contribute to crime by unleashing greed. Some criminologists have argued that economic inequality itself worsens crimes of the poor and of the well-off by increasing the opportunities for the well-off and increasing the humiliation of the poor.[72] And inequality has worsened in recent years.

The gap between rich and poor worsened during the 1980s and 1990s. In 1970, the poorest fifth of the nation's families received 5.5 percent of the aggregate income, and the richest fifth received 41.6 percent. In 1980, the share of the poorest fifth was 5.3 percent of aggregate income, and that of the richest fifth was 41.1 percent. By 2004, the share of the poorest fifth had declined to 3.4 percent, while that of the richest fifth had risen to 50.1 percent. In the period from 1980 to 2002, the share of the top 5 percent rose from 14.6 to 20.8 percent. By 2004, the number of poor Americans was 37 million (about 1 in 8 Americans), up from 30.1 million in 1990, and from 25.2 million in 1980.[73] And, due to cuts in welfare,

> from 1995 to 1997, despite continued economic growth, the average incomes of the poorest 20 percent of female-headed households fell . . . an average of $580 per family. Among the poorest 10 percent of female-headed families with children, income fell an average of $810 between 1995 and 1997.[74]

Moreover, these developments were the predictable outcome of the Reagan administration's strategy of fighting inflation by cutting services to the poor while reducing the taxes of the wealthy. In September 1982, a group of 34 prominent economists sharply criticized Reagan's economic policy as "extremely regressive in its impact on our society, redistributing wealth and power from the middle class and the poor to the rich, and shifting more of the tax burden away from business and onto low-and middle-income consumers."[75] In that same month, a study released by the Urban Institute concluded that "the Reagan administration's policies are not only aiding upper-income families at the expense of the working poor, but also are widening the gulf between affluent and poorer regions of the country."[76] The study maintained that the combined effect of the administration's tax and social service spending cuts was "to penalize working families near the poverty line who receive some federal benefits . . . creating 'major work disincentives.'"

Edward Wolff writes that the

> equalizing trends of the 1930s–1970s reversed sharply in the 1980s. The gap between the haves and have-nots is greater now than at any time since 1929. The sharp increase in inequality since the late 1970s has made wealth distribu-

tion in the United States more unequal than in what used to be perceived as the class-ridden societies of northwestern Europe.[77]

By 2004, 17 percent of American children were living in poverty, with 33 percent of black children and 28 percent of Latino children living in families below the poverty level, compared with 10 percent of white children.[78]

The tax cuts recently enacted by President George W. Bush had much the same effect because 25 percent of the benefits went to those with incomes in the top 1 percent, and nearly 50 percent of the benefits went to those with incomes in the top 10 percent. Using data from the Congressional Budget Office (CBO), the nonpartisan Center on Budget and Policy Priorities calculated that "the top one percent of households (whose incomes average nearly $1.2 million) will receive an average tax cut of approximately $40,990 in 2004"—a figure "more than 40 times the average tax break for those in the middle fifth of the income distribution." They further note that between 1979 and 2001,

> the average after-tax income of the top one percent of households rose by a stunning $409,000, or 139 percent, after adjusting for inflation. This dwarfed the $6,300, or 17 percent, average increase among the middle fifth of the population, over this 22-year period, and the $1,100, or 8 percent, increase among the bottom fifth of the population.[79]

Furthermore, as unemployment has gone up and down over the past decades, unemployment at the bottom of society remains strikingly worse than the national average. For example, over the past 35 years, black unemployment has remained slightly more than twice the rate of white unemployment. In 1967, when 3.4 percent of white workers were unemployed, 7.4 percent of black workers were jobless. By 2000, when overall unemployment was about 4 percent, 3.5 percent of white workers were unemployed and 7.6 percent of blacks were. Among those in the crime-prone ages of 16 to 19, 11.4 percent of white youngsters and 24.7 percent (almost one in every four) black youngsters were jobless.[80] The pattern held true for the economic slump starting in 2002, and for all of 2003—when the overall unemployment rate was 6 percent—the white jobless rate was 5.2 percent and the black rate was almost 11 percent.[81]

In his important book, *A Theory of Justice*, John Rawls—the late Harvard moral and political philosopher called by some the John Stuart Mill of the twentieth century—argued for a principle of economic justice called the *difference principle*.[82] According to this principle, economic inequalities are unjust unless they work to maximize the share of the worst-off group in society, say, by providing incentives that increase production overall.[83] This implies that the inequalities are only just if reducing them would further reduce the share of the worst-off group. This is as egalitarian as a distributive principle can be without simply insisting on equal shares for everyone.

In a later work, *Justice as Fairness: A Restatement*, Rawls compares two models of society, "property-owning democracy" and "welfare-state capitalism."[84] A property-owning democracy is a capitalist society governed by the difference principle along with other principles that guarantee equal liberty, in both form and substance, and fair equality of opportunity. Welfare-state capitalism is a capitalist society where equal liberties are guaranteed formally in the law, but little is done to guarantee their substance, that is, to make sure that people have adequate means to exercise those liberties. Moreover, in welfare-state capitalism, economic and other inequalities are limited only by the existence of a social safety net, providing for the basic needs of those at the bottom of society.

Rawls characterizes the difference principle as a principle of reciprocity. Its requirement that inequalities work to the maximum advantage of the worst off means that the greater than equal economic benefits for the better off are matched by increased benefits for those at the bottom of society. Moreover, the principle guaranteeing the substance of equal liberties requires that, where necessary, the government intervene to make sure that economic inequalities are not reducing the equal liberties of the poor to empty legal forms, or giving the rich disproportionate influence on political decisions. Rawls contends that citizens of a property-owning democracy, even the poorest citizens, will feel allegiance to the society because they will see that, though others are doing better, those others are only doing better on terms that also improve the shares of those who are less well off. By contrast, writes Rawls, in a capitalist welfare state, "there may develop a discouraged and depressed underclass many of whose members are chronically dependent on welfare. This underclass feels left out and does not participate in the public political culture."[85]

Can there be any doubt that Rawls is describing the United States here? Is there any wonder why a society that does no more than provide for the most basic needs of its poorest members (when it even does that much!)[86] also finds that those individuals commit crimes? Rawls's analysis shows us that economic inequality may result in crime, not simply from need, but by producing an impoverished class that feels "left out" of society and thus does not develop allegiance to its major institutions.

Writes Todd Clear, professor of criminal justice at Rutgers University, "Let's start investing in things that really reduce crime: good schools, jobs and a future for young parents and their children."[87] Why don't we?

Prison

We know that prison produces more criminals than it cures. We know that more than 70 percent of the inmates in the nation's prisons or jails are not there for the first time. A study from the Bureau of Justice Statistics indicates that, of inmates released in 1994, 67.5 percent were rearrested within three years, "almost exclusively for a felony or serious misdemeanor."[88] We know that prison inmates are denied autonomy and privacy and are subjected to indignities and acts of violence as regular features of their confinement, all of which is heightened by overcrowding. As of the last day of 2004, 24 state prison systems were operating above the most generous measure of their reported capacity; the federal prison system was operating at 40 percent above capacity.[89] A study of prisons in four Midwestern states found that about one-fifth of male inmates reported "a pressured or forced sex incident while incarcerated. About nine percent of male inmates reported that they had been raped."[90]

The predictable result, as delineated by Robert Johnson and Hans Toch in *The Pains of Imprisonment*, "is that the prison's survivors become tougher, more pugnacious, and less able to feel for themselves and others, while its nonsurvivors become weaker, more susceptible, and less able to control their lives."[91] Prisoners are thus bereft of both training and capacity to handle daily problems in competent and socially constructive ways, inside or outside of prison. The organization Stop Prison Rape reports, "Upon release, male prisoner rape survivors may bring with them emotional scars and learned violent behavior that continue the cycle of harm. Feelings of rage can be suppressed until release, when survivors may engage in violent, antisocial behavior."[92] According to a Human Rights Watch report entitled "No Escape: Male Rape in U.S. Prisons," "[T]he only way to avoid the repetition of sexual abuse, many prisoners assert, is to strike back violently." The report quotes a victim of prison rape saying, "People start to treat you right, once you become deadly."[93] In this way, prison makes inmates a greater harm to society than they were when they entered.

Once on the outside, burdened with the stigma of a prison record and rarely trained in a marketable skill, they find few opportunities for noncriminal employment open to them. Nor does this affect all groups in America alike. According to Professor Michael Tonry, author of *Malign Neglect: Race, Crime and Punishment in America*, "By affecting so many young black men, American criminal laws have further undermined the black family and made it harder for black men to get an education and find good jobs." A recent study by the Sentencing Project indicates that the enormous number of African American men who have been convicted of felonies, and therefore deprived of their right to vote, is "having a profound [negative!] impact on the black community's ability to participate in the political process."[94]

What's more, because so much of the recent increase in imprisonment has been of inner-city black men who were involved in families and who had at least part-time legitimate employment at the time of their arrest and incarceration, social scientists are beginning to study the ways in which massive imprisonment is undermining the family and other community institutions, depriving children of male role models, and depriving women of potential husbands and support. Several criminologists have found limited evidence suggesting that massive imprisonment may weaken inner-city institutions of informal social control *and thus lead to more crime in the long run.* Others argue that high levels of incarceration can weaken the stigma and thus the deterrent value of punishment in prison, and massive incarceration can strengthen ties between prison gangs and offenders on the street.[95]

Can we honestly act as if we do not know that our prison system (including our failure to ensure a meaningful postrelease noncriminal alternative for the ex-con) is a *source* of crime? Should we really pretend, then, that we do not *know* why ex-cons turn to crime? Recidivism does not happen because ex-cons miss their alma mater. In fact, if prisons are supposed to deter people from crime, one would expect that ex-prisoners would be the most deterred, because the deprivations of prison are more real to them than to the rest of us. Recidivism is thus a doubly poignant testimony to the job that prison does in preparing its graduates for crime, yet we do little to change the nature of prisons or to provide real services to ex-convicts.

In his 2004 State of the Union Address, President Bush seemed to indicate that he understood at least a small part of the recidivism problem when he discussed the 600,000 inmates released back into society each year. He said, "We know from long experience that if they can't find work, or a home, or help, they are much more likely to commit more crimes and return to prison." His proposed Prisoner Re-entry Initiative would expand job training and placement, and help with transitional housing and mentoring. But the $300 million he proposed to spend over four years, divided into the 2,400,000 inmates who would be released over that period, amounts to about $125 per inmate. That is hardly enough to ensure that America is "the land of the second chance—and when the gates of the prison open, the path ahead should lead to a better life."[96] (Two years later, the Republican-led U.S. Congress has not scheduled hearings on this bill.)

Guns

President Bush noted in 2001, "In America, a teenager today is more likely to die from a gunshot than from all natural causes of death combined."[97] Our firearm death rate is higher by far than that of any other modern nation. And, because the fatality rate for robberies using a gun is three times higher than for robberies with knives and ten times higher than for robberies with other weapons, countries like Italy and Australia that have robbery rates comparable to the United States' have far fewer robberies that end up as homicides.[98]

Speaking about the extraordinary spate of deadly violence that we had in the late 1980s and early 1990s, Garen Wintemute puts it bluntly: "the entire increase in homicide in the United States through 1993 was attributable to firearm homicide."[99] Increasingly, this was due to highly lethal semiautomatic pistols (during the same period, the percentage of homicides with regular revolvers declined significantly). Hospitals reported an increase in gunshot wounds per victim, and in the size of bullets removed. This phenomenon is closely linked to trends in handgun production. Starting in the late 1980s, American gun manufacturers started producing "high capacity, medium-caliber semiautomatic pistols that were also very inexpensive." Almost all were produced "by a small group of manufacturers in Southern California."[100]

Gary Kleck estimates that, by 1990, the civilian stock of guns in the United States had passed the 200 million mark. This estimate is corroborated by a 1993 report from the Bureau of Alcohol, Tobacco, and Firearms, which estimated 200 million guns, about 1 percent of which were assault rifles. They also note that the "number of large caliber pistols produced annually increased substantially after 1986."[101] A more recent review by the nonpartisan National Research Council suggests that by 1999, the civilian gun stock climbed to 258 million. The United States has 925 guns for every 1,000 people, with about 43 percent of households owning at least one.[102]

The President's Crime Commission reported that, in 1965, "5,600 murders, 34,700 aggravated assaults and the vast majority of the 68,400 armed robberies were committed by means of firearms. All but 10 of 278 law enforcement officers murdered during the period 1960–65 were killed with firearms." The commission concluded almost 40 years ago that

> more than one-half of all willful homicides and armed robberies, and almost one-fifth of all aggravated assaults, involve use of firearms. As long as there is no effective gun-control legislation, violent crimes and the injuries they inflict will be harder to reduce than they might otherwise be.[103]

The situation has worsened since the commission's warning. The FBI states, "In 1975, 66 percent of murders of persons (aged 15 to 19) were attributable to guns, while in 1992 the figure rose to 85 percent. This increase supports the theory that today's high-school-aged youths are exposed to an environment that includes guns."[104] The Office of Juvenile Justice reports, "By 1997, the homicide rate for 15- to 24-year-olds was 15.2 per 100,000, which is higher than the combined total homicide rate of eleven industrialized nations," and goes on to point out, "Firearms were the weapons of choice in nearly two-thirds of all murders."[105]

Furthermore, guns kill and maim outside of crime as well. "Every 14 minutes someone in America dies from a gunshot wound. Slightly more than half of those deaths are suicides, about 44 percent are homicides and 4 percent are unintentional shootings."[106] The Centers for Disease Control report that in 1997, "32,436 deaths resulted from firearm-related injuries, making such injuries the second leading cause of injury mortality in the United States after motor-vehicle-related incidents," and, further, that "an estimated 64,207 persons sustained nonfatal firearm-related injuries."[107] Guns also take a grave and worsening toll among our children. According to a report from the Children's Defense Fund, nearly 50,000 children were killed by guns between 1979 and 1991.[108]

In the face of facts like these—indeed, in the face of his own nearly fatal shooting by a would-be assassin—President Reagan refused to support any legislative attempts to control the sale of handguns.[109] His successor, President George H. W. Bush, followed suit.[110] On Thanksgiving Day 1993, Bush's successor, Bill Clinton, signed into law the so-called Brady Bill, which goes only so far as imposing a five-day waiting period for gun purchases to enable checks to see whether would-be gun purchasers have criminal records. The Brady Law leaves it to the states to enforce the waiting period and to get their police to make a "reasonable effort" to conduct the background checks. However, the bill provides no sanctions for states that do not comply, and it leaves it effectively up to the states to provide funding for the checks and to determine what is a "reasonable effort."[111] From 1994, when the Brady Law went into effect, until 2003, over 1.1 million applications for firearms have been rejected, but as Blumstein notes, "it is not known how many of those customers eventually bought guns from an unregulated source."[112] Moreover, while the Brady Law prohibits sales of guns to individuals with prior felony convictions, the sad fact is that, as different studies show, between half and three-quarters of those arrested for crimes involving weapons had *no prior felony conviction.*[113]

Can we believe that our leaders sincerely want to cut down on violent crime and the injuries it produces when they oppose even as much as *registering* guns or *licensing* gun owners, much less actually restricting the sale and movement of guns as a matter of national policy? Can we really believe that if guns were less readily available, violent criminals would simply switch to other weapons to commit the same number of crimes and do the same amount of damage? Is there a weapon other than the handgun that works as quickly, that allows its user so safe a distance, or that makes the criminal's physical strength (or speed or courage, for that matter) irrelevant? Could a bank robber hold a row of tellers at bay with a switchblade? Studies indicate that, if gun users switched to the next deadliest weapon—the knife—and attempted the same number of crimes, we could still expect *two-thirds fewer fatalities* because the fatality rate of the knife is roughly one-third that of the gun. In other words, even if guns were eliminated and the number of crimes held steady, we could expect to save as many as two out of every three persons who are now the victims of firearm homicide.

Drugs

Finally, the United States has an enormous drug abuse and addiction problem. There is considerable evidence, however, that our attempts to cure it are worse than the disease itself. Consider first heroin. Some people think this drug is out of fashion and no longer widely used. Far from it! Its use is widespread and persistent. The number of heroin users is hard to estimate because we only know about the ones who get caught and because there is a large but unknown number of individuals who (contrary to popular mythology) shoot up occasionally without becoming addicts, a practice known as "chipping." In his book, *The Heroin Solution,* Arnold Trebach suggests that this number may be as high as 3.5 million.[114] For 1999, the Office of National Drug Control Policy estimated about 1 million chronic heroin users and another 140,000 to 600,000 occasional users. The number of chronic users decreased earlier in the 1990s, "Perhaps due to the AIDS epidemic and increased incarceration, but that decrease had largely abated by the latter part of the decade, perhaps because new users were attracted by the availability of high-quality low-cost heroin."[115]

As shocking as these numbers may be, it must be at least as shocking to discover that there is little evidence proving that heroin is a *dangerous* drug. James Q. Wilson, a defender of the prohibition of heroin and other drugs, admits that "there are apparently no specific pathologies—serious illnesses or physiological deterioration—that are known to result from heroin use per se."[116] On the basis of available scientific evidence, there is every reason to suspect that we do our bodies more damage, more *irreversible* damage, by smoking cigarettes and drinking liquor than by using heroin. Most of the physical damage associated with heroin use is probably attributable to the trauma of withdrawal, a product not so much of heroin as of its occasional unobtainability.

It remains the case that most drug arrests are for marijuana use or possession, and that marijuana is a relatively safe drug.[117] The 1988 surgeon general's report lists tobacco as a more dangerous drug than marijuana.[118] According to the findings and conclusions of Francis Young, administrative law judge for the Drug Enforcement Administration, there are no documented marijuana user fatalities ("despite [its 5,000-year-]long history of use and the extraordinarily high numbers of social smokers, there are simply no credible medical reports to suggest that consuming marijuana has caused a single death"!), and no amount of marijuana that a person could possibly eat or smoke would constitute a lethal dose. By contrast, aspirin overdoses cause hundreds of deaths a year.[119]

Regarding the illicit drugs that can cause death from overdose, the dangers have been blown wildly out of proportion. Trebach points out that, although federal authorities documented 2,177 deaths from the most popular illicit drugs in 1985, between 400,000 and 500,000 people died from alcohol and tobacco during that same year. He adds that 59 children aged 17 and under died from drug overdoses in 1987, while "408 American children (from infants through the age of 14) were murdered by their parents in 1983"![120]

It might be said that the evil of drugs such as heroin is that they are *addicting,* because this is a bad thing even if the addicting substance is not itself harmful. It is hard to deny that the image of a person enslaved to a chemical is ugly and repugnant to our sense that the dignity of human beings lies in their capacity to control their destinies. More questionable, however, is whether this is, in the case of adults, anybody's business but their own. Even so, suppose we agree that addiction is an evil worthy of prevention. Doesn't that make us hypocrites? What about all our other addictions? What about cigarette smoking, which, unlike heroin, contributes to cancer and heart disease? Nicotine's addictiveness—according to former Surgeon General C. Everett Koop—is similar to that of heroin, and *more addicting than cocaine*, more likely to addict the new user, and more difficult to quit once addicted.[121] What about the roughly 15 million alcoholics in the nation working their way through their livers and into their graves? What about the people who cannot get started without a caffeine fix in the morning and those who, once started, cannot slow down without their alcohol fix in the evening? What of the folks who can't face daily life without their Prozac? Are they not all addicts?[122]

Suffice it to say, then, at the very least, our attitudes about heroin are inconsistent and irrational, and there is reason to believe they are outrageous and hypocritical. Even if this were not so, even if we could be much more certain that heroin addiction is a disease worth preventing, the fact would remain that the "cure" we have chosen is worse than the disease. We *know* that treating the possession of heroin as a criminal offense produces more crime than it prevents.

Alfred Blumstein provides a useful categorization of the relationship between drugs and crime:

- *Pharmacological/psychological consequences:* The chemical properties of the drug directly cause criminal activity.
- *Economic/compulsive crimes:* Drug users commit crimes to get money to support their habit.
- *Systemic crime:* Crime, violence, and corruption are committed as part of the regular means of doing business in the drug industry because there is no regulation and because formal dispute-resolution mechanisms are unavailable.[123]

About the pharmacological consequences of drugs, says Blumstein, the drug "that has the strongest pharmacological effect is alcohol. . . . Heroin is a downer, so heroin doesn't do much. And there hasn't been shown to be much pharmacological effect of the other serious drugs on crime, not anything comparable to that of alcohol, which has been shown to be a strong stimulator of violence."[124] PCP tends to be one of the only other drugs to have a pharmacological link to violence. High doses of cocaine and methamphetamine can lead to some psychoses that include paranoia and delusion, which can lead to violence. But most of the violence associated with drugs falls under the second and third of Blumstein's categories. As for systemic crime, we have already seen the link between the crack trade and the murder epidemic of the late 1980s and early 1990s. Both systemic crimes and the economic/compulsive crimes that are engaged in by drug users to support their habits are due to the fact that drugs are so costly, and that is due to the fact that the drugs are illegal.

Prior to 1914, when anyone could go into a drugstore and purchase heroin and other opiates the way we buy aspirin today, hundreds of thousands of upstanding, law-abiding citizens were hooked.[125] Opiate addiction is not in itself a *cause* of crime. If anything, it is a pacifier.[126] There is, writes Trebach, "nothing in the pharmacology, or physical and psychological impact, of the drug that would propel a user to crime."[127] Nor is there anything about heroin itself that makes it extremely costly. The heroin for which an addict pays $100 or more a day could be produced legally at a cost of a few cents for a day's supply. However, once sale or possession of heroin is made a serious criminal offense, a number of consequences follow. First, the prices go up because those who supply it face grave penalties, and those who want it want it bad. Second, because the supply (and the quality) of the drug fluctuates, depending on how vigorously the agents of the law try to prevent it, the addict's life is continuously unstable. Addicts live in constant uncertainty about the next fix and must devote much of their wit and energy to getting it and to getting enough money to pay for it. They do not, then, fit easily into the routines of a nine-to-five job, even if they could get one that would pay enough to support their habits. Finally, all the difficulties of securing the drug add up to an incentive to be not merely a user of heroin but a dealer as well, because this both earns money and makes one's own supply more certain. Addicts thus have an incentive to find and encourage new addicts, which they would not have if heroin were legally and cheaply available. If we add to this the fact that heroin addiction has remained widespread, and possibly even increased in spite of all our law enforcement efforts, can we doubt that the cure is worse than the disease? Can we doubt that the cure is a *source* of crime?

Says former Washington, D.C., Police Chief Maurice Turner,

> If you see an addict going through withdrawal, he's in some kind of damn pain. . . . When they get pretty well strung out, they have about a $100- to $120-a-day habit. When they get that type of habit, they're going to have to steal approximately six times that much [because fences don't pay list price].[128]

Professor Blumstein agrees that "you need money to buy drugs, so the higher the price of the drug, the greater the incentive to commit the crime."[129] The result is a recipe for large-scale and continual robbery and burglary, which would not exist if the drug were available legally. A recent study by Anglin and Speckart of the relationship between narcotics use and crime concludes that there is "strong evidence that there is a strong causal relationship, at least in the United States, between addiction to narcotics and property crime levels."[130]

Do a little arithmetic. Suppose that there are half a million addicts with $100-a-day habits. And let's make some conservative assumptions about these addicts. Suppose that they fill their habits only 250 days a year (sometimes they're in jail or in the hospital). Suppose that they have to steal for half their drug needs, and that they must steal three times the dollar value of what they need because they must convert their booty into cash through a fence. (These conservative assumptions are similar to those made in a report of the U.S. Department of Health, Education, and Welfare, entitled *Social Cost of Drug Abuse,* estimating the amount of theft in which heroin addicts had to engage to support their habits in 1974.)[131] If you've done your arithmetic, you have seen that our half-million addicts need to steal $18,750,000,000 a year to support their habits. This is more than the $16.1 billion that the FBI estimates as the loss due to property crimes during 2004,[132] and it doesn't even take into consideration theft by those addicted to other drugs, such as crack cocaine.

The Bureau of Justice Statistics reports that, in 1997, roughly one of every six prisoners—19 percent of state inmates, 15 percent of federal inmates—said that they had committed their current offense in order to get money for drugs.[133] Because heroin doesn't produce crime through its pharmacological effects, and because it is so costly only because it's illegal, it is not the "disease" of heroin addiction but its "cure" that leads to property crime. *It is our steadfast refusal to provide heroin through legal sources that, for a significant number of the approximately 1 million heroin addicts, translates a physical need for a drug into a physical need to steal billions of dollars worth of property a year.*

Against this conclusion, it is sometimes countered that studies show that a large proportion of criminal heroin addicts were criminals before they were addicts. Such studies would only refute the claim that the illegality of heroin is a source of crime if the claim was that heroin addiction turns otherwise law-abiding citizens into thieves. Rather, the claim is that the illegality of heroin (and, thus, its very high price) places addicts in situations in which they *must* engage in theft, continually and at a high level, to keep a step ahead of the pains of withdrawal. Anglin and Speckart affirm that "while involvement in property crime activities generally precedes the addiction career, after addiction occurs the highly elevated property crime levels demonstrated by addicts appear to be regulated by similarly high narcotics use levels."[134] Thus, even for addicts who already were criminals, heroin addiction increases the amount they need to steal and works to make them virtually immune to attempts to wean them from a life of crime. Consequently, even if all heroin addicts were criminals before they were addicts, the illegality of heroin would still be a source of crime because of the increased pressure it places on the addict to steal a lot and to steal often. Much the same reasoning applies to other illegal addictive drugs.

Recently, attention has shifted from heroin to "crack," a highly addictive derivative of cocaine. The Office of National Drug Control Policy (ONDCP) reports that there were 2.8 million hard-core cocaine users in 1999.[135] Having learned nothing from our experience with heroin, we have applied to cocaine and crack the same policy that failed with heroin, with predictable results. A report from the ONDCP indicates that in 2000, Americans spent $64 billion on these illegal drugs: "$36 billion on cocaine, $10 billion on heroin, $5.4 billion on methamphetamine, $11 billion on marijuana, and $2.4 billion on other substances."[136] Because the price per pure gram of cocaine and of heroin has generally gone down between 1980 and the present, we can only conclude that, for all the hoopla of the war on drugs, not to mention the enormous increase in the number of persons sent to prison for drug offenses, there is a plentiful supply and these drugs remain popular.

According to the ONDCP, during the decade of the 1990s, "cocaine users consumed somewhere between 270 and 450 metric tons of pure cocaine each year," while "heroin users consumed 14 metric tons at the beginning and end of the decade."[137] According to an earlier United Nations estimate, illicit drugs account for some $400 billion worldwide, nearly one-tenth of world trade in all products![138] The General Accounting Office reports that U.S. efforts to reduce cultivation of drug crops in Bolivia and Colombia "have been almost entirely ineffective and the cultivation of drug crops has increased dramatically in both countries."[139] This caps a long history of failure, starting with President Richard Nixon's (successful) attempt to pressure Turkey into eradicating local cultivation of poppies (the source of opium and thus of heroin, an opium derivative) in 1971 and continuing with both Reagan's and Bush Sr.'s largely futile attempts to pressure foreign countries to reduce domestic production of narcotic substances. Even when such pressure works, it serves only to displace production elsewhere. And when the pressure lets up, production rebounds.

In spite of three U.S.-led international drug wars since 1971, worldwide illicit opium production rose from 990 tons in 1971 to 4,200 tons in 1989 and 4,500 tons in 2002. Andean coca leaf (the source of cocaine and thus of crack) production went from 319,200 metric tons in 1990 down to 294,400 in 2002, but UN estimates of total world cocaine manufacture increased from 774 metric tons in 1990 to 800 in 2002.[140] Likewise, attempts to use the U.S. Coast Guard and Navy to interdict cocaine coming into the United States by sea have failed to put a dent in the traffic. After all, America has over 88,000 miles of coastline.[141] *The Wall Street Journal* reports that a kilogram of cocaine that cost between $55,000 and $65,000 in 1981 cost between $20,000 and $40,000 in 1987.[142] The National Narcotics Intelligence Consumers' Committee reports cocaine prices as low as $10,500 per kilogram in 1994.[143] In a summary of these trends, a 2004 ONDCP report indicated "very sharp (roughly 70 percent) price declines during the 1980s through 1989" and "gradual declines during the 1990s," with occasional years of price increases. Prices continued declining through 2003, "reaching all-time lows that are roughly 12 to 21 percent below prices in 1999. Cumulatively, powder cocaine prices have declined by roughly 80 percent since 1981," and "purity-adjusted prices were at or near all-time lows in 2003."[144] All of this testifies to the general failure of our costly "war on drugs" to make these drugs harder to obtain—a conclusion endorsed by the conservative American Enterprise Institute in a 2005 book on drug policy.[145]

In 1988, the *National Law Journal* surveyed 181 chief prosecutors or their top drug deputies throughout the United States and reported that "nearly two-thirds of the country's top state and local prosecutors say they are having little to no impact in the fight against illegal narcotics."[146] The American Enterprise Institute study stated that "on the whole, then, there is now less reason than ever to believe that current policies are an efficient and effective response to the problem of illicit drugs."[147] This failing drug war cost federal, state, and local governments approximately $33 billion in 1999, up nearly $5 billion from 1994.[148] The National Drug Control Budget alone is $12.1 billion for fiscal year 2005.[149]

To that must be added the *nonfinancial* costs, such as increased violence among competing drug traffickers and increased corruption among law enforcement officials on the front line in the drug war. The year 1988 saw the nation's capital reach and overtake its annual homicide record, with all experts attributing the surge in murders to the struggle to capture the lucrative drug market.[150] *The New York Times* reports that "researchers say there are now more than 100 cases each year in state and Federal courts in which law enforcement officials are charged or implicated in drug corruption."[151] Says William Green, assistant commissioner for internal affairs at the U.S. Customs Service, "The money that's being offered by the drug dealers is so big it is just hard to visualize."[152] The Mollen Commission report on police corruption in New York City found "willful blindness" to corruption throughout the police department, resulting in networks of rogue officers who dealt in drugs and preyed on black and Hispanic neighborhoods.[153]

In sum, we have an antidrug policy that is failing at its own goals and succeeding only in adding to crime. First, there are the heroin and crack addicts, who must steal to support their habits. Then, there are the drug merchants who are offered fabulous financial incentives to provide illicit substances to a willing body of consumers. This in turn contributes to the high rate of inner-city murders and other violence as drug gangs battle for the enormous sums of money available. Next, there are the law enforcement officials who, after risking their lives for low salaries, are corrupted by nearly irresistible amounts of money. Finally, there are the otherwise law-abiding citizens who are made criminals because they use cocaine, a drug less harmful than tobacco, and those who are made criminals because they use marijuana, a drug that is safer than alcohol and less deadly than aspirin.

Much of the recent dramatic growth in our prison population (documented above) is the result of the hardening of drug enforcement policy starting in the Reagan years and continuing into the present: In 1968 there were 162,000 drug arrests nationwide, in 1977 there were 569,000, and in 1989 there were 1,150,000 drug arrests.[154] In 2004 there were more than 1.7 million drug arrests, and the Bureau of Justice Statistics reports that 55 percent of federal inmates were serving sentences for drug violations in 2003.[155] The absolute numbers are even more striking. In 2003, federal prisons held 86,972 drug offenders, compared to 30,470 in 1990.[156] On the state level, there were less than 20,000 drug offenders in state prisons in 1990, but by 2000, there were over 250,000.[157] Because numerous studies show that arrested drug dealers in inner-city neighborhoods are quickly replaced, it was apparent from the start that this policy would have little success in reducing the availability of illicit drugs.[158]

All this is occurring at a time when there is increasing evidence that what does work to reduce substance abuse is public education. Because this has succeeded in reducing alcohol and tobacco consumption and, in some cases, marijuana and cocaine consumption as well, it's time that we take the money we are wasting in the "war on drugs" and spend it on public education instead. Because that would be far less costly than the "war," this would leave over money to fight a more effective war against muggers and rapists rather than recreational drug users. Evidence from the 11 states that decriminalized marijuana possession in the 1970s suggests that decriminalization does not lead to increased use. And President Clinton's former surgeon general, Joycelyn Elders, recommended that we study seriously the possibility of decriminalizing drugs as a means to reducing violence, noting that "other countries had decriminalized drug use and had reduced their crime rates without increasing the use of narcotics."[159] Baltimore Mayor Kurt Schmoke has called for consideration of decriminalization, and so has Jerry Wilson, former chief of police of Washington, D.C. (where 42 percent of murders were drug-related in 1990).[160] A draft of a report commissioned by the American Medical Association recommended legalization of marijuana and decriminalization of other illicit drugs. The report was shelved when some doctors "expressed outrage at its recommendation."[161] Some form of decriminalization of marijuana, heroin, and cocaine would reduce the criminalization of otherwise law-abiding users; it would drive down the price of drugs, which would reduce the need for addicts to steal, and reduce as well the incentives to drug traffickers and smugglers to ply their trades and to find new users; and it would free up personnel and resources for a more effective war against the crimes that people fear most.

In the face of all this, it is hard not to share the frustration expressed by Norval Morris, former dean of the University of Chicago Law School: "It is trite but it remains true that the main causes of crime are social and economic. The question arises whether people really care. The solutions are so obvious. *It's almost as if America wished for a high crime rate.*"[162] If this is so, then *the system's failure is only in the eye of the victim: For those in control, it is a roaring success!*

WHAT WORKS TO REDUCE CRIME

Surveying the programs that might contribute to reducing crime, criminologist Elliot Currie concludes that "four priorities seem especially critical: preventing child abuse and neglect, enhancing children's intellectual and social development, providing support and guidance to vulnerable adolescents, and working extensively with juvenile offenders." About these programs, Currie observes that "the best of them work, and they work remarkably well given how limited and underfunded they usually are."[163] A study entitled *Diverting Children from a Life of Crime: Measuring Costs and Benefits*, issued in June 1996 by the Rand Corporation, concluded,

> Programs that try to steer the young from wrongdoing—the training of parents whose children often misbehave, for example, or incentives to graduate from high school—are far more cost-effective in preventing crime over the long term than are mandatory sentences that imprison repeat adult offenders for long periods.[164]

A more recent report from the Rand Corporation, entitled *Investing in Our Children: What We Know and Don't Know about the Costs and Benefits of Early Childhood Interventions*, reached a similar conclusion. Evaluating nine programs in which early interventions were targeted at disadvantaged children, the study concludes that such programs lead to decreased criminal activity and save taxpayer dollars at the same time.[165] Similar results were found for Head Start programs: "At age 27, those who participated [in Head Start programs as children] had lower arrest rates, higher education rates, earned more money, [and] were more likely to be homeowners and less likely to receive social services."[166]

The National Treatment Improvement Study, "the largest study of its kind, which followed more than 5,300 clients in programs funded by the federal Center for Substance Abuse Treatment," concludes that

> drug and alcohol treatment programs significantly reduced substance use, crime, and homelessness. . . . Use of most illicit substances in the year after treatment entry declined about 50 percent compared with the year before. . . . Arrest rates fell substantially in the sample—from 48 percent to 17 percent.[167]

And a study by the Rand Corporation Drug Policy Research Center, entitled *Controlling Cocaine: Supply versus Demand Programs*, found that "[t]reatment is seven times more cost-effective than domestic drug enforcement in reducing cocaine use and 15 times more cost-effective in reducing the social costs of crime and lost productivity."[168] The study also concluded that "treatment is the most effective way to reduce violent crime."[169]

A recent review of more than 500 crime-prevention program evaluations yielded a list of what works. Among the programs that appear effective in reducing crime, the report lists family therapy and parent training for delinquent and at-risk adolescents; teaching of social competency skills in schools, and coaching of high-risk youth in "thinking skills"; vocational training for older male ex-offenders; extra police patrols in high-crime hot spots; monitoring of high-risk repeat offenders by specialized police forces as well as incarceration; rehabilitation programs with risk-focused treatments for convicted offenders; and therapeutic community treatment fo. using offenders in prisons.[170]

In short, there is a growing body of knowledge showing that early childhood intervention, drug treatment, and numerous other programs can work to reduce crime. As Professor Blumstein observed, "If you intervene early, you not only save the costs of incarceration, you also save the costs of crime and gain the benefits of an individual who is a taxpaying contributor to the economy."[171] But, as Peter Greenwood, author of the Rand Corporation Study, *Diverting Children from a Life of Crime*, says, "The big policy question is, Who will act on this?"[172]

HOW CRIME PAYS: ERIKSON AND DURKHEIM

Kai T. Erikson has suggested in his book, *Wayward Puritans*, that societies derive benefit from the existence of crime, and thus there is reason to believe that social institutions work to maintain rather than to eliminate crime. Because the Pyrrhic defeat theory draws heavily upon this insight, it will serve to clarify my own view if we compare it with Erikson's.

Professor Erikson's theory is based on the view of crime that finds expression in one of the classic works of sociological theory, *The Division of Labor in Society*, by Émile Durkheim. Writing toward the end of the nineteenth century, Durkheim

> had suggested that crime (and by extension other forms of deviation) may actually perform a needed service to society by drawing people together in a common posture of anger and indignation. The deviant individual violates rules of conduct which the rest of the community holds in high respect; and when these people come together to express their outrage over the offense and to bear witness against the offender, they develop a tighter bond of solidarity than existed earlier.[173]

The solidarity that holds a community together, in this view, is a function of the intensity with which the members of the community share a living sense of the group's cultural identity, of the boundary between acceptable and unacceptable behavior that gives the group its distinctive character. It is necessary, then, for the existence of a community as a *community* that its members learn and constantly relearn the location of its "boundaries." Erikson writes that these boundaries are learned in dramatic confrontations with

> policing agents whose special business it is to guard the cultural integrity of the community. Whether these confrontations take the form of criminal trials, excommunication hearings, courts-martial, or even case conferences, they act

as boundary-maintaining devices in the sense that they demonstrate to whatever audience is concerned where the line is drawn between behavior that
belongs in the special universe of the group and behavior that does not.[174]

In brief, this means not only that a community makes good use of unacceptable behavior *but also that it positively needs unacceptable behavior.* Not only
does unacceptable behavior cast in relief the terrain of behavior acceptable to
the community; it also reinforces the intensity with which the members of
the community identify that terrain as their shared territory. On this view,
deviant behavior is an ingredient in the glue that holds a community together.
"This," Erikson continues,

> raises a delicate theoretical issue. If we grant that human groups often derive
> benefit from deviant behavior, can we then assume that they are organized in
> such a way as to promote this resource? Can we assume, in other words, *that
> forces operate in the social structure to recruit offenders and to commit them to long
> periods of service in the deviant ranks?* . . .
>   Looking at the matter from a long-range historical perspective, it is fair to
> conclude that prisons have done a conspicuously poor job of reforming the
> convicts placed in their custody; but the very consistency of this failure may
> have a peculiar logic of its own. Perhaps we find it difficult to change the worst
> of our penal practices because we expect the prison to harden the inmate's com-
> mitment to deviant forms of behavior and draw him more deeply into the
> deviant ranks.[175]

Drawing on Durkheim's recognition that societies benefit from the existence of deviants, Erikson entertains the view that societies have institutions
whose unannounced function is to recruit and maintain a reliable supply of
deviants. Modified for our purposes, Erikson's view would become the
hypothesis that the American criminal justice system fails to reduce crime
because a visible criminal population is essential to maintaining the "boundaries" that mark the cultural identity of American society and to maintaining
the solidarity among those who share that identity. In other words, in its failure, the criminal justice system succeeds in providing some of the cement
necessary to hold American society together as a society.
    As I said in the Introduction, this is one of the ideas that contributes to the
Pyrrhic defeat theory, but it is also transformed in the process. Here, then, my
aim is to acknowledge my debt to the Durkheim–Erikson thesis and to state
the difference between it and the view that I will defend. The debt is to the
insight that societies may promote behavior that they seem to desire to stamp
out, and that failure to eliminate deviance may be a success of some sort.
    The difference, on the other hand, is this: Both Durkheim and Erikson
jump from the *general* proposition that the failure to eliminate deviance promotes social solidarity to the *specific* conclusion that the form in which this
failure occurs in a particular society can be explained by the contribution the
failure makes to promoting consensus on shared beliefs and thus feelings of

social solidarity. This is a "jump" because it leaves out the important question of how a social group forms its particular consensus around one set of shared beliefs rather than another; that is, Durkheim and Erikson implicitly assume that a consensus already exists (at least virtually) and that deviance is promoted to manifest and reinforce it. This leads to the view that social institutions reflect beliefs already in people's heads and already largely and spontaneously shared by all of them.

In my view, even if it is granted that societies work to strengthen feelings of social solidarity, the set of beliefs about the world around which those feelings will crystallize are by no means already in people's heads and spontaneously shared. A consensus is made, not born, although, again, I do not mean that it is made intentionally. It is created, not just reflected, by social institutions. Thus, the failure to stamp out deviance does not simply reinforce a consensus that already exists; it is part of the process by which a very particular consensus is created.[176] In developing the Pyrrhic defeat theory, I try to show how the failure of criminal justice works to create and reinforce a very particular set of beliefs about the world, about what is dangerous and what is not, and about who is a threat and who is not. This does not merely shore up general feelings of social solidarity; it allows those feelings to be attached to a social order characterized by striking disparities of wealth, power, and privilege, and by considerable injustice.

A WORD ABOUT FOUCAULT

Michel Foucault is another thinker who has suggested that the failure of the criminal justice system—prisons in particular—serves a function for society. His view of this failure and its function is, at points, close to the one for which I argue here, but there are differences as well. In his book, *Discipline and Punish*, Foucault notes that complaints about the failure of prisons to curb crime, indeed their tendency to increase crime by promoting recidivism, have accompanied the prison throughout its history—so much so that Foucault asks, "Is not the supposed failure part of the functioning of the prison?"[177] In response, Foucault writes that the prison "has succeeded extremely well . . . in producing delinquents, in an apparently marginal, but in fact centrally supervised milieu; in producing the delinquent as a pathologized subject."[178] That is, the prison regime transforms the offender from a lawbreaker into a *delinquent in need of correction*, an abnormal individual in need of treatment. And this development licenses a permanent policing of the potentially troublesome classes.

Foucault suggests that the new prison regime that emerged in France in the nineteenth century was a response to a "new threat" posed by peasants and workers against the "new system of the legal exploitation of labour,"[179] by which he means capitalism. This is a class-based explanation of the new prison regime, in which criminality gets identified "almost exclusively [with] a certain social class . . the bottom rank of the social order."[180] Among the advantages produced by this prison regime and the policing that accompanies it are the maintenance of illegality at a sufficiently low level so that it does not pose a general threat to the social order, and the weakening of the poorer classes—from whom both the delinquents and their victims tend to come—by dividing the poor against themselves. Moreover, says Foucault, "[d]elinquency, controlled illegality, is an agent for the illegality of the dominant groups."[181] Here he has in mind the profits to be made from drugs and prostitution, alongside a general toleration of the "delinquency of wealth."[182] This much is generally in accord with the thesis of this book, which argues that the failure of the criminal justice system to significantly reduce crime, as well as the identification of crime with the harmful acts of poor people, serves the interests of the rich and powerful by creating the general belief that the greatest threat to the well-being of ordinary folks comes from the poor rather than from the rich.[183]

But Foucault goes further. He contends that delinquency, "with the generalized policing that it authorizes, constitutes a means of perpetual surveillance of the population: an apparatus that makes it possible to supervise, through the delinquents themselves, the whole social field."[184] For Foucault, then, the prison is part of "general tactics of subjection" that amount to a system of permanent social surveillance. Stretching from the "Panopticon" model of a prison in which a single guard can watch a large number of inmates without himself being seen to the emergence of a "scientific" criminological establishment that observes and studies delinquents, and from there to the modern medical-psychological establishment that keeps records on just about everyone, ubiquitous surveillance works to make people feel observed and thus makes them into the agents of their own normalizing discipline. Thus, the prison spreads out into a "carceral archipelago," a whole system of institutions and practices, including the disciplines such as psychology and medicine, aimed at "normalization."[185] In sum, writes Foucault,

> the normalizing power has spread. Borne along by the omnipresence of the mechanisms of discipline, basing itself on all the carceral apparatuses, it has become one of the major functions of our society. The judges of normality are everywhere. We are in the society of the teacher-judge, the doctor-judge, the educator-judge, the 'social-worker'-judge; it is on them that the universal reign of the normative is based; and each individual, wherever he may find himself, subjects to it his body, his gestures, his behaviour, his aptitudes, his achievements.[186]

With this, Foucault has left criminal justice behind and spun a theory of the nature of modern society generally. Also left behind is the class structure of the exercise of power that was present in the origins of the prison system as Foucault described it. Now, power is everywhere, exercised by everyone on him or herself and on everyone else.[187] No doubt, this captures something of the flavor of modern life, in which people at all levels of society are subjected to myriad pressures to be "normal," from the tsk-tsks of teachers and doctors to the self-help books and advice columns that offer to make us better earners and better lovers and better parents. The judges of normality are, indeed, everywhere.

But this account also mystifies the exercise of power, and renders resistance and thus amelioration unintelligible. Rather than operating along a class axis that might be eliminated, and to serve interests that might be identified and critiqued, power now seems its own goal, a universal fact of modern life, driven by no particular interest beyond that of discipline—"the policing of normality" as an end in itself.[188] Not only is the class structure of the exercise of power—particularly criminal justice power—flattened out here, the moral status of the exercise is obscured as well. Absent from Foucault's analysis is any sense of the difference between those forms of discipline that are necessary for the freedom of each to coexist peacefully with the freedom of the rest and those forms of discipline that simply serve the interests of the rich and powerful.[189] The analysis that I shall present in this book will strive to keep the class nature of the criminal justice system in view, while recognizing the importance of distinguishing between those exercises of power that are necessary for the protection of freedom and those that simply serve the interests of the wealthy.

SUMMARY

In this chapter, I have tried to establish the first part of the Pyrrhic defeat theory, namely, that the war on crime is a failure and an avoidable one: The American criminal justice system—by which I mean the entire process from lawmaking to law enforcing—has failed to eliminate the high rates of crime that characterize our society and threaten our citizens. Over the last several decades, crime has generally risen, although in recent years it has declined. I have shown that numerous causes—economic and social—have contributed to this, such that serious observers agree that criminal justice policy and practice cannot be credited with more than a fraction of the recent declines. At the same time, however, neither should it be thought on this basis that public policy cannot reduce the crime we have. To support this, I have shown that crime is not a simple and unavoidable consequence of either the number of youngsters in our populace or the degree of urbanization of our society. I have pointed out a number of policies we have good reason to believe would succeed in reducing crime—effective gun control, decriminalization of illicit drugs, amelioration of poverty, prevention of child abuse and neglect, and early intervention with at-risk youngsters—that we refuse to implement. I indicated that the Pyrrhic defeat theory shares, with the Durkheim–Erikson view of the functional nature of crime, the idea that societies may promote behavior that they seem to want to eliminate. However, my theory differs from their view in insisting that the failure to stamp out crime doesn't simply reflect an existing consensus but contributes to creating one, one that is functional for only a certain part of our society. I concluded by discussing Foucault's claim that the failure of the prison is part of a larger structure of disciplinary surveillance that pervades modern society. I pointed out how Foucault's account of the beginnings of this regime parallels the class analysis for which I shall argue. However, in its later development Foucault leaves class structure behind and thus, in my view, mystifies the nature of the power exercised in the criminal justice system.

STUDY QUESTIONS

1. Why do crime rates rise and fall?

2. What causes crime? How, and why, does the author distinguish a "cause" from a "source" of crime? What conditions make crime more likely?

3. What excuses have been given for our inability to reduce the amount of crime we have? How do you evaluate these excuses?

4. How do you think we could reduce the amount of crime? To what extent are these solutions within the criminal justice system, or do non-criminal-justice policies have a greater impact on crime?

5. What does it mean to say that "crime is functional for a society"? How does the Pyrrhic defeat theory differ on this from the Durkheim–Erikson theory?

6. List the costs and benefits of our current war on drugs. Is it worth it? Do you think that legalizing all or some illicit drugs would reduce crime? If so, would you agree to legalization?

7. What is meant by saying that the criminal justice system is "designed to fail"?

   A companion website to this book, with a chapter outline and summary, links to additional information, and Internet-based exercises is available at "Rich Get Richer," *www.paulsjusticepage.com*.

ADDITIONAL READINGS

Chambliss, William. *Power, Politics, and Crime*. Boulder, CO: Westview Press, 1999.

Christie, Nils. *Crime Control as Industry: Toward Gulags, Western Style?* 3rd ed. London: Routledge, 2000.

Conklin, John. *Why Crime Rates Fell*. Boston: Allyn & Bacon, 2003.

Currie, Elliot. *Crime and Punishment in America*. New York: Henry Holt, 1998.

Diaz, Tom. *Making a Killing: The Business of Guns in America*. New York: New Press, 1999.

Dyer, Joel. *The Perpetual Prisoner Machine: How America Profits from Crime*. Boulder, CO: Westview Press, 2000.

Irwin, John, and James Austin. *It's about Time: America's Imprisonment Binge,* 3rd ed. Belmont, CA: Wadsworth, 2000.

Kappeler, Victor, Mark Blumberg, and Gary Potter. *The Mythology of Crime and Criminal Justice,* 4th ed. Long Grove, IL: Waveland, 2005.

Mauer, Marc, and Meda Chesney-Lind. *Invisible Punishment: The Collateral Consequences of Mass Imprisonment.* New York: New Press/W. W. Norton, 2002.

Messerschmidt, J. *Capitalism, Partriarchy and Crime.* Totowa, NJ: Rowman & Littlefield, 1985.

Quinney, Richard. *Class, State and Crime.* New York: Longman, 1997.

Ross, Jeffrey, and Stephen Richards. *Convict Criminology.* Belmont, CA: Wadsworth, 2002.

Shelden, Randall. *Controlling the Dangerous Classes: A Critical Introduction to the History of Criminal Justice.* Boston: Allyn & Bacon, 2001.

NOTES

1. Franklin Zimring, "The New Politics of Criminal Justice," *Perspectives on Crime and Justice: 1999-2000 Lecture Series,* NCJ 184245, March 2001, p. 3.

2. State of the Union Message, January 25, 1994, as reported in *The Washington Post,* January 26, 1994, p. A13.

3. Fox Butterfield, "A Large Drop in Violent Crime Is Reported," *The New York Times,* September 18, 1996, p. A14.

4. "Popgun Politics," *U.S. News & World Report,* September 30, 1996, p. 41.

5. David H. Bayley (professor of criminal justice at the State University of New York at Albany), "The Cop Fallacy," *The New York Times,* August 13, 1993, p. A17.

6. The White House, Office of the Press Secretary, "Radio Address of the President to the Nation," January 11, 1997.

7. State of the Union Address, January 20, 1999, *www.washingtonpost.com/wp-srv/politics.*

8. President George Bush, "Remarks by the President on Project Safe Neighborhoods" May 14, 2001, *www.whitehouse.gov.*

9. *A Blueprint for New Beginnings: A Responsible Budget for America's Priorities* (Washington, DC: U.S. Government Printing Office, 2001), ch. 9, "Combat Crime and Drug Abuse, *www.whitehouse.gov/news/usbudget/blueprint/budtoc.html.*

10. Executive Office of the President, "Statement of Administration Policy: H.R. 1279: Gang Deterrence and Community Protection Act of 2005" May 11, 2005, *www.whitehouse.gov.*

11. Office of Management and Budget, *Fiscal Year 2006: Department of Justice,* *www.whitehouse.gov/omb/budget/fy2006/justice.html.* The document does find that federal funding to continue support for the 100,000 police was cut because an assessment rated the program as "Results Not Demonstrated."

12. Elliot Currie, *Crime and Punishment in America* (New York: Metropolitan Books, Henry Holt, 1998), p. 12; BJS, *Prisoners in 2004,* NCJ210677, October 2005; and *StatAbs 2004–5,* Table 17, p. 20.

13. BJS, *Criminal Offender Statistics,* *www.ojp.usdoj.gov/bjs/crimoff.htm* (last revised June 27, 2005).

14. *UCR–2004,* p. 11; and *Sourcebook–2003,* Table 3.106.

15. Elliott Currie, "Reflections on Crime and Criminology at the Millenium," *Western Criminology Review* 2, no. 1 (1999): *http://wcr.sonoma.edu/v2n1/currie.html.*

16. Lorraine Adams and David Vise, "Crime Rates Down for 7th Straight Year," *The Washington Post,* October 18, 1999, p. A2 (emphasis in original).

17. David Vise and Lorraine Adams, "Despite Rhetoric, Violent Crime Climbs," *The Washington Post,* December 5, 1999, p. A3.

18. Quoted in ibid.

19. Quoted in ibid.

20. *Sourcebook–1998*, p. 502, Table 6.48; and *Prisoners in 2004*, p. 1. See also Vise and Adams, "Despite Rhetoric, Violent Crime Climbs."

21. William Spelman, "The Limited Importance of Prison Expansion," in *The Crime Drop in America*, ed. Alfred Blumstein and Joel Wallman (New York: Cambridge University Press, 2000), p. 123.

22. Quoted in Raspberry, "2 Million and Counting," *Washington Post*, January 26, 1994, p. A13.

23. Vincent Schiraldi, "Spend More Money on Education, Not Prisons," *Newsday*, August 29, 2002, p. A39.

24. Jeremy Travis and Sarah Lawrence, *Beyond the Prison Gates: The State of Parole in America*. (Washington, DC: Urban Institute, 2002), pp. 21–22, *www.urban.org/url.cfm?ID=310583*.

25. Alfred Blumstein, "Why Is Crime Falling—or Is It?" in National Institute of Justice, *Perspectives on Crime and Justice: 2000–2001 Lecture Series*, p. 16.

26. Blumstein, "Why Is Crime Falling—or Is It?" pp. 19–21.

27. Blumstein, "The Recent Rise and Fall of American Violence," in Blumstein and Wallman, *The Crime Drop in America*, pp. 4–5.

28. Molly Moore, "Drugs Flood in from Mexico," *The Washington Post*, November 19, 1999, p. A15.

29. William J. Chambliss, *Power, Politics, and Crime* (Boulder, Colo.: Westview Press, 1999), p. 127; see also Currie, *Crime and Punishment in America*, pp. 30–36.

30. J. Austin, M. Bruce, L. Carroll, P. McCall, and S. Richards, "The Use of Incarceration in the United States," *Critical Criminology* 10 (2001): 20.

31. John Conklin, *Why Crime Rates Fell* (Boston: Allyn & Bacon, 2003), p. 200.

32. Quoted in Pierre Thomas, "In a Reversal, U.S. Homicide Numbers Fall," *The Washington Post*, December 31, 1995, p. A8.

33. "Popgun Politics," *U.S. News & World Report*, September 30, 1996, p. 33.

34. Blumstein, "Why Is Crime Falling—or Is It?" pp. 17–18, 12, 24.

35. Conklin, *Why Crime Rates Fell*, p. 69.

36. Eric Pooley, "One Good Apple," *Time*, January 15, 1996, pp. 54–56.

37. Currie, "Reflections on Crime and Criminology at the Millenium."

38. Conklin, *Why Crime Rates Fell*, p. 71.

39. *UCR–1992*, p. 58; and *UCR–1993*, p. 5, quote is on p. 287.

40. *UCR–2001*, p. 5.

41. *Sourcebook–2001*, Table 3.120; and *UCR-2004*, p. 15.

42. Currie, *Crime and Punishment in America*, pp. 24–25.

43. David Garland, *Punishment and Modern Society* (Chicago: University of Chicago Press, 1990), pp. 165–66.

44. *Challenge*, p. 35.

45. *Sourcebook 2003*, Table 3.106; and *UCR 2004*, pp. 11, 41.

46. BJS, *Justice Expenditures and Employment in the U.S., 1999*, NCJ191746, February 2002, p. 1; and BJS, *Justice Expenditures and Employment in the U.S., 2001*, NCJ202792, May 2004, p. 1.

47. Private security is one of the fastest growing industries in the nation. For 1990, expenditure on private security was $52 billion, and the number of people employed in some form of private security work was "more than 1.5 million people, outnumbering police officers by a 2:1 margin. In that year, more than 2.6 percent of the workforce was employed in the private security industry, double the percentage it was in 1970. The latest figures show that this ratio is now about 3:1, with more than $100 billion, dwarfing law enforcement expenditures [on police] of around $40 billion." Randall Shelden, *Controlling the Dangerous Classes* (Boston: Allyn & Bacon, 2001), p. 280.

48. On this issue, I have made ample use of the discussion and references in Victor Kappeler, Mark Blumberg, and Gary Potter, *The Mythology of Crime and Criminal Justice*, 3rd ed. (Prospect Heights, IL: Waveland, 2000), pp. 257–72.

49. *Sourcebook–2002*, p. 141, Table 2.43; and Ernest van den Haag, "When Felons Go Free: Worse than a Crime," *National Review*, January 20, 1992, p. 50.

50. Victor Kappeler, Mark Blumberg, and Gary Potter, *The Mythology of Crime and Criminal Justice*, 1st ed. (Prospect Heights, IL: Waveland, 1993), pp. 195–96.

51. BJS, *Prisoners in 2003*, p. 2.

52. International Centre for Prison Studies, *www.kcl.ac.uk/depsta/rel/icps/home.html*.

53. According to James Lynch,

> When the range of crimes examined is made more comparable in terms of seriousness and when the rates are standardized for differences in the level of crime cross-nationally, the extreme differences in the use of incarceration between the United States and several other Western democracies are lessened considerably and, in some cases, disappear. (James Lynch, "A Comparison of Prison Use in England, Canada, West Germany, and the United States: A Limited Test of the Punitiveness Hypothesis," Journal of Criminal Law and Criminology 79, no. 1 [1988]: 196, cf. 181)

This conclusion is based on cross-national comparison of the rates at which convicted persons are sentenced to prison, regardless of the length of the sentence or eventual time actually served. Cross-national comparisons of actual time served show the United States to be roughly comparable to other Western democracies. See James Lynch, "A Cross-National Comparison of the Length of Custodial Sentences for Serious Crimes," *Justice Quarterly* 10, no. 4 (December 1993): 801–23.

54. David Montgomery, "Whoa! Canada! Legal Marijuana. Gay Marriage. Peace. What the Heck's Going on Up North, Eh?" *The Washington Post*, July 1, 2003, p. C01; and DeNeen L. Brown, "A Tolerance for IV Drug Users: Vancouver Seeks to Protect Addicts, Not Punish Them," *The Washington Post*, August 21, 2001, p. A01.

55. Clifford Krauss, "Senate Approves Broad Crime Bill; Split over Guns," *The New York Times*, November 20, 1993, p. 1.

56. BJS, *Capital Punishment in 2003*, NCJ 206627, November 2004, p. 1.

57. International Centre for Prison Studies; see note 38, above.

58. BJS, *Probation and Parole in the U.S.–2003*, NCJ205336, p. 1; and BJS press release, "U.S. Corrections Population Reaches 5.9 Offenders," August 22, 1999.

59. Elliott Currie, *Confronting Crime: An American Challenge* (New York: Pantheon, 1985), p. 12; cited in Kappeler et al., *The Mythology of Crime and Criminal Justice*, 2nd ed., p. 207.

60. See "Penal Code Crime Cases Known to the Police, Cases Cleared up and Arestees by Type of Crime (1980–2002)," *Japan Statistical Yearbook 2005*. Japan Ministry of Internal Affairs and Communications, p. 769, *www.stat.go.jp/english/data/nenkan/index.htm*. Crime totals were based on the sum for homicide, robbery, rape, and "violence" (which translates to aggravated assault) to make them comparable with UCR categories for violent crime. Population for 2002 was 127,435,000 from Chart 2.1 of the yearbook. (Thanks to Satoko Motohara for help clarifying the meanings of the categories.) *UCR 2002*, p. 15.

61. Louise I. Shelley, *Crime and Modernization* (Carbondale: Southern Illinois University Press, 1981), p. 76.

62. INTERPOL, *International Crime Statistics*, *www.interpol.int/Public/Statistics/ICS/downloadList.asp*; and *UCR–2000*, pp. 14, 74.

63. *UCR–2004*, pp. 76ff.

64. Quoted in K. Taylor and F. Soady, eds., *Violence: An Element of American Life* (Boston: Holbrook Press, 1972), p. 49.

65. *UCR–2004*, Table 4 (pp. 76–84) and Table 6 (pp. 97–134).

66. *Time*, June 30, 1975, p. 11.

67. *StatAbst—2004–5*, Table 12, p. 13; and *UCR–2003*, computed from Table 38, pp. 280–81.

68. *UCR–1990*, p. 50, Table 1; *UCR–1985*, p. 41, Table 1; and *StatAbst—1992*, p. 14, Table 12.

69. I have calculated the population of 16 to 24 year olds from *Economic Report of the President* (Washington, DC: U.S. Government Printing Office, 1988), p. 283, Table B-31, and *StatAbst—1998*, p. 21, Table 21; the victimization figures are from *Sourcebook–1987*, p. 240; and *Sourcebook–1998*, p. 172.

70. "Serious Crime Rises Again in New York," *The New York Times*, March 22, 1988, pp. B1, B6.

71. Research reviewed by Conklin also notes that in Japan and Scotland, there was no correlation between the proportion of young males and homicide rates between 1901 and 1970. Conklin, *Why Crime Rates Fell*, p. 155.

72. See, for example, John Braithwaite, "Poverty, Power, and White-Collar Crime," in *White-Collar Crime Reconsidered*, ed. Kip Schlegel and David Weisburd (Boston: Northeastern University Press, 1992), pp. 78–107.

73. *StatAbst—2004–5*, Table 672, p. 447; *StatAbst—1972*, Table 528, p 324; Carmen DeNavas-Walt, Bernadette Proctor, and Cheryl Hill Lee, U.S. Census Bureau, *Current Population Reports*, P60-229, *Income, Poverty & Health Insurance Coverage in the United States: 2004* (Washington, DC: U.S. Government Printing Office, 2005).

74. Kathy Sawyer, "Poorest Families Are Losing Ground," *The Washington Post*, August 22, 1999, p. A7. The article goes on to point out that a "report from the House Ways and Means Committee . . . acknowledged that the poorest families are losing ground."

75. *The Washington Post*, September 6, 1982, p. 2; the report was issued by the Full Employment Action Council (a coalition of religious, civil rights, and union groups) and the National Policy Exchange (an economic research and educational organization).

76. *The Washington Post*, September 14, 1982, pp. 1, 4.

77. Edward Wolff, *Top Heavy: A Study of the Increasing Inequality of Wealth in America* (New York: Twentieth Century Fund Press, 1995), p. 2.

78. National Center for Children in Poverty at Columbia University, "Who Are America's Poor Children?" *www.nccp.org/pub_cpt05b.html*.

79. David Kamin and Isaac Shapiro, "Studies Shed New Light on Effects of Administration's Tax Cuts," Center on Budget and Policy Priorities, 2004, *www.cbpp.org/8-25-04tax.htm*.

80. *StatAbst—2001*, p. 386, Table 598. See also *"Racial Gulf:* Blacks' Hopes, Raised by '68 Kerner Report, Are Mainly Unfulfilled," *The Wall Street Journal*, February 26, 1988, pp. 1, 9; and "Today's Native Sons," *Time*, December 1, 1986, pp. 26–29.

81. *StatAbst—2004–5*, p. 393, Table 603; and John Berry, "Jobless Rate Rose to 6% in November," *The Washington Post*, December 7, 2002, pp. E1, E2.

82. John Rawls, *A Theory of Justice* (Cambridge, MA: Harvard University Press, 1971; rev. ed., 1999).

83. See ch. 4, n. 52 below (and accompanying text) for more on this principle of distributive justice.

84. John Rawls, *Justice as Fairness: A Restatement* (Cambridge, MA: Harvard University Press, 2001), pp. 138–40.

85. Rawls, *Justice as Fairness*, p. 146. Note that Rawls is not using the term *underclass* in the technical sense in which it is used in some sociological literature. For him, it simply refers to the economically worst-off group in a society, and emphasizes their likely sense of exclusion.

86. An article in the *American Journal of Public Health* in March 1998 reported on the Third National Health and Nutrition Examination Survey (NHANES III), the most comprehensive health examination survey in the United States, which found that 10 million Americans, including 4 million children, suffer from hunger; see K. Alaimo et al., "Food Insufficiency Exists in the United States: Results from the Third National Health and Nutrition Examination Survey (NHANES III)," *American Journal of Public Health* 88, no. 3 (March 1998): 419–26.

87. Todd R. Clear, "'Tougher' Is Dumber," *The New York Times*, December 4, 1993, p. 21.

88. BJS, *Recidivism of Prisoners Released in 1994*, NCJ 193427, June 2002, p. 1.

89. BJS, *Prisoners in 2004*, p. 7.

90. Stop Prison Rape (STP), *Prisoner Rape Factsheet*, *www.spr.org*.

91. Robert Johnson and Hans Toch, "Introduction," in *The Pains of Imprisonment*, ed. Robert Johnson and Hans Toch (Beverly Hills, CA: Sage, 1982), pp. 19–20.

92. STP, *Prisoner Rape Factsheet*.

93. Human Rights Watch, "No Escape: Male Rape in U.S. Prisons," *www.hrw.org/reports/2001/prison*.

94. Fox Butterfield, "More Blacks in Their 20's Have Trouble with the Law," *The New York Times*, October 5, 1995, p. A18; and Pierre Thomas, "Study Suggests Black Male Prison Rate Impinges on Political Process," *The Washington Post*, January 30, 1997, p. A3. See Jeffrey Reiman, "Liberal and Republican Arguments against the Disenfranchisement of Felons," *Criminal Justice Ethics* 24, no. 1 (Winter–Spring 2005): 3–18.

95. James P. Lynch and William J. Sabol, "Prison Use and Social Control," U.S. Department of Justice, Office of Justice Programs, *Policies, Processes, and Decisions of the Criminal Justice System*, vol. 3 of *Criminal Justice 2000*, pp. 7–44; Conklin, *Why Crime Rates Fell*, pp. 83–84; and Todd Clear, "The Problem with 'Addition by Subtraction,'" in *Invisible Punishment: The Collateral Consequences of Mass Imprisonment*, ed. Mark Mauer and Meda Chesney-Lind (New York: New Press, 2002).

96. State of the Union Message, January 21, 2004, as provided by the Republican National Committee, *www.gop.com*.

97. Bush, "Remarks by the President on Project Safe Neighborhoods."

98. Philip J. Cook and Jens Ludwig, *Gun Violence: The Real Costs* (New York: Oxford University Press, 2000), pp. 15, 34, 35.

99. Garen Wintemute, "Guns and Gun Violence," in Blumstein and Wallman, *The Crime Drop in America*, p. 52.

100. Wintemute, "Guns and Gun Violence," pp. 54–57.

101. Gary Kleck, *Point Blank: Guns and Violence in America* (New York: Aldine de Gruyter, 1991), p. 17. Kleck's estimate of the number of guns is supported by the Bureau of Alcohol, Tobacco, and Firearms, which calculated 200 million in 1990 (cited in Albert Reiss and Jeffrey Roth, eds., *Understanding and Preventing Violence* [Washington, DC: National Academy Press, 1993], p. 256). See also BJS, *Guns Used in Crime*, NCJ-148201, July 1995, pp. 3, 6.

102. National Research Council, *Firearms and Violence: A Critical Review*, Committee to Improve Research Information and Data on Firearms, ed. Charles Wellford, John Pepper, and Carol Petrie, Committee on Law and Justice, Division of Behavioral and Social Sciences and Education (Washington, DC: National Academies Press, 2005), pp. 57–58.

103. *Challenge*, p. 239 (emphasis added).

104. *UCR–1995*, p. 36.

105. Office of Juvenile Justice and Delinquency Prevention, "Fact Sheet," February 1999, no. 93, *www.ncjrs.org/jjfact.htm*.

106. Don Colburn and Abigail Trafford, "Guns at Home: Doctors Target Growing Epidemic of Violence," *The Washington Post Health*, October 12, 1993, p. 12.

107. National Center for Injury Prevention and Control, "Nonfatal and Fatal Firearm-Related Injuries: United States, 1993-1997," November 19, 1999 , *www.cdc.gov/mmwr/preview/mmwrhtml/mm4845a1.htm*.

108. Barbara Vobejda, "Children's Defense Fund Cites Gun Violence," *The Washington Post*, January 21, 1994, p. A3.

109. Presidential news conference, June 16, 1981; see also "Reagan Denounces Gun Control Laws," *The Washington Post*, May 7, 1983, p. A8.

110. "Whenever there is a crime involving a firearm, there are various groups, some of them quite persuasive in their logic, that think you can ban certain kinds of guns, and I am not in that mode" (George H. W. Bush, quoted in George Will, "Playing with Guns," *Newsweek*, March 27, 1989, p. 78).

111. Pierre Thomas, "Brady Gun Law Contains No Penalties, Little Money for States," *The Washington Post*, December 3, 1993, p. A3.

112. BJS, *Background Checks for Firearm Transfers, 2003*, NCJ 204428, September 2004, p. 1; and Blumstein, "The Recent Rise and Fall of American Violence," p. 5.

113. Lawrence W. Sherman, "Reducing Gun Violence: What Works, What Doesn't, What's Promising," *NIJ Perspectives on Crime and Justice: 1999-2000 Lecture Series*, NCJ 184245, March, 2001, p. 74.

114. Arnold S. Trebach, *The Heroin Solution* (New Haven, CT: Yale University Press, 1982), pp. 3–24, 246.

115. Office of National Drug Control Policy, *What America's Users Spend on Illegal Drugs*, NCJ 192334, December 2001, pp 8, 1.

116. Quoted in Doug Bandow, "War on Drugs or War on America?" p. 246.

117. Marvin D. Miller, National Organization for the Reform of Marijuana Laws, testimony at the Hearings on Proposals to Legalize Drugs held by the House Select Committee on Narcotics Abuse and Control, September 29, 1988, pp. 12–13; *UCR–2004*, pp. 178, 180.

118. Miller, testimony, p. 19.

119. U.S. Department of Justice, Drug Enforcement Administration, Opinion and Recommended Ruling, Findings of Fact, Conclusions of Law and Decision of Administrative Law Judge Francis L. Young, in the Matter of MARIJUANA RESCHEDULING PETITION, Docket no. 86-22, September 6, 1988, pp. 56–57.

120. Arnold S. Trebach, Testimony at the Hearings on Proposals to Legalize Drugs Held by the House Select Committee on Narcotics Abuse and Control, September 29, 1988 (Washington, DC: U.S. Government Printing Office, 1988), pp. 11–12. Doug Bandow of the Cato Institute confirms Trebach's numbers:

> *Tobacco kills roughly 390,000 people annually and alcohol is responsible for some 150,000 deaths a year. . . . In contrast, all illicit drugs combined account for about 5,000 deaths, most of which, as explained below, are caused by the effects of prohibition. For 100,000 users, tobacco kills 650, alcohol 150, heroin 80, and cocaine 4. (Bandow, "War on Drugs or War on America?" p. 245)*

In a footnote, the author mentions that these figures have been reduced to reflect only the drug use, not the effects of prohibition.

121. Surgeon General C. Everett Koop quoted, and reports on the relative addictiveness of cigarettes and cocaine, in Bandow, "War on Drugs or War on America?" p. 249.

122. "The largest study ever made of drug abuse in this country shows that two widely available legal drugs—alcohol and the tranquilizer Valium—are responsible for the greatest amount of drug-related illness, the government reported yesterday." Stuart Auerbach, "2 Drugs Widely Abused," *The Washington Post*, July 9, 1976, p. A1.

123. Blumstein, "Why Is Crime Falling—or Is It?," p. 13.

124. "A LEN Interview with Professor Alfred Blumstein of Carnegie Mellon University," *Law Enforcement News* 21, no. 422 (April 30, 1995): p. 11.

125. Troy Duster, *The Legislation of Morality: Law, Drugs, and Moral Judgment* (New York: Free Press, 1970), pp. 3, 7, inter alia.

126. Cf. Philip C. Baridon, *Addiction, Crime, and Social Policy* (Lexington, MA: Lexington Books, 1976), pp. 4–5.

127. Trebach, *The Heroin Solution*, p. 246.

128. Quoted in Doug Bandow, "War on Drugs or War on America?" p. 250.

129. "A LEN interview with Professor Alfred Blumstein of Carnegie Mellon University," p. 11.

130. M. Douglas Anglin and George Speckart, "Narcotics Use and Crime: A Multisample, Multimethod Analysis," *Criminology* 26, no. 2 (1988): 226.

131. U.S. Department of Health, Education, and Welfare, Public Health Service, National Institute on Alcohol Abuse and Alcoholism, Special Action Office for Drug Abuse Prevention, *Social Cost of Drug Abuse* (Washington, DC: U.S. Government Printing Office, 1974), pp. 20–21.

132. *UCR–2004*, p. 42.

133. Christoper Mumola, *Substance Abuse and Treatment, State and Federal Prisoners, 1997*, Bureau of Justice Statistics Special Report NCI 172871, January 1997, p. 5.

134. Anglin and Speckart, "Narcotics Use and Crime," p. 197.

135. Office of National Drug Control Policy (ONDCP), *What America's Users Spend on Illegal Drugs*, December (Washington, DC: Office of National Drug Control Policy, 2001), p. 1.

136. Ibid., p. 2.

137. Ibid., p. 18.

138. "U.S. Anti-drug Effort Criticized," *The Washington Post*, November 12, 1988, p. A15.

139. Ibid.

140. McCoy and Block, "U.S. Narcotics Policy: An Anatomy of Failure," p. 3; and United Nations Office on Drugs and Crime, *Global Illicit Drug Trends 2003* (New York: United Nations, 2003), pp. 8 and 23, *www.unodc.org/unodc/global_illicit_drug_trends.html*.

141. Bandow, "War on Drugs or War on America?" p. 244; and BJS, *Drugs, Crime, and the Justice System*, December 1992, p. 44.

142. "Cocaine Down: Signs Indicate That America's Cocaine Habit Is Easing," *The Wall Street Journal*, July 20, 1987, p. 21.

143. National Narcotics Intelligence Consumers' Committee, *The NNICC 1994: The Supply of Illegal Drugs to the United States*, DEA-95051 August (Washington, DC: NNICC, 1995), p. 1.

144. ONDCP, *The Price and Purity of Illicit Drugs: 1981 through the Second Quarter of 2003*, NCJ 207768, November 2004, pp. v–vi.

145. David Boyum and Peter Reuter, *An Analytic Assessment of U.S. Drug Policy* (Washington, DC: AEI Press, 2005). "Yet despite the incarceration of hundreds of thousands of drug dealers and steadfast attempts to stop overseas cultivations and trafficking, drugs have become substantially cheaper, casting doubt on the effectiveness of this strategy" (p. 2).

146. "Prosecutors Admit: No Victory in Sight," *National Law Journal*, August 8, 1988, p. S-2.

147. Boyum and Reuter, *An Analytic Assessment of U.S. Drug Policy*, p. 2.

148. BJS Fact Sheet, *Drug Data Summary*, NCJ-167246, February 1998.

149. ONDCP, *National Drug Control Strategy*, February (Washington, DC: Office of National Drug Control Policy, 2005), p. 61.

150. "Drug Wars Push D.C. to Brink of Homicide Record: Police Efforts Futile as Turf Disputes Raise 1988 Slaying Total to 285," *The Washington Post*, October 26, 1988, p. A1. By year's end the record was soundly broken, with the number of murders reaching 372! And the carnage continued: In 1991, there were 482 homicides in the nation's capital; *UCR–1991*, p. 64.

151. "Enemy Within: Drug Money Is Corrupting the Enforcers," pp. A1, A12.

152. Ibid.

153. Clifford Krauss, "2-Year Corruption Inquiry Finds a 'Willful Blindness' in New York's Police Dept," *The New York Times*, July 7, 1994, p. A1.

154. Bandow, "War on Drugs or War on America?" p. 243; and McCoy and Block, "U.S. Narcotics Policy," p. 6.

155. *UCR 2004*, p 280; and BJS, *Prisoners in 2004*, p. 10.

156. BJS, *Prisoners in 2001*, p. 14; and BJS, *Prisoners in 2004*, p. 10.

157. Boyum and Reuter, *An Analytic Assessment of U.S. Drug Policy*, p. 10.

158. Michael Tonry, "Racial Politics, Racial Disparities, and the War on Crime," *Crime & Delinquency* 40, no. 4 (October 1994): 487.

159. BJS, *Correctional Populations in the U.S., 1992*, p. 31; Surgeon General Joycelyn Elders's statement was reported in *International Herald Tribune*, December 8, 1993, p. 1. She reiterated the suggestion after "reviewing many studies," and even after President Clinton's opposition to the idea was reported. "Elders Reiterates Her Support for Study of Drug Legalization," *The Washington Post*, January 15, 1994, p. A8.

160. Jerry V. Wilson, "Our Wasteful War on Drugs," *The Washington Post*, January 18, 1994, p. A20.

161. Christopher Wren, "A.M.A. Shelves Disputed Report on Drugs," *The New York Times,* June 23, 1996, p. A22.

162. *Time,* June 30, 1975, p. 17 (emphasis added).

163. Currie, *Crime and Punishment in America,* pp. 81, 98.

164. Fox Butterfield, "Intervening Early Costs Less than '3-Strikes' Laws, Study Says," *The New York Times,* June 23, 1996, p. A24.

165. Peter W. Greenwood, "Costs and Benefits of Early Childhood Intervention," OJJDP Fact Sheet no. 94, February (Washington, DC: U.S. Department of Justice, Office of Juvenile Justice and Delinquency Prevention, 1999).

166. Steven Donziger, ed., *The Real War on Crime: The Report of the National Criminal Justice Commission* (New York: HarperPerenniel, 1966), p. 216.

167. "Federally Funded Drug and Alcohol Programs Found Effective in Reducing Drug Use, Crime, Homelessness," *Psychiatric Services* 47, no. 11 (November 1996): 1280.

168. *The National Report on Substance Abuse* 8, no. 15 (July 1, 1994): p. 2.

169. Rand Corporation Press Release, *www.ndsn.org/JULY94/RAND.html.*

170. Lawrence Sherman et al., "Preventing Crime: What Works, What Doesn't, What's Promising," *NIJ Research in Brief,* NIJ171676, July (Washington, DC: National Institute of Justice, 1988).

171. Quoted in Butterfield, "Intervening Early Costs Less than '3-Strikes' Laws," p. A24.

172. Ibid. For an extensive list of promising programs aimed at reducing crime, see Donziger, *The Real War on Crime,* app. B. StopViolence.com, "Resources for a Just Peace," *http://stopviolence.com,* contains a growing collection of information about nonrepressive responses to crime and violence.

173. Kai T. Erikson, *Wayward Puritans* (New York: Wiley, 1966), p. 4. Reprinted by permission of John Wiley & Sons, Inc.

174. Ibid., p. 11.

175. Ibid., pp. 13–15 (emphasis added).

176. Garland suggests that this is true of Erikson's study even if Erikson does not highlight this aspect. Garland writes that Erikson's study

> is a description of the deep social and religious tensions within [Puritan] community. . . . In this context, it becomes clear that the exercise of criminal punishments . . . was also the forceful imposition of a particular framework of politico-religious authority on a society riven by factions and deep tensions. (*Garland,* Punishment and Modern Society, *p. 79*)

177. Michel Foucault, *Discipline and Punish: The Birth of the Prison,* trans. Alan Sheridan (London: Allen Lane, 1977), p. 271.

178. Ibid., p. 277.

179. Ibid., p. 274.

180. Ibid., p. 275.

181. Ibid., p. 279.

182. Ibid., p. 288.

183. Foucault writes that the system includes an attempt to shape "the common perception of delinquents: to present them as close by, everywhere present and everywhere to be feared" (ibid., p. 286).

184. Ibid., p. 281.

185. Ibid., pp. 296–97.

186. Ibid., p. 304.

187. "Foucault's description of Western liberal democracy as a society of surveillance, disciplined from end to end, is deliberately reminiscent of . . . totalitarianism" (Garland, *Punishment and Modern Society,* p. 151).

188. According to Nicos Poulantzas,

Now, for Foucault, the power relation never has any other basis than itself: it becomes a pure 'situation' in which power is always immanent; and the question what power *and* power to do what *appears as a mere obstacle. This leads Foucault into a particular logical impasse from which there is no possible escape. . . . For if power is always already there, if every power situation is immanent in itself,* why should there ever be resistance? From where *would resistance come, and* how would it be even possible? *(Nicos Poulantzas,* State, Power, Socialism, *trans. P. Camiller [London: NLB, 1978], p. 149)*

189. According to David Garland,

Foucault's vision of power may be a positive conception in the sense that power moulds, trains, builds up, and creates subjects, but it also involves a thoroughly negative evaluation. Foucault writes as someone who is absolutely 'against' power. His critique is not of one form of power in favour of another but is rather an attack upon power itself. . . . [However, t]here is an important sense in which discipline can create freedom as well as control. As Foucault's own subsequent work shows, discipline is necessary to the development of self-control. (Garland, Punishment and Modern Society, *p. 174)*

CHAPTER 2

A CRIME BY ANY OTHER NAME . . .

If one individual inflicts a bodily injury upon another which leads to the death of the person attacked we call it manslaughter; on the other hand, if the attacker knows beforehand that the blow will be fatal we call it murder. Murder has also been committed if society places hundreds of workers in such a position that they inevitably come to premature and unnatural ends. Their death is as violent as if they had been stabbed or shot. . . . Murder has been committed if society knows perfectly well that thousands of workers cannot avoid being sacrificed so long as these conditions are allowed to continue. Murder of this sort is just as culpable as the murder committed by an individual.

—Frederick Engels, *The Condition of the Working Class in England*

WHAT'S IN A NAME?

If it takes you an hour to read this chapter, by the time you reach the last page, two of your fellow citizens will have been murdered. *During that same time, more than six Americans will die as a result of unhealthy or unsafe conditions in the workplace!* Although these work-related deaths could have been prevented, they are not called murders. Why not? Doesn't a crime by any other name still cause misery and suffering? What's in a name?

The fact is that the label "crime" is not used in America to name all or the worst of the actions that cause misery and suffering to Americans. It is reserved primarily for the dangerous actions of the poor.

In the February 21, 1993, edition of *The New York Times*, an article appeared with the headline "Company in Mine Deaths Set to Pay Big Fine." It reported an agreement by the owners of a Kentucky mine to pay a fine for safety misconduct that may have led to "the worst American mining accident in nearly a decade." Ten workers died in a methane explosion, and the company pleaded guilty to "a pattern of safety misconduct" that included falsifying reports of methane levels and requiring miners to work under

unsupported roofs. The company was fined $3.75 million. The acting fore-
man at the mine was the only individual charged by the federal government,
and for his cooperation with the investigation, prosecutors were recommending that he receive the minimum sentence: probation to six months in
prison. The company's president expressed regret for the tragedy that
occurred, and the U.S. attorney said he hoped the case "sent a clear message
that violations of Federal safety and health regulations that endanger the
lives of our citizens will not be tolerated."[1] Compare this with the story of
Colin Ferguson, who prompted an editorial in *The New York Times* of December 10, 1993, with the headline "Mass Murder on the 5:33."[2] A few days earlier, Colin had boarded a commuter train in Garden City, Long Island, and
methodically shot passengers with a 9mm pistol, killing 5 and wounding 18.
Colin Ferguson was surely a murderer, maybe a mass murderer. My question
is, why wasn't the death of the miners also murder? Why weren't those
responsible for subjecting ten miners to deadly conditions also "mass murderers"? Why do ten dead miners amount to an "accident" and a "tragedy,"
and five dead commuters a "mass murder"? "Murder" suggests a murderer,
whereas "accident" and "tragedy" suggest the work of impersonal forces.
But the charge against the company that owned the mine said that they
"repeatedly exposed the mine's work crews to danger and that such conditions were frequently concealed from Federal inspectors responsible for
enforcing the Mine Safety Act." And the acting foreman admitted to falsifying records of methane levels only two months before the fatal blast. Someone was responsible for the conditions that led to the death of ten miners. Is
that person not a murderer, perhaps even a *mass murderer?*

These questions are at this point rhetorical. My aim is not to discuss this
case but rather to point to the blinders we wear when we look at such an
"accident." There was an investigation. One person, the acting foreman, was
held responsible for falsifying records. He was to be sentenced to six months
in prison (at most). The company was fined. But no one was tried for *murder.*
No one was thought of as a murderer. *Why not?* Would the miners not be
safer if such people were treated as murderers? Might they not still be alive?
Will a president of the United States address the Yale Law School and recommend mandatory prison sentences for such people? Will he mean these people when he says,

> These relatively few, persistent criminals who cause so much misery and fear
> are really the core of the problem. The rest of the American people have a right
> to protection from their violence[?][3]

Didn't those miners have a right to protection from the violence that took
their lives? *And if not, why not?*

Once we are ready to ask this question seriously, we are in a position to
see that the reality of crime—that is, the acts we label crime, the acts we think

of as crime, and the actors and actions we treat as criminal—is *created:* It is an image shaped by decisions as to *what* will be called crime and *who* will be treated as a criminal.

THE CARNIVAL MIRROR

It is sometimes coyly observed that the quickest and cheapest way to eliminate crime would be to throw out all the criminal laws. There is a sliver of truth to this view. Without criminal laws, there would indeed be no "crimes." There would, however, still be dangerous acts. This is why we cannot solve our crime problem quite so simply. The criminal law *labels* some acts "crimes." In doing this, it identifies those acts as so dangerous that we must use the extreme methods of criminal justice to protect ourselves against them. This does not mean that criminal law *creates* crime—it simply "mirrors" real dangers that threaten us. What is true of the criminal law is true of the whole justice system. If police did not arrest or prosecutors charge or juries convict, there would be no "criminals." This does not mean that police or prosecutors or juries create criminals, any more than legislators do. They *react* to real dangers in society. The criminal justice system—from lawmakers to law enforcers—is just a mirror of the real dangers that lurk in our midst. *Or so we are told.*

How accurate is this mirror? We need to answer this in order to know whether or how well the criminal justice system is protecting us against the real threats to our well-being. The more accurate a mirror is, the more the image it shows is created by the reality it reflects. The more misshapen a mirror is, the more the distorted image it shows is created by the mirror, not by the reality reflected. It is in this sense that I will argue that the image of crime is *created:* The American criminal justice system is a mirror that shows a distorted image of the dangers that threaten us—an image created more by the shape of the mirror than by the reality reflected. What do we see when we look in the criminal justice mirror?

On the morning of September 16, 1975, *The Washington Post* carried an article in its local news section headlined "Arrest Data Reveal Profile of a Suspect." The article reported the results of a study of crime in Prince George's County, a suburb of Washington, D.C. It read in part as follows:

> The typical suspect in serious crime in Prince George's County is a black male, aged 14 to 19, who lives in the area inside the Capital Beltway where more than half of the county's 64,371 reported crimes were committed in 1974. [The study] presents a picture of persons, basically youths, committing a crime once every eight minutes in Prince George's County.[4]

This report is hardly a surprise. The portrait it paints of "the typical suspect in serious crime" is probably a pretty good rendering of the image lurking in the back of the minds of most Americans who fear crime. Furthermore, although the crime rate in Prince George's County is somewhat above the national average and its black population somewhat above that of the average suburban county, the portrait generally fits the national picture presented in the FBI's *Uniform Crime Reports* for the same year, 1974. In Prince George's County, "youths between the ages of 14 and 19 were accused of committing nearly half [45.5 percent] of all 1974 crimes."[5] For the nation in 1974, the FBI reported that persons in this age group accounted for 39.5 percent of arrests for the FBI Index crimes (criminal homicide, forcible rape, robbery, aggravated assault, burglary, larceny, and motor vehicle theft).[6] These youths were male and disproportionately black. In Prince George's County, males "represented three of every four serious crime defendants."[7] In the nation in 1974, of 1,289,524 persons arrested for FBI Index crimes, 1,043,155, or more than 80 percent, were males.[8] In Prince George's County, where blacks made up approximately 25 percent of the population, "blacks were accused of 58 percent of all serious crimes."[9] In the nation, where blacks made up 11.4 percent of the population in 1974, they accounted for 34.2 percent of arrests for Index crimes.[10]

This was the *Typical Criminal* in 1974; but little has changed since. In his 1993 book, *How to Stop Crime,* retired Police Chief Anthony Bouza writes, "Street crime is mostly a black and poor young man's game."[11] And listen to the sad words of the Reverend Jesse Jackson: "There is nothing more painful to me at this stage of my life than to walk down the street and hear footsteps and start thinking about robbery—and then look around and see someone white and feel relieved."[12] In 2005, William Bennett, President Reagan's secretary of education (1985–1988) and the first President Bush's "drug czar" (1989–1990), commented, "I do know that it's true that if you wanted to reduce crime, you could—if that were your sole purpose—you could abort every black baby in this country, and your crime rate would go down."[13] In *The Color of Crime*, Kathryn Russell speaks of the "criminalblackman."[14] Marjorie Zatz characterizes this notion as follows: "The 'criminalblackman' is a composite of white fears of black men's criminality. It may become so strong and so widespread that it allows for racial hoaxes, in which a white offender blames an African American, usually male, for the offense in question and is readily believed by criminal justice agents and/or the general public."[15]

Let us look more closely at the face in today's criminal justice mirror, and we shall see much the same Typical Criminal.

He is, first of all, a *he*. Of 10 million persons arrested for crimes in 2004, 76 percent were males. Of persons arrested for violent crimes, 82 percent were men. Second, he is *young*. Nearly half (45 percent) of men arrested for all crimes were under the age of 25; and the same is true of violent crimes. Third, he is predominantly *urban*. Cities with populations over 250,000 had a rate of 322 arrests for violent crimes per 100,000 inhabitants, while cities with populations under 10,000 had 165 such arrests per 100,000 inhabitants;

arrests for property crimes were 735 per 100,000 in big cities, compared with 613 for smaller ones. "Half of all homicides occur in the 63 largest cities, which house only 16 percent of the population."[16] Fourth, he is disproportionately *black:* Blacks are arrested for Index crimes at a rate more than twice that of their percentage in the national population. In 2004, with blacks representing 13 percent of the nation's population, they made up 27 percent of all crime arrests.[17] Finally, he is *poor:* Almost one-third (29 percent) of 2002 jail inmates were unemployed (without full- or part-time work) prior to being arrested, an unemployment rate considerably higher than that of adults in the general population, and almost half (45 percent) reported prearrest incomes below $7,200 a year.[18] As the President's Commission reported nearly 40 years ago, "The offender at the end of the road in prison is likely to be a member of the lowest social and economic groups in the country."[19]

This is the Typical Criminal feared by most law-abiding Americans. Poor, young, urban, (disproportionately) black males make up the core of the enemy forces in the crime war. They are the heart of a vicious, unorganized guerrilla army, threatening the lives, limbs, and possessions of the law-abiding members of society, necessitating recourse to the ultimate weapons of force and detention in our common defense.

How do we know who the criminals are who so seriously endanger us that we must stop them with force and lock them in prisons? "From the arrest records, probation reports, and prison statistics," the President's Commission on Law Enforcement and Administration of Justice, authors of *The Challenge of Crime in a Free Society,* tells us, the "'portrait' of the offender emerges."[20] *These sources are not merely objective readings taken at different stages in the criminal justice process: Each of them represents human decisions.* "Prison statistics" and "probation reports" reflect *decisions* of juries on who gets convicted and decisions of judges on who gets probation or prison and for how long. "Arrest records" reflect decisions about which crimes to investigate and which suspects to take into custody. All these decisions rest on the most fundamental of all decisions: the *decisions* of legislators as to which acts shall be labeled "crimes" in the first place.

The reality of crime as the target of our criminal justice system and as perceived by the general populace is not a simple objective threat to which the system reacts: *It is a reality that takes shape as it is filtered through a series of human decisions running the full gamut of the criminal justice system*—from the lawmakers who determine what behavior shall be in the province of criminal justice to the law enforcers who decide which individuals will be brought within that province. And it doesn't end with the criminal justice system as such, because the media—particularly television and daily newspapers— contribute as well to the image that people have of crime in our society.[21] Here, too, human decisions are fundamental. The news media do not simply report the facts. There are too many facts out there. A selection must be made. People working in the news media must choose which facts are *news,* and they must choose how to represent those facts.

Note that by emphasizing the role of "human decisions," I do not mean to suggest that the reality of crime is voluntarily and intentionally "created" by individual "decision makers." Their decisions are themselves shaped by the social system, much as a child's decision to become an engineer rather than a samurai warrior is shaped by the social system in which he or she grows up. Thus, to have a full explanation of how the reality of crime is created, we have to understand how our society is structured in a way that leads people to make the decisions they do. In other words, these decisions are part of the social phenomena to be explained, they are not the explanation.

For the present, however, I emphasize the role of the decisions themselves for the following reasons: First, they are conspicuous points in the social process, relatively easy to spot and verify empirically. Second, because they are decisions aimed at protecting us from the dangers in our midst, we can compare the decisions with the real dangers and determine whether they are accurately responding to the real dangers. Third, because the reality of crime—the real actions labeled crimes, the real individuals identified as criminals, and the real faces we watch in the news as they travel from arrest to court to prison—results from these decisions, we can determine whether that reality corresponds to the real dangers in our society. Where that reality does correspond to the real dangers, we can say that the reality of crime simply reflects the real dangers in society. Where the reality of crime does not correspond to the real dangers, we can say that it is a reality *created* by those decisions. Then we can investigate the role played by the social system in encouraging, reinforcing, and otherwise shaping those decisions.

It is to capture this way of looking at the relation between the reality of crime and the real dangers "out there" in society that I refer to the criminal justice system as a "mirror." Whom and what we see in this mirror are functions of the decisions about who and what is criminal. Our poor, young, urban, black male, who is so well represented in arrest records and prison populations, appears not simply because of the threat he poses to the rest of society. As dangerous as he may be, he would not appear in the criminal justice mirror *if* it had not been decided that the acts he performs should be labeled "crimes," *if* it had not been decided that he should be arrested for those crimes, *if* he had had access to a lawyer who could persuade a jury to acquit him and a judge to expunge his arrest record, and *if* it had not been decided that he is the type of individual and his the type of crime that warrant imprisonment. *The shape of the reality we see in the criminal justice mirror is the outcome of all these decisions.* We want to know how accurately the reality we see in this mirror reflects the real dangers that threaten us in society.

It is not my view that this reality is created out of nothing. The mugger, the rapist, the murderer, the burglar, and the robber all pose a definite threat to our well-being, and they ought to be dealt with in ways that effectively reduce that threat to the minimum level possible (without making the criminal justice system itself a threat to our lives and liberties). Of central importance, however, is that the threat posed by the Typical Criminal is not the greatest threat to which we are exposed. The acts of the Typical Criminal are not the only acts that endanger us, nor are they the acts that endanger us the most. As I shall show in this chapter, we have as great and sometimes even a greater chance of being killed or disabled by an occupational injury or disease, by unnecessary surgery, or by shoddy medical services than by aggravated assault or even homicide! Yet even though these threats to our well-being are graver than that posed by our poor young criminals, they do not show up in the FBI's Index of serious crimes. The individuals responsible for them do not turn up in arrest records or prison statistics. *They never become part of the reality reflected in the criminal justice mirror, although the danger they pose is at least as great and often greater than the danger posed by those who do!*

Similarly, the general public loses more money *by far* (as I show below) from price fixing and monopolistic practices and from consumer deception and embezzlement than from all the property crimes in the FBI's Index combined. Yet these far more costly acts are either not criminal, or, if technically criminal, not prosecuted, or, if prosecuted, not punished, or if punished, only mildly. In any event, although the individuals responsible for these acts take more money out of the ordinary citizen's pocket than our Typical Criminal, they rarely show up in arrest statistics and almost never in prison populations. *Their faces rarely appear in the criminal justice mirror, although the danger they pose is at least as great and often greater than that of those who do.*

The inescapable conclusion is that the criminal justice system does not simply *reflect* the reality of crime; it has a hand in *creating* the reality we see.

The criminal justice system is like a mirror in which society can see the face of the evil in its midst. Because the system deals with some evils and not with others, because it treats some minor evils as grave and treats some of the gravest evils as minor, the image it throws back is distorted, like the image in a carnival mirror. Thus, the image cast back is false, not because it is invented out of thin air but because the proportions of the real are distorted: Large becomes small, and small large; grave becomes minor, and minor grave. Like a carnival mirror, although nothing is reflected that does not exist in the world, the image is more a creation of the mirror than a picture of the world.

If criminal justice really gives us a carnival-mirror image of "crime," we are doubly deceived. First, we are led to believe that the criminal justice system is protecting us against the gravest threats to our well-being when, in fact, the system is protecting us against only some threats and not necessarily the gravest ones. We are deceived about how much protection we are receiving, and thus are left vulnerable. The second deception is just the other side of this one. If people believe that the carnival mirror is a true mirror—that is, if they believe the criminal justice system simply reacts to the gravest threats to their well-being—they come to believe that whatever is the target of the criminal justice system must be the greatest threat to their well-being. In other words, if people believe that the most drastic of society's weapons are wielded by the criminal justice system *in reaction to* the gravest dangers to society, they will believe the reverse as well: that those actions that call forth the most drastic of society's weapons *must be* those that pose the gravest dangers to society.

A strange alchemy takes place when people accept uncritically the legitimacy of their institutions: What *needs* justification becomes *proof* of justification. People come to believe that prisoners must be criminals *because* they are in prison and that the inmates of insane asylums must be *crazy* because they are in insane asylums.[22] The criminal justice system's use of extreme measures—such as force and imprisonment—is thought to be justified by the extreme gravity of the dangers it combats. By this alchemy, these extreme measures become *proof* of the extreme gravity of those dangers, and the first deception, which merely misleads the public about how much protection the criminal justice system is actually providing, is transformed into the second, which deceives the public into believing that the acts and actors that are the targets of the criminal justice system pose the gravest threats to its well-being. Thus, the system may not only fail to protect us from dangers as great as or greater than those listed in the FBI Crime Index; it may also do still greater damage by creating the false security of the belief that only the acts on the FBI Index really threaten us and require control.

In the following discussion, I describe how and why the criminal justice carnival mirror distorts the image it creates.

CRIMINAL JUSTICE AS CREATIVE ART

The Pyrrhic defeat explanation for the "failure" of criminal justice in America holds that criminal justice *fails* (or, what amounts to the same thing, high crime rates are allowed to persist) in order to project a particular *image* of crime. In Chapter 1, I described the failure to adopt policies that could eliminate our high crime rates. It is the task of this chapter and the next to prove that the reality of crime is *created* and that it is created in a way that promotes a particular *image* of crime: *the image that serious crime—and therefore the greatest danger to society—is the work of the poor.*

The notion that the reality of crime is created is derived from Richard Quinney's theory of the *social reality of crime*.[23] Here as elsewhere, however, an idea that contributes to the Pyrrhic defeat theory is transformed along the way. Because I understand the idea that the social reality of crime is created in a way different from its meaning for Quinney, it will help in presenting my view to compare it with Quinney's.

Quinney maintains that crime has a "social reality" rather than an objective reality. What he means can be explained with an example. Wherein lies the reality of money? Certainly not in the "objective" characteristics of green printed paper. It exists rather in the "social" meaning attributed to that paper and the pattern of "social" behavior that is a consequence of that meaning. If people did not act as if that green printed paper had value, it would be just green paper, not real money. The reality of a crime as *a crime* does not lie simply in the objective characteristics of an action. It lies in the "social" meaning attached to that action and the pattern of "social" behavior—particularly the behavior of criminal justice officials—that is a product of that meaning. I think Quinney is right in this. When I speak of the reality of crime, I am referring to much more than physical actions such as stabbing or shooting. I mean as well the reality that a society gives those physical actions by labeling them and treating them as criminal.

Quinney further maintains that this reality of crime is *created*. By this, he means that crime is a definition of behavior applied by lawmakers and other criminal justice decision makers. "Crime," Quinney writes,

> is a definition of behavior that is conferred on some persons by others. Agents of the law (legislators, police, prosecutors, and judges), representing segments of a politically organized society, are responsible for formulating and administering criminal laws. Persons and behaviors, therefore, become criminal because of the formulation and application of criminal definitions. Thus, crime is created.[24]

This is *not* what I have in mind when I say that the reality of crime is created. Here is the difference. Quinney's position amounts to this: Crimes are established by the criminal law, and the criminal law is a human creation; ergo, crime is created. This is true, but it does not take us very far. After all, who can deny that crime is created *in this sense*? Only someone who has been hypnotized into forgetting that law books are written by lawmakers could deny that "crime" is a label that human beings apply to certain actions. What *is* controversial, however, is whether the label is applied appropriately. "Crime," after all, is not merely a sound—it is a word with a generally accepted meaning. Roughly speaking, it means at least "an intentional action that is harmful to society." (Of course, "crime" has a technical definition, namely, "an act prohibited by a criminal law." The point of prohibiting an act by the criminal law is to protect society from an injurious act. Thus, though any act prohibited by criminal law is rightly labeled a crime in the technical sense, not every act so prohibited is rightly prohibited, and thus not every act labeled "crime" is labeled appropriately. To determine whether the label "crime" is applied appropriately, we must use the more general definition.) The label is applied appropriately when it is used to identify all, or at least the worst, acts that are harmful to society. The label is applied inappropriately when it is attached to harmless acts or when it is not attached to seriously harmful acts. When I argue that the reality of crime is created, I mean that the label "crime" has not been applied appropriately.

One might ask why the inappropriate use of the label "crime" is a reason for saying that crime is created. My answer is this: By calling something *created*, we call attention to the fact that human actors are responsible for it.

By calling crime created, I point to human actors *rather than objective dangers* as determining the shape that the reality of crime takes in our society. If the label "crime" is applied consistently to the most dangerous or harmful acts, then it is misleading to point to the fact that human decision makers are responsible for how the label is applied because their decisions are dictated by compelling objective reasons. Rather than creating a reality, their decisions trace a reality that already exists. On the other hand, if the label is not applied appropriately, it is sensible to assume that it is applied for reasons that lie with the decision makers and not in the realm of objective dangers. This means that when the label "crime" is applied inappropriately, it is essential to call attention to the fact that human actors are responsible for it. Thus, it is precisely when the label "crime" is applied inappropriately that it is important to point out that the reality of crime is *created*.

By calling crime created, I want to emphasize the human responsibility for the shape of crime, not in the trivial sense that humans write the criminal law, *but rather to call attention to the fact that decisions as to what to label and treat as crime are not compelled by objective dangers, and thus that, to understand the reality of crime, we must look to the social processes that shape those decisions.*

By calling crime created, I suggest that our picture of crime—the portrait that emerges from arrest statistics, prison populations, politicians' speeches, news media, and fictionalized presentations, the portrait that in turn influences lawmakers and criminal justice policy makers—is not a photograph of the real dangers that threaten us. Its features are not simply traced from the real dangers in the social world. Instead, it is a piece of creative art. It is a picture in which some dangers are portrayed, and others omitted. Because it cannot be explained as a straight reflection of real dangers, we must look elsewhere to understand the shape it takes.

This argument, which will occupy us in this chapter and the next, leads to *five hypotheses* about the way in which the public's image of crime is created. To demonstrate that the reality of crime is created, and that the criminal justice system is a carnival mirror that gives us a distorted image of the dangers that threaten us, I will try to prove that, at each of the crucial decision-making points in criminal justice, the decisions made do not reflect the real and most serious dangers we face. The five hypotheses are as follows.

1. **Of the decisions of legislators:** That the definitions of crime in the criminal law do not reflect the only or the most dangerous of antisocial behaviors
2. **Of the decisions of police and prosecutors:** That the decisions on whom to arrest or charge do not reflect the only or the most dangerous behaviors legally defined as "criminal"
3. **Of the decisions of juries and judges:** That criminal convictions do not reflect the only or the most dangerous individuals among those arrested and charged

4. **Of the decisions of sentencing judges:** That sentencing decisions do not reflect the goal of protecting society from only or the most dangerous of those convicted by meting out punishments proportionate to the harmfulness of the crime committed
5. **Of all these decisions taken together:** That what criminal justice policy decisions (in hypotheses 1 through 4) do reflect is the implicit identification of crime with the dangerous acts of the poor, an identification amplified by media representations of crime

The Pyrrhic defeat theory is composed of these five hypotheses, *plus* the proposition that the criminal justice system is failing in avoidable ways to eliminate our high crime rates (argued in Chapter 1), *plus* the *historical inertia* explanation of how this failure is generated and left uncorrected because of the ideological benefits it produces (argued in Chapter 4). Note that the fifth hypothesis goes beyond the criminal justice system to point to the role of the media. That is, while the structure of criminal justice practice enables it to create an image of crime as the work of the poor, the media serve as the conveyor of that image to the wider public. Moreover, this conveyor adds a twist of its own, not merely conveying an accurate picture of the whole of criminal justice practice with its biases, but actually magnifying those biases. So, we shall see that the media portray crime—in reality and in fiction—in ways that overrepresent the types of crimes committed by poor people (whether they are committed by poor or rich folks) and that obscure the social factors that lead to crime in reality (argued in this chapter and in Chapter 4). Finally, I tie this theory of how and why the criminal justice system functions as it does together with the *historical inertia* explanation: That is, I will try to show how the decisions that create the biased image of crime are caused by historical forces and left unchanged because the particular distribution of costs and benefits to which those decisions give rise serves to make the system self-reinforcing.

A CRIME BY ANY OTHER NAME . . .

Think of a crime, any crime. Picture the first "crime" that comes into your mind. What do you see? The odds are you are not imagining a mining company executive sitting at his desk, calculating the costs of proper safety precautions, and deciding not to invest in them. Probably what you do see with your mind's eye is one person attacking another physically or robbing something from another via the threat of physical attack. Look more closely. What does the attacker look like? It's a safe bet he (and it is a *he*, of course) is not wearing a suit and tie. In fact, my hunch is that you—like me, like almost anyone else in America—picture a young, tough, lower-class male when the thought of crime first pops into your head. You (we) picture someone like the

Typical Criminal described above. The crime itself is one in which the Typical Criminal sets out to attack or rob some specific person.

This last point is important. It indicates that we have a mental image not only of the Typical Criminal but also of the *Typical Crime*. If the Typical Criminal is a young, lower-class male, the Typical Crime is *one-on-one harm*—where "harm" means physical injury, loss of something valuable, or both. If you have any doubts that this is the Typical Crime, look at any random sample of police or private eye shows on television. How often do you see the officers on the TV show *COPS* investigate consumer fraud or failure to remove occupational hazards? When *Law & Order* detectives Green and Fontana happen to track down a well-heeled criminal, it is almost always for violent crimes such as murder. A study of TV crime shows by the Media Institute in Washington, D.C., indicates that, while the fictional criminals portrayed on television are on average both older and wealthier than the real criminals who figure in the FBI *Uniform Crime Reports*, "TV crimes are almost 12 times as likely to be violent as crimes committed in the real world."[25] A review of several decades of research confirms that violent crimes are overrepresented on TV news and fictional crime shows, and that "young people, black people, and people of low socioeconomic status are underrepresented as offenders or victims in television programs"—exactly opposite from the real world, in which nonviolent property crimes far outnumber violent crimes, and young, poor, and black folks predominate as offenders and victims.[26]

Notice, then, that TV crime shows focus on the crimes typically committed by poor people, but they do not present these as uniquely committed by poor people. Rather than contradict the Pyrrhic defeat theory, this combination confirms it in a powerful way. The result is that TV crime shows broadcast the double-edged message that the one-on-one crimes of the poor are the typical crimes that rich and poor criminals commit and thus they are not caused uniquely by the pressures of poverty; *and* that the criminal justice system pursues rich and poor alike—thus, when the criminal justice system happens mainly to pounce on the poor in real life, it is not from any class bias.[27] In other words, what is most important about the televised portrayals of crime is the *kinds* of crimes that are shown, not *who* is typically shown to be guilty. By overrepresenting violent one-on-one crimes, television confirms the commonsense view that these are the crimes that threaten us. Then, since in the real world those crimes are disproportionately committed by poor people, that is enough to create the image that it is the poor who pose the greatest danger to law-abiding Americans.

In addition to the steady diet of fictionalized TV violence and crime, there has been an increase in the graphic display of crime on many TV news programs. Crimes reported on TV news are also far more frequently violent than real crimes are.[28] An article in *The Washingtonian* says that the word around two prominent local TV news programs is "If it bleeds, it leads."[29]

The Center for Media and Public Affairs reports a dramatic increase in homicide coverage on evening news programs starting in 1993, just as homicide rates were falling significantly. Other researchers found that news programs were highly selective in the homicides they reported. The murders that were chosen for coverage tended to be committed by strangers in neighborhoods where average household income was over $25,000 a year, while we know that most murders occur between people known to each other and take place in low-income neighborhoods. The effect is to magnify the risk of lower-class crime to middle-class individuals. Is it any wonder that fear of crime has persisted even as crime rates have gone down sharply?[30]

What's more, a new breed of nonfictional "tabloid" TV show has appeared in which viewers are shown films of actual violent crimes—blood, screams, and all—or reenactments of actual violent crimes, sometimes using the actual victims playing themselves! Among these are COPS and America's Most Wanted. The Wall Street Journal, reporting on the phenomenon of tabloid TV, informs us, "Television has gone tabloid. The seamy underside of life is being bared in a new rash of true-crime series and contrived-confrontation talk shows."[31] Here, too, the focus is on crimes of one-on-one violence, rather than, say, deadly industrial pollution.

It is important to identify this model of the Typical Crime because it functions like a set of blinders. It keeps us from calling a mine disaster a mass murder even if ten men are killed, even if someone is responsible for the unsafe conditions in which they worked and died. One study of newspaper reporting of a food-processing plant fire, in which 25 workers were killed and criminal charges were ultimately brought, concludes that "the newspapers showed little consciousness that corporate violence might be seen as a crime."[32] I contend that this is due to our fixation on the model of the Typical Crime. This particular piece of mental furniture so blocks our view that it keeps us from using the criminal justice system to protect ourselves from the greatest threats to our persons and possessions.

What keeps a mine disaster from being a mass murder in our eyes is that it is not a one-on-one harm. What is important in one-on-one harm is not the numbers but the *desire of someone (or ones) to harm someone (or ones) else.* An attack by a gang on one or more persons or an attack by one individual on several fits the model of one-on-one harm; that is, for each person harmed, there is at least one individual who wanted to harm that person. Once he selects his victim, the rapist, the mugger, or the murderer all want the person they have selected to suffer. A mine executive, on the other hand, does not want his employees to be harmed. He would truly prefer that there be no accident, and no injured or dead miners. What he does want is something legitimate. It is what he has been hired to get: maximum profits at minimum costs. If he cuts corners to save a buck, he is just doing his job. If ten men die because he cut corners on safety, we may think him crude or callous, but not a murderer. He is, at most, responsible for *indirect harm,* not one-on-one harm. For this, he may even be criminally indictable for violating safety regulations, but not for murder. The ten men are dead as an unwanted consequence of his (perhaps overzealous or undercautious) pursuit of a legitimate goal. So, unlike the Typical Criminal, he has not committed the Typical Crime, or so we generally believe. As a result, ten men are dead who might be alive now if cutting corners of the kind that leads to loss of life, whether suffering is specifically aimed at or not, were treated as murder.

This is my point. Because we accept the belief—encouraged by our politicians' statements about crime and by the media's portrayal of crime—that the model for crime is one person specifically trying to harm another, we accept a legal system that leaves us unprotected against much greater dangers to our lives and well-being than those threatened by the Typical Criminal. Before developing this point further, let us anticipate and deal with some likely objections. Defenders of the present legal order are likely to respond to my argument at this point with irritation. Because this will surely turn to outrage in a few pages, let's talk to them now, while the possibility of rational communication still exists.

The "Defenders of the Present Legal Order" (I'll call them "the Defenders" for short) are neither foolish nor evil people. They are not racists, nor are they oblivious to the need for reform in the criminal justice system to make it more even-handed and for reform in the larger society to make equal opportunity a reality for all Americans. Their response to my argument at this point is that the criminal justice system *should* occupy itself with one-on-one harm. Harms of the sort exemplified in the "mine tragedy" are really *not* murders and are better dealt with through stricter government enforcement of safety regulations. The Defenders admit that this enforcement has been rather lax and recommend that it be improved. Basically, though, they think this division of labor is right because it fits our ordinary moral sensibilities.

The Defenders maintain that, according to our common moral notions, someone who tries to do another harm and does is really more evil than someone who jeopardizes others while pursuing legitimate goals but doesn't aim to harm anyone. The one who jeopardizes others in this way doesn't want to hurt them. He or she doesn't have the goal of hurting someone in the way that a mugger or a rapist does. Moreover, being directly and purposely harmed by another person, the Defenders believe, is terrifying in a way that being harmed indirectly and impersonally, say, by a safety hazard, is not, even if the resultant injury is the same in both cases. And we should be tolerant of the one responsible for lax safety measures because he or she is pursuing a legitimate goal—that is, his or her dangerous action occurs as part of a productive activity, something that ultimately adds to social wealth and thus benefits everyone—whereas doers of one-on-one harm benefit no one but themselves. Thus, the latter are rightfully in the province of the criminal justice system with its drastic weapons, and the former are appropriately dealt with by the milder forms of regulation (or, perhaps, treated legally as responsible for *torts*).[33]

Further, the Defenders insist, the crimes targeted by the criminal justice system are imposed on their victims totally against their will, whereas the victims of occupational hazards chose to accept their risky jobs and thus have, in some degree, consented to subject themselves to the dangers. Where dangers are consented to, the appropriate response is not blame but requiring improved safety, and this is most efficiently done by regulation rather than with the guilt-seeking methods of criminal justice.

In sum, the Defenders make four objections: (1) Someone who purposely tries to harm another is really more evil than someone who harms another without aiming to, even if the degree of harm is the same; (2) being harmed directly by another person is more terrifying than being harmed indirectly and impersonally, as by a safety hazard, even if the degree of harm is the same; (3) someone who harms another in the course of an illegitimate and purely self-interested action is more evil than someone who harms another as a consequence of a legitimate and socially productive endeavor; (4) the harms of typical crimes are imposed on their victims against their wills, whereas harms such as those due to occupational hazards are consented to by workers when they agree to a job.

All four of these objections are said to reflect our common moral beliefs, which are a fair standard for a legal system to match. Together they are said to show that the typical criminal does something worse than the one responsible for an occupational hazard and thus deserves the special treatment provided by the criminal justice system. Some or all of these objections may have already occurred to the reader. Thus, it is important to respond to the Defenders. For the sake of clarity, I shall number the paragraphs in which I start to take up each objection in turn.

1. Defenders' first objection: Someone who purposely tries to harm another is really more evil than someone who harms another without aiming to, even if the degree of harm is the same. Thus, the typical criminal is rightly subject to criminal justice, while the cost-cutting executive who endangers his workers is rightly subject to noncriminal safety regulations.

Response: The Defenders' first objection confuses intention with aim or purpose, and it is intention that brings us properly within the reach of the criminal law. It is true that a mugger aims to harm his victim in a way that a corporate executive who maintains an unsafe workplace does not. But the corporate executive acts intentionally nonetheless, and that's what makes his actions appropriately subject to criminal law. What we intend is not just what we want to make happen but what we do on purpose knowing what is likely to happen as the normal result of what we have done. As criminal law theorist Hyman Gross points out, "What really matters here is whether conduct of a particular degree of dangerousness was done intentionally."[34] Whether the actor wants or aims for that conduct to harm someone is a different matter, which is relevant to the actor's *degree* of culpability (not to whether he or she is culpable at all).

Here's an example (adapted from one given by Gross) to help understand the legally recognized degrees of culpability: Suppose a construction worker digs a trench in a neighborhood where children regularly play, and leaves the trench uncovered. One rainy day, children are killed while playing in the trench when its walls cave in on them. If the construction worker dug the trench and left it uncovered in order to kill the children, then their deaths were caused *purposely*. But suppose that the trench was dug and left uncovered not in order to harm the children, but knowing that children played in the area. Then, their deaths were brought about *knowingly*. If digging the ditch and leaving it uncovered were done without knowledge that children played in the area, but without making sure that they did not, then their deaths were brought about *recklessly*. Finally, if the trench was dug and left uncovered without knowledge that children played in the area and some, but inadequate, precautions were taken to make sure no children were there, then their deaths were brought about *negligently*.[35]

How does this apply to the executive who imposes dangerous conditions on his workers, conditions that, as in the mine explosion, finally do lead to death? The first thing to note is that the difference between purposely, knowingly, recklessly, or negligently causing death is a difference within the range of intentional (and thus to some degree legally culpable) action. What is done recklessly or negligently is still done intentionally. Second, culpability decreases as we go from purposely to knowingly to recklessly to negligently killing because, according to Gross, the outcome is increasingly due to chance and not to the actor; that is, the one who kills on purpose leaves less to chance that the killing will occur than the one who kills knowingly (the one who kills on purpose will take precautions against the failure of his killing, while the one who kills knowingly won't), and likewise the one who kills recklessly leaves wholly to chance whether there is a victim at all. And the one who kills negligently reduces this chance, but insufficiently.

The kernel of truth in the Defenders' first objection is that the common street mugger harms on purpose, while the executive harms only knowingly or recklessly or negligently. This does not justify refusing to treat the executive killer as a criminal, however, because we have criminal laws against reckless or even negligent harming. Thus the kid-glove treatment meted out to those responsible for occupational hazards and the like is no simple reflection of our ordinary moral sensibilities, as the Defenders claim. Moreover, don't be confused into thinking that, because all workplaces have some safety measures, all workplace deaths are at most due to negligence. To the extent that precautions are not taken against particular dangers (such as leaking methane), deaths due to those dangers are—by Gross's standard—caused recklessly or even knowingly (because the executive knows that potential victims are in harm's way from the danger he fails to reduce). Nancy Frank concludes from a review of state homicide statutes that "a large number of states recognize unintended deaths caused by extreme reckless-ness as murder."[36]

There is more to be said. Remember that Gross attributes the difference in degrees of culpability to the greater role left to chance as we descend from purposely to knowingly to recklessly to negligently harming. In this light, it is important to note that the executive (say, the mine owner) imposes danger on a larger number of individuals than the typical criminal typically does. So, while the typical criminal purposely harms a particular individual, the exec-utive knowingly subjects a large number of workers to a risk of harm. As the risk becomes greater and the number of workers increases, it becomes increasingly likely that one or more workers will be harmed. This means that the gap between the executive and the typical criminal shrinks. By not harm-ing workers purposely, the executive leaves more to chance; but by subject-ing large numbers to risk, he leaves it less and less to chance that *someone* will be harmed, and, thus, he rolls back his moral advantage over the typical criminal. If you keep your workers in mines or factories with high levels of toxic gases or chemicals, you start to approach 100 percent likelihood that at least one of them will be harmed as a result. That means that the culpability of the executive approaches that of the typical criminal.

A different way to make the Defenders' first objection is to say that the executive has failed to protect his workers, while the typical criminal has acted positively to harm his victim. In general, we think it is worse to harm someone than to fail to prevent their being harmed (perhaps you should feed starving people on the other side of town or of the world, but few people will think you are a murderer if you don't and the starving die). But in at least some cases, we are responsible for the harm that results from our failure to act (for example, parents are responsible when they fail to provide for their children). Some philosophers go further and hold that we are responsible for all the foreseeable effects of what we do, including the foreseeable effects of failing to act in certain ways.[37] Although this view supports the position for which I am arguing here, I think it goes too far. It entails that we are murder-ers every time we are doing anything other than saving lives, which surely goes way beyond our ordinary moral beliefs. My view is that in most cases, we are responsible only for the foreseeable effects likely to be caused by our action, and are not responsible for those caused by our inaction. We are responsible, however, for the effects of our inaction in at least one special type of case: when we have a special obligation to aid people. This covers the parent who causes his child's death by failing to feed him, the doctor who causes her patient's death by failing to care for her, and the coal mine owner who causes his employees' death by failing to take legally mandated safety precautions. It may also cover the society that fails to rectify harm-producing injustices in its midst. This is another way in which the moral difference between the safety-cutting executive and the typical criminal shrinks away.

Further on this first objection, I think the Defenders overestimate the importance of specifically trying to do evil in our moral estimate of people.

The mugger who aims to hurt someone is no doubt an ugly character, but so too is the well-heeled executive who calmly and callously chooses to put others at risk. Most murders, we know, are committed in the heat of some passion such as rage or jealousy. Two lovers or neighbors or relatives find themselves in a heated argument. One (often it is a matter of chance *which* one) picks up a weapon and strikes the other a fatal blow. Such a person is clearly a murderer and rightly subject to punishment by the criminal justice system. Is this person more evil than the executive who, knowing the risks, calmly chooses not to pay for safety equipment?

The one who kills in a heated argument kills from passion. What she does she probably would not do in a cooler moment. She is likely to feel "she was not herself." The one she killed was someone she knew, a specific person who at the time seemed to her to be the embodiment of all that frustrated her, someone whose very existence made life unbearable. I do not mean to suggest that this is true of all killers, although there is reason to believe that it is true of many. Nor do I mean to suggest that such a state of mind justifies murder. What it does do, however, is suggest that the killer's action, arising out of anger at a particular individual, does not show general disdain for the lives of her fellows. Here is where she is different from our mine executive. Our mine executive wanted to harm no one in particular, but *he knew his acts were likely to harm someone.* Once someone is harmed, the victim is someone in particular. Nor can our executive claim that "he was not himself." His act is done not out of passion but out of cool reckoning. It is precisely here that his evil shows. In his willingness to jeopardize the lives of unspecified others who pose him no real or imaginary threat in order to make a few dollars, he shows his general disdain for all his fellow human beings. Can it really be said that he is less evil than one who kills from passion? The Model Penal Code includes within the definition of murder any death caused by "extreme indifference to human life."[38] Is our executive not a murderer by this definition?

It's worth noting that, in answering the Defenders here, I have portrayed harms from occupational hazards in their best light. They are not, however, all just matters of well-intentioned but excessive risk taking. Consider, for example, the Manville (formerly Johns Manville) asbestos case. It is predicted that 240,000 Americans working now or who previously worked with asbestos will die from asbestos-related cancer over a period of 30 years. But documents made public during congressional hearings in 1979 show "that Manville and other companies within the asbestos industry covered up and failed to warn millions of Americans of the dangers associated with the fireproof, indestructible insulating fiber."[39] An article in the *American Journal of Public Health* attributes thousands of deaths to the cover-up.[40] Later in this chapter I document similar intentional cover-ups, such as the falsification of reports on coal-dust levels in mines, which leads to crippling and often fatal black lung disease. Surely someone who knowingly subjects others to risks and tries to hide those risks from them is culpable in a high degree.

2. Defenders' second objection: Being harmed directly by another person is more terrifying than being harmed indirectly and impersonally, as by a safety hazard, even if the degree of harm is the same.

Response: I think the Defenders are largely right in believing that direct personal assault is terrifying in a way that indirect impersonal harm is not. I say "largely right" here because deaths from some safety hazards—slowly suffocating to death in a collapsed mine, or living in fear of an occupational cancer's spreading and becoming fatal—may well be as terrifying as or more terrifying than some direct personal assaults. Nonetheless, even granting the Defenders their general point that direct assault is usually more terrifying than indirect harm, it does not follow that indirect harms should be treated as noncriminal regulatory matters. This difference in terrifyingness is no stranger to the criminal justice system. Prosecutors, judges, and juries constantly have to consider how terrifying an attack is in determining what to charge and what to convict offenders for. This is why we allow gradations in charges of homicide or assault and allow particularly grave sentences for particularly grave attacks. In short, the difference the Defenders are pointing to here might justify treating a one-on-one murder as graver than murder due to lax safety measures, but it doesn't justify treating one as a grave crime and the other as a mere regulatory (or very minor criminal) matter. After all, although it is worse to be injured with terror than without, it is still the injury that constitutes the worst part of violent crime. Given the choice, seriously injured victims of crime would surely rather have been terrorized and not injured than injured and not terrorized. If that is so, then the worst part of violent crime is still shared by the indirect harms that the Defenders would relegate to regulation.

3. Defenders' third objection: Someone who harms another in the course of an illegitimate and purely self-interested action is more evil than someone who harms another as a consequence of a legitimate and socially productive endeavor.

Response: There is also something to the Defenders' claim that indirect harms, such as ones that result from lax safety measures, are part of legitimate productive activities, whereas one-on-one crimes generally are not. No doubt, we must tolerate the risks that are necessary ingredients of productive activity (unless those risks are so great as to outweigh the gains of the productive activity). But this doesn't imply we shouldn't identify the risks that are excessive and use the law to protect innocent people from them. If those risks are great enough, the fact that they may further a productive or otherwise legitimate activity is no reason against making them crimes if that's what's necessary to protect workers. A person can commit a crime to further an otherwise legitimate endeavor and it is still a crime. If a manager threatens to assault his workers if they don't work faster, the fact that getting them to work faster is a legitimate goal for a manager doesn't make the manager's act any less criminal. If acts that endanger others ought to be crimes, then the fact that the acts are means to legitimate aims doesn't change the fact that they ought to be crimes.

4. Defenders' fourth objection: The harms of typical crimes are imposed on their victims against their wills, whereas harms such as those due to occupational hazards are consented to by workers when they agree to a job.

Response: Cases like the Manville asbestos case show that the Defenders overestimate the reality of the "free consent" with which workers take on the risks of their jobs. You can consent to a risk only if you know about it, and often the risks are concealed. Moreover, the Defenders overestimate generally the degree to which workers freely consent to the conditions of their jobs. Although no one is forced at gunpoint to accept a particular job, virtually everyone is forced by the requirements of necessity to take some job. Moreover, workers can choose jobs only where there are openings, which means they cannot simply pick their place of employment at will. At best, workers can choose among the dangers present at various worksites, but rarely can they choose to face no danger at all. For nonwhites and women, the choices are further narrowed by discriminatory hiring and long-standing occupational segregation (funneling women into nursing or food-processing jobs and blacks into janitorial and other menial occupations), not to mention subtle and not-so-subtle practices that keep nonwhites and women from advancing within their occupations. Consequently, for all intents and purposes, most workers *must* face the dangers of the jobs that are available to them. What's more, remember that, while here we have been focusing on harms due to occupational hazards, much of the indirect harm that I shall document in what follows is done not to workers but, for example, to hospital patients (subjected to careless medical care) or to neighbors of industrial sites (breathing dangerous concentrations of pollutants). And these victims surely don't consent to these risks.

Finally, recall that the basis of all the Defenders' objections is that the idea that one-on-one harms are more evil than indirect harms is part of our common moral beliefs, and that this makes it appropriate to treat the former with the criminal justice system and the latter with milder regulatory measures. Here I think the Defenders err by overlooking the role of legal institutions in shaping our ordinary moral beliefs. Many who defend the criminal justice system do so precisely because of its function in educating the public about the difference between right and wrong. The great historian of English law, Sir James Fitzjames Stephens, held that a

> great part of the general detestation of crime which happily prevails amongst the decent part of the community in all civilized countries arises from the fact that the commission of offences is associated in all such communities with the solemn and deliberate infliction of punishment wherever crime is proved.[41]

One cannot simply appeal to ordinary moral beliefs to defend the criminal law because the criminal law has already had a hand in shaping ordinary moral beliefs. At least one observer has argued that making narcotics use a crime at the beginning of the twentieth century *caused* a change in the public's ordinary moral notions about drug addiction, which prior to that time had been viewed as a medical problem.[42] It is probably safe to say that, in our own time, civil rights legislation has sharpened the public's moral condemnation of racial discrimination. Hence, we might speculate that if the criminal justice system began to prosecute—and if the media began to portray—those who inflict *indirect harm* as serious criminals, our ordinary moral notions would change on this point as well.

I think this disposes of the Defenders for the time being. We are left with the conclusion that there is no moral basis for treating *one-on-one harm* as criminal and *indirect harm* as merely a regulatory affair (or only as a tort). What matters, then, is whether the purpose of the criminal justice system will be served by including, in the category of serious crime, actions that are predictably likely to produce serious harm, yet that are done in pursuit of otherwise legitimate goals and without the desire to harm anyone.

What is the purpose of the criminal justice system? No esoteric answer is required. Norval Morris and Gordon Hawkins write that "the prime function of the criminal law is to protect our persons and our property."[43] *The Challenge of Crime in a Free Society,* the report of the President's Commission on Law Enforcement and Administration of Justice, tells us that "any criminal justice system is an apparatus society uses to enforce the standards of conduct necessary to protect individuals and the community."[44] Whatever else we think a criminal justice system should accomplish, I doubt if anyone would deny that its central purpose is to protect us against the most serious threats to our well-being. *This purpose is seriously undermined by taking one-on-one harm as the model of crime.* Excluding harm caused without the desire to harm someone in particular prevents the criminal justice system from protecting our persons and our property from dangers at least as great as those posed by one-on-one harm. This is so because, as I will show, a large number of actions that are not labeled *criminal* lead to loss of life, limb, and possessions on a scale comparable to those actions that are represented in the FBI Crime Index. A crime by any other name still causes misery and suffering.

***

In the remainder of this chapter, I identify some acts that are *crimes by other names:* acts that cause harm and suffering comparable to that caused by acts called crimes. My purpose is to confirm the first hypothesis: that the definitions of crime in the criminal law do not reflect the only or the most dangerous behaviors in our society. To do this, we will need some measure of the harm and suffering caused by crimes with which we can compare the harm and suffering caused by noncrimes. Our measure need not be too refined because my point can be made if I can show that there are some acts that we do not treat as crimes but that cause harm *roughly comparable* to that caused by acts we do treat as crimes. For that, it is not necessary to compare the harm caused by noncriminal acts with the harm caused by *all* crimes. I need only show that the harm produced by some type of noncriminal act is comparable to the harm produced by *any* serious crime. Because the harms caused by noncriminal acts fall into the categories of death, bodily injury (including the disabling effects of disease), and property loss, I will compare the harms done by noncriminal acts with the injuries caused by the crimes of murder, aggravated assault, and theft.

In order to compare the harms produced by both criminal and noncriminal acts, I will generally use statistics for 2003, the most recent year for which there are ample statistics from both categories. Where figures for 2003 are not available, I will use the most recent figures that are available unless there is reason to think that significant changes have occurred in the interim. According to the FBI's *Uniform Crime Reports,* in 2003 there were 16,503 murders and nonnegligent manslaughters and 857,921 aggravated assaults. "Murder and nonnegligent manslaughter" includes all "willful (nonnegligent) killing of one human being by another." "Aggravated assault" is defined as an "attack by one person on another for the purpose of inflicting severe or aggravated bodily injury."[45] Thus, as measures of the harm done by crime in 2003, we can say that serious crimes led to roughly 16,500 deaths and 850,000 instances of serious bodily injury short of death a year. As a measure of monetary loss due to property crime, we can use $17 billion, the figure the FBI estimates to be the total lost due to property crime in 2003.[46] Whatever the shortcomings of these reported crime statistics, they are the statistics on which public policy has traditionally been based.[47] Thus, I will consider any actions that lead to loss of life, physical harm, and property loss comparable to the figures in the *UCR* as actions that pose grave dangers to the community comparable to the threats posed by crimes. They are surely precisely the kinds of harmful actions from which a criminal justice system whose purpose is to protect our persons and property ought to protect us, but *they are crimes by other names.*

In making this case, the following sections review a number of research reports, both historical and contemporary. The continued inclusion of older reports—sometimes seen as "outdated"—is meant to underscore that these harms are neither new nor recently discovered. The harms are not transient, but ongoing, and the inclusion of findings reported over several decades should bolster confidence in the validity of sometimes scarce contemporary research.

Work May Be Dangerous to Your Health

When the *President's Report on Occupational Safety and Health*[48] was published in 1972, the government estimated the number of job-related illnesses at 390,000 per year and the number of annual deaths from industrial disease at 100,000. Since that time, numerous studies have documented the alarmingly high incidence of disease, injury, and death due to hazards in the workplace *and* the fact that much or most of this carnage is the consequence of the refusal of management to pay for safety measures, of government to enforce safety standards, and sometimes of management's willful defiance of existing law.[49]

For 2003, the U.S. Department of Labor's Bureau of Labor Statistics (BLS) reports 4.4 million workplace injuries and illnesses, about half of which (2.3 million) resulted in lost workdays or restricted duties at work. BLS also indicates "269,500 newly reported cases of [nonfatal] occupational illnesses in private industry."[50]

Complete data on occupational fatalities are difficult to come by. BLS says about its data on fatal occupational diseases that

> [i]t is difficult to compile a complete count of fatal occupational diseases because the latency period [the delay between contracting a fatal disease on the job and the appearance of symptoms, and from these to death] for many of these conditions may span years. In addition, there is some difficulty in linking illnesses to work exposures. Data presented are incomplete, therefore, and do not represent all deaths that result from occupational diseases.[51]

Moreover, the Occupational Safety and Health Administration (OSHA) relies on employer reporting for its figures, and there are many incentives for underreporting. Writing in the journal *Occupational Hazards*, Robert Reid states that

> OSHA concedes that many factors—including insurance rates and supervisor evaluations based on safety performance—are incentives to underreport. And the agency acknowledges that recordkeeping violations have increased more than 27 percent since 1984, with most of the violations recorded for not maintaining the injuries and illnesses log examined by compliance officers and used for BLS' annual survey.[52]

A study by the National Institute for Occupational Safety and Health (NIOSH) concludes that "there may be several thousand more workplace deaths each year than employers report."[53]

For these reasons, we must look elsewhere for accurate figures. In testimony before the Senate Committee on Labor and Human Resources, Dr. Philip Landrigan, director of the Division of Environmental and Occupational Medicine at the Mount Sinai School of Medicine in New York City, stated,

> Recent data indicate that occupationally related exposures are responsible each year in New York State for 5,000 to 7,000 deaths and for 35,000 new cases of illness (not including work-related injuries). These deaths due to occupational disease include 3,700 deaths from cancer. . . .
>   Crude national estimates of the burden of occupational disease in the United States may be developed by multiplying the New York State data by a factor of 10. New York State contains slightly less than 10 percent of the nation's workforce, and it includes a broad mix of employment in the manufacturing, service and agricultural sectors. Thus, it may be calculated that occupational disease is responsible each year in the United States for 50,000 to 70,000 deaths, and for approximately 350,000 new cases of illness.[54]

Landrigan's estimates of deaths from occupational disease are corroborated by a study reported by the National Safe Workplace Institute, which estimates that the number of occupational disease deaths is between 47,377 and 95,479. Mark Cullen, director of the occupational medicine program at the Yale University School of Medicine, praised this study as "a very balanced, very comprehensive overview of occupational health."[55]

In a 1997 article in the AMA journal *Archives of Internal Medicine*, researchers at San Jose State University in California aggregated the national and large regional data sets collected by BLS, the National Council on Compensation Insurance, the National Center for Health Statistics, the Health Care Financing Administration, and other government agencies and private firms, and came up with an estimate, for 1992, of 60,300 deaths from occupational illness.[56]

Dr. Samuel Epstein, professor emeritus of environmental and occupational medicine at the University of Illinois School of Public Health, and chairman of the Cancer Prevention Coalition, states, "Over 10 percent of adult cancer deaths result from occupational exposures, which are also a recognized cause of cancer in children: parents exposed to carcinogens on the job often expose their unborn children to the same cancer-causing chemicals."[57] With current estimates of annual cancer deaths running above 570,000, this translates into approximately 57,000 adult deaths a year from occupationally caused cancer alone. A 1999 report estimates approximately 55,000 annual deaths from occupational disease, though noting that the number may be as high as 94,000.[58]

In light of these various estimates, we can hardly be overestimating the actual death toll if we take the conservative route and set it at 50,000 deaths a year resulting from occupational disease.

As for nonfatal occupational illness, BLS reports 269,500 new cases for 2003, and the San Jose State University researchers estimate 862,200 cases (based on data from 1992). These illnesses are of varying severity. Because I want to compare these occupational harms with those resulting from aggravated assault, I shall stay on the conservative side here, too, as with deaths from occupational diseases, and say that there are annually in the United States approximately 250,000 job-related serious illnesses. This is a conservative figure in light of the San Jose State University researchers' estimate of 862,200 cases, as well as the likelihood of underreporting. Note also that these figures don't include the effects of workers' exposure to occupational illnesses on the health of their families.[59] Taken together with 50,000 deaths from occupational diseases, how does this compare with the threat posed by crime?

Before jumping to any conclusions, note that the risk of occupational disease and death falls only on members of the labor force, whereas the risk of crime falls on the whole population, from infants to the elderly. Because the civilian labor force is about half (50.6 percent) of the total population (146,500,000 in 2003 out of a total civilian population of 289,558,000),[60] to get a true picture of the *relative* threat posed by occupational diseases compared with that posed by crimes, we should multiply the crime statistics by half (0.5) when comparing them with the figures for occupational disease and death. Using the crime figures for 2003 (cited earlier in this chapter), we note that the *comparable* figures would be:

	OCCUPATIONAL DISEASE	CRIME (X 0.5)
Death	50,000	8,250
Other physical harm	250,000	425,000

If it is argued that this paints an inaccurate picture because so many crimes go unreported, my answer is this: First of all, homicides are by far the most completely reported of crimes. For obvious reasons, the general underreporting of crimes is not equal among crimes. It is easier to avoid reporting a rape or a mugging than a corpse. Second, although not the best, aggravated assaults are among the better-reported crimes. Estimates from the Justice Department's National Crime Victimization Survey indicate that 57 percent of aggravated assaults were reported to the police in 2002, compared with 33 percent of thefts.[61] On the other hand, we should expect more, not less, underreporting of industrial than criminal victims because diseases and deaths are likely to cost firms money in the form of workdays lost and insurance premiums raised, occupational diseases are frequently first seen by company physicians who have an incentive to diagnose complaints as either malingering or not job related, and many occupationally caused diseases do not show symptoms or lead to death until after the employee has left the job.

In sum, both occupational and criminal harms are underreported, though there is reason to believe that the underreporting is worse for occupational than for criminal harms. Those who doubt this should bear in mind that I have accepted the statistics on criminal harms as reported, while I have reduced substantially the reported estimates for occupational harms. However one may quibble with figures presented here, I think it is fair to say that, if anything, they understate the extent of occupational harm compared with criminal harm.

Note further that the estimates in the last chart are *only* for occupational *diseases* and deaths from those diseases. They do not include death and disability from work-related injuries. Here, too, the statistics are gruesome. The San Jose State University researchers estimated 6,500 job-related deaths from injuries in 1992.[62] BLS's *National Census of Fatal Occupational Injuries* reports 4,928 workplace fatalities in 2003 (not counting work-related homicides).[63] I will use the lower of these figures. Added to the previous figure, this brings the number of occupation-related deaths to 54,928 a year.

The BLS reported that, in 2003, there were 4.4 million recordable cases of nonfatal injuries and illnesses. A recordable case involves days away from work, medical treatment other than first aid, loss of consciousness, restriction of work or motion, transfer to another job, or "cancer, chronic irreversible disease, a fracture or cracked bone, or a punctured eardrum."[64] Of these, BLS says that 2.3 million entailed lost workdays, restricted activities on the job, or both. To make sure that we are counting more serious harms, I will use this figure of 2.3 million. Note that this figure includes physical harms from both disease and injury. Thus it replaces our previous figure of 250,000.

If, on the basis of these additional figures, we recalculated our table comparing occupational harms from both disease and accident with criminal harms, it would look like this:

	OCCUPATIONAL DISEASE AND INJURY	CRIME (X 0.5)
Death	54,928	8,250
Other physical harm	2,300,000	425,000

Can there be any doubt that workers are more likely to stay alive and healthy in the face of the danger from the underworld than from the work-world? If any doubt lingers, consider this: Lest we falter in the struggle against crime, the FBI includes in its annual *Uniform Crime Reports* several "crime clocks," which illustrate graphically the extent of the criminal menace. For 2003, the crime clock shows a murder occurring every 31.8 minutes.[65] If a similar clock were constructed for occupational deaths—using the conservative estimate of 54,928 cited above, and remembering that this clock ticks for only that half of the population that is in the labor force—this clock would show an occupational death about every 10 minutes! In other words, in about the time it takes for two murders on the crime clock, more than six workers have died *just from trying to make a living.*

To say that some of these workers died from accidents due to their own carelessness is about as helpful as saying that some of those who died at the hands of murderers deserved it. It overlooks the fact that, when workers are careless, it is not because they love to live dangerously. They have production quotas to meet, quotas that they themselves do not set. If quotas were set with an eye to keeping work at a safe pace rather than keeping the production-to-wages ratio as high as possible, it might be more reasonable to expect workers to take the time to be careful. Beyond this, we should bear in mind that the vast majority of occupational deaths result from disease, not accident, and disease is generally a function of conditions outside a worker's control.

Examples of such conditions are the level of coal dust in the air ("260,000 miners receive benefits for [black lung] disease, and perhaps as many as 4,000 retired miners die from the illness or its complications each year"; about 10,000 currently working miners "have X-ray evidence of the beginnings of the crippling and often fatal disease"),[66] or textile dust (some 100,000 American cotton textile workers presently suffer breathing impairments caused by acute byssinosis, or brown lung, and another 35,000 former mill workers are totally disabled with chronic brown lung),[67] or asbestos fibers (it has been estimated that, under the lenient asbestos standard promulgated by OSHA in 1972, anywhere from 18,400 and 598,000 deaths from lung cancer would result from exposure to asbestos),[68] or coal tars ("workers who had been employed five or more years in the coke ovens died of lung cancer at a rate three and a half times that for all steelworkers"; coke oven workers develop cancer of the scrotum at a rate five times that of the general population).[69] According to the National Academy of Sciences, there are more than 1 million repetitive motion injuries annually.[70] Repetitive strain disease "is, by all accounts, the fastest-growing health hazard in the U.S. workplace, reportedly afflicting about 1,000 keyboard operators, assembly-line workers, meat processors, grocery check-out clerks, secretaries and other employees everyday. . . . OSHA officials argue that . . . carpal tunnel problems lead the list in average time lost from work (at a median of 30 days per case), well above amputations (24 days) and fractures (20)."[71]

To blame the workers for occupational disabilities and deaths is to ignore the history of governmental attempts to compel industrial firms to meet safety standards that would keep dangers (such as chemicals or fibers or dust particles in the air) that are outside the worker's control down to a safe level. This has been a continual struggle, with firms using everything from their own "independent" research institutes to more direct and often questionable forms of political pressure to influence government in the direction of loose standards and lax enforcement. So far, industry has been winning because OSHA has been given neither the personnel nor the mandate to fulfill its purpose. It is so understaffed that, in 1973, when 1,500 federal sky marshals guarded the nation's airplanes from hijackers, only 500 OSHA inspectors toured the nation's workplaces. As of 2003, there are some 7.2 million worksites in the United States, and federal OSHA's 1,100 inspectors carried out some 40,000 inspections, while its state counterparts carried out some 58,000.[72] Currently, OSHA reports 51,666 "serious" violations for which fines were issued totalling $54,526,440, an average fine of $1,055 per *serious* violation. OSHA defines a serious violation as one "where there is substantial probability that death or serious physical harm could result and the employer knew, or should have known, of the hazard."[73] The problem does not lie with OSHA alone, but starts with the legislators who decided in 1970 that causing the death of an employee by willfully violating safety laws was a misdemeanor. As noted by a recent *New York Times* investigation: "The maximum sentence, six months in jail, is half the maximum for harassing a wild burro on federal lands." Although Congress has rarely voted down tougher sentences for street crime, it has rejected every attempt to get tougher with those who willfully (and sometimes repeatedly) violate safety laws, in spite of evidence that stricter laws could save lives. On top of lax laws, OSHA discourages prosecutions and criminal referrals to such an extent that a 1988 congressional report noted, "A company official who willfully and recklessly violates federal OSHA laws stands a greater chance of winning a state lottery than being criminally charged."[74]

Is a person who kills another in a bar brawl a greater threat to society than a business executive who refuses to cut into his profits to make his plant a safe place to work? By any measure of death and suffering, the latter is by far a greater danger than the former. However, because he wishes his workers no harm, and because he is only indirectly responsible for death and disability while pursuing legitimate economic goals, his acts are not labelled "crimes." Once we free our imagination from the blinders of the one-on-one model of crime, can there be any doubt that the criminal justice system does *not* protect us from the gravest threats to life and limb? It seeks to protect us when danger comes from a young, lower-class male in the inner city. When a threat comes from an upper-class business executive in an office, the criminal justice system looks the other way. This is in the face of growing evidence that for every two American citizens murdered by thugs, more than six American workers are killed by the recklessness of their bosses and the indifference of their government.

Health Care May Be Dangerous to Your Health

A recent article in *The Journal of the American Medical Association* estimates that there are 225,000 deaths a year due to medical treatment, making medical treatment "the third leading cause of death in the United States, after deaths from heart disease and cancer."[75] Hospital infections alone were said to cause about 1,500 preventable deaths in Pennsylvania during 2004. Since Pennsylvania has about 4 percent of the U.S. population, the

Pennsylvania data suggest that hospital infections may cause some 37,500 preventable deaths nationwide, more than double the number of homicides reported by the FBI.[76] Estimates from the Centers for Disease Control and other studies put the numbers at 90,000 to 100,000 deaths,[77] deaths that could have been prevented by following established hygiene protocols. And this is only the beginning.

On July 15, 1975, Dr. Sidney Wolfe, of Ralph Nader's Public Interest Health Research Group, testified before the House Commerce Oversight and Investigations Subcommittee that there "were 3.2 million cases of unnecessary surgery performed each year in the United States." These unneeded operations, Wolfe added, "cost close to $5 billion a year and kill as many as 16,000 Americans."[78] Wolfe's estimates of unnecessary surgery were based on studies comparing the operations performed and surgery recommended by doctors who are paid for the operations they do with those performed and recommended by salaried doctors who receive no extra income from surgery.

The figure accepted by Dr. George A. Silver, professor of public health at the Yale University School of Medicine, is 15,000 deaths a year "attributable to unnecessary surgery."[79] Silver places the annual cost of excess surgery at $4.8 billion.[80] In an article on an experimental program by Blue Cross and Blue Shield aimed at curbing unnecessary surgery, *Newsweek* reported that

> a Congressional committee earlier this year [1976] estimated that more than 2 million of the elective operations performed in 1974 were not only unnecessary—but also killed about 12,000 patients and cost nearly $4 billion.[81]

Because the number of surgical operations performed in the United States rose from 16.7 million in 1975 to 27.6 million in 2002,[82] there is reason to believe that at least somewhere between (the congressional committee's estimate of) 12,000 and (Dr. Wolfe's estimate of) 16,000 people a year still die from unnecessary surgery. In 2003, the FBI reported that 1,816 murders (in which the weapon is known) were committed with a "cutting or stabbing instrument."[83] Obviously, the FBI does not include the scalpel as a cutting or stabbing instrument. If it did, it would have had to report that between 13,816 and 17,816 persons were killed by "cutting or stabbing" in 2003, depending on whether you take Congress's figure or Wolfe's. No matter how you slice it, the scalpel may be more dangerous than the switchblade.

This is only a fraction of the problem. A report issued on November 29, 1999, by the National Academy of Sciences's Institute of Medicine (IOM) stated that up to "98,000 hospitalized Americans die every year and 1 million more are injured as a result of preventable medical errors that cost the nation an estimated $29 billion a year."[84] The report goes on to predict that, if a "centralized system for keeping tabs on medical errors" were put in place, "the number of deaths from medical mistakes could be cut in half within five years."[85] However, due to resistance by doctors and hospitals to mandatory reporting of errors and to other recommendations in the IOM report, no significant progress has been made. "As a result, experts contend, it's doubtful that patients checking into most of America's 5,200 hospitals [in 2002] are any less likely to be killed or injured than they were on November 29, 1999, when the report was issued."[86] Indeed, things may be worse. "Operations on the wrong body part or the wrong patient have increased according to the Joint Commission on the Accreditation of Healthcare Organizations, which inspects hospitals."[87] Bear in mind as well that "[t]he IOM considered only errors committed in hospitals, and not in other medical settings where they undoubtedly abound: clinics, outpatient surgery centers and doctors' offices."[88] Recall the example of digging a trench: "Suppose that the trench was dug and left uncovered, knowing that children played in the area. Then, their deaths were brought about *knowingly.*" *Knowingly* was the second degree of culpability, right below *purposely*—and is more culpable than *recklessly* or *negligently.* Suppose that preventable and deadly potential hospital errors were identified but left unprevented, knowing that vulnerable patients would be in the area. Didn't the doctors and hospitals who resisted correcting previously identified dangerous practices bring about 98,000 deaths *knowingly*?

While it is at it, the FBI should probably add the hypodermic needle and the prescription drug to the list of potential murder weapons. Silver points out that these are also death-dealing instruments:

> Of the 6 billion doses of antibiotic medicines administered each year by injection or prescription, it is estimated that 22 percent are unnecessary. Of the doses given, 10,000 result in fatal or near-fatal reactions. Somewhere between 2,000 and 10,000 deaths probably would not have occurred if the drugs, meant for the patient's benefit, had not been given.[89]

These estimates are supported by the Harvard Medical Practice Study. Its authors write that, of the 1.3 million medical injuries (which they estimated on the basis of hospital records for 1984), 19 percent (247,000) were related to medications, and 14 percent of these (34,580) resulted in permanent injury or death.[90] Another report estimates that, in part due to faulty warning labels on prescription drugs, "100,000 hospital patients die [annually] of adverse reactions to medication and 2.2 million are injured."[91] Further, "experts have estimated that more than one million serious drug errors occur annually in hospitals alone." One drug that has figured frequently in cases of deadly overdoses is potassium chloride, which, in low doses, restores electrolyte balance and, in high doses, stops the heart instantly. Potassium chloride is the drug used by states that administer the death penalty by lethal injection![92]

If someone had the temerity to publish a *Uniform Crime Reports* that really portrayed the way Americans are murdered, the FBI's statistics on the *type* of weapon used in murder would have to be changed for 2003, from those shown in Table 2.1 to something like those shown in Table 2.2.

The figures shown in Table 2.2 would give American citizens a much more honest picture of what threatens them. Nonetheless, we are not likely to see such a table published by the criminal justice system, perhaps because it would also give American citizens a more honest picture of *who* threatens them.

We should not leave this topic without noting that, aside from the other losses it imposes, unnecessary surgery was estimated to have cost between $4 billion and $5 billion in 1974. The price of medical care has increased about sevenfold between 1974 and 2000. Thus, assuming that the same number of unneeded operations was performed in 2003, the cost of unnecessary surgery would be between $28 and $35 billion. To this we should add the unnecessary 22 percent of the 6 billion doses of medication administered. Even at an extremely conservative estimate of $3 a dose, this adds about $4 billion. In short, assuming that earlier trends have continued, there is reason to believe that unnecessary surgery and medication cost the public between $28 and $34 billion annually, far outstripping the $17 billion taken by the thieves that concern the FBI.[93] This gives us yet another way in which we are robbed of more money by practices that are not treated as criminal than by practices that are.

TABLE 2.1   **How Americans Are Murdered, 2003**

TOTAL MURDERS WHERE WEAPON IS KNOWN	FIREARMS	KNIFE OR OTHER CUTTING INSTRUMENT	OTHER WEAPON: BLUNT OBJECTS, ARSON, STRANGULATION, POISON, etc.	PERSONAL WEAPONS: HANDS, FISTS, etc.
14,408*	9,638	1,816	2,008	946

*This figure is lower than the number of murders and nonnegligent manslaughters used elsewhere in the text, due to the fact that the FBI lacks data on the weapons used in roughly one-sixth of the homicides it reports. "Other Weapon" represents all the other categories in the UCR's Table 2.9 that are not reported separately here, including the category "Other Weapon/Not Stated."

Source: UCR–2003, Table 2.9, p. 19.

TABLE 2.2   How Americans Are *Really* Murdered, 2003

TOTAL MURDERS WHERE WEAPON IS KNOWN	OCCUPATIONAL HAZARD OR DISEASE	FIREARMS	KNIFE OR OTHER CUTTING INSTRUMENT, INCLUDING SCALPEL	OTHER WEAPON: BLUNT OBJECTS, POISON, STRANGULATION, PRESCRIPTION DRUG, OTHER MEDICAL TREATMENT, etc.	PERSONAL WEAPONS: HANDS, FISTS, etc.
133,336*	54,928	9,638	13,816	53,008	946

*These figures represent the relevant figures in Table 2.1 plus the most conservative figures for the relevant categories discussed in the text. Note in particular that, under the category "Other Weapon," I have included the low estimate of the number of people who die from unnecessary prescription drugs (2,000) according to Dr. Silver, plus the 50 percent of the 98,000 hospital deaths due to error that the IOM predicted could have been prevented within five years of their report (49,000).

Waging Chemical Warfare against America

One in four Americans can expect to contract cancer during his or her lifetime. The American Cancer Society estimated that 420,000 Americans would die of cancer in 1981. The Society's estimate for 2005 is 570,280 deaths from cancer, with more than 1.3 million new cases diagnosed that year.[94] "A 1978 report issued by the President's Council on Environmental Quality (CEQ) unequivocally states that 'most researchers agree that 70 to 90 percent of cancers are caused by environmental influences and are hence theoretically preventable.'"[95] This means that a concerted national effort could result in saving 350,000 or more lives a year and reducing each individual's chances of getting cancer in his or her lifetime from 1 in 4 to 1 in 12 or fewer. If you think this would require a massive effort in terms of money and personnel, you are right. How much of an effort, though, would the nation make to stop a foreign invader who was killing 1,500 people a day and bent on slaughtering one-quarter of the present population? And how has the "cancer establishment"—the publicly funded National Cancer Institute (NCI) and the private American Cancer Society (ACS)—responded? A group of experts writes,

> The cancer establishment's funding for primary prevention is trivial. While the NCI has made wildly varying estimates for prevention research—up to 50 percent of its budget—independent estimates are closer to 2.5 percent. . . . The ACS's "Environmental Research" funding is less than 0.1 percent of revenues.
>
> The cancer establishment conducts minimal research on avoidable exposures to a wide range of occupational and environmental industrial

carcinogens, including nationwide cancer clusters in the vicinity of nuclear power plants, petrochemical industries, and Superfund hazardous waste sites that are disproportionately located in ethnic and low-socioeconomic communities, and exposures to ionizing radiation and persistant organic pollutants contaminating the entire environment: air, water, soil, the workplace, and consumer products.[96]

Chemical warfare is being waged against us on three fronts:

- pollution
- cigarette smoking
- food additives

Not only are we losing on all three fronts, but it also looks as if we do not even have the will to fight. A 2002 article in *The Washington Post* reports that "the Bush administration has begun a broad restructuring of the scientific advisory committees that guide federal policy in areas such as patient rights and public health, eliminating some committees that were coming to conclusions at odds with the president's views." One committee, "which had been assessing the effects of environmental chemicals on human health[,] has been told that nearly all of its members will be replaced—in several instances by people with links to the industries that make those chemicals. One new member is a California scientist who helped defend Pacific Gas and Electric Co. against the real-life Erin Brockovitch."[97]

The evidence linking *air pollution* and cancer, as well as other serious and often fatal diseases, has been accumulating rapidly in recent years. In 1993, *The Journal of the American Medical Association* reported research that found "'robust' associations between premature mortality and air pollution levels."[98] They estimate that pollutants cause about 2 percent of all cancer deaths (at least 10,000 a year).[99] In 2002, the same journal published a study that concludes "that people living in the most heavily polluted metropolitan areas have a 12 percent higher risk of dying of lung cancer than people in the least polluted areas."[100]

During 1975, the epidemiological branch of the National Cancer Institute did a massive county-by-county analysis of cancer in the United States, mapping the "cancer hotspots" in the nation. The result was summed up by Dr. Glenn Paulson, assistant commissioner of science in the New Jersey Department of Environmental Protection: "If you know where the chemical industry is, you know where the cancer hotspots are."[101] What distinguishes these findings from the material on occupational hazards discussed above is that NCI investigators found higher death rates for *all* those living in the cancer hotspots, not just the workers in the offending plants.

Another study by two NCI researchers found that in *all* U.S. counties with smelters, the incidence of lung cancer is above the national average.

"The researchers found high lung cancer death rates not only in men—who are often exposed to arsenic on their jobs inside smelters—but also among women, who generally never went inside smelters and were not previously believed to have been exposed to arsenic." Explanation: "neighborhood air pollution from industrial sources of inorganic arsenic."[102]

New Jersey, however, took the prize for having the highest cancer death rate in the nation. NCI investigators found that "19 of New Jersey's 21 counties rank in the top 10 percent of all counties in the nation for cancer death rates." Salem County, home of E. I. Du Pont de Nemours and Company's Chambers Works, which has been manufacturing chemicals since 1919, "has the highest bladder cancer death rate in the nation—8.7 deaths per 100,000 persons."[103]

Pollution kills in other ways than by causing lung cancer. A 1996 study by the Natural Resources Defense Council (NRDC) concludes,

> Every year, some 64,000 people may die prematurely from cardiopulmonary causes linked to particulate air pollution. . . . Tens of thousands of these deaths could be averted each year if the Environmental Protection Agency set stringent health standards for fine-particle pollution.
>
> In the most polluted cities, lives are shortened by an average of one to two years. Los Angeles tops the list with an estimated 5,873 early deaths, followed by New York (4,024), Chicago (3,479), Philadelphia (2,599) and Detroit (2,123).[104]

This chemical war is not limited to the air. The National Cancer Institute has identified as carcinogens or suspected carcinogens 23 of the chemicals commonly found in our drinking water.[105] Moreover, according to one observer, we are now facing a "new plague—toxic exposure." Of the extent of contamination, he says that

> this country generates between 255 million and 275 million metric tons of hazardous waste annually, of which as much as 90 percent is improperly disposed of. . . . The Office of Technology Assessment estimates that there are some 600,000 contaminated sites in the country, of which 888 sites have been designated or proposed by the Environmental Protection Agency for priority cleanup under the Superfund program.[106]

Studies have borne out the correlation between nearness to toxic wastes and above-average cancer mortality rates, as well as the positive correlation between residential poverty and nearness to toxic wastes.[107] Other studies indicate that race is an even more important determinant of the location of toxic waste dumps. Writes Robert Bullard,

> Toxic time bombs are not randomly scattered across the urban landscape. . . . The Commission for Racial Justice's landmark study, *Toxic Wastes and Race in the United States*, found race to be the most important factor

(i.e., more important than income, home ownership rate, and property values) in the location of abandoned toxic waste sites. . . . [T]hree out of five African Americans live in communities with abandoned toxic waste sites.[108]

As it did with OSHA, the Reagan administration instituted a general slowing down of enforcement of EPA regulations. Reagan tried to cut the EPA's enforcement budget by 45 percent during his first two years in office. By 1983, the EPA's regional offices were staffed at levels substantially lower than needed to enforce the law effectively, according to the agency's own studies. The president also signaled his tolerant attitude toward environmental hazards in his appointments to top-level posts at the EPA of such people as Anne Burford, "who fiercely opposed any legislation regulating hazardous-waste disposal."[109] President Bush Sr. followed suit. The EPA's research and development staff, whose work provides the scientific basis for such regulations, was reduced by nearly 25 percent between 1981 and 1992.[110] The EPA Superfund spearheads cleanups of large-scale toxic waste with money collected from polluters and from taxes on certain businesses. But increasingly, companies that have toxic waste responsibilities use bankruptcy to escape them and the taxes expired in 1995, so "Superfund's current budget is lower than at any time since 1988."[111]

So the chemical war goes on. No one can deny that we know the enemy. No one can deny that we know the toll it is taking. Indeed, we can compute the number of deaths that result every day that we refuse to mount an offensive. Yet we still refuse. Thus, for the time being, the only advice we can offer someone who values his or her life is "If you must breathe our air, don't inhale."

The evidence linking *cigarette smoking* and cancer is overwhelming and need not be repeated here. The American Cancer Society simply notes, "Smoking remains the most preventable cause of death in our society."[112] Cigarettes are widely estimated to cause 30 percent of all cancer deaths,[113] and 87 percent of lung cancers, which according to the surgeon general translate into 125,000 deaths each year between 1995 and 1999.[114] Cigarettes are also blamed for other lung diseases such as emphysema, they play a substantial role in heart disease, and their addictive nature is now well established.

Tobacco continues to kill an estimated 440,000 Americans a year and costs taxpayers $18 billion annually. Some estimates go as high 600,000 to 700,000 annual deaths due to smoking, with total annual costs estimated at $150 billion.[115] According to the National Cancer Institute, current and former smokers are responsible over their lifetimes for half a trillion dollars in excess health care costs. Tobacco use costs Medicare $10 billion annually, and Medicaid about $13 billion.[116]

This is enough to expose the hypocrisy of running a full-scale war against heroin (which produces no degenerative disease) while allowing cigarette sales and advertising to flourish. It also should be enough to underscore the point that, once again, there are threats to our lives much greater than criminal homicide. Indeed, not only does our government fail to protect us against this threat, but it also promotes it! The government provided a price-support program for the tobacco industry (making up the difference when market price fell below a target price) from 1933 to 1982, and in 1986 it wrote off $1.1 billion in loans that it had made to tobacco farmers.[117] Moreover, the Reagan administration first supported and then, under intense lobbying pressure from the tobacco industry, withdrew its support for more and stronger warnings on cigarettes.[118] The former president is not the only offender here. The U.S. Congress has turned down more than 1,000 proposed tobacco control bills since 1964, the year of the first Surgeon General's Report on the dangers of tobacco. This may be related to the enormous generosity of the tobacco industry. Common Cause reports, "Since 1995, tobacco interests have given more than $32 million in political donations to state and federal candidates and political parties." The Phillip Morris Companies alone gave over $10,000,000 between 1995 and 2000. Common Cause adds that "analysis of recent tobacco-related votes in Congress shows a strong correlation between the amount that Members received and how they voted."[119]

If you think that tobacco harms only people who knowingly decide to take the risk, consider the following. In 1995, *The Journal of the American Medical Association* devoted a special issue to the so-called Brown and Williamson Documents, several thousand pages of internal documents from the Brown and Williamson Tobacco Corporation and BAT Industries (formerly British American Tobacco Company). Brown and Williamson (B&W) is the third-largest cigarette maker in the United States. It is a wholly owned subsidiary of BAT, the world's second-largest private producer of cigarettes. An editorial in this issue states that "[t]he documents show . . . that executives at B&W knew early on that tobacco use was harmful and that nicotine was addictive . . . that the industry decided to conceal the truth from the public . . . that despite their knowledge to the contrary, the industry's public position was (and continues to be) that the link between smoking and ill health was not proven . . . and that nicotine was not addictive." The editorial concludes that "the evidence is unequivocal—the U.S. public has been duped by the tobacco industry."[120]

Moreover, the cigarette industry intentionally targets young people—who are not always capable of assessing the consequences of their choices—with its ads, and it is successful. Some 2.6 million youngsters between the ages of 12 and 18 are smokers.[121] A 2001 report indicates that smoking among American teenagers increased 73 percent over the previous ten years.[122]

In addition, the Environmental Protection Agency has released data on the dangers of "secondhand" tobacco smoke (which nonsmokers breathe when smoking is going on around them). They report that each year, second-hand smoke causes 3,000 lung cancer deaths, contributes to 150,000 to 300,000 respiratory infections in babies, exacerbates the asthmatic symptoms of 400,000 to 1,000,000 children with the disease, and triggers 8,000 to 26,000 new cases of asthma in children who don't yet have the disease.[123] A 1993 issue of *The Journal of the American Medical Association* reported that tobacco contributes to 10 percent of infant deaths.[124]

Let's be clear: I do not advocate making cigarette smoking illegal on the model of our failed attempts to make drugs like heroin illegal. Restrictions on advertising aimed at youngsters, as well as measures to protect nonsmokers from secondhand smoke, and perhaps higher insurance premiums for those who choose to smoke, seem reasonable, however.

The average American consumes *one pound* of chemical *food additives* per year.[125] Speaking on the floor of the U.S. Senate in 1972, Senator Gaylord Nelson said,

> People are finally waking up to the fact that the average American daily diet is substantially adulterated with unnecessary and poisonous chemicals and frequently filled with neutral, nonnutritious substances. We are being chemically medicated against our will and cheated of food value by low nutrition foods.[126]

A hard look at the chemicals we eat and at the federal agency empowered to protect us against eating dangerous chemicals reveals the recklessness with which we are being "medicated against our will." Beatrice Hunter has taken such a hard look and reports her findings in a book aptly titled *The Mirage of Safety*, a catalog of the possible dangers that lurk in the foods we eat. More than this, however, it is a description of how the Food and Drug Administration, through a combination of lax enforcement and uncritical acceptance of the results of the food industry's own "scientific" research, has allowed a situation to exist in which the American public is the real guinea pig for nearly 3,000 food additives. As a result, we are subjected to chemicals strongly suspected of producing cancer,[127] gallbladder ailments,[128] hyperkinesis in children,[129] and allergies;[130] to others that inhibit "mammalian cell growth" and "may adversely affect the rate of DNA, RNA, and protein synthesis";[131] and to still others that are capable of crossing the placental barrier between mother and fetus and are suspected causes of birth defects and congenital diseases.[132]

The food additives are, of course, only some of the dangerous chemicals that we eat. During the 1980s, American farmers normally used about 800 million pounds of the active ingredients in pesticides per year.[133] In 1993, *The New York Times* reported that farmers now use 1 billion pounds of chemicals on crops each year.[134] Dr. Landrigan of the Mount Sinai School of Medicine, writing in a 1992 issue of *The American Journal of Public Health*, points to

> recent data from the US Environmental Protection Agency (EPA) showing that infants and young children are permitted to have dietary exposures to potentially carcinogenic and neurotoxic pesticides that exceed published standards by a factor of more than 1000.[135]

Landrigan also estimates that between 3 and 4 million American preschool children have dangerously elevated blood-lead levels, which could result in long-term neuropsychological impairment.

To call government and industry practices reckless is mild in view of the fact that, in spite of the growth in knowledge about the prevention and cure of cancer, "between 1950 and 1988, for U.S. Whites, age-adjusted incidence of cancer rose by 43.5 percent."[136]

Based on the knowledge we have, there can be no doubt that air pollution, tobacco, and food additives amount to a chemical war that makes the crime wave look like a football scrimmage. Even with the most conservative estimates, it is clear that *the death toll in this war is far higher than the number of people killed by criminal homicide!*

Poverty Kills

We are long past the day when we could believe that poverty was caused by forces outside human control. Poverty is "caused" by lack of money, which means that once a society reaches a level of prosperity at which many enjoy a relatively high standard of living, then poverty can be eliminated or at least reduced significantly by transferring some of what the "haves" have to the "have-nots." In other words, regardless of what caused poverty in the past, what causes it to continue in the present is the refusal of those who have more to share with those who have less. Now you may think these remarks trite or naïve. They are not offered as an argument for redistribution of income, although I think such a redistribution is long overdue. These remarks are presented to make a much simpler point, which is that poverty exists in a wealthy society like ours *because we allow it to exist.* Therefore, we[137] share responsibility for poverty and for its consequences.

The poverty for which we are responsible "remains," in the words of *Business Week,* "stubbornly high." Moreover, it has particularly nasty features. For example, it affects blacks and children at a rate higher than the national average. Whereas 10.8 percent of white Americans were below the poverty level in 2004, 24.7 percent of black Americans were. Among children in 2002, about 13 percent of white children live in poverty, while nearly 32 percent of black children do.[138] A study published by the Urban Institute ranked the United States highest in child poverty among eight industrialized nations studied. The other nations were Switzerland, Sweden, Norway, Germany, Canada, the United Kingdom, and Australia. Moreover, the Urban Institute estimates that 2.3 million Americans experience homelessness each year, including 1 million children who are also exposed to interruptions in, or lack of, education each year.[139] Of the homeless, some 25 to 40 percent work, which means that at least half a million working Americans cannot afford shelter.[140]

We are prone to think that the consequences of poverty are fairly straightforward: Less money means fewer things. So poor people have fewer clothes or cars or appliances, go to the theater less often, and live in smaller homes with less or cheaper furniture. This is true and sad, but perhaps not intolerable. In addition, however, one of the things poor people have less of is *good health*. Less money means less nutritious food, less heat in winter, less fresh air in summer, less distance from other sick people or from unhealthy work or dumping sites, less knowledge about illness or medicine, fewer doctor visits, fewer dental visits, less preventive health care, and (in the United States at least) less first-quality medical attention when all these other deprivations take their toll and a poor person finds him- or herself seriously ill. The result is that the poor suffer more from poor health and die earlier than do those who are well-off. Poverty robs them of their days while they are alive and kills them before their time. A prosperous society that allows poverty in its midst is a party to murder.

A review of more than 30 historical and contemporary studies of the relationship of economic class to life expectancy affirms the conclusion that "class influences one's chances of staying alive. Almost without exception, the evidence shows that classes differ on mortality rates."[141] An article in the November 10, 1993, issue of *The Journal of the American Medical Association* confirms the existence of this cost of poverty:

> People who are poor have higher mortality rates for heart disease, diabetes mellitus, high blood pressure, lung cancer, neural tube defects, injuries, and low birth weight, as well as lower survival rates from breast cancer and heart attacks.[142]

A July 30, 1998, news release from the U.S. Department of Health and Human Services confirms the continued "strong relationship between socioeconomic status and health in the United States for every race and ethnic group studied."[143] A 2005 *Washington Post* article headlined "Race Gap Persists in Health Care, Three Studies Say" reports on a study by a Harvard School of Public Health researcher published in *The New England Journal of Medicine*. The researcher is quoted as commenting, "We have known for 20 years that we have a problem in our health care system: blacks and whites do not receive equal care. We hoped all the attention paid to this topic would result in some improvement. What we found is that we have not made much progress."[144]

Interestingly, the poor have higher mortality rates even in countries such as Canada and Great Britain, which guarantee access to medical care. The difference can be attributed in large measure to the other disabilities of poverty, such as lower education levels and less healthy work and residential environments. A study of lower respiratory illness in infants found its incidence correlated directly to socioeconomic status (SES), with lower-SES infants showing greater incidence than middle-SES infants and more than twice that of higher-SES infants. A large portion of the difference was attributed to the unhealthy environmental conditions in which poor infants grow up.[145]

Another indication of the correlation between low income and poor health is found in statistics on the number of days of reduced activity due to illness or injury suffered by members of different income groups. In 1995, persons from families earning less than $10,000 a year suffered an average of 30 such days, persons from families earning from $10,000 to $19,999 suffered 21 days, persons from families earning between $20,000 and $34,999 suffered 15 days, and persons from families earning $35,000 and above suffered 10.6 days of reduced activity.[146]

Here, too, things have gotten worse rather than better recently. The number of poor Americans continues to grow each year. By 2004 it was 37 million, up from 30.1 million in 1990 and from 25.2 million in 1980.[147] In 2004, the Census Department records 45.8 million people without health insurance coverage (and that doesn't include those who are inadequately covered).[148] The percentage of the poor covered by Medicaid has gone from 65 percent to less than 40 percent. Hardest hit have been poor women and their children, many of whom have been removed from Medicaid coverage because income eligibility rules have not kept up with inflation. "In 1986, the average state income cutoff for Medicaid was 48 percent of the federal poverty level, compared to 71 percent in 1975."[149] Estimates indicate that only one-third of those who lose Medicaid benefits get private insurance; the rest do without. Moreover, the percent of nonelderly Americans doing without has grown in the past decade: It was 14.8 percent of the population in 1987, 17.3 percent in 1993, and 18.3 percent in 1997. According to the National Academy of Sciences, lack of health insurance results in some 18,000 premature deaths a year because people without insurance don't get the health care they need.[150] Sadly, inadequate health insurance also often leads to poverty because "the leading cause of personal bankruptcy in the United States is unpaid medical bills."[151]

A comparison of the health and mortality of blacks and whites in America yields further insight into the relationship of health and mortality to economic class. In 2004, one of every four blacks lived below the poverty line, as compared with one of every ten whites. In 2001, black infant mortality (during the first year of life) was 14 per 1,000 live births, compared with 5.7 per 1,000 for whites.[152] In short, black mothers lost their babies within the first year of life more than twice as often as white mothers did. In the face of this persistent disparity, the Reagan administration reduced funding for maternal and child health programs by more than 25 percent and attempted to reduce support for immunization programs for American children.[153] In 1987, only 48 percent of American one year olds had received the standard immunizations, and every Western European nation was at least ten percentage points higher, with France and the United Kingdom in the 80s.[154]

Numerous studies have suggested that allocation of health services is marked by racial bias. A 1992 study of patients under Medicare said that older whites are 3.5 times more likely than older blacks to get bypass surgery for blocked arteries. Black kidney patients are 45 percent less likely than whites to get transplants, according to a 1991 New York State Health Department study. There is evidence also of discrimination against Hispanic patients and women.[155] A study of surgery rates in Maryland hospitals by race and income of patients asserts, "The more discretionary the procedure, the lower is the relative incidence among Blacks."[156] Other studies confirm that health care delivery in the United States remains segregated by race and class.[157] A 2004 study in *The American Journal of Public Health* found that almost 900,000 deaths could have been prevented during the decade of the 1990s if African Americans received the same care as whites.[158]

Cancer survival statistics show a similar picture. Between 2000 and 2005, 55.2 percent of blacks diagnosed with cancer were still alive five years after the diagnosis, compared with 65.5 percent of whites. This disparity has been noted since at least the early 1970s.[159] One important cause of this difference is that "white patients tended to have higher percentages of cancers diagnosed while localized,"[160] that is, earlier in their development. This means, at a minimum, that at least some of the difference turns out to be due to such things as better access to medical care, higher levels of education about the early-warning signs of cancer, and so on, all of which correlate strongly with higher income levels. Data reported in the journal *Science* suggest that "blacks get more cancer not because they're black, but because they're poor."[161] A study of the stage at which women had breast cancer diagnosed found that white and black women living in areas characterized by lower average income and educational attainment were diagnosed later than those in areas marked by higher income and educational attainment. Within the same areas, black women were diagnosed later than whites, except in the areas of highest income and education, where the black disadvantage disappeared.[162] "And while black women show a lower incidence of breast cancer than white women, they nevertheless die from it more often."[163]

Life expectancy figures paint the most tragic picture of all. For 2001, life expectancy among blacks born that year was 72.2 years, whereas among whites it was 77.5 years.[164] That this difference cannot be attributed wholly to genetic factors is borne out by a "study of the relative contribution of various risk factors and income levels to mortality among blacks" reported recently in *The Journal of the American Medical Association*. The study "estimated that 38 percent of excess [of black over white] mortality could be accounted for by family income."[165] A stronger conclusion is reached by a study reported in a 1992 issue of *The American Journal of Public Health*, whose authors concluded, "In no instance were Black–White differences in all-cause or coronary mortality significantly different when socioeconomic status was controlled."[166]

In short, *poverty hurts, injures, and kills—just like crime.* A society that could remedy its poverty but does not is an accomplice in crime.

SUMMARY

The criminal justice system does not protect us against the gravest threats to life, limb, or possessions. Its definitions of crime are not simply a reflection of the objective dangers that threaten us. The workplace, the medical profession, the air we breathe, and the poverty we refuse to rectify lead to far more human suffering, result in far more death and disability, and take far more dollars from our pockets than the murders, aggravated assaults, and thefts reported annually by the FBI. What is more, this human suffering is preventable. A government really intent on protecting our well-being would treat many of these harmful behaviors as criminal, and turn the massive powers of the state against their perpetrators in the way that they are turned against the perpetrators of the so-called common crimes. But it does not. A government really intent on protecting us would enforce work safety regulations, police the medical profession, require that clean-air standards be met, and devote sufficient resources to the poor to alleviate the major disabilities of poverty. But it does not. Instead we hear a lot of cant about law and order and a lot of rant about crime in the streets. It is as if our leaders were not only refusing to protect us from the major threats to our well-being but also trying to cover up this refusal by diverting our attention to crime, as if this were the only real threat.

As we have seen, the criminal justice system is a carnival mirror that presents a distorted image of what threatens us. The distortions do not end with the definitions of crime. As we will see in what follows, new distortions enter at every level of the system, so that, in the end, when we look in our prisons to see who really threatens us, virtually all we see are poor people. By that time, most of the well-to-do people who endanger us have been discreetly weeded out of the system. As we watch this process unfold in the next chapter, we should bear in mind the conclusion of the present chapter: All the mechanisms by which the criminal justice system comes down more frequently and more harshly on the poor criminal than on the well-off criminal take place *after most of the dangerous acts of the well-to-do have been excluded from the definition of crime itself.* The bias against the poor within the criminal justice system is all the more striking when we recognize that the door to that system is shaped in a way that excludes in advance the most dangerous acts of the well-to-do. Demonstrating this has been the purpose of the present chapter.

STUDY QUESTIONS

1. What should be our definition of the term "crime"? Why does it matter what we call things? Should there be an overlap between the acts we label crimes and the acts we think are morally wrong?

2. Quickly—without thinking about it—picture to yourself a criminal. Describe what you see. Where did this picture come from? Are there people in our society who pose a greater danger to you than the individual you pictured? Why or why not?

3. What is meant by likening the criminal justice system to a "carnival mirror"?

4. Do you think a business executive who refuses to invest in safety precautions with the result that several workers die is morally better than, equal to, or worse than a mugger who kills his victim after robbing him? What if the executive knowingly violated a safety regulation? What if the mugger was high on drugs? Explain your response.

5. What is meant by speaking of criminal justice as "creative art"? How does the view presented here differ from that of Quinney?

6. Give examples of social practices that are more dangerous to your well-being than common crime. How should these practices be dealt with?

    A companion website to this book, with a chapter outline and summary, links to additional information, and Internet-based exercises, is available at "Rich Get Richer," *www.paulsjusticepage.com.*

ADDITIONAL READINGS

Barlett, Donald, and James Steele. *Critical Condition: How Health Care in America Became Big Business and Bad Medicine.* New York: Doubleday, 2004.

Glantz, Stanton, et al. *The Cigarette Papers.* Berkeley: University of California Press, 1996. (The original documents on which this book is based can be found at *www.library. ucsf.edu/tobacco/.*)

Hills, Stuart, ed. *Corporate Violence: Injury and Death for Profit.* Totowa, N.J.: Rowman & Littlefield, 1987.

Kennedy, Robert. *Crimes against Nature.* New York: Harper Perennial, 2004.

Lofgren, Don. *Dangerous Premises: An Insider's View of OSHA Enforcement.* Ithaca, N.Y.: ILR Press/Cornell University, 1989.

Messner, Steven, and Richard Rosenfeld. *Crime and the American Dream*, 3rd ed. Belmont, Calif.: Wadsworth, 2000.

Pearce, Frank, and Laureen Snider. *Corporate Crime: Contemporary Debates.* Toronto: University of Toronto Press, 1995.

Quinney, Richard. *The Social Reality of Crime.* Boston: Little, Brown, 1970.

Robinson, James. *Toil and Toxics: Workplace Struggles and Political Strategies for Occupational Health.* Berkeley: University of California Press, 1991.

Winslow, George. *Capital Crimes.* New York: Monthly Review Press, 1999.

NOTES

1. "Company in Mine Deaths Set to Pay Big Fine," *The New York Times*, February 21, 1993, p. A19.

2. "Mass Murder on the 5:33," *The New York Times*, December 10, 1993, p. A34.

3. Gerald R. Ford, "To Insure Domestic Tranquility: Mandatory Sentence for Convicted Felons," speech delivered at the Yale Law School Sesquicentennial Convocation, New Haven, Conn., April 25, 1975, in *Vital Speeches of the Day* 41, no. 15 (May 15, 1975): p. 451.

4. "Arrest Data Reveal Profile of Suspect," *The Washington Post*, September 16, 1975, p. C1.

5. Ibid.; see also Maryland–National Capital Parks and Planning Commission, *Crime Analysis 1975: Prince George's County* (August 1975), p. 86.

6. *UCR–1974*, p. 186.

7. Maryland–National Capital Parks and Planning Commission, *Crime Analysis 1975*, p. 3.

8. See *UCR–1974*, p. 190.

9. "Arrest Data Reveal Profile of Suspect," p. C1; and Maryland–National Capital Parks and Planning Commission, *Crime Analysis 1975*, p. 86.

10. *UCR–1974*, p. 190.

11. Anthony Bouza, *How to Stop Crime* (New York: Plenum, 1993), p. 57.

12. Quoted in George Will, "A Measure of Morality," *The Washington Post*, December 16, 1993, p. A25.

13. Brian Faler, "Bennett under Fire for Remark on Crime and Black Abortions," *The Washington Post*, September 30, 2005, A05.

14. Kathryn Russell, *The Color of Crime: Racial Hoaxes, White Fear, Black Protectionism, Police Harassment, and Other Macroaggressions* (New York: New York University Press, 1998), p. 3; cited in Marjorie S. Zatz, "The Convergence of Ethnicity, Gender, and Class on Court Decisionmaking: Looking toward the 21st Century," in NIJ, *Criminal Justice 2000, volume 3: Policies, Processes, and Decisions of the Criminal Justice System*, NCJ 182410, p. 507.

15. Zatz, "The Convergence of Ethnicity, Gender, and Class on Court Decisionmaking," p. 509.

16. Lawrence W. Sherman, "Reducing Gun Violence: What Works, What Doesn't, What's Promising," NIJ *Perspectives on Crime and Justice: 1999–2000 Lecture Series*, March 2001, NCJ 184245, p. 75.

17. *UCR–2004*, Table 31, p. 282, Table 39, pp. 292–93, Table 42, p. 297, Table 43, p. 298; and *StatAbst–2004–5*, Table 13, p. 14. New census procedures allow for counting of multiple races, so those who identify as black only are 12.7 percent; those who identify as black and some other race are 13.3 percent.

18. BJS, *Profile of Jail Inmates 2002*, July 2004, NCJ 201932.

19. *Challenge*, p. 44; see also p. 160.

20. Ibid.

21. "Mass news representations in the 'information age' have become the most significant communication by which the average person comes to know the world outside his or her immediate experience"; Gregg Barak, *Media, Process and the Social Construction of Crime* (New York: Garland, 1994), p. 3.

22. This transformation has been noted by Erving Goffman in his sensitive description of total institutions, *Asylums* (Garden City, N.Y.: Doubleday, 1961):

> *The interpretative scheme of the total institution automatically begins to operate as soon as the inmate enters, the staff having the notion that entrance is prima facie evidence that one must be the kind of person the institution was set up to handle. A man in a political prison must be traitorous; a man in a prison must be a law-breaker; a man in a mental hospital must be sick. If not traitorous, criminal, or sick, why else would he be here? (p. 84)*

So, too, a person who calls forth the society's most drastic weapons of defense must pose the gravest danger to its well-being. Why else the reaction? The point is put well and tersely by D. Chapman: "There is a circular pattern in thinking: we are hostile to wicked people, wicked people are punished, punished people are wicked, we are hostile to punished people because they are wicked" ("The Stereotype of the Criminal and the Social Consequences," *International Journal of Criminology and Penology* 1 [1973]: p. 16).

23. Richard Quinney, *The Social Reality of Crime* (Boston: Little, Brown, 1970). In his later work, for example, *Critique of Legal Order: Crime Control in Capitalist Society* (Boston: Little, Brown, 1973), and *Class, State & Crime* (New York: McKay, 1977), Quinney moves clearly into a Marxist problematic and his conclusions dovetail with many in this book. In my own view, however, Quinney has not yet accomplished a satisfactory synthesis between the "social reality" theory and his later Marxism. Elsewhere, I have examined Quinney's theory from the standpoint of moral philosophy. See Jeffrey H. Reiman, "Doing Justice to Criminology: Reflections on the Implications for Criminology of Recent Developments in the Philosophy of Justice," in Marc Riedel and Duncan Chappell, eds., *Issues in Criminal Justice: Planning and Evaluation* (New York: Praeger, 1976), pp. 134–42.

24. Quinney, *Social Reality of Crime*, p. 15.

25. *The Washington Post*, January 11, 1983, p. C10.

26. Lydia Voigt et al., *Criminology and Justice* (New York: McGraw-Hill, 1994), pp. 11–15; the quotation is on p. 15.

27. This answers Graeme Newman, who observes that most criminals on TV are white and wonders what the "ruling class" or conservatives "have to gain by denying the criminality of Blacks." Graeme R. Newman, "Popular Culture and Criminal Justice: A Preliminary Analysis," *Journal of Criminal Justice* 18 (1990): pp. 261–74.

28. Newman, "Popular Culture and Criminal Justice," pp. 263–64.

29. Barbara Matusow, "If It Bleeds, It Leads," *Washingtonian*, January 1988, p. 102.

30. Victor Kappeler, Mark Blumberg, and Gary Potter, *Mythology of Crime and Criminal Justice*, 3rd ed. (Prospect Heights, Ill: Waveland, 2000), pp. 41–42.

31. "Titillating Channels: TV Is Going Tabloid as Shows Seek Sleaze and Find Profits, Too," *The Wall Street Journal*, May 18, 1988, p. 1.

32. John P. Wright, Francis T. Cullen, and Michael B. Blankenship, "The Social Construction of Corporate Violence: Media Coverage of the Imperial Food Products Fire," *Crime & Delinquency* 41, no. 1 (January 1995): p. 32. I discuss this case in Chapter 3.

33. Another way to put the Defenders' claim here is that one-on-one harms are appropriately "crimes," while indirect harms are appropriately "torts." *Torts* are noncriminal harms that justify civil suits for damages, but not criminal prosecution and punishment. Since our dispute with the Defenders is about whether indirect harms *should* be crimes, these legal labels cannot resolve our dispute. They may, however, give readers familiar with legal terminology a different way of understanding what as at stake: The Defenders think that indirect harms are rightly treated as torts, while I think that many of them should count as crimes, and serious ones at that.

34. Hyman Gross, *A Theory of Criminal Justice* (New York: Oxford University Press, 1979), p. 78. See generally Chapter 3, "Culpability, Intention, Motive," which I have drawn on in making the argument of this and the following two paragraphs.

35. I owe this example, modeled on one by Hyman Gross, to Andrew W. Austin of the University of Wisconsin–Green Bay.

36. Nancy Frank, "Unintended Murder and Corporate Risk-Taking: Defining the Concept of Justifiability," *Journal of Criminal Justice* 16 (1988): p. 18.

37. For example, see John Harris, "The Marxist Conception of Violence," *Philosophy & Public Affairs* 3, no. 2 (Winter 1974): pp. 192–220; Jonathan Glover, *Causing Death and Saving Lives* (Hammondsworth, UK: Penguin, 1977), pp. 92–112; and James Rachels, *The End of Life* (Oxford: Oxford University Press, 1986), pp. 106–50.

38. *Model Penal Code*, final draft (Philadelphia: American Law Institute, 1962).

39. Russell Mokhiber, *Corporate Crime and Violence: Big Business Power and the Abuse of Public Trust* (San Francisco: Sierra Club, 1988), pp. 278, 285.

40. David E. Lilienfeld, "The Silence: The Asbestos Industry and Early Occupational Cancer Research—A Case Study," *American Journal of Public Health* 81, no. 6 (June 1991), p. 791. This article shows how early the asbestos industry knew of the link between asbestos and cancer and how hard they tried to suppress this information. See also Paul Brodeur, *Outrageous Misconduct: The Asbestos Industry on Trial* (New York: Pantheon, 1985).

41. Sir James Fitzjames Stephen, from his *History of the Criminal Law of England 2* (1883), excerpted in Abraham S. Goldstein and Joseph Goldstein, eds., *Crime, Law and Society* (New York: Free Press, 1971), p. 21.

42. Troy Duster, *The Legislation of Morality: Law, Drugs and Moral Judgment* (New York: Free Press, 1970), pp. 3–76.

43. Norval Morris and Gordon Hawkins, *The Honest Politician's Guide to Crime Control* (Chicago: University of Chicago Press, 1970), p. 2.

44. Challenge, p. 7.

45. *UCR–2003*, pp. 15, 37.

46. *UCR–2003*, p. 42.

47. See Willard Oliver, "The Power to Persuade: Presidential Influence over Congress on Crime Control Policy" *Criminal Justice Review* 28, no. 1 (2003). The author finds *UCR* reported crime "to have the most impact on congressional committees and subcommittees initiating hearings on crime and drugs" (p. 125), and this factor remains significant across several variations in model specifications.

48. White House, *President's Report on Occupational Safety and Health* (Washington, D.C.: U.S. Government Printing Office, 1972).

49. "James Messerschmidt, in a comprehensive review of research studies on job-related accidents, determined that somewhere between 35 and 57 percent of those accidents occurred because of direct safety violations by the employer. Laura Shill Schraeger and James Short Jr. found 30 percent of industrial accidents resulted from safety violations and another 20 percent resulted from unsafe working conditions." Kappeler et al., *Mythology of Crime and Criminal Justice*, p. 104. See James Messerschmidt, *Capitalism, Patriarchy, and Crime: Toward a Socialist Feminist Criminology* (Totowa, N.J.: Rowman & Littlefield, 1986); and Laura Shill Schraeger and James Short, "Toward a Sociology of Organizational Crime," *Social Problems* 25 (April 1978): pp. 407–19. See also Joseph A. Page and Mary-Win O'Brien, *Bitter Wages: Ralph Nader's Study Group Report on Disease and Injury on the Job* (New York: Grossman, 1973); Rachel Scott, *Muscle and Blood* (New York: Dutton, 1974); Jeanne M. Stellman and Susan M. Daum, *Work Is Dangerous to Your Health* (New York: Vintage, 1973); Fran Lynn, "The Dust in Willie's Lungs," *Nation* 222, no. 7 (February 21, 1976): pp. 209–12; and Joel Swartz, "Silent Killers at Work," *Crime and Social Justice* 3 (Summer 1975): pp. 15–20.

50. BLS, "Workplace Injury and Illness in 2003," December 14, 2004, p. 1, 2, 4, *www.bls.gov/iif/home.htm*. Note that this "survey excludes the self-employed; farms with fewer than 11 employees . . . [and] federal [and state] government agencies."

51. BLS, *National Census of Fatal Occupational Injuries, 1991–93*, app. C.

52. Robert Reid, "How Accurate Are Safety and Health Statistics?" *Occupational Hazards* (March 1987): p. 49.

53. "Is OSHA Falling Down on the Job?" *The New York Times*, August 2, 1987, pp. A1, A6.

54. Philip Landrigan, testimony before the Senate Committee on Labor and Human Resources, April 18, 1988, p. 2. For cancer deaths, see *StatAbst–1988*, p. 77, Table 117, and p. 80, Table 120.

55. "Safety Group Cites Fatalities Linked to Work," *The Wall Street Journal*, August 31, 1990, p. B8; and Sally Squires, "Study Traces More Deaths to Working than Driving," *The Washington Post*, August 31, 1990, p. A7.

56. J. P. Leigh, S. B. Markowitz, M. Fahs, C. Shin, and P. J. Landrigan, "Occupational Injury and Illness in the United States: Estimates of Costs, and Morbidity, and Mortality," *Archives of Internal Medicine* 157, no. 14 (July 1997): pp. 1557–68.

57. Cancer Prevention Coalition, "U.S. National Cancer Institute," *www.preventcancer.com/losing/nci/why_prevent.htm.*

58. J. Paul Leigh and John Robbins, "Occupational Disease and Workers, Compensation: Coverage, Costs and Consequences," *The Milbank Quarterly* 82, no. 4 (2004): p. 694.

59. NIOSH, "Worker Health Chartbook, 2000: Nonfatal Illness," April 2002. See also NIOSH, "Protecting Workers' Families: A Research Agenda," May 2002.

60. *StatAbst—2004–2005*, Table 2, p. 7, Table 570, p. 371.

61. *Sourcebook—2003*, Table 3.33, p. 207 (figures rounded to nearest whole percentage point).

62. J. P. Leigh et al., "Occupational Injury and Illness in the United States"; see note 53, above.

63. BLS, *National Census of Fatal Occupational Injuries in 2003*, p. 1 (BLS reports a total of 5,559 workplace fatalities, of which 631 are homicides.)

64. BJS, *Workplace Injuries and Illnesses in 2003*. Definitions from BLS, "Occupational Health and Safety Definitions," *www.bls.gov/iif/oshdef.htm#occupinjury.*

65. *UCR–2003*, p. 7.

66. Philip J. Hilts, "U.S. Fines Mine Companies for False Air Tests," *The New York Times*, April 5, 1991, p. A12. The fines, by the way, amounted to a total of $5 million distributed among 500 mining companies found to have tampered with the coal-dust samples used to test for the risk of black lung disease.

67. Joan Claybrook and the Staff of Public Citizen, *Retreat from Safety: Reagan's Attack on America's Health* (New York: Pantheon, 1984), p. 83. Chronic brown lung is a severely disabling occupational respiratory disease. See also Page and O'Brien, *Bitter Wages*, p. 18.

68. Claybrook, *Retreat from Safety*, p. 97. See also Page and O'Brien, *Bitter Wages*, p. 23; and Scott, *Muscle and Blood*, p. 196.

69. Scott, *Muscle and Blood*, pp. 45–46; cf. Page and O'Brien, *Bitter Wages*, p. 25.

70. Cindy Skrzycki, "Alarm over a Sheepish Non-rule," *The Washington Post*, October 29, 2002, p. E1.

71. Curt Suplee, "House to Consider 'Ergo Rider' Restraints on OSHA," *The Washington Post*, July 11, 1996, p. A4.

72. "OSHA Facts," December 2004, *www.osha.gov/as/opa/oshafacts.html.*

73. "OSHA Facts."

74. Barstow, David. "When Workers Die: U.S. Rarely Seeks Charges for Deaths in Workplace" *The New York Times*, December 22, 2003, A1, *http://reclaimdemocracy.org.* Barstow found 1,242 cases of deaths related to willful violations between 1982 and 2002, but OSHA declined prosecution in 93 percent of the cases. Recently, "OSHA began to accede to employer demands that it replace the word 'willful' with 'unclassified' in citations involving workplace deaths."

75. Barbara Starfield, MD, MPH, "Is US Health Really the Best in the World?" *Journal of the American Medical Association* 284, no. 4 (July 26, 2000): *http://jama.ama-assn.org/issues/v284/ffull/jco00061.html.*

76. Ceci Connolly, "Data Show Scourge of Hospital Infections," *The Washington Post*, July 13, 2005, p. A1 (citing a report by the Pennsylvania Health Care Cost Containment Council and an interview with its executive director).

77. Betsy McCaughey, "Hospital Infection Fact Sheet," *http://hospitalinfectionrates.org;* see also "Coming Clean," *The New York Times*, June 6, 2005, p. A19.

78. *The Washington Post*, July 16, 1975, p. A3.

79. George A. Silver, "The Medical Insurance Disease," *Nation* 222, no. 12 (March 27, 1976): p. 369.

80. Ibid., p. 371.

81. *Newsweek*, March 29, 1976, p. 67. Lest anyone think this is a new problem, compare this passage written in a popular magazine over 40 years ago:

> *In an editorial on medical abuse, the* Journal of the Medical Association of Georgia *referred to "surgeons who paradoxically are often cast in the role of the supreme hero by the patient and family and at the same time may be doing the greatest amount of harm to the individual." Unnecessary operations on women, stemming from the combination of a trusting patient and a split fee, have been so deplored by honest doctors that the phrase "rape of the pelvis" has been used to describe them. The American College of Surgeons, impassioned foe of fee-splitting, has denounced unnecessary hysterectomies, uterine suspensions, Caesarian sections.* (Howard Whitman, "Why Some Doctors Should Be in Jail," *Colliers*, October 30, 1953, p. 24)

82. *StatAbst–2004-5*, Table 160, p. 113.

83. *UCR–2003*, Table 2.9, p. 19.

84. Sandra G. Boodman, "No End to Errors," *The Washington Post Health*, December 3, 2002, p. F1. The original report was L. Kohn, J. Corrigan, and M. Donaldson, eds., *To Err Is Human: Building a Safer Health System* (Washington, D.C.: National Academy Press, 1999).

85. Rick Weiss, "Medical Errors Blamed for Many Deaths: As Many as 98,000 a Year in U.S. Linked to Mistakes," *The Washington Post*, November 30, 1999, p. A1.

86. Boodman, "No End to Errors," p. F1.

87. Ibid., p. F6.

88. Ibid., p. F6.

89. Silver, "The Medical Insurance Disease," p. 369. Silver's estimates are extremely conservative. Some studies suggest that between 30,000 and 160,000 individuals die as a result of drugs prescribed by their doctors. See Boyce Rensberger, "Thousands a Year Killed by Faulty Prescriptions," *The New York Times*, January 28, 1976, pp. A1, A17. If we assume with Silver that at least 20 percent are unnecessary, this puts the annual death toll from unnecessary prescriptions at between 6,000 and 32,000 persons. For an in-depth look at the recklessness with which prescription drugs are put on the market and the laxness with which the Food and Drug Administration exercises its mandate to protect the public, see the series of eight articles by Morton Mintz, "The Medicine Business," *The Washington Post*, June 27–30, July 1–4, 1976.

90. Paul Weiler, Howard Hiatt, Joseph Newhouse, William Johnson, Troyen Brennan, and Lucian Leape, *A Measure of Malpractice: Medical Injury, Malpractice Litigation and Patient Compensation* (Cambridge, Mass.: Harvard University Press, 1993), p. 54. The data given here come from the Harvard Medical Practice Study. See also Christine Russell, "Human Error: Avoidable Mistakes Kill 100,000 Patients a Year," *The Washington Post Health*, February 18, 1992, p. 7.

91. Sheryl Gay Stohlberg, "Faulty Warning Labels Add to Risk in Prescription Drugs," *The New York Times*, June 4, 1999, p. A27.

92. Boodman, "No End to Errors," p. F6.

93. The rate of increase of medical costs is calculated from *StatAbst—1995*, Table 167, p. 117, and *StatAbst—2004–5*, Table 124, p. 97. Note that the assumption that the *number* of unnecessary operations and prescriptions has remained the same between 1974 and 2003 is a conservative assumption in that it effectively assumes that the rate of these practices relative to the population has declined because population has increased in the period.

94. American Cancer Society, "Cancer Facts & Figures 2005," p. 1, *www.cancer.org*.

95. Lewis Regenstein, *America the Poisoned* (Washington, D.C.: Acropolis Books, 1982), pp. 246–47; American Cancer Society, *United States Cancer Statistics: 1999 Incidence*; and National Institutes of Health, *NCI 1995 Budget Estimate*, September 1993, p. 3.

96. Samuel S. Epstein, Nicholas A. Ashford, Brent Blackwelder, Barry Castleman, Gary Cohen, Edward Goldsmith, Anthony Mazzocchi, and Quentin D. Young, "The Crisis in U.S. and International Cancer Policy," *International Journal of Health Services* 32, no. 4 (2002): p. 693.

97. Rick Weiss, "HHS Seeks Science Advice to Match Bush Views," *The Washington Post,* September 17, 2002, p. A1.

98. Paul Cotton, "'Best Data Yet' Say Air Pollution Kills below Levels Currently Considered Safe," *Journal of the American Medical Association* 269, no. 24 (June 23–30, 1993): p. 3087.

99. J. Michael McGinnis and William H. Foege, "Actual Causes of Death in the United States," *Journal of the American Medical Association* 270, no. 18 (November 10, 1993): p. 2209.

100. Cited in Eric Pianin, "Study Ties Pollution, Risk of Lung Cancer," *The Washington Post,* March 6, 2002, p. A1.

101. Quoted in Stuart Auerbach, "N.J.'s Chemical Belt Takes Its Toll: $4 Billion Industry Tied to Nation's Highest Cancer Death Rate," *The Washington Post,* February 8, 1976, p. A1.

102. Bill Richards, "Arsenic: A Dark Cloud over 'Big Sky Country,'" *The Washington Post,* February 3, 1976, pp. A1, A5.

103. Quotations in this paragraph are from Auerbach, "N.J.'s Chemical Belt Takes Its Toll," p. A1.

104. "Air and Atmosphere at NRDC: Danger in the Air," *www.nrdc.org/find/aibresum.htm.*

105. Toxic Substances Strategy Committee, Council on Environmental Quality, *Toxic Chemicals and Public Protection: A Report to the President,* Washington, D.C., May 1980, p. 6; quoted by Regenstein, *America the Poisoned,* p. 184. See also p. 170 in Regenstein.

106. Michael Edelstein, *Contaminated Communities: The Social and Psychological Impacts of Residential Toxic Exposure* (Boulder, Colo.: Westview Press, 1988), p. 3.

107. Jay M. Gould, *Quality of Life in American Neighborhoods: Levels of Affluence, Toxic Waste, and Cancer Mortality in Residential Zip Code Areas* (Boulder, Colo.: Westview Press, 1986), pp. 22 and 28.

108. Robert Bullard, "Environmental Justice for All," in *Unequal Protection: Environmental Justice and Communities of Color,* ed. Robert Bullard (San Francisco: Sierra Club Books, 1994), p. 17.

109. Joan Claybrook, *Retreat from Safety,* pp. 117–29.

110. Walter A. Rosenbaum, "The Clenched Fist and the Open Hand: Into the 1990s at EPA," in N. Vig and M. Kraft, eds., *Environmental Policy in the 1990s: Toward a New Agenda* (Washington, D.C.: CQ Press, a division of Congressional Quarterly Inc., 1994), p. 132.

111. Juliet Eilperin, "Lack of Funds Delaying Toxic Waste Cleanups," *The Washington Post,* July 28, 2004, p. A6.

112. American Cancer Society, "Cancer Facts and Figures 2005," p. 40.

113. Edward Sondik, "Progress in Cancer Prevention and Control," in *Unnatural Causes: Three Leading Killer Diseases in America,* ed. Russell Maulitz (New Brunswick, N.J.: Rutgers University Press, 1988, 1989), p. 117; and CNN, "Second-hand Smoke Price Tag: $10 Billion" August 17, 2005, *http://money.cnn.com/2005/08/17/news/economy/secondhand_smoke/index.html.*

114. Rebecca Perl, "30 Years after the Surgeon General's Report, Cigarettes Still Kill More than 1,000 Americans a Day . . . and Make Money for More than Just the Tobacco Companies," *The Washington Post Health,* January 11, 1994, p. 11. U.S. Department of Health and Human Services, *The Health Consequences of Smoking: A Report of the Surgeon General* (Atlanta: Centers for Disease Control and Prevention, 2004), p. 858, *www.cdc.gov/tobacco/sgr/sgr_2004/.*

115. U.S. Department of Health and Human Services, *The Health Consequences of Smoking,* p. 861 (440,00 yearly deaths since 1995). See also David Simon, *Elite Deviance* (Boston: Allyn & Bacon, 1999), p. 140; McGinnis and Foege, "Actual Causes of Death in the United States," p. 2207; and Perl, "30 Years after the Surgeon General's Report," p. 11.

116. *Scientific Priorities for Cancer Research: NCI's Extraordinary Opportunities: Research on Tobacco and Tobacco-Related Cancers, http://2001.cancer.gov/tobacco.htm.*

117. "The Price of Tobacco: The Basics," *The New York Times,* March 23, 1993, p. A14.

118. Robbins, "Can Reagan Be Indicted?" p. 12.

119. Common Cause, the Campaign for Tobacco-Free Kids, the American Heart Association, and the American Lung Association, "Buying Influence, Selling Death: How Big Tobacco's Campaign Contributions Harm Public Health," March 14, 2001, pp. 1, 2; *www.commoncause.org.*

120. Dr. James S. Todd et al., "The Brown and Williamson Documents: Where Do We Go From Here?" *Journal of the American Medical Association* 274, no. 3 (July 19, 1995): pp. 256, 258.

121. "U.S. Urged to Escalate Tobacco War," *The Washington Post,* January 12, 2002, p. A17.

122. *Scientific Priorities for Cancer Research;* see note 116.

123. Geoffrey Cowley, "Poison at Home and at Work: A New Report Calls Secondhand Smoke a Killer," *Newsweek,* June 29, 1992, p. 55.

124. McGinnis and Foege, "Actual Causes of Death in the United States," p. 2208.

125. Hunter, *The Mirage of Safety,* p. 4.

126. Quoted in ibid., p. 2.

127. Ibid., pp. 40–41, 64–65, 85, 148–51, inter alia.

128. Ibid., p. 119.

129. Ibid., pp. 123–24.

130. Ibid., pp. 127–40.

131. Ibid., pp. 102–3.

132. Ibid., pp. 162–76.

133. Public Voice for Food and Health Policy, *A Blueprint for Pesticide Policy* (Washington, D.C.: Public Voice for Food and Health Policy, 1989), p. 22.

134. "Pesticide Plan Could Uproot U.S. Farming," *The New York Times,* October 10, 1993, p. A6.

135. Philip Landrigan, "Commentary: Environmental Disease—A Preventable Epidemic," *American Journal of Public Health* 82, no. 7 (July 1992): p. 942.

136. Landrigan, "Commentary," p. 942.

137. At the very least, "we" includes all those who earn considerably above the median income for the nation (around $44,436 for a household in 2004) and who resist, or who vote for candidates who resist, moves to redistribute income significantly.

138. Karen Pennar, "The Rich Are Richer—and America May Be the Poorer," *Business Week,* November 18, 1991, pp. 85–88. Carmen DeNavas-Walt, Bernadette Proctor, and Cheryl Hill Lee, U.S. Census Bureau, *Income, Poverty & Health Insurance Coverage in the United States: 2004,* Current Population Reports, P60-229 (Washington, D.C.: U.S. Government Printing Office, 2005), p. 10; and *StatAbst—2004–5,* Table 684 (Children in Poverty), p. 452.

139. The Urban Institute, *A New Look at Homelessness in America,* February 1, 2000, *www.urban.org/url.cfm?ID=900302.*

140. National Law Center on Homelessness and Poverty, "Homelessness in America: Fact Sheet," June 1996; *www.nlchp.org.*

141. Aaron Antonovsky, "Class and the Chance for Life," in *Inequality and Justice,* ed. Lee Rainwater (Chicago: Aldine, 1974), p. 177.

142. McGinnis and Foege, "Actual Causes of Death in the United States," p. 2211.

143. *HHS News,* "Health in America Tied to Income and Education," July 30, 1998, *www.cdc.gov/nchs/releases/98news/98news/huspr98.htm.* See also R. Wilkinson, *Unhealth Societies: The Afflictions of Inequality* (London: Routledge, 1996).

144. Rob Stein, "Race Gap Persists in Health Care, Three Studies Say," *The Washington Post* August 18, 2005, p. A1.

145. Peter A. Margolis et al., "Lower Respiratory Illness in Infants and Low Socioeconomic Status," *American Journal of Public Health* 82, no. 8 (August 1992): p. 1119.

146. *StatAbst—1998,* p. 144, Table 220.

147. *Income, Poverty & Health Insurance Coverage in the United States: 2004,* p. 9; *StatAbst—1996,* p. 48, Table 49.

148. *Income, Poverty & Health Insurance Coverage in the United States: 2004,* p. 16.

149. David Stipp, "The Tattered Safety Net"; see also Dan Goodgame, "Ready to Operate," *Time,* September 20, 1993, p. 55.

150. Ceci Connolly, "Study: Uninsured Don't Get Needed Health Care: Delayed Diagnoses, Premature Deaths Result," *The Washington Post,* May 22, 2002, p. A3.

151. Malcolm Gladwell, "The Moral-Hazard Myth: The Bad Idea Behind Our Failed Health Care System" *The New Yorker*, August 29, 2005, *http://newyorker.com*.

152. *Income, Poverty & Health Insurance Coverage in the United States: 2004*, p. 10; and *StatAbst—2004–5*, p. 78, Table 100.

153. Robbins, "Can Reagan Be Indicted?" pp. 12–13. See also "Infant Mortality Down; Race Disparity Widens," *The Washington Post*, March 12, 1993, p. A11.

154. United Nations Development Programme, *Human Development Report 1990* (New York: Oxford University Press, 1990), p. 147.

155. Sonia Nazario, "Curing Doctors of Bedside Bias," *International Herald Tribune*, December 23, 1993, p. 8.

156. Alan M. Gittelsohn et al., "Income, Race, and Surgery in Maryland," *American Journal of Public Health* 81, no. 11 (November 1991): p. 1435.

157. See Jane Perkins, "Race Discrimination in America's Health Care System," *Clearinghouse Review* 27, no. 4 (1993): p. 371.

158. January Payne, "Dying for Basic Care," *The Washington Post*, December 21, 2004, p. HE1. The report itself notes that "socioeconomic conditions represent a more pertinent cause of disparities than race."

159. *StatAbst—2004–5*, p. 127, Table 191.

160. National Institutes of Health, *Cancer Patient Survival Experience*, June 1980, pp. 4–5.

161. Ann Gibbons, "Does War on Cancer Equal War on Poverty?" *Science* 253 (July 19, 1991): p. 260.

162. Barbara L. Wells and John W. Horm, "Stage at Diagnosis in Breast Cancer: Race and Socioeconomic Factors," *American Journal of Public Health* 82, no. 10 (October 1992): p. 1383.

163. Gibbons, "Does War on Cancer Equal War on Poverty?" p. 260.

164. *StatAbst—2004–5*, p. 71, Table 92. Although the difference between white and black life expectancy has generally shrunk in recent times, this tendency is by no means uniform: "Since 1984, life expectancy increased each year for white males; for white females, it increased for 3 of the 5 years; for black females, for only 2 of five years; and for black males, life expectancy decreased for 4 of the 5 years, and remained unchanged for one year" (*Vital Statistics of the United States, 1989, vol. 2, Mortality*, pt. A, sec. 6, p. 3). Richard Allen Williams reports that "there is no reason why the life span of the White should differ from that of the Black," in his *Textbook of Black-Related Diseases* (New York: McGraw-Hill, 1975), p. 2.

165. McGinnis and Foege, "Actual Causes of Death in the United States," p. 2211.

166. Julian E. Keil et al., "Does Equal Socioeconomic Status in Black and White Men Mean Equal Risk of Mortality?" *American Journal of Public Health* 82, no. 8 (August 1992): p. 1133.

CHAPTER 3

... AND THE POOR GET PRISON

*When we come to make an intelligent study of the prison at first hand ...
we are bound to conclude that after all it is not so much crime in its
general sense that is penalized, but that it is poverty which is punished.*

*Take a census of the average prison and you will find that a large majority
of people are there not so much because of the particular crime they are
alleged to have committed, but for the reason that they are poor
and ... lacked the money to engage the services of first class and
influential lawyers.*

—Eugene V. Debs, *Walls and Bars*

*Laws are like spiders' webs: they catch the weak and the small, but the
strong and the powerful break through them.*

—Scythian, one of the Seven Wise Men of Ancient Greece

WEEDING OUT THE WEALTHY

The offender at the end of the road in prison is likely to be a member of the lowest social and economic groups in the country.[1]

This statement in the *Report of the President's Commission on Law Enforcement and Administration of Justice* is as true today as it was almost four decades ago when it was written. Our prisons are indeed, as Ronald Goldfarb has called them, the "national poorhouse."[2] To most citizens, this comes as no surprise—recall the Typical Criminal and the Typical Crime. Dangerous crimes, they think, are committed mainly by poor people. Seeing that prison populations are made up primarily of the poor only makes them surer of this. They think, in other words, that the criminal justice system gives a true reflection of the dangers that threaten them.

In my view, it also comes as no surprise that our prisons and jails predominantly confine the poor. This is not because these are the individuals who most threaten us. It is because the criminal justice system effectively weeds out the well-to-do, so that *at the end of the road in prison,* the vast majority of those we find there come from the lower classes. This weeding-out process starts before the agents of law enforcement go into action. In Chapter 2, I argued that our very definition of crime *excludes* a wide variety of actions at least as dangerous as those included and often worse. Is it any accident that the kinds of dangerous actions excluded are the kinds most likely to be performed by the affluent in America? Even before we mobilize our troops in the war on crime, we have already guaranteed that large numbers of upper-class individuals will never come within their sights.

This process does not stop at the definition of crime. It continues throughout each level of the criminal justice system. At each step, from arresting to sentencing, the likelihood of being ignored or released or treated lightly by the system is greater the better off one is economically. As the late U.S. Senator Philip Hart wrote,

> Justice has two transmission belts, one for the rich and one for the poor. The low-income transmission belt is easier to ride without falling off and it gets to prison in shorter order. The transmission belt for the affluent is a little slower and it passes innumerable stations where exits are temptingly convenient.[3]

This means that the criminal justice system functions from start to finish in a way that makes certain that "the offender at the end of the road in prison is likely to be a member of the lowest social and economic groups in the country."

For the same criminal behavior, the poor are more likely to be arrested; if arrested, they are more likely to be charged; if charged, more likely to be convicted; if convicted, more likely to be sentenced to prison; and if sentenced, more likely to be given longer prison terms than members of the middle and upper classes.[4] In other words, the image of the criminal population one sees in our nation's jails and prisons is distorted by the shape of the criminal justice system itself. It is the face of evil reflected in a carnival mirror, but it is no laughing matter.

The face in the criminal justice carnival mirror is also, as we have already noted, very frequently a black face. Although blacks do not make up the majority of the inmates in our jails and prisons, they make up a proportion that far outstrips their proportion in the population.[5] Here, too, the image we see is distorted by the processes of the criminal justice system itself. Edwin Sutherland and Donald Cressey write, in their widely used textbook *Criminology,* that

> numerous studies have shown that African-Americans are more likely to be arrested, indicted, convicted, and committed to an institution than are whites who commit the same offenses, and many other studies have shown that blacks

have a poorer chance than whites to receive probation, a suspended sentence, parole, commutation of a death sentence, or pardon.[6]

William Wilbanks has attacked this conclusion in *The Myth of a Racist Criminal Justice System*, and many still believe the larger point that blacks are overrepresented in prison *only* because they commit more than their share of crimes.[7] Wilbanks uses, as "perhaps the most important criticism" of the charge that there is discrimination against blacks in arrests, the work of Michael Hindelang, which compares the rate at which respondents to the *National Crime Victimization Survey* report being victimized by assailants perceived to be black with the rate at which blacks are arrested for the relevant crimes according to the *UCR*, and finds "that the racial gap in *offending* for robbery, assault, and rape (whether or not an arrest occurred) was almost equal to that found for *arrest* statistics." Wilbanks concludes that "these results indicate that police select black and white arrestees in approximately the same proportion as they are found in the pool of offenders," and thus "argue against police bias in the arrest process."[8] Recent statistics, however, suggest quite the opposite. Consider the following.

In 2003, respondents to the *National Criminal Victimization Survey* (*NCVS*) reported that approximately 23 percent of their assailants in violent victimizations (rape, robbery, and simple and aggravated assault) were perceived to be black. That same year, the *UCR* indicates that 37 percent of the individuals arrested for these crimes were black. These figures indicate that police are arresting blacks almost two times more frequently than the occurrence of their perceived offenses.[9] Because arrest determines the pool from which charged, convicted, and imprisoned individuals are selected, this suggests that deep bias persists throughout the criminal justice system.

There are various problems with comparing *UCR* and *NCVS* statistics, and various possible explanations for the divergence of black–white arrest rates from the rates at which blacks and whites are perceived offenders. Thus, I do not claim that the results just presented prove definitively the presence of racism. Nonetheless, because they come from the statistics that Wilbanks uses as "the most important criticism" of the discrimination thesis, I think they suffice to cast significant doubt on Wilbanks's claim. Thus, I shall treat his thesis as currently unsubstantiated and continue to follow the majority of researchers in holding that the criminal justice system is widely marked by racial discrimination as well as by economic bias.[10] Moreover, numerous studies substantiate this point. Cassia Spohn reviewed 40 "recent and methodologically sophisticated studies investigating the linkages between race/ethnicity and sentence severity," and found that

these studies suggest that race and ethnicity do play an important role in contemporary sentencing decisions. Black and Hispanic offenders—and particularly those who are young, male, or unemployed—are more likely than their white counterparts to be sentenced to prison; in some jurisdictions, they also receive longer sentences . . . than do similarly situated white offenders.[11]

Spohn and others have pointed to the fact that the studies that led some researchers to conclude that racial discrimination was neglible often ignored *indirect* and *interaction* effects. For example, some recent studies have shown that black defendants are less likely than whites to be released on bail prior to trial. Because it is generally recognized that pretrial detention increases the likelihood of eventual incarceration, discrimination at the bail decision will *indirectly* produce greater likelihoods of prison sentences for blacks than whites.[12] Moreover, numerous studies have shown that blacks who victimize whites receive harsher sentences than whites who victimize whites, and other studies suggest that blacks who victimize blacks receive lighter sentences than whites who victimize whites. Thus, race of victim *interacts* with offender race to produced biased sentences. This will be so even if, overall, sentences for black criminals are no worse than those for white criminals due to the fact that harshness for black-on-white crimes and leniency for black-on-black crimes may cancel each other out.[13] Such facts have led Spohn to conclude that the question should no longer be "'does race make a difference?' but, rather '*when* does race make a difference—under what conditions, for what types of offenders, and in interaction with what other factors?'"[14]

Marvin Free offers a list of common methodological shortcomings in research on race in the criminal justice system that will tend to hide racial bias. His list includes mixing of racial and ethnic groups (identification of Hispanics as whites will tend to reduce or eliminate black–white differences), failure to study presentencing decisions (e.g., the decision to release an accused on bail) that affect the fairness of later decisions, aggregating data from different crimes (which hides discrimination that is tied to specific types of crimes, such as drug offenses, for which blacks are characteristically treated more harshly than whites), failure to consider the impact of the race of the victim (such that leniency to blacks who victimize blacks cancels out harshness to blacks who victimize whites, though both policies are racially discriminatory), use of aggregated national data (which hides or reduces the significance of geographic differences in the degree of racial discrimination), and failure adequately to distinguish legal from extralegal factors (for example, evidence suggests that blacks are more likely than whites to be arrested without sufficient legal evidence, thus blacks will have inflated "prior arrest records" compared to whites who do the same acts, with the consequence that blacks will receive harsher sentences than whites for similar behavior due to the extralegal factor of "racial selectivity in policing").[15]

Interestingly, statistics on differential treatment of races are available in abundance while statistics on differential treatment of economic classes are rare and getting rarer. Although the FBI tabulates arrest rates by race (as well as by sex, age, and geographic area), it omits class or income. The *Sourcebook of Criminal Justice Statistics* shows household income categories only for crime victims, and both the President's Crime Commission report and Sutherland and Cressey's *Criminology* have index entries for race or racial discrimination but none for class or income of offenders. It would seem that both independent and government data gatherers are more willing to own up to America's racism than to its class bias. Writes Majorie Zatz, "Class is one of the paramount sociological variables, yet our measures of it in criminal justice data are abysmal." She continues, "There is general recognition among scholars that some of the race effects that have been found [in research on sentencing] may be due in part to class effects."[16]

I will take advantage of this last hint and use race as a rough proxy for class. I believe that racism is a distinct, resilient, and powerful form of bias in our system, and it often targets well-off blacks. Indeed, I grant that racism has a long, inglorious history in American society, in which the massive imprisonment of young black men in the last decades is but the latest in a series of policies controlling and isolating blacks that spans slavery, Jim Crow, and northern ghettoization.[17] With these important provisos noted, I will try to make up in part for our society's blindness to class by using evidence of differential treatment of blacks—and of Hispanics—as evidence for differential treatment of members of the lower classes. There are five reasons for this.

1. First and foremost, black Americans are disproportionately poor. In 2004, while 8.6 percent of white non-Hispanic Americans received income below the poverty line, 24.7 percent of black Americans did.[18] The picture is even worse when we shift from income to wealth (property such as a home, land, and stocks). On average, blacks in America own one-fifth to one-sixth of the wealth that white non-Hispanics do.[19] Only about 11 percent of nonwhite and Hispanic families owned stocks, compared to 25 percent of white non-Hispanic families. While this ownership gap has narrowed, the median value in 2001 of stock holdings was $22,000 for white non-Hispanic families and $8,000 for nonwhite and Hispanic families. Ownership of business is another important measure of economic power, and here 13.2 percent of white non-Hispanic families have business equity compared to only 5.4 percent of nonwhite or Hispanic families; the median amount was $76,200 for whites, and $32,700 for nonwhites and Hispanics.[20] Unemployment figures give a similarly dismal picture: In 2003, 5.2 percent of white workers were unemployed and 10.8 percent of blacks were. Among those in the crime-prone ages of 16 to 24 in 2000, 11.2 percent of white youngsters (with no college) and 24.6 percent of black youngsters (with no college)—one of every four!—were jobless.[21]

2. The factors most likely to keep one out of trouble with the law and out of prison, such as a suburban living room instead of a tenement alley to gamble in or legal counsel able to devote time to one's case instead of

an overburdened public defender, are the kinds of things that money can buy regardless of one's race, creed, or national origin. Writes Zatz, "[S]ome of the racial differences found in processing and sanctioning decisions may be attributable to class differences in access to resources."[22] Moreover, as we shall see, arrests of blacks for illicit drug possession or dealing have skyrocketed in recent years, rising way out of proportion to drug arrests for whites, though research shows no greater drug use among blacks than among whites. However, drug arrests are most easily made in "disorganized inner-city" areas, where drug sales are more likely to take place out-of-doors, and dealers are more willing to sell to strangers. Blacks and Hispanics are more likely than whites to live in such inner-city areas and thus more likely than whites to be arrested on drug charges.[23] And, though racism surely plays a major role here, one very important reason that blacks and Hispanics are more likely than whites to live in disorganized inner-city areas is that a greater percentage of blacks than whites are poor and unemployed. What might at first look like a straightforward racial disparity turns out to reflect lower economic status as well.

3. Blacks who travel the full route of the criminal justice system and end up in jail or prison are close in economic condition to whites who do. In 1978, 53 percent of black jail inmates had prearrest incomes below $3,000, compared with 44 percent of whites.[24] In 1983, the median pre-arrest income of black jail inmates was $4,067 and that of white jail inmates was $6,312. About half of blacks in jail were unemployed before arrest, and 44 percent of whites were.[25] In 1991, 30 percent of whites in the prison population and 38 percent of blacks reported no full- or part-time employment during the month before their arrest.[26]

4. Some studies suggest that race works to heighten the effects of economic conditions on criminal justice outcomes, so that "being unemployed *and* black substantially increase[s] the chances of incarceration over those associated with being either unemployed or black."[27] This means that racism will produce a kind of selective economic bias, making a certain segment of the unemployed even more likely to end up behind bars.

5. Finally, in light of the relatively high incidence of poverty and/or unemployment among blacks and Hispanics, both racially biased criminal justice policies and economically biased criminal justice policies will result in poor people being disproportionately arrested and imprisoned. I am more concerned with this consequence than with the intention behind it.

For all these reasons, racism will be treated here as a form of economic bias or a tool that achieves the same end.

In the remainder of this chapter, I show how the criminal justice system functions to *weed out the wealthy* (meaning both middle- and upper-class offenders) at each stage of the process and, thus, produces a distorted image of the crime problem. Before entering into this discussion, however, three points are worth noting.

First, it is not my view that the poor are all innocent victims persecuted by the evil rich. The poor do commit crimes, and my own assumption is that the vast majority of the poor who are confined in our prisons are guilty of the crimes for which they were sentenced. In addition, there is good evidence that the poor do commit a greater portion of the crimes against persons and property listed in the FBI Index than the middle and upper classes do, relative to their numbers in the national population. What I have already tried to prove is that the crimes in the FBI Index are not the only acts that threaten us, nor are they the acts that threaten us the most. What I will try to prove in what follows is that the poor are arrested and punished by the criminal justice system much more frequently than their contribution to the crime problem would warrant. Thus, the criminals who populate our prisons as well as the public's imagination are disproportionately poor.

Second, the following discussion has been divided into three sections that correspond to the major criminal justice decision points and that also correspond to hypotheses 2, 3, and 4 stated on pages 69–70 in Chapter 2. As always, such classifications are a bit neater than reality, and so they should not be taken as rigid compartments. Many of the distorting processes operate at all criminal justice decision points. The section in which a given issue is treated is a reflection of the point in the criminal justice process at which the disparities are the most striking. Suffice it to say, however, that the disparities between the treatment of the poor and the nonpoor are to be found at all points of the process.

Third, it must be borne in mind that the movement from arrest to sentencing is a funneling process, so that discrimination that occurs at any early stage shapes the population that reaches later stages. Thus, for example, some recent studies find little economic bias in sentence length for people convicted of similar crimes.[28] When reading such studies, however, one should remember that the population that reaches the point of sentencing has already been subject to whatever discrimination exists at earlier stages. If, for example, among people with similar offenses and records, poor people are more likely to be charged and more likely to be convicted, then, even if the sentencing of convicted criminals is evenhanded, it will reproduce the discrimination that occurred before.

Arrest and Charging

Most official records of who commits crime are really statistics on who gets arrested and convicted. If, as I will show, the police are more likely to arrest some people than others, these official statistics may tell us more about police than about criminals. In any event, they give us little reliable data about those who commit crimes and do not get caught. Some social scientists, suspicious of the bias built into official records, have tried to devise other methods of determining who has committed a crime. Most often, these methods involve an interview or questionnaire in which the respondent is assured of anonymity and asked to reveal whether he or she has committed any offenses for which he or she could be arrested and convicted. Techniques to check the reliability of these self-reports also have been devised; however, if their reliability is still in doubt, common sense dictates that they would understate rather than overstate the number of individuals who have committed crimes and never come to official notice. In light of this, the conclusions of these studies are rather astounding. It seems that crime is the national pastime. The President's Crime Commission conducted a survey of 10,000 households and discovered that "91 percent of all Americans have violated laws that could have subjected them to a term of imprisonment at one time in their lives."[29]

A number of other studies support the conclusion that serious criminal behavior is widespread among middle- and upper-class individuals, although these individuals are rarely, if ever, arrested. Some of the studies show that there are no significant differences between economic classes in the incidence of criminal behavior.[30] The authors of a recent review of literature on class and delinquency conclude, "Research published since 1978, using both official and self-reported data suggests . . . that there is no pervasive relationship between SES [socioeconomic status] and delinquency."[31] This conclusion is echoed by Dunaway, Cullen, Burton, and Evans, who conclude, from a study based on questionnaires given to 550 adults in a midwestern urban area, that "direct class impact on general crime is relatively weak."[32]

Others conclude that while lower-class individuals do commit more than their share of crimes, arrest records overstate their share and understate that of the middle and upper classes.[33] Still other studies suggest that some forms of serious crime—forms usually associated with lower-class youth—show up *more frequently* among higher-class persons than among lower-class ones.[34] For instance, Empey and Erikson interviewed 180 white males aged 15 to 17 who were drawn from different economic strata. They found that "virtually all respondents reported having committed not one but a variety of different offenses." Although youngsters from the middle classes constituted 55 percent of the group interviewed, they admitted to 67 percent of the instances of breaking and entering, 70 percent of the instances of property destruction, and an astounding 87 percent of all the armed robberies admitted to by the entire sample.[35]

Even those who conclude "that more lower status youngsters commit delinquent acts more frequently than do higher status youngsters"[36] also recognize that lower-class youth are significantly overrepresented in official records. Gold writes that "about five times more lowest than highest status boys appear in the official records; if records were complete and unselective, we estimate that the ratio would be closer to 1.5:1."[37] The simple fact is that for the same offense, *a poor person is more likely to be arrested and, if arrested, charged than a middle- or upper-class person.*[38]

This means, first of all, that poor people are more likely to come to the attention of the police. Furthermore, once apprehended, the police are more likely to formally charge a poor person and release a higher-class person *for the same offense.* Gold writes that

> boys who live in poorer parts of town and are apprehended by police for delinquency are four to five times more likely to appear in some official record than boys from wealthier sections who commit the same kinds of offenses. These same data show that, at each stage in the legal process from charging a boy with an offense to some sort of disposition in court, boys from different socioeconomic backgrounds are treated differently, so that those eventually incarcerated in public institutions, that site of most of the research on delinquency, are selectively poorer boys.[39]

From a study of self-reported delinquent behavior, Gold finds that, when individuals were apprehended, "if the offender came from a higher status family, police were more likely to handle the matter themselves without referring it to the court."[40]

Terence Thornberry reached a similar conclusion in his study of 3,475 delinquent boys in Philadelphia. Thornberry found that among boys arrested *for equally serious offenses* and who had *similar prior offense records,* police were more likely to refer the lower-class youths than the more affluent ones to juvenile court. The police were more likely to deal with the wealthier youngsters informally, for example, by holding them in the station house until their parents came rather than instituting formal procedures. Of those referred to juvenile court, Thornberry found further that, for *equally serious offenses* and with *similar prior records,* the poorer youngsters were more likely to be institutionalized than were the affluent ones. The wealthier youths were more likely to receive probation than the poorer ones. As might be expected, Thornberry found the same relationships when comparing the treatment of black and white youths apprehended for equally serious offenses.[41]

Recent studies continue to show similar effects. For example, Sampson found that, for the same crimes, juveniles in lower-class neighborhoods were more likely to have some police record than those in better-off neighborhoods. Again, for similar crimes, lower-class juveniles were more likely to be referred to court than better-off juveniles. If you think these differences are not so important because they are true only of young offenders, remember that this group accounts for much of the crime problem. Moreover, other studies not limited to the young tend to show the same economic bias. McCarthy found that, in metropolitan areas, for similar suspected crimes, unemployed people were more likely to be arrested than employed people.[42]

As I indicated above, I take racial bias as either a form of bias against the poor or a means to the same result. And blacks are more likely to be suspected or arrested than whites. A 1988 *Harvard Law Review* overview of studies on race and the criminal process concludes that "most studies . . . reveal what many police officers freely admit: that police use race as an independently significant, if not determinative, factor in deciding whom to follow, detain, search, or arrest."[43] Furthermore, according to Jerome Miller, "A 1994 study of juvenile detention decisions found that African American and Hispanic youths were more likely to be detained at each decision point, even after controlling for the influence of offense seriousness and social factors (e.g., single-parent home). Decisions by both police and the courts to detain a youngster were highly influenced by race."[44] The study states that "[n]ot only were there direct effects of race, but indirectly, socioeconomic status was related to detention, thus putting youth of color again at risk for differential treatment."[45] Reporting the results of University of Missouri criminologist Kimberly Kempf's study of juvenile justice in 14 Pennsylvania counties, Miller says that "Black teenagers were more likely to be detained, to be handled formally, to be waived to adult court, and to be adjudicated delinquent."[46] And there is some evidence that charges against blacks are thrown out more frequently than charges against whites because blacks are arrested on the basis of less evidence.[47]

There is also the disturbing finding that many black people are arrested for the crime of "driving while black." John Lamberth of Temple University set out to study whether the police arrest black drivers on the New Jersey Turnpike out of proportion to their percentage in the driving population and to their rate of committing traffic violations. Lamberth and his team "recorded data on more than forty-two thousand cars." They found that

> blacks and whites violated the traffic laws at almost exactly the same rate; there was no statistically significant difference in the way they drove. Thus, driving behavior alone could not explain differences in how police might treat black and white drivers. With regard to arrests, 73.2 percent of those stopped and arrested were black, while only 13.5 percent of the cars on the road had a black driver or passenger. Lamberth notes that the disparity between these two numbers is 'statistically vast.'[48]

Similar studies, with similar results, were carried out in Maryland and Ohio.

One official government study that found no evidence of blacks being disproportionately pulled over, noted "evidence of black drivers having worse experiences—more likely to be arrested, more likely to be searched, more likely to be have force used against them—during traffic stops than white drivers."[49] Though the study contained the information mentioned above, "political supervisors within the Office of Justice Programs ordered Mr. Greenfeld [head of the Bureau of Justice Statistics] to delete certain references to the disparities from a news release that was drafted to announce the findings, according to more than a half-dozen Justice Department officials with knowledge of the situation." According to a report in *The New York Times*, Greenfeld refused and "was initially threatened with dismissal and the possible loss of some pension benefits," an event that "caps more than three years of simmering tensions over charges of political interference at the agency." He was ultimately transferred to a lower position, and the report was posted to the BJS website without a news release or congressional briefing, leading to charges that the results were being buried.[50]

For reasons mentioned earlier, a disproportionately large percentage of the casualties in the recent war on drugs are poor inner-city minority males. Michael Tonry writes that "according to National Institute on Drug Abuse (1991) surveys of Americans' drug use, [Blacks] are not more likely than Whites ever to have used most drugs of abuse. Nonetheless, the . . . number of drug arrests of Blacks more than doubled between 1985 and 1989, whereas White drug arrests increased only by 27 percent."[51] A study conducted by the Sentencing Project, based mainly on Justice Department statistics, indicates that "Blacks make up 12 percent of the United States' population and constitute 13 percent of all monthly drug users . . . but represent 35 percent of those arrested for drug possession, 55 percent of those convicted of drug possession and 74 percent of those sentenced to prison for drug possession."[52]

The greater likelihood of arrest that minorities face is matched by a greater likelihood of being charged with a serious offense. For example, Huizinga and Elliott report, "Minorities appear to be at greater risk for being charged with more serious offenses than whites when involved in comparable levels of delinquent behavior."[53] Bear in mind that, once an individual has a criminal record, it becomes harder for that person to obtain employment, thus increasing the likelihood of future criminal involvement and more serious criminal charges.

Numerous studies of police use of deadly force show that blacks are considerably more likely than whites or Hispanics to be shot by the police. For example, using data from Memphis, Tennessee, covering the years from 1969 through 1974, James Fyfe found that blacks were 10 times more likely than whites to have been shot at by police, 18 times more likely to have been wounded, and 5 times more likely to have been killed.[54] A nation that has watched the videotaped beating meted out to Rodney King, a black man, by baton-wielding California police officers will not find this surprising. Does anyone think this would have happened if King were a white man?

Any number of reasons can be offered to account for the differences in police treatment of poor versus well-off citizens. Some argue that they reflect that the poor have less privacy.[55] What others can do in their living rooms or backyards, the poor do on the street. Others argue that a police officer's decision to book a poor youth and release a middle-class youth reflects either the officer's judgment that the higher-class youngster's family will be more likely and more able to discipline him or her than the lower-class youngster's, or differences in the degree to which poor and middle-class complainants demand arrest. Others argue that police training and police work condition police officers to be suspicious of certain kinds of people, such as lower-class youth, blacks, Hispanics, and so on,[56] and thus more likely to detect their criminality. Still others hold that police mainly arrest those with the least political clout,[57] those who are least able to focus public attention on police practices or bring political influence to bear, and these happen to be the members of the lowest social and economic classes.

Regardless of which view one takes, and probably all have some truth in them, one conclusion is inescapable: One of the reasons the offender "at the end of the road in prison is likely to be a member of the lowest social and economic groups in the country" is that the police officers who guard the access to the road to prison make sure that more poor people make the trip than well-to-do people.

Likewise for prosecutors. A recent study of prosecutors' decisions shows that lower-class individuals are more likely to have charges filed against them than upper-class individuals.[58] Racial discrimination also characterizes prosecutors' decisions to charge. The *Harvard Law Review* overview of studies on race and the criminal process asserts, "Statistical studies indicate that prosecutors are more likely to pursue full prosecution, file more severe charges, and seek more stringent penalties in cases involving minority defendants than in cases involving nonminority defendants."[59] One study of whites, blacks, and Hispanics arrested in Los Angeles on suspicion of having committed a felony found that, among defendants with equally serious charges and prior records, 59 percent of whites had their charges dropped at the initial screening, compared with 40 percent of blacks and 37 percent of Hispanics.[60]

The *weeding out of the wealthy* starts at the very entrance to the criminal justice system: The decision about whom to investigate, arrest, or charge is not made simply on the basis of the offense committed or the danger posed. It is a decision distorted by a systematic economic bias that works to the disadvantage of the poor.

This economic bias is a two-edged sword. Not only are the poor arrested and charged out of proportion to their numbers for the kinds of crimes poor people generally commit—burglary, robbery, assault, and so forth—but also, when we reach the kinds of crimes poor people almost never have the opportunity to commit, such as antitrust violations, industrial safety violations, embezzlement, and serious tax evasion, the criminal justice system shows an increasingly benign and merciful face. The more likely that a crime is the type committed by middle- and upper-class people, the less likely it is that it will be treated as a criminal offense. When it comes to crime in the streets, where the perpetrator is apt to be poor, he or she is even more likely to be arrested and formally charged. When it comes to crime in the suites, where the offender is apt to be affluent, the system is most likely to deal with the crime noncriminally, that is, by civil litigation or informal settlement. When it does choose to proceed criminally, as we will see in the section on sentencing, it rarely goes beyond a slap on the wrist. Not only is the main entry to the road to prison held wide open to the poor, but the access routes for the wealthy are largely sealed off. Once again, we should not be surprised at whom we find in our prisons.

Many writers have commented on the extent and seriousness of "white-collar crime," so I will keep my remarks to a minimum. Nevertheless, for those of us trying to understand how the image of crime is created, four points should be noted.

1. White-collar crime is costly; it takes far more dollars from our pockets than all the FBI Index crimes combined.
2. White-collar crime is widespread, probably much more so than the crimes of the poor.
3. White-collar criminals are rarely arrested or charged; the system has developed kindlier ways of dealing with the more delicate sensibilities of its higher-class clientele.
4. When white-collar criminals are prosecuted and convicted, their sentences tend to be lenient when judged by the cost their crimes have imposed on society.

The first three points will be discussed here, and the fourth will be presented in the sections that follow.

Everyone agrees that the cost of white-collar crime is enormous. In 1985, *U.S. News & World Report* reported, "Experts estimate that white-collar criminals rake in a minimum of $200 billion annually."[61] Marshall Clinard also cites the $200 billion estimate in his recent book, *Corporate Corruption: The Abuse of Corporate Power*.[62] That $200 billion is equivalent to $320 billion in 2003 dollars. Nonetheless, it underestimates the cost. Some experts place the cost of white-collar crime for firms doing business in the government sector alone at $500 billion a year.[63] Tax evasion has been estimated to cost from 5 to 7 percent of the gross national product. For 2003, that would be between $550 and $770 billion.[64] A 2004 study by the Association of Certified Fraud Examiners has found that "the typical organization loses six percent of its annual revenues to occupational fraud, the same result . . . obtained from . . . studies in 1996 and 2002. . . . If multiplied by the U.S. Gross National Product, which in 2003 totaled just under $11 trillion, it would translate into $660 billion in annual fraud losses."[65] A survey conducted by the National White Collar Crime Center between January and April 1999 found that one in three American households had been the victim of white-collar crime.[66]

In some areas of the economy, white-collar crime is growing dramatically. For example, the North American Securities Administrators Association conducted a survey of state enforcement actions and found that $400 million had been lost to investors as a result of fraud and abuse in the financial planning industry during the period from 1986 to 1988. Most striking, however, was their finding that "the number of state actions against financial planners rose 155 percent and the amount of lost investor funds climbed 340 percent" since their previous survey in 1985.[67] Then, of course, there was the outbreak of fraud in the savings and loan industry, followed by the corporate scandals starting with Enron, which we look at later in this chapter.

We need a rough estimate of the cost of white-collar crime so that we can compare its impact with that of the crimes reported on by the FBI. For this purpose, we can start with the conservative estimates in the U.S. Chamber of Commerce's *A Handbook on White-Collar Crime*.[68] Because the *Handbook* was issued in 1974, we will have to adjust its figures to take into account both inflation and growth in population to compare these figures with losses reported for 2004 by the FBI. (In light of the avalanche of statistics the government puts out on street crimes, it's worth wondering why the Chamber has not seen fit to revise its more than 30-year-old figures, and why no other private or public institution—neither the FBI nor the U.S. Department of Commerce—keeps up-to-date statistics on the overall cost of white-collar crime.) In some categories, I shall modify the Chamber's figures in light of more recent estimates. As usual, I use conservative estimates when there is a choice. The result will be a rough estimate of the costs of different categories of white-collar crime, as well as of the overall total.

First, the modifications: As might be expected, the cost of computer crime is far beyond the $0.1 billion estimated by the Chamber in 1974. A report from ZDNet News says, "No comprehensive records on computer-related crime are public, but it is estimated to drain as much as $11 billion per year from consumers and corporations in the U.S. alone."[69] A 2001 study of online sales concluded that $700 million was lost due to fradulent sales, including auction fraud, nondelivery of goods or services, and credit card fraud.[70] The theft of intellectual property is a hotly contested topic, with ongoing battles over what constitutes illegal copying and sharing of software, music, and movies. A 2004 Department of Justice report notes, "According to the Office of the United States Trade Representative, intellectual property theft worldwide cost American companies $250 billion a year."[71] While there are legitimate concerns about computer crime potentially having substantial overlap with credit card fraud, the $11 billion figure is conservative in that lost productivity from computer viruses—like the 2000 "I Love You" virus—were estimated at $10 billion alone.[72] I will use this $11 billion estimate for computer crime.

Telemarketing fraud is said to cost consumers $40 billion a year.[73] I will use this figure as a conservative estimate for the cost of fraud against consumers, though it represents only one among many forms that consumer fraud can take.[74] As for business victims of consumer fraud, illegal competition, and deceptive practices, "figures ranging between $50 and $240 billion have been posited as the amounts 'lost' in the United States through industrial espionage."[75] I will use the low estimate here—$50 billion—noting again that it covers only one form of illegal competition. Government revenue loss has also outstripped the Chamber's estimate of $12 billion annually. An article in *U.S. News & World Report* maintains that "25 percent of Americans admit to tax cheating which costs $100 billion annually."[76] Because this doesn't include defense and other procurement fraud, we can take $100 billion as a conservative estimate.

Credit card fraud has also exceeded the Chamber's expectations, with several sources estimating its annual cost at over $1 billion, a figure we can safely use.[77] According to a 2003 National White Collar Crime Center report on credit card fraud, "Research figures indicate the total cost of fraud was as high as $1.5 billion in 1999 and could grow to an estimated $30 billion in 2005."[78] "The FBI estimates that if commercial banks and other institutions combined their check fraud losses, the total would be $12 to $15 billion annually."[79] I will use the $12 billion figure.

The cost of pilferage has increased as well. "The Bureau of National Affairs estimates total employee theft at $15 billion to $25 billion, while the U.S. Chamber of Commerce [recently] says it may be as high as $20 billion to $40 billion. And that's not including theft by government workers, which can be significant."[80] More recent estimates place the range between $20 and $90 billion. The Food Marketing Association put the loss from *organized* retail theft to be "as high as $15 billion annually in the supermarket industry alone—and $34 billion across all retail."[81] I'll use $30 billion for the cost of pilferage, in the middle of the range recently given by the Chamber.

Insurance fraud has also gone far beyond the Chamber's 1974 estimates. The Coalition against Insurance Fraud estimates that insurance fraud costs more than $85 billion a year and is still growing.[82] I will use the $85 billion figure, which is surely an underestimate in light of government estimates of $100 billion a year in health care fraud—much of which is insurance fraud.[83] This is also conservative in light of a recent study that concluded the American public paid more than $96 billion in increased insurance premiums because of fraud in 1999; recent studies place the cost of auto insurance to consumers to cover fraud at $30 billion.[84] It will also come as no surprise, after the era of Ivan Boesky and Michael Milken (two stockbrokers who served time in prison for illegal stock manipulations), that security thefts and frauds have far outstripped the Chamber's 1974 estimate of $4 billion. The FBI's Economic Crimes Unit estimates the cost of securities and commodities fraud at $40 billion,[85] and there is now a new category, not even dreamt of by the Chamber in 1974: theft of cellular phone services, estimated to cost $1 billion a year.[86]

For the remainder of the Chamber's figures, I will assume that the rate of white-collar crime relative to the population remained constant from 1974 to 2003 and that its real dollar value remained constant as well (two conservative assumptions in light of the evidence just cited, which shows considerable growth in many white-collar crimes). Thus, I will simply adjust these figures to reflect the growth in population and inflation since 1974. Between 1974 and 2003, the population of the United States increased 36 percent, and the Consumer Price Index increased 273 percent.[87] (That is, 2003's population is 136 percent of 1974's, and 2003's prices are 373 percent of 1974's.) Thus, we can bring the Chamber of Commerce's figures up-to-date by multiplying them by 5.07 (1.36 x 3.73 = 5.07). This, taken together with the modifications indicated in the previous paragraphs, gives us an estimated total cost of white-collar crime in 2003 of nearly *$419 billion* (ten times higher than the Chamber's 1974 estimated total cost of $41.78 billion). (See Table 3.1 for the total cost and the breakdown into costs per category of white-collar crime.) The $419 billion figure jibes with the estimates quoted earlier, but it is surely on the conservative side. Nonetheless, it is more than 24 *times* the $17 billion that the FBI states is the total amount stolen in all property crimes reported in the *Uniform Crime Reports* for 2003.

In addition to the standard forms of white-collar crime by individuals, corporate crime is also rampant. Sutherland, in a study published in 1949 that has become a classic, analyzed the behavior of 70 of the 200 largest U.S. corporations over a period of some 40 years:

> The records reveal that every one of the seventy corporations had violated one or more of the laws, with an average of about thirteen adverse decisions per corporation and a range of from one to fifty adverse decisions per corporation. . . . Thus, generally, the official records reveal that these corporations violated the trade regulations with great frequency. The 'habitual criminal' laws of some states impose severe penalties on criminals convicted the third or fourth time. If this criterion were used here, about 90 percent of the large corporations studied would be considered habitual white-collar criminals.[88]

Nevertheless, corporate executives rarely end up in jail, where they would find themselves sharing cells with poorer persons who had stolen less from their fellow citizens. What Sutherland found in 1949 continues up to the present. In his 1990 book, *Corporate Corruption: The Abuse of Power,* Marshall Clinard writes,

> Many government investigations, both federal and state, have revealed extensive law violations in such industries as oil, autos, and pharmaceuticals. . . . [O]ver one two-year period, the federal government charged nearly two-thirds of the Fortune 500 corporations with law violations; half were charged with a serious violation. . . . According to a 1982 *U.S. News & World Report* study, more than one out of five of the *Fortune 500* companies had been convicted of at least one major crime or had paid civil penalties for serious illegal behavior between 1970 and 1979.[89]

A recent study of offenders convicted of federal white-collar crimes found "that white-collar criminals are often repeat offenders."[90] As for the treatment of these repeat offenders, Clinard says "a large-scale study of

TABLE 3.1   The Cost of White-Collar Crime, 2003

	$ (IN BILLIONS)	
Bankruptcy fraud		0.41
Bribery, kickbacks, and payoffs		15.21
Computer- and Internet-related crime		11.00
Consumer fraud, illegal competition, and deceptive practices		190.00
Consumer victims	40.00	
Business victims	50.00	
Government revenue loss	100.00	
Credit card and check fraud		13.00
Credit card	1.00	
Check	12.00	
Embezzlement and pilferage		45.21
Embezzlement (cash, goods, and services)	15.21	
Pilferage	30.00	
Insurance fraud		85.00
Receiving stolen property		17.75
Securities thefts and frauds		40.00
Cellular phone fraud		1.00
Total (billions)		**$418.58**

Source: Chamber of Commerce of the United States, *Handbook on White-Collar Crime, 1974* (Washington, D.C.: Chamber of Commerce of the United States, 1974); figures adjusted for inflation and population growth through 2000, and supplemented from other sources documented in the text.

sanctions imposed for corporate law violations found that administrative [that is, noncriminal] penalties were employed in two-thirds of serious corporate law violations, and that slightly more than two-fifths of the sanctions . . . consisted simply of a warning to the corporation not to commit the offense again."[91]

The continued prevalence of these practices is confirmed in a recent study of white-collar crime prosecutions by Susan Shapiro, titled "The Road Not Taken: The Elusive Path to Criminal Prosecution for White-Collar Offenders." Focusing on the enforcement practices of the Securities and Exchange Commission (SEC), Shapiro writes that

> while criminal dispositions are often appropriate, they are rarely pursued to the sentencing stage. Out of every 100 suspects investigated by the SEC, 93 have committed securities violations that carry criminal penalties. Legal action is taken against 46 of them, but only 11 are selected for criminal treatment. Six of these are indicted; 5 will be convicted and 3 sentenced to prison. Thus, for Securities and Exchange Commission enforcement, criminal prosecution most often represents the road not taken. Of those found to have engaged in securities fraud, 88 percent never have to contend with the criminal justice system at all.[92]

Russell Mokhiber reports that "less than one half of one percent (250) of the criminal indictments brought by the Department [of Justice] in 1994 involved environmental crimes, occupational safety and health crimes, and crimes involving product and consumer safety issues."[93] With upper-class law-breakers, the authorities prefer to sue in civil court for damages or for an injunction rather than treat the wealthy as common criminals. Judges have, on occasion, stated in open court that they would not make criminals of reputable businessmen. One would think it would be up to the businessmen to make criminals of themselves by their actions, but, alas, this privilege is reserved for the lower classes.

Examples of reluctance to use the full force of the criminal process for crimes not generally committed by the poor can be multiplied ad nauseam. We shall see later that a large number of potential criminal cases arising out of the savings and loan scandals has been dismissed by federal law enforcement agencies because they lack the personnel to pursue them, even as thousands of new police officers were being hired to fight street crime.

Let me close with one final example that typifies this particular distortion of criminal justice policy. Embezzlement is the crime of misappropriating money or property entrusted to one's care, custody, or control. Because the poor are rarely entrusted with tempting sums of money or valuable property, this is predominantly a crime of the middle and upper classes. The U.S. Chamber of Commerce estimate of the annual economic cost of embezzlement, adjusted for inflation and population growth, is $15.21 billion, nearly nine-tenths of the total value of all property and money stolen in all FBI Index property crimes in 2003. (Don't be fooled into thinking that this cost is imposed only on the rich or on big companies with lots of resources. They pass on their losses—and their increased insurance costs—to consumers in the form of higher prices. Embezzlers take money out of the very same pockets that muggers do: yours!) Nevertheless, the FBI reports that, in 2003, when there were 1,605,127 arrests for property crimes, there were 16,826 arrests for embezzlement nationwide.[94] Although their cost to society is comparable, the number of arrests for property crimes was *more than 95 times greater* than the number of arrests for embezzlement. Roughly, this means there was one property crime arrest for every $10,600 stolen, and one embezzlement arrest for every $904,000 "misappropriated": Note that even the language becomes more delicate as we deal with a "better" class of crook.

The clientele of the criminal justice system forms an exclusive club. Entry is largely a privilege of the poor. The crimes they commit are the crimes that qualify one for admission, and they are admitted in greater proportion than their share of those crimes. Curiously enough, the crimes the affluent commit are not the kind that easily qualify one for membership in the club.

And as we have seen, the reluctance to use the full force of the criminal justice system in pursuit of white-collar criminals is matched by a striking reluctance to use the full force of current public and private research organizations to provide up-to-date estimates of its cost. This coincidence is worth pondering by anyone interested in how criminal justice policy gets made and how research and statistics function in the process.

Adjudication and Conviction

Between arrest and imprisonment lies the crucial process that determines guilt or innocence. Studies of individuals accused of similar offenses and with similar prior records show that the poor defendant is more likely to be adjudicated guilty than is the wealthier defendant.[95] In the adjudication process the only thing that *should* count is whether the accused is guilty and whether the prosecution can prove it beyond a reasonable doubt. Unfortunately, at least two other factors that are irrelevant to the question of guilt or innocence significantly affect the outcome: One is the ability of the accused to be free on bail prior to trial, and the second is access to legal counsel able to devote adequate time and energy to the case. Because both bail and high-quality legal counsel cost money, it should come as no surprise that here, as elsewhere, the poor do poorly.

Being released on bail is important in several respects. First and foremost is that those who are not released on bail are kept in jail like individuals who have been found guilty. They are thus punished while they are still legally innocent. Of the 713,990 inmates in American jails in 2004, a little more than 60 percent were not convicted, which means 428,000 people were locked up though they had not yet been found guilty.[96] Beyond the obvious ugliness of punishing people before they are found guilty, confined defendants suffer from other disabilities. Specifically, they cannot actively aid in their own defense by seeking out witnesses and evidence. Several studies have shown that among defendants accused of the same offenses, those who make bail are more likely to be acquitted than those who do not.[97] In a recent study of unemployment and punishment, Chiricos and Bales found that "after the effects of other factors [seriousness of crime, prior record, etc.] were controlled, an unemployed defendant was 3.2 times more likely to be incarcerated before trial than his employed counterpart."[98]

Marvin Free reports on 12 studies that show racial disparities in bail and pretrial release decisions even when legally relevant variables (prior record, etc.) were held constant. Some studies showed interaction effects, such that "being lower class [is] a greater disadvantage for African Americans than for whites." Another such study revealed that "while overall African American defendants were 1.6 times more likely than white defendants to be detained prior to trial . . . young, unemployed African American males were six times more likely than their white counterparts to be detained."[99]

Furthermore, because the time spent in jail prior to adjudication of guilt may count as part of the sentence if one is found guilty, the accused are often placed in a ticklish position. Suppose the accused believes he or she is innocent, and that he or she has been in the slammer for two months awaiting trial. Along comes the prosecutor to offer a deal: If you plead guilty to such-and-such (usually a lesser offense than has been charged, say, possession of burglar's tools instead of burglary), the prosecutor promises to ask the judge to sentence you to two months. In other words, plead guilty and walk out of jail today (free, but with a criminal record that will make finding a job hard and ensure a stiffer sentence next time around), or maintain your innocence, stay in jail until trial, and then be tried for the full charge instead of the lesser offense! In fact, not only does the prosecutor threaten to prosecute for the full charge, this is often accompanied by the implied but very real threat to press for the most severe penalty as well—for taking up the court's time.

Plea bargaining such as this is an everyday occurrence in the criminal justice system. Contrary to the Perry Mason image, the vast majority of criminal convictions in the United States are reached without a trial. It is estimated that between 70 and 95 percent of convictions are the result of a negotiated plea,[100] that is, a bargain in which the accused agrees to plead guilty (usually to a lesser offense than he or she is charged with or to one offense out of many he or she is charged with) in return for a promise of leniency from the prosecutor with the consent of the judge. If you were the jailed defendant offered a deal like this, how would you choose? Suppose you were a poor black man not likely to be able to retain someone like Johnny Cochran or F. Lee Bailey for your defense?

The advantages of access to adequate legal counsel during the adjudicative process are obvious but still worthy of mention. In 1963, the U.S. Supreme Court handed down the landmark *Gideon v. Wainwright* decision, holding that the states must provide legal counsel to the indigent in all felony cases. As a result, no person accused of a serious crime need face his or her accuser without a lawyer. However, the Supreme Court has not held that the Constitution entitles individuals to lawyers able to devote equal time and resources to their cases. Even though *Gideon* represents significant progress in making good on the constitutional promise of equal treatment before the law, we still are left with two transmission belts of justice: one for the poor, and one for the affluent. There is an emerging body of case law on the right to effective assistance of counsel;[101] however, this is yet to have any serious impact on the assembly-line legal aid handed out to the poor.

The problem of adequate legal representation is particularly acute in capital cases. According to Robert Johnson, "Most attorneys in capital cases are provided by the state. Defendants, as good capitalists, routinely assume that they will get what they pay for: next to nothing." Their perceptions, he concludes, "may not be far from right."[102] Indeed, Stephen Gettinger maintains that an inadequate defense was "the single outstanding charac-teristic" of the condemned persons he studied. The result: Capital defen-dants appeared in court as "creatures beyond comprehension, virtually gagged and masked in preparation for the execution chamber."[103] Writes Linda Williams in *The Wall Street Journal,*

> The popular perception is that the system guarantees a condemned person a lawyer. But most states provide counsel only for the trial and the automatic review of the sentence by the state appeals court. Indigent prisoners—a description that applies to just about everybody on death row—who seek fur-ther review must rely on the charity of a few private lawyers and on cash-starved organizations like the Southern Prisoners Defense Committee.[104]

A *Time* magazine article on this topic is entitled "You Don't Always Get Perry Mason." Says the author, "Because the majority of murder defendants are . . . broke . . . many of them get court-appointed lawyers who lack the resources, experience or inclination to do their utmost. . . . Some people go to traffic court with better prepared lawyers than many murder defendants get."[105] In 2004, Johnny Lee Bell was convicted of second degree murder and "received an automatic mandatory sentence of life in prison, despite his public defender's admission that she had spent only 11 minutes prepar-ing for his trial." The National Association of Criminal Defense Attorneys notes that the "case is egregious, but not unsymptomatic given the trend of substandard legal representation that has become common in many states."[106]

Needless to say, the distinct legal advantages that money can buy become even more salient when we enter the realm of corporate and other white-collar crime. Indeed, it is often precisely the time and cost involved in bringing to court a large corporation with its army of legal eagles that is offered as an excuse for the less formal and more genteel treatment accorded to corporate crooks. This excuse is, of course, not equitably distributed to all economic classes, any more than quality legal service is. This means that, regardless of actual innocence or guilt, one's chances of beating the rap increase as one's income increases. A case in point is the epidemic of corpo-rate crime that broke out in 2002, with the corporate giant Enron in the lead, to which we now turn. Many of these cases are in the adjudication stage, and so we must watch to see how justice is meted out to the wealthy.

Enron and a year of corporate financial scandals   2002's big crime story was a long and complicated saga of corporate financial shenanigans that caused a significant drop in stock market prices. Although the economic losses were widespread, *Fortune* magazine notes, "The not-so- secret dirty secret of the crash is that even as investors were losing 70 percent, 90 per-cent, even in some cases *all* of their holdings, top officials of many of the companies that have crashed the hardest were getting immensely, extraordinarily, obscenely wealthy."[107]

At center stage was Enron, a multibillion-dollar energy-rights trading company, which declared one of the largest bankruptcies in history on December 2, 2001, with debts of over $31 billion! Enron was subsequently accused of having perpetrated a massive "disinformation" campaign, hiding the degree of its indebtedness from investors by treating loans as revenue, and hiding company losses by creating new firms with company capital and then attributing losses to them rather than Enron. As Enron shares were tanking, then-CEO Ken Lay was e-mailing concerned employees, advising them to hold their shares and buy new ones. Meanwhile, he himself cashed in $103 million of his own shares in the company. Enron executives unloaded nearly a *billion dollars* worth of stock while employees were locked out of selling the holdings in their pensions during much of the period in which the company's stock fell from $80 a share to $0.30. Enron investors collectively lost about $60 billion, which included many large pension plans and the retirement savings of up to 20,000 employees.[108]

Enron turned out not to be an isolated incident, and the list of companies touched by financial scandal soon included Tyco, Global Crossing, Quest, Worldcom, Xerox, Adelphia, MicroStrategy, ImClone and homemaker Martha Stuart, AOL–Time Warner, K-Mart, and some major banks, such as Citigroup and J. P. Morgan Chase.

Investor confidence plummeted along with stock prices, and politicians tripped over themselves trying to appear tough on corporate crime. Numerous critics claimed that President Bush was too close to the problem to deal effectively with the wrongdoing: Enron had contributed about $2 million to Bush over the course of his political career.[109] Congress passed the Sarbanes-Oxley Act, touted as the most sweeping financial reform since the Depression Era. Federal agents did the "perp walk" with several handcuffed executives before the press and American public; but, considering the number of people and the amounts of money involved, arrests and indictments have been few.

The so-called questionable bookkeeping and misstatements that Enron and others engaged in were not mere technical rule violations without real victims. One important consequence of the current spate of corporate crime and financial trickery is the elimination of many people's retirement nest eggs, forcing many older people to put off retirement and many retirees to go back to work: "In this age of the 401(k), when the retirement dreams of middle-class America are tied to the integrity of the stock market, crooks in the corner office are everybody's problem."[110] Other families had college tuition money tied up in stocks, along with their dreams of a more comfortable future.

The scams perpetrated by executives and companies during 2002 are a diverse collection. Some, like those of which Adelphia Communications stands accused, appear to involve relatively straightforward looting by the founding family, which allegedly used the company as its personal bank to enrich themselves. Others, like Enron's, involve complicated financial trans-actions to inflate earnings, and thus stock prices, artificially. The SEC charged Adelphia with fraudulently excluding $2.3 billion in debt from its earnings report. AES, AOL–Time Warner, Cedent, Haliburton, K-Mart, Lucent Technologies, MicroStrategy, Rite Aid, and Waste Management are all said to have misstated revenues in different ways at more than $100 million in each case.

Arthur Andersen accountants served as auditors for Enron while taking in millions of dollars from consulting deals with the company. This dual role of auditor and consultant created an obvious conflict of interest. Andersen audi-tors would surely be reluctant to bite the hand that was feeding them by letting the market know the real extent of Enron's losses and indebtedness. Andersen is, of course, quite experienced at this sort of thing, having audited such other corporate suspects as Global Crossing, Halliburton Oil, Qwest, Waste Man-agement, and WorldCom, and, before that, Charles Keating's Lincoln Savings and Loan, "which became a symbol of the nation's savings-and-loan crisis when it failed in 1989 at an eventual cost to taxpayers of $2.9 billion."[111]

Further, financial service firms like J. P. Morgan Chase and Citigroup appear to have loaned money to corporations and helped them to hide their level of indebtedness from investors who lack an inside track. *Fortune* approvingly quoted a *Wall Street Journal* editorial that called the banks "Enron Enablers" and went further, "They appear to have behaved in a guileful way and helped their corporate clients undertake unsavory prac-tices. And they appear to have had an entire division that, among other things, helped corporations avoid taxes and manipulate their balance sheets through something called structured finance, which is a huge profit center for each bank."[112] In addition, brokerage firms came under fire because their high-profile analysts enthusiastically endorsed stocks publicly that they were disparaging privately (in e-mails), all because their firms derived underwriting fees or other business from the troubled companies.[113] Merrill Lynch Internet analyst Henry Blodgett privately described some stocks as a "piece of shit" while recommending them to small investors.[114]

A summary of the most serious examples of alleged (and sometimes admitted) corporate wrongdoing is provided in Table 3.2, "Scoundrel Capi-talism, 2005." Because of the large amount of such wrongdoing, the table focuses on the most harmful incidents and highlights the multiple dimen-sions of corporate misbehavior. At the moment, charges have been filed in some, but by no means all, of the troubled companies; and, frequently, it is underlings in the organization who are the targets of indictments. Massive frauds require widespread cooperation, but the indictments have been highly selective. It remains to be seen whether this narrow and selective prosecution is part of a strategy to get information to build cases against others—especially top executives—or whether the charges are meant only to give the appearance of getting tough while top executives get off unscathed.

TABLE 3.2   Scoundrel Capitalism, 2005*

NAME/COMPANY	ALLEGED WRONGDOING
Adelphia The sixth-largest cable company declared bankruptcy soon after announcing it was responsible for $2.3 billion in off-balance-sheet loans to the founding Rigas family. Investors lost $60 billion in value when stock fell to $0.15 from a high of $66.00; the company has filed for bankruptcy and restated earnings for the last several years.	The founding Rigas family allegedly used the company as their personal bank and improperly took money and loans, then created sham transactions and forged financial documents to cover it up. A Securities and Exchange Commission (SEC) official describes this as "one of the most extensive financial frauds ever to take place at a public company." They found "rampant self-dealing," including the use of $252 million in Adelphia funds to repay stock market losses; other company money was used to purchase $28 million in timber rights, a $12.8 million golf club, the Buffalo Sabres hockey team ($150 million), and "luxury condominiums in Colorado, Mexico, and New York City for the Rigas Family." The family also used, without reimbursement, three airplanes owned by Adelphia, including for a safari vacation in Africa. At one point, Timothy Rigas grew concerned about his father John's "unacceptably large" spending of company money and put him on an allowance of $1 million a month.
Arthur Andersen Accountants and financial consultants.	Andersen audited many companies that had to restate earnings in the current scandal and has settled with the SEC in numerous past cases involving deceptive bookkeeping: Enron, WorldCom ($8 billion restatement), Global Crossing, Qwest Communications, Baptist Foundation of Arizona ($217 million settlement), Sunbeam ($110 million settlement), and Colonial Realty ($90 million settlement). The Waste Management case ($1 billion overstated earnings) led to an SEC settlement of $7 million, a $229 million shareholder settlement, and an SEC "cease and desist" order on misleading accounting. Andersen officials allegedly ordered the shredding of important Enron documents after an SEC investigation started. To help dispose of 30 boxes of documents, Andersen called a company named Shred-It, whose motto is "Your secrets are safe with us." Andersen also deleted large numbers of e-mails relating to its internal debates on Enron's financial problems.

NAME/COMPANY	ALLEGED WRONGDOING

Enron
Described by executive Jeffrey Skilling as "the world's coolest company," Enron declared the largest corporate bankruptcy in history on December 2, 2001. It restated its earnings and assets downward by $1.5 billion, wiping out 4,200 jobs and $60 billion in market value lost to shareholders.

A special committee of Enron's board (the Powers Committee) concluded that partnership arrangements allowed high-level Enron executives to hide Enron's losses and liabilities, while earning tens of millions of dollars in fees for themselves. The report was based on a three-month review without subpoena power or access to many documents. Nevertheless, it "found a systematic and pervasive attempt by Enron's Management to misrepresent the Company's financial condition" and found that Enron employees involved in the partnerships received "tens of millions of dollars they should never have received." Investigators concluded that Enron manipulated the California power crisis for financial gain, entered into transactions presenting conflicts of interest, engaged in fraudulent transactions to book revenue, and punished whistleblowers and those who questioned the appropriateness of business transactions and practices. Enron executives and directors sold $1 billion worth of shares in the three years before the company collapsed. While executives were selling off shares just before the bankruptcy announcement, employees were locked out of selling their shares because of "administrative changes" to the stock plan. During this period, Enron stock lost 28 percent of its value. Ken Lay took $19 million in cash advances during this time, which he repaid with Enron stock that was rapidly losing value.

Global Crossing
Optical fiber company filed the fourth-largest bankruptcy under the weight of $12 billion in debt. This company is chartered in Bermuda to avoid U.S. corporate taxes, even though it is headquartered and run out of the United States, and enjoys all the rights and access to government contracts

Allegedly engaged in capacity swaps with Qwest Communications (see below) to improperly book revenue in order to inflate stock price. In one congressional hearing, Rep. Billy Tauzin (R-LA), said executives "pursued sham transactions to put revenue on the books, to mislead investors, and to prevent further drops in their stock prices." Many of these transactions were done in the last few days, sometimes the last minutes, of the financial quarter to help meet earnings expectations. CEO Thomas Casey may have misled Wall Street analysts when he denied on several occasions that Global Crossing used swaps.

(continued)

TABLE 3.2   Continued

NAME/COMPANY	ALLEGED WRONGDOING
that U.S. corporations enjoy.	Chairman Gary Winnick, who works out of a replica of the Oval Office inside a gated plaza, sold more than $730 million in shares before the announcement and devaluation of the stock.
Qwest Communications The dominant local telephone company in 14 states. Shares dropped to $1 each, down 89 percent from the start of the year and a high of $66.00.	Alleged to have improperly accounted for about $1 billion, may have to restate another $500 million in sales, and engaged in hollow trades and capacity swaps with Global Crossing and other telecoms to boost revenue and meet earnings expectations. "Investors in Global Crossing and Qwest lost billions of dollars when the truth came out about these companies' finances, while insiders walked away with billions of dollars," according to Rep. James Greenwood (R-PA), who chairs a congressional committee investigating the companies. On several occasions, executives asked that the details of the swaps not be put in writing to avoid scrutiny. An internal memo by Chief Financial Officer (CFO) Robin Szeliga indicated Qwest would penalize anyone who questioned the company's handling of swaps and followed through by blocking business to Morgan Stanley, which publicly questioned Qwest's reliance on swaps. Qwest lays the blame with Arthur Andersen, which it says approved the accounting related to the capacity swaps. Qwest's founder and largest shareholder, Philip Anschutz, sold $213.5 million in shares prior to the restated earnings report.
Tyco This large conglomerate is chartered in Bermuda to avoid U.S. corporate taxes, even though it is headquartered and run out of the United States, and enjoys all the rights and access to government contracts that U.S. corporations enjoy.	Former CEO Dennis Kozlowski and former CFO Mark Swartz allegedly looted company and shareholders of $600 million that went to themselves and others who helped them cover up improper secret loans that were forgiven without proper authorization. Tyco also seems to have taken losses on certain business transactions that it improperly booked as profit, which then justified bonuses for executives. The two men used the money to buy houses, art, and luxury items for themselves, including a $1 million birthday party for Kozlowski's wife on the Italian

NAME/COMPANY	ALLEGED WRONGDOING

island of Sardinia that included toga-clad waiters and an ice sculpture of Michelangelo's *David* with vodka pouring from his genitals.

Kozlowski also allegedly improperly bought valuable paintings by Renoir and Monet worth $13.2 million using funds borrowed from Tyco, only some of which has been repaid, and he evaded $1.1 million in New York State sales tax by falsifying documents related to the art purchases and sending empty boxes to the company's New Hampshire address.

WorldCom (now MCI)
Telecommunications giant announced a series of restatements totaling about $9 billion, and it displaced Enron as the largest bankruptcy filing in U.S. history. The stock price fell from a high of $64.00 to $0.09, reducing their total value from $120 billion to about $4.4 billion; 17,000 employees have been laid off. The New York State pension plan lost $300 million because of WorldCom investments.

Deputy U.S. Attorney General Larry Thompson said CFO Scott Sullivan and Controller David Myers "systematically flouted rules of accounting and lied outright to investors to perpetuate the false image that WorldCom was succeeding." In response to overbuilding and excess capacity in telecommunications, business was deteriorating, and executives put pressure on numerous others to, in Myers's words, engage in accounting adjustments for which "there was no justification or documentation and [that] were not in accordance with generally accepted accounting principles." WorldCom executives pressured whistleblowers to remain quiet, and Myers warned employees who had questions not to discuss their concerns with outside auditors.

CEO Bernard Ebbers was removed from his position when WorldCom declared bankruptcy, but he negotiated a severance package worth $1.5 million a year for life.

---

*The title comes from a phrase used by Simon Schama (source given below).

Source: See Simon Schama, "The Dead and the Guilty," *The Guardian,* September 11, 2002, *www.guardian.co.uk/september11/oneyearon/story/0,12361,789978,00.html.* In the article, he notes that "Enron Corporation['s] implosion began the unraveling of scoundrel capitalism." Other sources include Devin Leonard, "The Adelphia Story" *Fortune,* August 12, 2002, *www.fortune.com/indexw.jhtml?channel=artcol.jhtml&doc_id=208825; CNNMoney,* "Rigas and Sons Arrested," July 25, 2002, *http://money.cnn.com/2002/07/24/news/rigas/;* George Mannes, "Adelphia Charges Up the Ante," The Street.com, July 24, 2002, *www.thestreet.com/_yahoo/tech/georgemannes/10033900.html;* Carrie Johnson and Christopher Stern, "Adelphia Founder, Sons Charged," *Washington Post,* July 25, 2002, p. A1; "Swartz Got Rich Severance Deal," *Boston Globe,* September 26, 2002, *www.boston.com/dailyglobe2/269/business/Swartz_got_rich_severance_deal+.shtml;* Peter Behr and Dan Eggen, "Enron Is Target of Criminal Probe," *Washington Post,* January 10, 2002, p. A1; Peter Behr and April Witt, "Visionary's Dream Led to Risky Business," *Washington Post,* July 28, 2002, p. A1; Jonathan Krim, "Fast and Loose at WorldCom: Lack of Controls, Pressure to Grow Set

President Bush announced a new corporate fraud task force, although critics quickly pointed out that the official responsible for this "financial SWAT team" was a director of a credit card company that had been forced to pay more than $400 million to settle consumer and securities fraud suits. When Bush announced $100 million for the SEC, Laura Unger, a Republican who has served as acting chairman of the SEC, commented that "$100 million is not even close to enough to really make a significant difference" in regulatory effectiveness.[115] No provision was made to replace 500 FBI agents who had been transferred from white-collar crime enforcement to counterterrorism efforts. Leon E. Panetta, a co-chairman of a New York Stock Exchange panel on corporate reforms, was disappointed that Bush, as a former businessman, did not challenge his peers more earnestly "on a whole range of other issues that determine whether we really change the culture of American business. . . . It's not just the fraud we have to deal with—it's the whole get-rich-quick, boost-the-stock-price environment that invited it and encouraged it that we need to address."[116]

Panetta's comments also apply to the Sarbanes-Oxley Act, which was signed into law on July 30, 2002. It created a new board to oversee the accounting and auditing of publicly traded companies, limited the ability of accounting firms to be both auditors and consultants of the same firms, gave shareholders five rather than three years to sue companies that mislead them, and increased possible fines and jail sentences for those who violate new and existing corporate laws. Much of the law is a step in the right direction. However, political compromises in Congress led to changing the standard for holding executives liable for fraud from "reckless" (in allowing it to happen) to "knowing" (that it was happening). The new standard requires stronger evidence and makes the case more difficult for prosecutors. Another issue involves *disgorgement*, the technical term for the amount and conditions under which executives must repay money taken in fraud. Congress voted

Stage for Financial Deceptions," *Washington Post*, August 29, 2002, p. A1; Jonathan Krim, "WorldCom Staff Told Not to Talk to Auditor, E-Mails Show," *Washington Post*, August 27, 2002, p. E3; David M. Ewalt and John Kreiser, "Sidgmore Steps Down as WorldCom CEO; Ebbers May Lose Golden Parachute," *InformationWeek.com*, September 10, 2002, *www.informationweek.com/story/IWK20020910S0007*; Motley Fool, "The Motley Fool Take on Wednesday, Feb. 27, 2002," *www.fool.com/news/take/2002/take020227.htm*; Motley Fool, "The Motley Fool Take on Wednesday, June 5, 2002," *www.fool.com/news/take/2002/take020605.htm*; Robert O' Harrow, "Tyco Executives Free on Bond of $15 Million," *Washington Post*, September 28, 2002, p. E1; Carrie Johnson and Ben White, "WorldCom Arrests Made," *Washington Post*, August 2, 2002, p. A1; Ben White, "WorldCom Officer Pleads Guilty to Fraud," *Washington Post*, October 8, 2002, p. E1; and Citizen Works, "Corporate Crookbook: Corporate Scandal Sheet," *http://citizenworks.org/enron/corp-scandal.php*; and Mark Gimein, "You Bought: They Sold," *Fortune*, September 2, 2002, pp. 64–65.

not to apply this to company officers and directors who knew about misconduct but were not directly involved in it.[117]

As soon as the ink was dry on the legislation, *The Washington Post* reported, "Members of Congress from both parties accused the administration of undermining or narrowing the scope of provisions covering securities fraud, whistleblower protection and punishment for shredding documents." Critics, including the bill's authors, charged that the Justice Department drew up interpretations and prosecution guidelines that contradicted the legislative intent of the reform measure. Iowa Republican Senator Charles E. Grassley blasted the administration on whistleblower protection, saying, "Any dummy that reads the bill knows what we meant. We couldn't have written it any clearer." And Vermont Democratic Senator Patrick Leahy, Chair of the Senate Judiciary Committee, commented, "The president said all the right things at the signing ceremony. But now given the tough law, they're basically saying, 'We're not going to use it.'"[118] And a September 2002 article in *The·Washington Post* notes that Congress was quickly losing its zeal to correct the flaws that led to the Enron debacle:

> The recently devastated retirement accounts of employees from Enron Corp. and WorldCom Inc. initially fueled a wave of indignation among lawmakers in Washington and solemn vows to protect their investments. But the anger that pushed tough new accounting standards past corporate opponents this summer has already faded [by September!], lawmakers and lobbyists say, allowing businesses to regain their strength on Capitol Hill.[119]

Following up on Sarbanes-Oxley, the U.S. Sentencing Commission increased the penalties for some white-collar crimes. This was done under emergency powers and will only be effective through November 2003, by which point they will have something more permanent in place. According to the Commission's press release, "The emergency amendments provide significant sentencing enhancements for white collar offenses that affect a large number of victims or endanger the solvency or financial security of publicly traded corporations, other large employers, or 100 individual victims."[120] However, "the Justice Department promptly complained that the new guidelines do not go far enough, because the panel failed to crack down harder on lower-level offenders and failed to make it more difficult for white-collar criminals to avoid prison. The agency said it would ask Congress to pass legislation to assuage its concerns."[121] A recent article in *The Washington Post* reports,

> The Securities and Exchange Commission's staff, over objections from investor and consumer groups, is recommending that the commission back off from several auditing reforms it was considering in response to scandals at Enron Corp.

and other companies. The staff, at the urging of the accounting industry, will not propose limiting the industry's lucrative consulting work in finding tax shelters for clients they audit, staff members said at a briefing yesterday.

Said Lynn E. Turner, chief accountant at the SEC in the Clinton administration, 'How can you go through Enron, how can you go through Tyco, how can you go through WorldCom and still have an SEC that is putting accountants before investors?'[122]

In March 2002, after the disclosure of Enron's bankruptcy, but before a wave of other frauds was revealed, *Fortune* magazine observed, "The double standard in criminal justice in this country is starker and more embedded than many realize. Bob Dylan was right: Steal a little, and they put you in jail. Steal a lot, and you're likely to walk away with a lecture and a court-ordered promise not to do it again."[123] As a case in point, Enron's Chief Financial Officer Andy Fastow was charged with 109 felony counts including conspiracy, wire fraud, securities fraud, falsifying books, as well as obstruction of justice, money laundering, insider trading, and filing false income tax returns. He was sentenced to ten years in prison. Sounds pretty tough, doesn't it? However, at the same time, Leandro Andrade received a sentence of 50 years for two counts of stealing videocassettes from K-Mart—a sentence upheld by the Supreme Court as a not unreasonable application of a three-strikes law. As I noted in a pamphlet written with Paul Leighton (see Recommended Readings at the end of this chapter), a poor guy ends up in jail for life for stealing less than $200 worth of goods, and a rich guy ends up in jail for ten years for bringing about the financial ruin of thousands of Enron employees and investors, including pension funds that held the retirement hopes of many.[124]

Some of the sentences handed down to corporate executives who went to trial have been harsher than what Fastow received, although it is still too early to make a final judgment on the "toughness" of our criminal justice system on these corporate criminals. At this writing, the top officials at Enron—Ken Lay and Jeff Skilling—are on trial. Other sentences are still under appeal, including the 25 years for Bernard Ebbers, CEO of WorldCom, which filed for bankruptcy just after Enron and displaced it as the largest corporate bankruptcy in American history. The 24-year sentence of Jamie Olis has been overturned, and the case sent back for additional consideration about how to calculate economic losses. Olis was senior director of tax planning at Dynergy. He allegedly spearheaded a large-scale fraud that resulted in hundreds of millions of dollars in losses to shareholders when it was discovered. Accounting firm Arthur Andersen has had its conviction overturned by the Supreme Court because of an improper jury instruction.[125] More generally, while the government has put unprecedented effort into prosecuting corporate fraud, the fraud itself has dwarfed previous outbreaks of corporate crime. Enron and WorldCom were the two largest corporate bankrupticies in

U.S. history, and more than 50 firms were under investigation by October 2002.[126] The problem is not run-of-the-mill white-collar crime or a few bad apples, but systemic and widespread fraud that undermined trust in the financial system itself. Such episodes of fraud are relatively rare, but since they weaken the public's faith in the financial system, the government must react very strongly. Thus, to the extent the criminal justice system has really come down hard on these recent cases, it is a response to fraud that was unprecedented in size and scope and that threatened both the financial and the legal systems. Consequently, we cannot assume that the same toughness will be applied to less notorious white-collar crimes. (Indeed, remember from Chapter 2 that willful violations of health and safety laws that result in a death are still punishable by six months in prison—half the penalty for harassing a wild burro on federal land.)

Sentencing

On June 28, 1990, the House Subcommittee on Financial Institutions Supervision, Regulation, and Insurance met in the Rayburn House Office Building to hold hearings on the prosecution of savings and loan criminals. The chairman of the subcommittee, Congressman Frank Annunzio, called the meeting to order and said,

> The American people are furious with the slow pace of prosecutions involving savings and loan criminals. These crooks are responsible for 1/3, 1/2, or maybe even more, of the savings and loan cost. The American taxpayer will be forced to pay $500 billion or more over the next 40 years, largely because of these crooks. For many Americans, this bill will not be paid until their grandchildren are old enough to retire.
>
> We are here to get an answer to one question: "When are the S&L crooks going to jail?"
>
> The answer from the administration seems to be: "probably never."
>
> Frankly, I don't think the administration has the interest in pursuing Gucci-clad, white-collar criminals. These are hard and complicated cases, and the defendants often were rich, successful prominent members of their upper-class communities. It is far easier putting away a sneaker-clad high school dropout who tries to rob a bank of a thousand dollars with a stick-up note, than a smooth talking S&L executive who steals a million dollars with a fraudulent note.

Later in the hearing, Chairman Annunzio questioned the administration's representative:

> You cited, Mr. Dennis, several examples in your testimony of successful convictions with stiff sentences, but the average sentence so far is actually about 2 years, compared to an average sentence of about 9 years for bank robbery.

Why do we throw the book at people who rob a bank in broad daylight but we coddle people who . . . rob the bank secretly?[127]

Twelve years later, on July 11, 2002, at a hearing of the Crime and Drugs Subcommittee of the Senate Judiciary Committee on the subject of "Penalties for White Collar Crimes: Are We Really Getting Tough on Crime?" Senator Joseph Biden Jr. said,

Under federal law, if . . . you steal a car out of my driveway and you drive it across [the state line] into Pennsylvania, ten years. Ten years, federal guideline. You take a pension by violating ERISA, the federal system to safeguard pensions, misdemeanor, maximum one year. The pension may be worth $1,800,000. My car may be worth $2,000.[128]

The simple fact is that the criminal justice system reserves its harshest penalties for its lower-class clients and puts on kid gloves when confronted with a better class of crook.

We will come back to the soft treatment of the S&L crooks shortly. For the moment, note that the tendency to treat higher-class criminals more leniently than lower-class criminals has been with us for a long time. In 1972, *The New York Times* did a study on sentencing in state and federal courts. The *Times* stated that "crimes that tend to be committed by the poor get tougher sentences than those committed by the well-to-do," that federal "defendants who could not afford private counsel were sentenced nearly twice as severely as defendants with private counsel," and that a "study by the Vera Institute of Justice of courts in the Bronx indicates a similar pattern in the state courts."[129]

D'Alessio and Stolzenberg studied a random sample of 2,760 offenders committed to the custody of the Florida Department of Corrections during fiscal year 1985. They found that poor offenders received longer sentences for violent crimes, such as manslaughter, and for morals offenses, such as narcotics possession. Nor, by the way, did sentencing guidelines reduce this disparity.[130] A study of individuals convicted of drunk driving found that increased education (an indicator of higher economic status) "increase[d] the rate of movement from case filing to probation and decrease[d] the rate of movement to prison." And, though, when probation was given, better-educated offenders got longer probation, they also got shorter prison sentences, if sentenced to prison at all.[131]

Chiricos and Bales found that, for individuals guilty of similar offenses and with similar prior records, unemployed defendants were more likely to be incarcerated while awaiting trial, and for longer periods, than employed defendants. They were more than twice as likely as their employed counterparts to be incarcerated on a finding of guilt, and defendants with public defenders experienced longer periods of jail time than those who could afford private attorneys.[132] McCarthy noted a similar link between unemployment and greater likelihood of incarceration.[133] In his study of 28,315 felony defendants in Tennessee, Virginia, and Kentucky, Champion also found that offenders who could afford private counsel had a greater likelihood of probation, and received shorter sentences when incarceration was imposed.[134] A study of the effects of implementing Minnesota's determinate sentencing program shows that socioeconomic bias is "more subtle, but no less real" than before the new program.[135]

Tillman and Pontell examined the sentences received by individuals convicted of Medicaid-provider fraud in California. Because such offenders normally have no prior arrests and are charged with grand theft, their sentences were compared with the sentences of other offenders convicted of grand theft who also had no prior records. While 37.7 percent of the Medicaid defrauders were sentenced to some jail or prison time, 79.2 percent of the others convicted of grand theft were sentenced to jail or prison. This was so even though the median dollar loss due to the Medicaid frauds was $13,000, more than ten times the median loss due to the other grand thefts ($1,149). Tillman and Pontell point out that most of the Medicaid defrauders were health professionals, while most of the others convicted of grand theft had low-level jobs or were unemployed. They conclude that "differences in the sentences imposed on the two samples are indeed the result of the different social statuses of their members."[136]

As usual, data on racial discrimination in sentencing tell the same story of the treatment of those who cannot afford the going price of justice. A study of offender processing in New York State counties found that, for offenders with the same arrest charge and the same prior criminal records, minorities were incarcerated more often than comparably situated whites.[137] A study of 9,690 males who entered Florida prisons in 1992 and 1993, and who were legally eligible for stricter sentencing under the habitual offender statute, shows that, for similar prior records and seriousness of crime, race had a "significant and substantial" effect: Black defendants were particularly disadvantaged "for drug offenses and for property crimes."[138] After reviewing 22 recent studies estimating sentencing severity based on federal-level data, Spohn concluded that "more than two-thirds (15 of 22) of the estimates reveal that blacks [and Hispanics] were sentenced more harshly than whites." Based on a total of 40 recent studies of both federal and state data, Spohn concludes that "Black and Hispanic offenders—particularly those who are young, male, or unemployed—are more likely than their white counterparts to be sentenced to prison; they also may receive longer sentences than similarly situated white offenders."[139]

Most striking perhaps is that, in 2001, 46 percent of inmates in state and federal prisons were black and 40.6 percent of inmates of jails were black, whereas blacks make up only 32.9 percent of those arrested for serious (FBI Index) crimes.[140] Furthermore, when we look only at federal prisons, where there is reason to believe that racial and economic discrimination is less prevalent than in state institutions, we find that, in 2003, the average sentence for blacks found guilty of violent offenses was 109.7 months, while for whites it was 91.2 months—more than a year and a half less.[141]

Here must be mentioned the notorious "100-to-1" disparity between sentences for possession of cocaine in powder form (popular in the affluent suburbs) and in crack form (popular in poor inner-city neighborhoods). Federal laws require a mandatory five-year sentence for crimes involving 500 grams of powder cocaine or 5 grams of crack cocaine. This yields a sentence for first-time crack offenders (with no aggravating factors, such as possession of a weapon) that is longer than the sentence for kidnapping, and only slightly shorter than the sentence for attempted murder![142] About 86 percent of those convicted of federal crack offenses are black; about 5 percent are white.[143] In 1995, the United States Sentencing Commission recommended ending the 100-to-1 disparity between powder and crack penalties, and, in an unusual display of bipartisanship, both the Republican congress and the Democratic president rejected their recommendation.[144]

Sentencing disparities between the races are, of course, not new. An extensive study by the *Boston Globe* of 4,500 cases of armed robbery, aggravated assault, and rape found that "blacks convicted in the superior courts of Massachusetts receive harsher penalties than whites for the same crimes."[145] The authors of a study of almost 1,200 males sentenced to prison for armed robbery in a southeastern state found that "in 1977 whites incarcerated for armed robbery had a greater than average chance of receiving the least severe sentence, while nonwhites had a greater than average chance of receiving a moderately severe sentence."[146] A study of 229 adjudicated cases in a Florida judicial district yielded the finding that "whites have an 18 percent greater chance in the predicted probability of receiving probation than blacks when all other things are equal."[147] A recent study of criminal justice systems in California, Michigan, and Texas by Petersilia confirms the continuation of this trend. "Controlling for the factors most likely to influence sentencing and parole decisions," she writes, "the analysis still found that blacks and Hispanics are less likely to be given probation, more likely to receive *prison* sentences, more likely to receive longer sentences, and more likely to serve a greater portion of their original time."[148] Myers found that "harsher treatment of persons with fewer resources (e.g., female, unemployed, unmarried, black) is . . . pronounced in highly unequal counties."[149]

The federal government has introduced sentencing guidelines and mandatory minimum sentences that might be expected to eliminate discrimination, and many states have followed suit. The effect of this, however, has been not to eliminate discretion but to transfer it from those who sentence to those who decide what to charge—that is, from judges to prosecutors. Prosecutors can charge in a way that makes it likely that the offender will get less than the mandatory minimum sentence. Says U.S. District Judge J. Lawrence Irving of San Diego, "[T]he system is run by the U.S. attorneys. When they decide how to indict, they fix the sentence."[150] And discrimination persists. To examine the effects of mandatory minimum sentences, Barbara Meierhoefer studied 267,178 offenders sentenced in federal courts from January 1984 to June 1990. She found that whites were consistently more likely than blacks to be sentenced to less than the minimum sentence. The disparity varied from year to year, reaching a high point in 1988, when blacks were 30 percent more likely than whites to receive at least the minimum. Hispanics fared even worse than blacks. Concludes Meierhoefer,

> [D]espite the laws' emphasis on offense behavior, sentences still vary by offender characteristics. . . . Further, both black and Hispanic offenders now receive notably more severe sentences than their white counterparts.
>
> The latter trend suggests that there may be questions to be considered concerning the impact of shifting discretion affecting sentencing from the court to the prosecutor's office.[151]

A growing number of judges are speaking out against the system of sentencing guidelines and mandatory minimum sentences. According to U.S. District Judge Terry Hatter of Los Angeles, "[T]he toughest sentences are now strictly 'applied to basically one group of people: poor minority people.'" Appellate Judge Gerald W. Heaney of Duluth, Minnesota, conducted his own study "and found that young black men got longer sentences than their white counterparts for similar crimes. Using 1989 data, he compared sentences under the new system with those under the old. The average sentence for black males was 40 months longer, he found, while the average sentence for white males was 19 months longer."[152]

There is considerable evidence that *double discrimination*—by race of the victim and of the offender—affects death penalty sentencing. In Florida, for example, blacks "who kill whites are nearly forty times more likely to be sentenced to death than those who kill blacks." Moreover, among "killers of whites, blacks are five times more likely than whites to be sentenced to death." This pattern of double discrimination was also evidenced, though less pronouncedly, in Texas, Ohio, and Georgia, the other states surveyed.[153] Together, these four states account for the vast majority of American death sentences.

More recent studies have shown the same pattern. It was on the basis of such research that what may have been the last major constitutional challenge to the death penalty in our era was raised and rejected. In the 1987 case of *McCleskey v. Kemp*, evidence of discrimination on the basis of the victim's race was provided by a study by Professor David Baldus, of the University of Iowa, who examined 2,484 Georgia homicide cases that occurred between 1973 (when the current capital murder law was enacted) and 1979 (a year after McCleskey received his death sentence).[154] After controlling for all legitimate nonracial factors—such as severity of crime and the presence of aggravating factors—Baldus found that "murderers of white victims are still being sentenced to death 4.3 times more often than murderers of black victims."[155] The justices of the Supreme Court acknowledged the systemic disparities, but a majority held that the disparities would not invalidate death penalty convictions unless discrimination could be shown in the individual case at hand.

A recent study by criminologists at the University of Maryland looked at some 6,000 homicides committed between 1978 and 1999 in the state of Maryland and concluded the following:

- Black offenders who kill whites are *twice as likely* to get a death sentence as whites who kill whites.
- Black offenders who kill whites are *four times as likely* to get a death sentence as blacks who kill blacks.[156]

Note that all these discriminatory sentences were rendered under statutes that had passed constitutional muster and were therefore presumed free of the biases that led the Supreme Court to invalidate all American death penalty statutes in *Furman v. Georgia* in 1972.

Another study has shown that, among blacks and whites on death row, whites are more likely to have their sentences commuted. Also, blacks or whites who have private counsel are more likely to have their execution commuted than condemned persons defended by court-appointed attorneys.[157] A study appearing in the American Bar Association's *Criminal Justice* magazine examined 107 cases of people on death row who were wrongfully convicted. Of these exonerated inmates, 45 percent were black and another 13 percent were other minorities. In short, 58 percent of wrongful convictions were of minority defendants.[158]

As I have already pointed out, justice is increasingly tempered with mercy as we deal with a better class of crime. The Sherman Antitrust Act is a criminal law. It was passed in recognition of the fact that one virtue of a free enterprise economy is that competition tends to drive consumer prices down, so agreements by competing firms to refrain from price competition is the equivalent of stealing money from the consumer's pocket. Nevertheless, although such conspiracies cost consumers far more than lower-class theft, price fixing was a misdemeanor until 1974.[159] In practice, few conspirators end up in prison and, when they do, the sentence is a mere token, well below the maximum provided in the law.

In the historic *Electrical Equipment* cases in the early 1960s, executives of several major firms met secretly to fix prices on electrical equipment to a degree that is estimated to have cost the buying public well over $1 billion. The executives involved knew they were violating the law. They used plain envelopes for their communications, called their meetings "choir practice," and referred to the list of executives in attendance as the "Christmas card list." This case is rare and famous because it was an early case in which the criminal sanction was actually imposed. Seven executives received and served jail sentences. In light of the amount of money they had stolen from the American public, however, their sentences were more an indictment of the government than of themselves: *thirty days in jail!*

After the "anything goes" attitude of the Reagan era, which brought us such highly publicized white-collar skulduggery as the multibillion dollar savings and loan scandal, starting in the 1990s there has been a kind of backlash, with the government under pressure to up the penalties for corporate offenders. Here too, however, progress follows a slow and zigzagging course. Consider, for example, the following series of headlines from *The Washington Post:* March 2, 1990, "Criminal Indictments: Training Bigger Guns on Corporations"; April 1, 1990, "Going Soft on Corporate Crime"; April 28, 1990, "Justice Dept. Shifts on Corporate Sentencing" ("Attorney General Dick Thornburgh last month withdrew the Justice Department's longstanding support for tough mandatory sentences for corporate criminals following an intense lobbying campaign by defense contractors, oil companies and other *Fortune* 500 firms."); and April 27, 1991, "Corporate Lawbreakers May Face Tougher Penalties."[160] Lest this last one be taken as truly reversing the trend to leniency, note that it reports new sentencing guidelines approved by the U.S. Sentencing Commission, and it points out, "The only penalties set forth by the guidelines are fines and probation because the defendants in such cases are not individuals." Compare this with a statement from Ira Reiner, then the Los Angeles district attorney, quoted in the first of the articles just listed: "A fine, no matter how substantial, is simply a cost of doing business for a corporation. But a jail term for executives is different. What we are trying to do is to change the corporate culture." Good luck, Ira.

Studies have shown that, even though corporate and white-collar lawbreakers are being more frequently brought to justice and more frequently sanctioned, they still receive more lenient sentences than do those who are sentenced for common property crimes.[161] A study by Hagan and Palloni, which focuses particularly on the differences between pre- and post-Watergate (a major political scandal that occurred in the 1970s in which President Nixon as well as numerous of his political underlings were implicated in an attempt to compromise the integrity of the electoral process) treatment of white-collar offenders, concludes that likelihood of prosecution after Watergate was increased, but that the effect of this was canceled out by the leniency of the sentences meted out:

> [T]he new incarcerated white-collar offenders received relatively light sentences that counterbalanced the increased use of imprisonment. Relative to less-educated common criminals, white-collar offenders were more likely to be imprisoned after Watergate than before, but for shorter periods.[162]

Even after the heightened public awareness of white-collar crime that came in the wake of Watergate and the S&L scandals, it remains the case that the

TABLE 3.3   Federal Sentences Served for Different Classes of Crimes, Fiscal Year 2001

	PERCENT SENTENCED TO PRISON	AVERAGE TIME SERVED (IN MONTHS)
CRIMES OF THE POOR		
Robbery	96	59
Burglary	88	22
Auto theft	77	17
CRIMES OF THE AFFLUENT		
Fraud	64	17
Tax law violation and tax fraud	56	16
Embezzlement	59	9

Source: Sourcebook—2003 (compiled from Tables 5.19 and 6.58, and rounded off).

crimes of the poor lead to stiffer sentences than the crimes of the well-to-do (see Table 3.3). Keep in mind while looking at the figures in Table 3.3 that *each* of the "crimes of the affluent" costs the public more than *all* of the "crimes of the poor" put together.

There has been some toughening of the treatment of white-collar offenders in recent years. Nonetheless, this toughening has been relatively mild when compared with the treatment dealt out to lower-class offenders. Before turning to the major scandal in the savings and loan industry, here is a "minor" case that illustrates the new developments.

In September 1991, a fire destroyed a chicken-processing plant in Hamlet, North Carolina. When the 100 employees in the plant tried to escape, they found that the company executives had ordered the doors locked "to keep out insects and to keep employees from going outside for coffee breaks, or stealing chickens." Twenty-five workers died in the fire; some were found burned to death at the doors they clawed at but couldn't open. Another 50 people were injured. The owner of the company and two plant managers were charged with involuntary manslaughter. The outcome: The owner pleaded guilty and was sentenced to 19 years and 6 months in prison. You may or may not think this is severe as a punishment for someone responsible for 25 very painful deaths, but note three revealing facts. First, the sentence was "believed to be the harshest judgment ever handed out for a workplace safety violation." Second, as part of the plea agreement, the involuntary manslaughter cases against the two plant managers were dismissed, though they surely knew that the doors were locked and what the risks were. And third, the owner eventually served a little more than four years in prison and was released.[163]

The savings & loan scandal   We turn now to one of the greatest examples of upper-class crime in our era, the savings and loan scandal. The federally insured system of savings and loan banks (also known as "thrifts") was created in the 1930s to promote the building and sale of new homes during the Great Depression. The system had built into it important restrictions on the kinds of loans that could be made and was subject to federal supervision to prevent the bank failures that came in the wake of the Depression of 1929. Starting in the 1970s and speeding up in the early 1980s, this entire system of regulation and supervision was first loosened, and then essentially dismantled, as part of the Reagan administration's policy of deregulation. Although S&Ls could now make riskier investments, their deposits were still insured by the Federal Savings and Loan Insurance Corporation (FSLIC). Translation: The S&Ls could make risky investments shooting for windfall profits, with the taxpayers picking up the tab for losses. This combination proved to be financial dynamite. The thrifts made high-risk investments, and many failed. By 1982, the bill to the FSLIC for bailing out insolvent thrifts was over $2.4 billion. By 1986, the FSLIC was itself insolvent![164] In 1996, *The Wall Street Journal* announced that a Government Accounting Office report put the total cost to the American taxpayer of the S&L bailout at $480.9 billion![165]

Not all this loss is due to crime. Some is due to foolish but legal investments, some is due to inflation, and some is due to foot-dragging by federal agencies that allowed interest to accumulate. Nonetheless, there is evidence that fraud was a central factor in 70 to 80 percent of the S&L failures.[166] Much of this fraud took the form of looting of bank funds for the personal gain of bank officers at the expense of the institution. The commissioner of the California Department of Savings and Loans is quoted as saying in 1987, "The best way to rob a bank is to own one."[167] Says *Fortune* magazine, "Though yet perceived only in hazy outline, today's S&L fraud dwarfs every previous carnival of white-collar crime in America."[168]

In response to the enormity of this scandal, American public opinion hardened toward white-collar crime, and federal law enforcement agencies were prosecuting, fining, and even jailing offenders at unprecedented rates. Nonetheless, considering the size of the scandal and the far-reaching damage it did to the American economy, the treatment is still light-handed compared with that of even nonviolent "common" crime. According to a study conducted at the University of California, Irvine, "The average prison term for savings and loan offenders sentenced between 1988 and 1992 was 36 months, compared to 56 months for burglars and 38 months for those convicted of motor vehicle theft." The study goes on to point out that S&L offenders were given lengthier sentences than first-time property crime offenders (who received an average sentence of 26 months), but, lest we think that this shows a new severity, the study notes that the average loss in an S&L case was $500,000.[169] The average loss per property offense in 1995 was $1,251.[170]

These sentenced S&L offenders represent just a small fraction of the crooks involved in the S&L looting. One observer points out that "from 1987 to 1992, Federal bank and thrift regulators filed a staggering 95,045 criminal referrals with the FBI. The volume was so large that more than 75 percent of these referrals have been dropped without prosecution."[171] At the same time, the Justice Department advised against funding for 425 new agents requested by the FBI and 231 new assistant U.S. attorneys, and the administration recommended against increasing funds authorized by Congress for the S&L investigations from $50 million to $75 million.[172] But, soon after, we find the president and the Congress ready to spend $23 billion on criminal justice and hire thousands of new police officers to keep our streets safe!

To give you a concrete idea of what some of the S&L crooks did and the treatment they are getting, I have culled, from various sources, a roughly representative "rogues gallery" (see Table 3.4). In looking at these rogues, their acts, and their punishments, keep in mind the treatment meted out to the Typical Criminal when he steals a fraction of what they did.

We have seen in this chapter and the one before that the criminal justice system is triply biased against the poor. First, there is the economic class bias *among harmful acts* as to which get labeled crimes and which are treated as regulatory matters, as we saw in the previous chapter. Second, there is economic class bias *among crimes* that we have seen in this chapter. The crimes that poor people are likely to commit carry harsher sentences than the "crimes in the suites" committed by well-to-do people. Third, there is economic class bias *among defendants convicted of the same crimes*. The poor receive less probation and more years of confinement than well-off defendants, assuring us once again that the vast majority of those put behind bars are from the lowest social and economic classes in the nation. On either side of the law, the rich get richer . . .

. . . AND THE POOR GET PRISON

At 9:05 A.M. on the morning of Thursday, September 9, 1971, a group of inmates forced their way through a gate at the center of the prison, fatally injured a guard named William Quinn, and took 50 hostages. The Attica uprising had begun. It lasted four days, until 9:43 A.M. on the morning of Monday, September 13, when corrections officers and state troopers stormed the prison and killed 29 inmates and 10 hostages.[173] During those four days the nation saw the faces of its captives on television—the hard black faces of young men who had grown up on the streets of Harlem and other urban ghettos. Theirs were the faces of crime in America. The television viewers who saw them were not surprised. Here were faces of dangerous men who should be locked up. Nor were people outraged when the state launched its murderous attack on the prison, killing many more inmates and guards than

TABLE 3.4   The Savings and Loan Roster

Michael Hellerman aka Michael Rapp	Defrauded Flushing Federal S&L (New York) of $8.4 million and Florida Center Bank of $7.5 million.	Sentenced to 32 years for Florida theft and 15 years for New York theft, plus $1.75 million fine. Reduced on appeal to 15 years and a fine of $100,000. Released on parole in 1992 after serving 5½ years; has not paid any of fine, but lawyer claims $100 a month is being deducted from Hellerman/Rapp's salary.
Charles Bazarian	Convicted for "swindling $20 million from two California S&Ls and skimming at least $100,000 from a low-income H.U.D. project." Also convicted with Rapp in Florida case.	Sentenced to two years and $100,000 fine in Florida case; sentenced to two years in prison, three years probation, and $10,000 fine for other incidents. Served less than two years for cooperating with authorities, and has paid $18,000.
Mario Renda	As partner in a brokerage business, he stole about $16 million.	Sentenced to prison, ordered to pay $9.9 million in restitution and $125,000 in criminal fines; was given early parole after serving 21 months. As of his release from prison, he had paid only a small fraction of the required restitution.
Herman Beebe	Involved in widespread loan fraud involving more than $30 million.	Pleaded guilty to two counts under a bargain in which he received a sentence of one year and one day. Served 10 months and is immune from prosecution for fraud charges in Louisiana and Texas.
Richard Mariucci	As branch manager of Gibraltar Federal (California), stole	Sentenced to two years and three months.

(continued)

TABLE 3.4 Continued

	$3.4 million, which he spent on gambling and raising racehorses.	
Walter Vladovich	Video store owner; defrauded Westlake Thrift and Loan (California) out of $4 million and bribed First United Federal (California) vice president to approve a $556,269 loan, which he pocketed.	Sentenced to four years and $50,000 fine.
Arthur Kick	President of North Chicago Federal S&L; stole $1.2 million by misappropriating loans.	Sentenced to full restitution and three years of probation.
Jack Lee Odon	President of Sioux Valley Savings (Iowa), stole $1 million, took kickbacks from developers, and set up a slush fund to hide bad loans from examiners.	Sentenced to six years.
Edward Jolly Jr.	Assistant regional vice president and consumer loan manager at First Federal Savings and Loan (South Carolina); stole $4.5 million through fictitious loan applications and lost all the money playing the futures market.	Sentenced to two years and nine months.
Ted Musacchio	President of Columbus Marin S&L (California); stole $9.3 million and lied about it on federal disclosure forms.	Sentenced January 1990 to five years of probation and immediate restitution of $9.3 million, but had only paid $1,000 by the time of his death in 1993.
Gina Loren	Investment manager; together with stockbroker Daniel Burkhart and attorney Charles Lusin, "conned California thrifts, individuals, and an order of nuns out of $4.1 million."	Sentenced to six years; Lusin sentenced to five years, and Burkhart to four years.

Source: Stephen Pizzo and Paul Muolo, "Take the Money and Run: A Rogues Gallery of Some Lucky S&L Thieves," *The New York Times Magazine,* May 9, 1993; Alan Fomhan, "S&L Felons," *Fortune,* November 5, 1990, p. 93; "Former Columbus President Guilty of Misapplying Funds," *American Banker,* December 26, 1989; and "Why S&L Crooks Have Failed to Pay Millions of Dollars in Court-Ordered Restitution: Nineteen Case Studies," in *A Staff Report for the Subcommittee on Financial Institutions Supervision, Regulation and Insurance of the Committee on Banking, Finance and Urban Affairs, House of Representatives,* 102nd Congress, 2nd session, April (Washington, D.C.: U.S. Government Printing Office, 1992).

the prisoners had. Maybe they were shocked—but not outraged. Neither were they outraged when two grand juries refused to indict any of the attackers, nor when the mastermind of the attack, New York Governor Nelson Rockefeller, was named vice president of the United States three years after the uprising and massacre.[174]

They were not outraged because the faces they saw on the TV screens fit and confirmed their beliefs about who is a deadly threat to American society—and a deadly threat must be met with deadly force. How did those men get to Attica? How did Americans get their beliefs about who is a dangerous person? These questions are interwoven. People get their notions about who is a criminal at least in part from the occasional television or newspaper picture of who is inside our prisons. The individuals they see there have been put in prison because people believe certain kinds of individuals are dangerous and should be locked up.

I have argued in this chapter that this is not a simple process of selecting the dangerous and the criminal from among the peace-loving and the law-abiding. It is also a process of *weeding out the wealthy* at every stage, so that the final picture—a picture like the one that appeared on the TV screen on September 9, 1971—is not a true reflection of the real dangers in our society but a distorted image, the kind reflected in a carnival mirror.

It is not my view that the inmates in Attica were innocent of the crimes that sent them there. I assume they and and most of the individuals in prisons in America are probably guilty of the crime for which they were sentenced, and maybe more. My point is that people who are equally or more dangerous, equally or more criminal, are not there; that the criminal justice system works systematically not to punish and confine the dangerous and the criminal, *but to punish and confine the poor who are dangerous and criminal.*

It is successful at all levels. In 1973, there were 204,211 individuals in state and federal prisons, or 96 prisoners for every 100,000 individuals (of all ages) in the general population. By 1979, state and federal inmates numbered 301,470, or 133 per 100,000 Americans. By 2004, there were a total of 1,496,629 persons in state and federal prisons, or 138 per 100,000 Americans. Add in the 713,990 in local jails, and the result is a staggering 724 for every 100,000 in the population. One in 138 U.S. residents (of all ages and both sexes) was behind bars in 2004. However, of the 2,210,619 inmates in federal and state prisons and in jails, some 2,011,689 are men, virtually all above the age of 18. Because the adult male population in the United States is about 106 million, *this means that roughly one out of every 53 American adult men is behind bars.*[175] This enormous number of prisoners is, of course, predominantly from the bottom of society.

Of the estimated 1.2 million people in state prisons in 1998, one-third were not employed at all (full- or part-time) prior to their arrests. Nearly half were without full-time employment prior to arrest. These statistics are comparable to those in 1986, when 31 percent of state inmates had no prearrest employment at all, and 43 percent had no full-time prearrest employment.[176] Among jail inmates in 2002, 29 percent were not employed prior to arrest—15 percent were looking for work, and 14 percent were not. Approximately 45 percent of jail inmates reported prearrest incomes below $7,200 a year.[177]

To get an idea of what part of society is in prison, we should compare these figures with comparable figures for the general population. Because more than 90 percent of inmates are male, we can look at employment and income figures for males in the general population.

In 2002, 5.9 percent of males, 16 years old and above, in the labor force were unemployed and looking for work. That same year, 19.6 percent of jail inmates were unemployed (and looking for work) in the year prior to their arrest. Prisoners were unemployed at a rate more than three times that of their counterparts in the general population.[178] In 2002, the median income for males, 15 years old and above, with any income at all, was $29,238.[179] This means that half of these males in the general population with any income at all were earning this amount or less. Compare this to jail inmates, about half of whom earned $12,000 a year or less in the year before they were arrested. Since this figure includes only jail inmates with income, and 20 percent did not have income before they were arrested, we can say that fully 70 percent of inmates earned less than half the median income for American males with income![180]

Our prisoners are not a cross-section of America. They are considerably poorer and considerably less likely to be employed than the rest of Americans. Moreover, they are also less educated, which is to say less in possession of the means to improve their sorry situations. As of 1999, 41 percent of U.S. prison inmates had not graduated from high school, compared to 20 percent of the U.S. adult population.[181] In 2002, 44 percent of jail inmates were not high school graduates compared with 16 percent of the general population.[182]

The criminal justice system is sometimes thought of as a kind of sieve in which the innocent are progressively sifted out from the guilty, who end up behind bars. I have tried to show that the sieve works another way as well. It sifts the affluent out from the poor, so it is not merely the guilty who end up behind bars, but the *guilty poor.*

With this I think I have proven the hypotheses set forth in Chapter 2, in the section titled "Criminal Justice as Creative Art." The criminal justice system does not simply weed the peace-loving from the dangerous, the law-abiding from the criminal. At every stage, starting with the very definitions of crime and progressing through the stages of investigation, arrest, charging, conviction, and sentencing, the system *weeds out the wealthy.* It refuses to define as "crimes" or as serious crimes the dangerous and predatory acts of the well-to-do—acts that, as we have seen, result in the loss of thousands of lives and billions of dollars. Instead, the system focuses its attention on those crimes likely to be committed by members of the lower classes. Thus, it is no surprise to find that so many of the people behind bars are from the lower classes. The people we see in our jails and prisons are no doubt dangerous to society, but they are not *the danger* to society, not *the gravest danger* to society. Individuals who pose equal or greater threats to our well-being walk the streets with impunity.

In Chapter 1, I argued that the society fails to institute policies that have a good chance of reducing crime. In the present chapter and the previous one, I have argued that the criminal justice system works to make crime appear to be the monopoly of the poor by restricting the label "crime" to the dangerous acts of the poor and rarely applying it to the dangerous acts of the well off (previous chapter), and by more actively pursuing and prosecuting the poor rather than the well off for the acts that are labeled crime (present chapter). *The joint effect of all these phenomena is to maintain a real threat of crime that the vast majority of Americans believes is a threat from the poor.* The criminal justice system is a carnival mirror that throws back a distorted image of the dangers that lurk in our midst—and conveys the impression that those dangers are the work of the poor. In Chapter 4, I suggest who benefits from this illusion and how.

SUMMARY

In this chapter I have mainly tried to document that, *even among those dangerous acts that our criminal justice system labels as crimes,* the system works to make it more likely that those who end up in jail or prison will be from the bottom of society. This works in two broad ways:

1. *For the same crime,* the system is more likely to investigate and detect, arrest and charge, convict and sentence, and sentence to prison (and for a longer time) a lower-class individual than a middle- or upper-class individual. To support this, we reviewed a large number of studies performed over a long period of time comparing the treatment of high- and low-socioeconomic status offenders and of white and nonwhite offenders, from arrest through sentencing for the same crimes.
2. *Between crimes that are characteristically committed by poor people (street crimes) and those characteristically committed by the well-off (white-collar and corporate crimes),* the system treats the former much more harshly than the latter, even when the crimes of the well-off take far more money from the public or cause far more death and injury than the crimes of the poor. To support this, we compared the sentences meted out for robbery with those for embezzlement, grand theft, and Medicaid-provider fraud, and we looked at the treatment of those responsible for death and destruction in the workplace as well as those responsible for the savings and loan scandal and the recent financial cheating at Enron and other major corporations.

STUDY QUESTIONS

1. Who is in our jails and prisons? How do the people behind bars in America compare with the general population in employment, wealth, and level of education?

2. What is meant by "white-collar crime"? How costly is it compared with the crimes on the FBI's Index?

3. What factors make it likelier that a poor person who commits a crime such as shoplifting or nonaggravated assault will be arrested than a middle-class person who commits the same crime?

4. What factors make it likelier that a middle- or upper-class person charged with a crime will be acquitted than a lower-class person charged with the same crime?

5. Are the people responsible for white-collar crime, including crimes that result in serious injury, more or less blameworthy than muggers? Do we punish white-collar criminals justly?

6. Is the criminal justice system racist? What evidence would establish or refute your view?

7. If killers of whites are more likely to be sentenced to death than killers of blacks, what should we do? Should we abolish the death penalty? Do you agree with the Supreme Court's decision in *McCleskey v. Kemp?* Why?

A companion website to this book, with a chapter outline and summary, links to additional information, and Internet-based exercises, is available at "Rich Get Richer," *www.paulsjusticepage.com.*

ADDITIONAL READINGS

Anderson, David. *Crime and the Politics of Hysteria: How the Willie Horton Story Changed American Justice.* New York: Times Books, 1995.

Barak, Gregg, Jeanne Flavin, and Paul Leighton. *Crime (In)Equality and Justice: Understanding Class, Race and Gender.* Lanham, Md.: Rowman & Littlefield, 2006.

Clinard, Marshall. *Corporate Corruption: The Abuse of Power.* New York: Praeger, 1990.

Day, Kathleen. *S & L Hell: The People and the Politics behind the $1 Trillion Savings and Loan Scandal.* New York: Norton, 1993.

Lusane, Clarence. *Pipe Dream Blues: Racism and the War on Drugs.* Boston: South End Press, 1991.

McLean, Bethany, and Peter Elkind. *The Smartest Guys in the Room: The Amazing Rise and Scandalous Fall of Enron.* New York: Portfolio/Penguin, 2004.

Miller, Jerome. *Search and Destroy: African-American Males in the Criminal Justice System.* New York: Cambridge University Press, 1996.

Pearce, Frank, and Lauren Snider. *Corporate Crime.* Toronto: University of Toronto Press, 1995.

Pizzo, Stephen, et al. *Inside Job: The Looting of America's Savings and Loans.* New York: McGraw-Hill, 1989.

Reiman, Jeffrey, and Paul Leighton, *A Tale of Two Criminals: We're Tougher on Corporate Criminals, but They Still Don't Get What They Deserve.* Boston: Allyn & Bacon, 2005. *www.paulsjusticepage.com.*

Simon, David. *Elite Deviance*, 8th ed. Boston: Allyn & Bacon, 2005.

Timmer, Doug, and Stanley Eitzen. *Crimes in the Streets and Crimes in the Suites*. Boston: Allyn & Bacon, 1989.

NOTES

1. *Challenge*, p. 44.

2. Ronald Goldfarb, "Prisons: The National Poorhouse," *New Republic*, November 1, 1969, pp. 15–17.

3. Philip A. Hart, "Swindling and Knavery, Inc.," *Playboy*, August 1972, p. 158.

4. Compare the statement, written more than half a century ago, by Professor Edwin H. Sutherland, one of the major luminaries of twentieth-century criminology:

> *First, the administrative processes are more favorable to persons in economic comfort than to those in poverty, so that if two persons on different economic levels are equally guilty of the same offense, the one on the lower level is more likely to be arrested, convicted, and committed to an institution. Second, the laws are written, administered, and implemented primarily with reference to the types of crimes committed by people of lower economic levels.*

E. H. Sutherland, *Principles of Criminology* (Philadelphia: Lippincott, 1939), p. 179.

5. For example, in 1991, when blacks made up 12 percent of the national population, they accounted for 46 percent of the U.S. state prison population. In 1996, blacks made up 41 percent of U.S. jail inmates. BJS, *Survey of State Prison Inmates, 1991*, p. 3; and BJS, *Profile of Jail Inmates 1996*, p. 3, Table 3, NCJ 164620.

6. Edwin H. Sutherland and Donald R. Cressey, *Criminology*, 9th ed. (Philadelphia: Lippincott, 1974), p. 133. The following studies are cited in support of this point (p. 133 n. 4): Edwin M. Lemert and Judy Roseberg, "The Administration of Justice to Minority Groups in Los Angeles County," *University of California Publications in Culture and Society* 2, no. 1 (1948): pp. 1–28; Thorsten Sellin, "Race Prejudice in the Administration of Justice," *American Journal of Sociology* 41 (September 1935): pp. 212–217; Sidney Alexrad, "Negro and White Male Institutionalized Delinquents," *American Journal of Sociology* 57 (May 1952): pp. 569–74; Marvin E. Wolfgang, Arlene Kelly, and Hans C. Nolde, "Comparisons of the Executed and the Commuted among Admissions to Death Row," *Journal of Criminal Law, Criminology, and Police Science* 53 (September 1962): pp. 301–11; Nathan Goldman, *The Differential Selection of Juvenile Offenders for Court Appearance* (New York: National Council on Crime and Delinquency, 1963); Irving Piliavin and Scott Briar, "Police Encounters with Juveniles," *American Journal of Sociology* 70 (September 1964): pp. 206–14; and Robert M. Terry, "The Screening of Juvenile Offenders," *Journal of Criminal Law, Criminology, and Police Science* 58 (June 1967): pp. 173–81. See also Ramsey Clark, *Crime in America* (New York: Simon & Schuster, 1970), p. 51, which states, "Negroes are arrested more frequently and on less evidence than whites and are more often victims of mass or sweep arrests"; and Donald Taft, *Criminology*, 3rd ed. (New York: Macmillan, 1956), p. 134:

> *Negroes are more likely to be suspected of crime than are whites. They are also more likely to be arrested. If the perpetrator of a crime is known to be a Negro the police may arrest all Negroes who were near the scene—a procedure they would rarely dare to follow with whites. After arrest Negroes are less likely to secure bail, and so are more liable to be counted in jail statistics. They are more liable than whites to be indicted and less likely to have their case nol prossed* [to have prosecution dropped by entering a nolle prosequi in court records] *or otherwise dismissed. If tried, Negroes are more likely to be convicted. If convicted they are less likely to be given probation. For this reason they are more likely to be included in the count of prisoners. Negroes are also more likely than whites to be kept in prison for the full terms of their commitments and correspondingly less likely to be paroled.*

7. William Wilbanks, *The Myth of a Racist Criminal Justice System* (Monterey, Calif.: Brooks/Cole, 1987).

8. Ibid., pp. 64–65.

9. *Sourcebook–2003*, p. 204, Table 3.29; and *UCR–2003*, p. 268.

10. For an overview of this double distortion, see Thomas J. Dolan, "The Case for Double Jeopardy: Black and Poor," *International Journal of Criminology and Penology* 1 (1973): pp. 129–50.

11. Cassia C. Spohn, "Thirty Years of Sentencing Reform: The Quest for a Racially Neutral Sentencing Process," in NIJ, *Criminal Justice 2000, vol. 3: Policies, Processes, and Decisions of the Criminal Justice System*, pp. 427–28.

12. Ibid., pp. 435, 466.

13. Marvin D. Free Jr., "Racial Bias and the American Criminal Justice System: Race and Presentencing Revisited," *Critical Criminology* 10 (2001): p. 198. See also Spohn, "Thirty Years of Sentencing Reform," pp. 467–68.

14. Spohn, "Thirty Years of Sentencing Reform," p. 480.

15. Free, "Racial Bias and the American Criminal Justice System," pp. 197–98.

16. Marjorie S. Zatz, "The Convergence of Ethnicity, Gender, and Class on Court Decision-Making: Looking toward the 21st Century," in NIJ, *Criminal Justice 2000, vol. 3: Policies, Processes, and Decisions of the Criminal Justice System*, NCJ 182410, p. 515.

17. See, for example, Loic Wacquant, "Deadly Symbiosis: When Ghetto and Prison Meet and Mesh," in *Mass Imprisonment in the United States: Social Causes and Consequences*, ed. David Garland (London: Sage, 2001), pp. 82–120.

18. Carmen DeNavas-Walt, Bernadette Proctor, and Cheryl Hill Lee, U.S. Census Bureau, *Current Population Reports*, P60-229, *Income, Poverty & Health Insurance Coverage in the United States: 2004* (Washington, D.C.: U.S. Government Printing Office, 2005), p. 10.

19. Arthur Kennickell, "A Rolling Tide: Changes in the Distribution of Wealth in the U.S., 1989-2001," Federal Reserve Board, (2003), p. 34, *www.federalreserve.gov/pubs/oss/oss2/scindex.html.*

20. Ana Aizcorbe, Arthur Kennickell and Kevin Moore, "Recebt Changes in U.S. Family Finances" *Federal Reserve Bulletin* 89 (2003): pp. 13 and 18.

21. *StatAbst—2004–5*, p. 372, Table 571; and *StatAbst–2001*, p. 368, Table 569, and p. 371, Table 574.

22. Zatz, "The Convergence of Ethnicity, Gender, and Class on Court Decision-Making," p. 511.

23. Michael Tonry, "Racial Politics, Racial Disparities, and the War on Crime," *Crime & Delinquency* 40, no. 4 (October 1994): pp. 483, 485–86.

24. *Sourcebook—1981*, p. 463.

25. *StatAbst—1988*, p. 175, Table 304.

26. BJS, *Profile of Inmates in the United States and in England and Wales, 1991,* October 1994, NCJ-145863, p. 13.

27. Theodore Chiricos and William Bales, "Unemployment and Punishment: An Empirical Assessment," *Criminology* 29, no. 4 (1991): p. 718.

28. "An offender's socioeconomic status . . . did not impact sentence length for any of the property offenses." Stewart J. D'Alessio and Lisa Stolzenberg, "Socioeconomic Status and the Sentencing of the Traditional Offender," *Journal of Criminal Justice* 21 (1993): p. 73. The same study did find that lower-socioeconomic status offenders received harsher sentences for violent and moral-order crimes. Another study that finds no greater likelihood of incarceration based on socioeconomic status is Michael Benson and Esteban Walker, "Sentencing the White-Collar Offender," *American Sociological Review* 53 (April 1988): pp. 294–302. And yet another found higher-status offenders to be more likely to be incarcerated: David Weisburd, Elin Waring, and Stanton Wheeler, "Class, Status, and the Punishment of White Collar Criminals," *Law and Social Inquiry* 15 (1990): pp. 223–41. These last two studies are limited to offenders convicted of white-collar crimes, and so they deal with a sample that has already been subject to whatever discrimination exists in the arrest, charging, and conviction of white-collar offenders.

29. Isidore Silver, "Introduction," in President's Crime Commission, *The Challenge of Crime in a Free Society* (New York: Avon, 1968), p. 31.

30. This is the conclusion of Austin L. Porterfield, *Youth in Trouble* (Fort Worth; Tex.: Leo Potishman Foundation, 1946); Fred J. Murphy, M. Shirley, and H. L. Witmer, "The Incidence of Hidden Delinquency," *American Journal of Orthopsychiatry* 16 (October 1946): pp. 686–96; James F. Short Jr., "A Report on the Incidence of Criminal Behavior, Arrests, and Convictions in Selected Groups," in *Proceedings of the Pacific Sociological Society, 1954,* pp. 110–18, and in *Research Studies of the State College of Washington,* vol. 22, no. 2 (Pullman: State College of Washington, 1954); F. Ivan Nye, James F. Short Jr., and Virgil J. Olson, "Socioeconomic Status and Delinquent Behavior," *American Journal of Sociology* 63 (January 1958): pp. 381–89; Maynard L. Erickson and Lamar T. Empey, "Class Position, Peers and Delinquency," *Sociology and Social Research* 49 (April 1965): pp. 268–82; William J. Chambliss and Richard H. Nagasawa, "On the Validity of Official Statistics; A Comparative Study of White, Black, and Japanese High-School Boys," *Journal of Research in Crime and Delinquency* 6 (January 1969): pp. 71–77; Eugene Doleschal, "Hidden Crime," *Crime and Delinquency Literature* 2, no. 5 (October 1970): pp. 546–72; Nanci Koser Wilson, *Risk Ratios in Juvenile Delinquency* (Ann Arbor, Mich.: University Microfilms, 1972); and Maynard L. Erikson, "Group Violations, Socioeconomic Status, and Official Delinquency," *Social Forces* 52, no. 1 (September 1973): pp. 41–52.

31. Charles R. Tittle and Robert F. Meier, "Specifying the SES/Delinquency Relationship," *Criminology* 28, no. 2 (1990): p. 292.

32. R. Gregory Dunaway, Francis Cullen, Velmer Burton Jr., and David Evans, "The Myth of Social Class and Crime Revisited: An Examination of Adult and Class Criminality," *Criminology* 38, no. 2 (2002): p. 600.

33. This is the conclusion of Martin Gold, "Undetected Delinquent Behavior," *Journal of Research in Crime and Delinquency* 3, no. 1 (1966): pp. 27–46; and of Sutherland and Cressey, *Criminology,* pp. 137, 220.

34. Cf. Larry Karacki and Jackson Toby, "The Uncommitted Adolescent: Candidate for Gang Socialization," *Sociological Inquiry* 32 (1962): pp. 203–15; William R. Arnold, "Continuities in Research: Scaling Delinquent Behavior," *Social Problems* 13, no. 1 (1965): pp. 59–66; Harwin L. Voss, "Socio-economic Status and Reported Delinquent Behavior," *Social Problems,* 13, no. 3 (1966): pp. 314–24; LaMar Empey and Maynard L. Erikson, "Hidden Delinquency and Social Status," *Social Forces* 44, no. 4 (1966): pp. 546–54; Fred J. Shanley, "Middle-Class Delinquency as a Social Problem," *Sociology and Social Research* 51 (1967): pp. 185–98; and Jay R. Williams and Martin Gold, "From Delinquent Behavior to Official Delinquency," *Social Problems* 20, no. 2 (1972): pp. 209–29.

35. Empey and Erikson, "Hidden Delinquency and Social Status," pp. 549, 551. Nye, Short, and Olson also found destruction of property to be committed most frequently by upper-class boys and girls; see their "Socioeconomic Status and Delinquent Behavior," p. 385.

36. Gold, "Undetected Delinquent Behavior," p. 37.

37. Ibid., p. 44.

38. Comparing socioeconomic status categories, "scant evidence is found that would support the contention that group delinquency is more characteristic of the lower-status levels than other socioeconomic status levels. In fact, only arrests seem to be more characteristic of the low-status category than the other categories." Erikson, "Group Violations, Socioeconomic Status and Official Delinquency," p. 15.

39. Gold, "Undetected Delinquent Behavior," p. 28 (emphasis added).

40. Ibid., p. 38.

41. Terence P. Thornberry, "Race, Socioeconomic Status and Sentencing in the Juvenile Justice System," *Journal of Criminal Law and Criminology* 64, no. 1 (1973): pp. 90–98.

42. Robert Sampson, "Effects of Socioeconomic Context on Official Reaction to Juvenile Delinquency," *American Sociological Review* 51 (December 1986): pp. 876–85; and Belinda R. McCarthy, "Social Structure, Crime, and Social Control: An Examination of Factors Influencing Rates and Probabilities of Arrest," *Journal of Criminal Justice* 19, (1991): pp. 19–29.

43. Note, "Developments in the Law: Race and the Criminal Process," *Harvard Law Review* 101 (1988): p. 1496.

44. Jerome Miller, *Search and Destroy: African-American Males in the Criminal Justice System* (New York: Cambridge University Press, 1996), p. 76. The study reported is M. Wordes, T. Bynum, and C. Corley, "Locking Up Youth: The Impact of Race on Detention Decisions," *Journal of Research in Crime and Delinquency* 31, no. 2 (May 1994).

45. Wordes, Bynum, and Corley, "Locking Up Youth," p. 164; quoted in Miller, *Search and Destroy*, pp. 76–77.

46. Miller, *Search and Destroy*, p. 72. The study reported is Kimberly L. Kempf, *The Role of Race in Juvenile Justice Processing in Pennsylvania*, Study Grant #89-90/J/01/3615, Pennsylvania Commission on Crime and Delinquency, August 1992.

47. Free, "Racial Bias and the American Criminal Justice System," p. 209.

48. Cited in David A. Harris, "The Stories, the Statistics, and the Law: Why 'Driving while Black' Matters," *Minnesota Law Review* 84 (1999): pp. 265–326, *http://academic.udayton.edu/race/03/justice/dwb03/htm*.

49. Bureau of Justice Statistics, "Contacts between Police and the Public: Findings from the 2002 National Survey," April 2005, NCJ 207845, p. 9.

50. Eric Lichtblau, "Profiling Report Leads to a Demotion," *The New York Times*, August 24, 2005, *www.nytimes.com/2005/08/24/politics/24profiling.html*.

51. Michael Tonry, "Racial Politics, Racial Disparities, and the War on Crime," *Crime & Delinquency* 40, no. 4 (October 1994): p. 483.

52. Fox Butterfield, "More Blacks in Their 20's Have Trouble with the Law," *The New York Times*, October 5, 1995, p. A8.

53. David Huizinga and Delbert Elliott, "Juvenile Offenders: Prevalence, Offender Incidence and Arrest Rates by Race" (paper presented at Meeting on Race and the Incarceration of Juveniles, Racine, Wisconsin, December 1986); and University of Colorado, Boulder, Institute of Behavioral Science, *National Youth Survey*; reported in Miller, *Search and Destroy*, p. 73.

54. James Fyfe, "Blind Justice: Police Shootings in Memphis," *Journal of Criminal Law and Criminology* 73 (1982): p. 719.

55. See, for example, D. Chapman, "The Stereotype of the Criminal and the Social Consequences," *International Journal of Criminology and Penology* 1 (1973): p. 24.

56. This view is widely held, although the degree to which it functions as a self-fulfilling prophecy is less widely recognized. Versions of this view can be seen in *Challenge*, p. 79; Jerome Skolnick, *Justice without Trial* (New York: Wiley, 1966), pp. 45–48, 217–18; and Jessica Mitford, *Kind and Usual Punishment*, p. 53. Piliavin and Briar write in "Police Encounters with Juveniles,"

> *Compared to other youths, Negroes and boys whose appearance matched the delinquent stereotype were more frequently stopped and interrogated by patrolmen—often even in the absence of evidence that an offense had been committed—[and] usually were given more severe dispositions for the same violations. Our data suggest, however, that these selective apprehension and disposition practices resulted not only from the intrusion of long-held prejudices of individual police officers but also from certain job-related experiences of law-enforcement personnel. First, the tendency of police to give more severe dispositions to Negroes and to youths whose appearance correspond to that which police associated with delinquents partly reflected the fact, observed in this study, that these youths also were much more likely than were other types of boys to exhibit the sort of recalcitrant demeanor which police construed as a sign of the confirmed delinquent. Further, officers assumed, partly on the basis of departmental statistics, that Negroes and juveniles who "look tough" (e.g., who wear chinos, leather jackets, boots, etc.) commit crimes more frequently than do other types of youths. (p. 212)*

Cf. Albert Reiss, *The Police and the Public* (New Haven, Conn.: Yale University Press, 1971). Reiss attributes the differences to the differences in the actions of complainants.

57. Richard J. Lundman, for example, found higher arrest rates to be associated with "offender powerlessness." Richard J. Lundman, "Routine Police Arrest Practices: A Commonwealth Perspective," *Social Problems* 22, no. 1 (October 1974): pp. 127–41.

58. William Bales, "Race and Class Effects on Criminal Justice Prosecution and Punishment Decisions" (Ph.D. diss., Florida State University, Tallahassee, 1987).

59. Note, "Developments in the Law: Race and the Criminal Process," *Harvard Law Review* 101 (1988): p. 1520.

60. Cassia Spohn, John Gruhl, and Susan Welch, "The Impact of the Ethnicity and Gender of Defendants on the Decision to Reject or Dismiss Felony Charges," *Criminology* 25 (1987): pp. 175, 180, 185.

61. "Stealing $200 Billion the Respectable Way," *U.S. News & World Report*, May 20, 1985, p. 83.

62. Marshall B. Clinard, *Corporate Corruption: The Abuse of Corporate Power* (New York: Praeger, 1990), p. 15.

63. August Bequai, "High-Tech Security and the Failings of President Clinton's Commission on Critical Infrastructure Protection," *Computers and Security* 17 (1998): pp. 19–21.

64. Michael Levi, *Regulating Fraud: White-Collar Crime and the Criminal Process* (London: Tavistock, 1987), p. 33; and *StatAbst–2004–5*, p. 425, Table 641.

65. Association of Certified Fraud Examiners, "2004 Report to the Nation" p. 8, *www.acfe.com/documents/2004RttN.pdf*.

66. National White Collar Crime Center, "National Public Survey on White Collar Crime," *www.nw3c.org/surveyresults.htm*.

67. North American Securities Administrators Administration, *The NASAA Survey of Fraud and Abuse in the Financial Planning Industry: Report to the U.S. Senate Subcommittee on Consumer Affairs, Committee on Banking, Housing and Urban Affairs,* July (Washington, D.C.: NASAA, 1988), pp. 1–2.

68. Chamber of Commerce of the United States, *A Handbook on White Collar Crime* (Washington, D.C.: Chamber of Commerce of the United States, 1974), p. 6. Copyright © 1974 by the Chamber of Commerce of the United States. Table reprinted by permission of the Chamber of Commerce of the United States.

69. Sandeep Junnarkar, "Online Banks: Prime Targets for Attacks," *ZDNet News*, April 30, 2002, *http://zdnet.com.com/2100- 1106-895079.html*.

70. National White Collar Crime Center, "Internet Fraud" (2002), *www.nw3c.org/research_topics.html*.

71. U.S. Department of Justice, *Report of the Department of Justice Task Force on Intellectual Property* (Washington, D.C.: U.S. Department of Justice, 2004), p. 8.

72. Paul Festa and Joe Wilcox, "Experts Estimate Damages in the Billions for Bug," Cnet.com, May 5, 2000, *http://news.com.com/2100-1001-240112.html*; and National White Collar Crime Center, "'True' Computer Crime" (2003), *www.nw3c.org/research_topics.html*.

73. National White Collar Crime Center, "Telemarketing Fraud," White Collar Crime Topic Papers, *www.nw3c.org/research_topics.html*.

74. It is essential to be conservative in estimating costs of various white-collar crimes due to the possibility of overlap in the estimates. For example, telemarketing fraud might count some credit card or computer fraud, and vice versa. Nonetheless, working with such partial numbers as we have, we can be quite confident that we are far from overestimating the actual costs—indeed.

75. Peter Grabosky, Russell Smith, and Gillian Dempsey, *Electronic Theft: Unlawful Acquisition in Cyberspace* (Cambridge: Cambridge University Press, 2001), p. 143.

76. Harrison Rainies, "The State of Greed," *U.S. News & World Report*, June 17, 1996, p. 64.

77. Margaret Webb Pressler, "Signs of Fraud Go beyond Signature: Credit Card Companies Use Artificial Intelligence to Thwart Thieves," *The Washington Post*, July 21, 2002, p. H5.

78. National White Collar Crime Center, "Credit Card Fraud" (2003), *www.nw3c.org/research_topics.html*.

79. National White Collar Crime Center, "Check Fraud," White Collar Crime Topic Papers, *www.nw3c.org/topics_intro.htm.*

80. Robert McGough and Elicia Brown, "Thieves at Work," *Financial World* 159 (December 11, 1990): p. 18.

81. National White Collar Crime Center, "Embezzlement/Employee Theft" (2002), *www.nw3c.org/research_topics.html*; and Food Marketing Institute, "Organized Retail Theft," *www.fmi.org/loss/ORT/.*

82. Coalition against Insurance Fraud, "Insurance Fraud: The Hidden Tax," *www. insurancefraud.org.*

83. "It has been estimated by the General Accounting Office that fraud accounts for up to 10 percent of total health care expenditures"—which amounts to $100 billion. See National White Collar Crime Center, "Health Care Fraud," White Collar Crime Topic Papers, *www. nw3c.org/topics_intro.htm.*

84. National White Collar Crime Center, "Insurance Fraud" (2002), *www.nw3c.org/ research_topics.html*; and Nicholas Stein, "Inside Operation," *Fortune,* December 8, 2003, p. 130.

85. FBI Economic Crimes Unit, "Securities/Commodities Fraud," *http://fbi.gov/hq/cid/fc/ ec/about/about_scf.htm.*

86. "Numbers Game: A High-Tech Arrest Gives Unusual Glimpse of Cell-Phone Fraud," *The Wall Street Journal,* April 29, 1996, p. A16.

87. *StatAbst—2004–5,* p. 7, Table 2 (population), CPI for 1974 = 49.3 and 2003 = 184; *StatAbst—1995,* p. 492, Table 761; and *StatAbst—2004–5,* p. 463, Table 698.

88. Sutherland and Cressey, *Criminology,* p. 41 (emphasis added).

89. Clinard, *Corporate Corruption,* p. 15.

90. David Weisburd, Ellen F. Chayet, and Elin J. Waring, "White-Collar Crime and Criminal Careers: Some Preliminary Findings," *Crime & Delinquency* 36, no. 3 (July 1990): p. 352.

91. Clinard, *Corporate Corruption,* p. 15.

92. Susan Shapiro, "The Road Not Taken: The Elusive Path to Criminal Prosecution for White-Collar Offenders," *Law and Society Review* 19, no. 2 (1985): p. 182.

93. Russell Mokhiber, "Underworld, U.S.A.," *In These Times,* April 1, 1996, p. 15.

94. *UCR–2003,* p. 270, Table 29.

95. See, for example, Theodore G. Chiricos, Philip D. Jackson, and Gordon P. Waldo, "Inequality in the Imposition of a Criminal Label," *Social Problems* 19, no. 4 (Spring 1972): pp. 553–72.

96. BJS, *Prison and Jail Inmates Midyear 2004,* April 2005, NCJ 208801, p. 8, Tables 9 and 10.

97. See, for example, C. E. Ares, A. Rankin, and J. H. Sturz, "The Manhattan Bail Project: An Interim Report on the Use of Pre-trial Parole," *NYU Law Review* 38 (1963): p. 67; C. Foote, "Compelling Appearances in Court-Administration of Bail in Philadelphia," *University of Pennsylvania Law Review* 102 (1954): pp. 1031–79; and C. Foote, "A Study of the Administration of Bail in New York City," *University of Pennsylvania Law Review* 106 (1958): p. 693. For statistics on persons held in jail awaiting trial, see U.S. Bureau of the Census, *The Social and Economic Status of the Black Population in the U.S., 1974* (Washington, D.C.: U.S. Government Printing Office, 1975), p. 171; and USLEAA, *Survey of Inmates in Local Jails 1972: Advance Report* (Washington, D.C.: U.S. Government Printing Office, 1974), pp. 5, 8.

98. Chiricos and Bales, "Unemployment and Punishment," p. 712.

99. Free, "Racial Bias and the American Criminal Justice System," p. 203.

100. Blumberg, *Criminal Justice,* pp. 28–29; *Challenge,* p. 134; and Donald J. Newman, *Conviction: The Determination of Guilt or Innocence without Trial* (Boston: Little, Brown, 1966), p. 3.

101. A good summary of these developments can be found in Joel Jay Finer, "Ineffective Assistance of Counsel," *Cornell Law Review* 58, no. 6 (July 1973): pp. 1077–120.

102. Robert Johnson, *Condemned to Die: Life under Sentence of Death* (New York: Elsevier, 1981), p. 138.

103. Stephen Gettinger, *Sentenced to Die: The People, the Crimes, and the Controversy* (New York: Macmillan, 1979), p. 261.

104. Linda Williams, "Death-Row Inmates Often Lack Help for Appeals, but Few Lawyers Want to Do Distasteful Work," *The Wall Street Journal,* August 27, 1987, p. 48.

105. Richard Lacayo, "You Don't Always Get Perry Mason," *Time,* June 1, 1992, pp. 38–39.

106. National Association of Criminal Defense Attorneys, "Getting What They Pay For: The Fallacy of Quality Indigent Defense," *Indigent Defense* (May–June 2004): *www.nacdl.org/ public.nsf/DefenseUpdates/Louisiana029.*

107. Mark Gimein, "You Bought: They Sold," *Fortune,* September 2, 2002, pp. 64–65.

108. Allan Sloan, "Free Lessons on Corporate Hubris, Courtesy of Enron," *Washington Post,* December 4, 2001, p. E3; see also Gimein, "You Bought: They Sold," passim.

109. For a list of financial scandals matched to amounts contributed to the political parties by the suspect companies, go to Citizen Work, "Crookbook," *http://citizenworks.org/enron.*

110. Clifton Leaf, "White-Collar Criminals: Enough Is Enough," *Fortune Magazine,* March 2, 2002, p. 64.

111. David Hilzenrath, "Two Failures with a Familiar Ring: Arthur Andersen Audited Foundation, S&L That Collapsed" *The Washington Post,* December 6, 2001, p. A21.

112. Julie Creswell, "Banks on the Hot Seat," *Fortune,* September 2, 2002, p. 80.

113. In one recent case, the National Association of Securities Dealers fined the Salomon Smith Barney Unit of Citigroup $5 million for "materially misleading research reports" on Winstar Communications. Analysts kept a $50 target price and a "buy" rating on the company until the price of a share hit $0.14. An article for TheStreet.com notes Salomon made $24 million in fees from Winstar, and Citigroup CEO Sandy Weill made $70 million a year for the last three years, plus has holdings in Citigroup worth about $960 million. "Meanwhile, the NASD trumpets that this settlement is the third largest in NASD's history. Well, if we were the NASD and we wanted to strike fear in the hearts of brokerage firms, we would keep that little statistic a secret." George Mannes, "The Five Dumbest Things on Wall Street This Week," TheStreet.com, September 27, 2002, *www.thestreet.com/markets/dumbest/ 10044586.html.*

114. David Teather, "The Whores of Wall Street," *Guardian,* October 2, 2002, *www.guardian. co.uk/usa/story/0,12271,802926,00.html.*

115. Anitha Reddy, "$100 Million More for SEC Not Enough, Ex-Officials Say," *The Washington Post,* July 10, 2002, p. E1.

116. Stephen Pearlstein, "Measures Not Likely to End Abuses," *The Washington Post,* July 10, 2002, p. A1.

117. The particulars of the legislations and some of its limitations are from Citizen Works, *http://citizenworks.org/enron/accountinglaw.php.*

118. Jonathan Weisman, "Some See Cracks IN Reform Law," *The Washington Post,* August 7, 2002, p. E1.

119. Jonathan Weisman, "Efforts to Restrict Retirement Funds Lose Steam: Indignation Wanes as Congress Considers Limits on Company Stock Holdings," *The Washington Post,* September 7, 2002, p. A1.

120. U.S. Sentencing Commission, "Sentencing Commission Stiffens Penalties for White Collar Criminals," press release, January 8, 2003, *www.ussc.gov/PRESS/rel010803.htm.*

121. Carrie Johnson, "Panel Boosts Penalties for White-Collar Offenses," *The Washington Post,* January 9, 2003, p. E1.

122. Kathleen Day, "SEC Staff Urges Limit to Reforms: Vote Planned Today on Auditing Rules," *The Washington Post,* January 22, 2003, E1.

123. Leaf, "White-Collar Criminals," p. 63.

124. Jeffrey Reiman and Paul Leighton, *A Tale of Two Criminals: We're Tougher on Corporate Criminals, but They Still Don't Get What They Deserve* (Boston: Allyn & Bacon, 2005), *www.paulsjusticepage.com.*

125. Those who wish to keep up to date on these cases and related issues can read the White Collar Crime Blog, written by two law professors: *http://lawprofessors.typepad.com/whitecollarcrime_blog/*.

126. Geraldine Szott Moohr, "An Enron Lesson," *Florida Law Review* 55, no. 4 (2003): p. 967.

127. "When Are the Savings and Loan Crooks Going to Jail?" Hearing before the Subcommittee on Financial Institutions Supervision, Regulation and Insurance of the Committee on Banking, Finance, and Urban Affairs, House of Representatives, 101st Congress, 2nd Session, June 28, 1990 (Washington, D.C.: U.S. Government Printing Office, 1990), pp. 1, 21.

128. "Penalties for White Collar Offenses: Are We Really Getting Tough on Crime?" Hearing of the Crime and Drugs Subcommittee of the Judiciary Committee, U.S. Senate, 107th Congress, 2nd session, July 11, 2002 (Washington, DC: U.S. Government Printing Office 2002).

129. Lesley Oelsner, "Wide Disparities Mark Sentences Here," *The New York Times,* September 27, 1972, p. 1.

130. Stewart J. D'Alessio and Lisa Stolzenberg, "Socioeconomic Status and the Sentencing of the Traditional Offender," *Journal of Criminal Justice* 21 (1993): pp. 71–74.

131. Barbara C. Nienstedt, Marjorie Zatz, and Thomas Epperlein, "Court Processing and Sentencing of Drinking Drivers," *Journal of Quantitative Criminology* 4, no. 1 (1988): pp. 39–59.

132. Theodore Chiricos and William Bales, "Unemployment and Punishment: An Empirical Assessment," *Criminology* 29, no. 4 (1991): pp. 701–24.

133. Belinda R. McCarthy, "A Micro-Level Analysis of Social Control: Intrastate Use of Jail and Prison Confinement," *Justice Quarterly* 7, no. 2 (June 1990): pp. 334–35.

134. Dean J. Champion, "Private Counsels and Public Defenders: A Look at Weak Cases, Prior Records, and Leniency in Plea Bargaining," *Journal of Criminal Justice* 17, no. 4 (1989): p. 143.

135. T. Miethe and C. Moore, "Socioeconomic Disparities under Determinate Sentencing Systems: A Comparison of Preguideline and Postguideline Practices in Minnesota," *Criminology* 23, no. 2 (1985): p. 358.

136. Robert Tillman and Henry Pontell, "Is Justice 'Collar-Blind'? Punishing Medicaid Provider Fraud," *Criminology* 30, no. 4 (1992): pp. 547–73, quote on p. 560.

137. James F. Nelson, "Hidden Disparities in Case Processing: New York State, 1985–1986," *Journal of Criminal Justice* 20 (1992): pp. 181–200.

138. C. Crawford, T. Chiricos, and G. Kleck, "Race, Racial Threat, and Sentencing of Habitual Offenders," *Criminology* 36, no. 3 (1998): pp. 481–511.

139. Spohn, "Thirty Years of Sentencing Reform," pp. 455, 481.

140. BJS, *Prison and Jail Inmates at Midyear 2001,* p. 9; BJS, *Prisoners in 2001* (July 2002; NCJ195189) p. 11; and *Sourcebook 2000,* Table 4.10.

141. BJS, *Compendium of Federal Justice Statistics, 2003,* NCJ 205368, p. 77, Table 5.5.

142. *Criminal Justice Newsletter,* March 1, 1995, p. 3; and *Criminal Justice Newsletter,* April 17, 1995, p. 5.

143. BJS, *Federal Drug Offenders, 1999, with Trends 1984–1999,* November 2001, NCJ 187285, p. 11, Table 8.

144. Ronald Smothers, "Wave of Prison Uprisings Provokes Debate on Crack," *The New York Times,* October 24, 1995, p. A12.

145. "Blacks Receive Stiffer Sentences," *Boston Globe,* April 4, 1979, pp. 1, 50ff.

146. Randall Thomson and Matthew Zingraff, "Detecting Sentencing Disparity: Some Problems and Evidence," *American Journal of Sociology* 86, no. 4 (1981): pp. 869–80, especially p. 875.

147. J. Unnever, C. Frazier, and J. Henretta, "Race Differences in Criminal Sentencing," *Sociological Quarterly* 21 (Spring 1980): pp. 197–205, especially p. 204.

148. J. Petersilia, "Racial Disparities in the Criminal Justice System: A Summary," *Crime & Delinquency* 31, no. 1 (1985): p. 28. See also G. Bridges and R. Crutchfield, "Law, Social Standing and Racial Disparities in Imprisonment," *Social Forces* 66, no. 3 (1988): pp. 699–724.

149. M. Myers, "Economic Inequality and Discrimination in Sentencing," *Social Forces* 65, no. 3 (1987): p. 761.

150. Mary Pat Flaherty and Joan Biskupic, "Rules Often Impose Toughest Penalties on Poor, Minorities," *The Washington Post,* October 9, 1996, p. A26.

151. Barbara S. Meierhoefer, *The General Effect of Mandatory Minimum Prison Terms: A Longitudinal Study of Federal Sentences Imposed* (Washington, D.C.: Federal Judicial Center, 1992), esp. pp. 1, 20, 25. Between October 1989 and 1990, 46 percent of whites received federal sentences below the mandatory minimum, but 32 percent of blacks did; *Sourcebook—1991,* p. 542, Table 5.43.

152. Flaherty and Biskupic, "Rules Often Impose Toughest Penalties on Poor, Minorities," p. A26.

153. William J. Bowers and Glenn L. Pierce, "Racial Discrimination and Criminal Homicide under Post-Furman Capital Statutes," in *The Death Penalty in America,* ed. H. A. Bedau (New York: Oxford University Press, 1982), pp. 206–24.

154. *McCleskey v. Kemp,* 107 S. Ct. 1756 (1987). The research central to this case was that of David Baldus, reported in D. Baldus, C. Pulaski, and G. Woodworth, "Comparative Review of Death Sentences: An Empirical Study of the Georgia Experience," *Journal of Criminal Law and Criminology* 74 (1983): pp. 661–725. Other studies that support the notion of discrimination in capital sentencing based on race of victim are R. Paternoster, "Race of Victim and Location of Crime: The Decision to Seek the Death Penalty in South Carolina," *Journal of Criminal Law and Criminology* 74, no. 3 (1983): pp. 754–88; R. Paternoster, "Prosecutorial Discretion in Requesting the Death Penalty: A Case of Victim-Based Racial Discrimination," *Law and Society Review* 18 (1984): pp. 437–78; S. Gross and R. Mauro, "Patterns of Death: An Analysis of Racial Disparities in Capital Sentencing and Homicide Victimization," *Stanford Law Review* 37 (1984): pp. 27–120; and Michael L. Radelet and Glenn L. Pierce, "Race and Prosecutorial Discretion in Homicide Cases," *Law and Society Review* 19 (1985): pp. 587, 615–19.

155. Anthony G. Amsterdam, "Race and the Death Penalty," in *Moral Controversies,* ed. S. Gold (Belmont, Calif.: Wadsworth, 1993), pp. 268–69.

156. Susan Levine and Lori Montgomery, "Large Racial Disparity Found by Study of Md. Death Penalty," *The Washington Post,* January 8, 2003, pp. A1, A8. See also U.S. General Accounting Office, *Death Penalty Sentencing: Research Indicates Pattern of Racial Disparities,* Report to the Senate and House Committees on the Judiciary, February (Washington, D.C.: U.S. General Accounting Office, 1990), esp. p. 5.

157. Marvin E. Wolfgang, Arlene Kelly, and Hans C. Nolde, "Comparison of the Executed and the Commuted among Admissions to Death Row," in Richard Quinney, ed., *Crime and Justice in Society* (Boston: Little, Brown, 1969), 508, 513.

158. Karen Parker, Mari DeWees, and Michael Radelet, "Race, the Death Penalty and Wrongful Convictions," *Criminal Justice* 18, no. 1 (2003), *www.abanet.org.*

159. "Antitrust: Kauper's Last Stand," *Newsweek,* June 21, 1976, p. 70. On December 21, 1974, the Antitrust Procedures and Penalty Act was passed, striking out the language of the Sherman Antitrust Act, which made price fixing a misdemeanor punishable by a maximum sentence of one year in prison. According to the new law, price fixing is a felony punishable by up to three years in prison. Because prison sentences were a rarity under the old law and usually involved only 30 days in jail when actually imposed, there is little reason to believe the new law will strike fear in the hearts of corporate crooks.

160. *The Washington Post,* March 2, 1990, pp. A1, A20; April 1, 1990, p. C3; April 28, 1990, pp. A1, A14; and April 27, 1991, p. A6.

161. K. Johnson, "Federal Court Processing of Corporate, White Collar, and Common Crime Economic Offenders over the Past Three Decades," *Mid-American Review of Sociology* 11, no. 1 (1986): pp. 25–44.

162. J. Hagan and A. Palloni, " 'Club Fed' and the Sentencing of White-Collar Offenders before and after Watergate," *Criminology* 24, no. 4 (1986): pp. 616–17. See also J. Hagan and P. Parker, "White-Collar Crime and Punishment: The Class Structure and Legal Sanctioning of Securities Violations," *American Sociological Review* 50 (1985): pp. 302–16.

163. John P. Wright, Francis T. Cullen, and Michael B. Blankenship, "The Social Construction of Corporate Violence: Media Coverage of the Imperial Food Products Fire," *Crime & Delinquency* 41, no. 1 (January 1995): pp. 23–24; Laurie Grossman, "Owner Sentenced to Nearly 20 Years over Plant Fire," *The Wall Street Journal*, September 15, 1992, p. A10; and Wil Haygood, "Still Burning: After a Deadly Fire, a Town's Losses Were Just Beginning," *The Washington Post*, November 10, 2002, p. F4.

164. This summary of the history leading up to the S&L debacle is based on Henry Pontell and Kitty Calavita, "White-Collar Crime in the Savings and Loan Scandal," *Annals of the American Academy of Political and Social Science* 525 (January 1993): pp. 31–45.

165. "Indirect Costs Raise Total for S&L Bailout to $480.9 Billion," *The Wall Street Journal*, July 15, 1996, p. B8A.

166. Pontell and Calavita, "White-Collar Crime in the Savings and Loan Scandal," p. 32, citing U.S. General Accounting Office, "Failed Thrifts: Internal Control Weaknesses Create an Environment Conducive to Fraud, Insider Abuse and Related Unsafe Practices," Statement of Frederick D. Wolf, Assistant Comptroller General, before the Subcommittee on Criminal Justice, Committee on the Judiciary, House of Representatives, March 22, 1989; and U.S. Congress, House, Committee on Government Operations, "Combatting Fraud, Abuse and Misconduct in the Nation's Financial Institutions," 72nd report by the Committee on Government Operations, October 13, 1989.

167. Pontell and Calavita, "White-Collar Crime in the Savings and Loan Scandal," p. 37.

168. Alan Fornham "S&L Felons," *Fortune*, November 5, 1990, p. 92.

169. *Criminal Justice Newsletter*, December 15, 1994, p. 5.

170. *UCR–1995*, p. 36.

171. Stephen Pizzo and Paul Muolo, "Take the Money and Run: A Rogues Gallery of Some Lucky S&L Thieves," *The New York Times Magazine*, May 9, 1993, p. 26.

172. "When Are the Savings and Loans Crooks Going to Jail?" Hearing before the Subcommittee on Financial Institutions Supervision, Regulation and Insurance of the Committee on Banking, Finance, and Urban Affairs, House of Representatives, 101st Congress, 2nd Session, June 28, 1990 (Washington, D.C.: U.S. Government Printing Office, 1990), p. 2.

173. Tom Wicker, *A Time to Die* (New York: Quadrangle, 1975), pp. 311, 314.

174. Ibid., p. 310.

175. *Sourcebook—1987*, p. 486; *StatAbst—2004–5*, p. 12, Table 11; BJS, *Prisoners in 2004*, NCJ210677; and BJS, *Prison and Jail Inmates at Midyear 2004*, NCJ208801.

176. BJS, *Survey of State Prison Inmates*, 1991, p. 3.

177. BJS, *Criminal Offender Statistics, www.ojp.usdoj.gov/bjs/crimoff.htm*; and BJS, *Profile of Jail Inmates 2002*, July 2004, NCJ201932.

178. *StatAbst—2003*, Table 589, p. 386; and BJS, *Profile of Jail Inmates 2002*, p. 9.

179. U.S. Census Bureau, *Current Population Survey*, 2003 Annual Social and Economic Supplement, Table PINC-o1, *http://pubdb3.census.gov/macro/032003/perinc/new01_010.htm*.

180. BJS, *Profile of Jail Inmates 2002*, p. 9.

181. BJS, "Comparing Federal and State Prison Inmates," in *Criminal Offender Statistics*.

182. BJS, *Profile of Jail Inmates 2002*, p. 2; and *StatAbst—2003*, Table 229, p. 154.

CHAPTER 4

TO THE VANQUISHED BELONG THE SPOILS

Who Is Winning the Losing War against Crime?

In every case the laws are made by the ruling party in its own interest; a democracy makes democratic laws, a despot autocratic ones, and so on. By making these laws they define as "just" for their subjects whatever is for their own interest, and they call anyone who breaks them a "wrongdoer" and punish him accordingly.

—Thrasymachus, in Plato's *Republic*

WHY IS THE CRIMINAL JUSTICE SYSTEM FAILING?

The streams of my argument flow together at this point in a question: *Why is it happening?* I have shown how it is no accident that "the offender at the end of the road in prison is likely to be a member of the lowest social and economic groups in the country."[1] I have shown that this is not an accurate group portrait of who threatens society—it is a picture of whom the criminal justice system *selects* for arrest and imprisonment from among those who threaten society. It is an image distorted by the shape of the criminal justice carnival mirror. This much we have seen, and now we want to know why: *Why is the criminal justice system allowed to function in a fashion that neither protects society nor achieves justice? Why is the criminal justice system failing?*

My answer to these questions will require looking at who benefits from this failure and who suffers from it. More particularly, I will argue that the rich and powerful in the United States—those who derive the greatest advantage from the persistence of the social and economic system as it is currently organized—reap benefits from the failure of criminal justice that has been documented in this book. However—as I cautioned early on—this should not lead the reader to think that my explanation for the current shape of the criminal justice system is a "conspiracy theory."

A conspiracy theory would argue that the rich and the powerful, seeing the benefits to be derived from the failure of criminal justice, consciously set out to use their wealth and power to make it fail. There are many problems with such a theory. First, it is virtually impossible to prove. If the conspiracy succeeds, then this is possible only to the extent that it is kept secret. Thus, evidence for a conspiracy would be as difficult to obtain as the conspiracy was successful. Second, conspiracy theories strain credibility precisely because the degree of secrecy they would require seems virtually impossible in a society as open and fractious as our own. If there is a "ruling elite" in the United States that comprises a group as small as the richest *one-thousandth of 1 percent* of the population, it would still be made up of more than 2,000 people. To think that a conspiracy to make the criminal justice system fail in the way it does could be kept secret among this number of people in a country like ours is just unbelievable. Third, conspiracy theories are not plausible because they do not correspond to the way most people act most of the time. Although there is no paucity of conscious mendacity and manipulation in our politics, most people most of the time seem sincerely to believe that what they are doing is right. Whether this is a tribute to human beings' creative capacities to rationalize what they do or just a matter of shortsightedness, it seems a fact. For all these reasons, it is not plausible that so fateful and harmful a policy as the failure of criminal justice could be purposely maintained by the rich and powerful. Rather, we need an explanation that is compatible with believing that policy makers, on the whole, are simply doing what they sincerely believe is right.

To understand how the Pyrrhic defeat theory explains the current shape of our failing criminal justice policy, note that this failure is really *three* failures that work together. First, there is the failure to implement policies that stand a good chance of reducing crime and the harm it causes. (This was argued in Chapter 1.) Second, there is the failure to identify as crimes the harmful acts of the rich and powerful. (This is the first of the hypotheses listed on pages 69–70 in Chapter 2, and it is confirmed by the evidence presented in Chapter 2.) Third, there is the failure to eliminate economic bias in the criminal justice system, so that the poor continue to have a substantially greater chance than better-off people of being arrested, charged, convicted, and penalized for committing the acts that are treated as crimes. (This corresponds to the second through fourth hypotheses listed in Chapter 2, and is confirmed by the evidence presented in Chapter 3.) The effect of the first failure is that there remains a large amount of crime—even if crime rates dip largely as a result of factors outside the control of the criminal justice system, such as the decline in unemployment or the routinization of the illicit drug trade. The effect of the second failure is that the acts identified as crimes are those done predominantly by the poor. The effect of the third failure is that the individuals who are arrested and convicted for crimes are predominantly poor people. The effect of the three failures working together is that we are largely unprotected against the harmful acts of the well-off, while at the same time we are confronted on the streets and in our homes with a real and large threat of crime and in the courts and prisons with a large and visible population of poor criminals. And lest it be thought that the public does not feel threatened by crime, consider that a recent poll shows that, though crime is down, 40 percent of Americans believe that there is more crime than there was the year before.[2] In short, the effect of current criminal justice policy is at once to narrow the public's conception of what is dangerous to acts of the poor and to present a convincing embodiment of this danger.

The Pyrrhic defeat theory aims to explain the *persistence* of this failing criminal justice policy, rather than its origins. The criminal justice system we have today originated as a result of complex historical factors that have to do with the development of the common law tradition in England, the particular form in which this was transplanted on American soil, and the zigzagging course of reform and reaction that has marked our history since the English colonies were transformed into an independent American nation. The study of these factors would surely require another book longer than this one—but, more important, for our purposes it would be unnecessary because it is not the origin of criminal justice policy and practices that is puzzling. The focus on one-on-one harm reflects the main ways in which people harmed each other in the days before large-scale industrialization; the refusal to implement policies that might reduce crime (such as gun control or legalization of heroin or amelioration of poverty) reflects a defensive and punitive response to crime that is natural and understandable, if not noble and farsighted; and the existence of economic bias in the criminal justice system reflects the real economic and political inequalities that characterize the society in which that system is embedded. What is puzzling, then, is not how these policies came to be what they are, but why they persist in the face of their failure to achieve either security or justice. The explanation I shall offer for this persistence I call "historical inertia."

The historical inertia explanation argues that current criminal justice policy persists because it fails in a way that does not give rise to an effective demand for change, for two reasons. First, this failing system provides benefits for those with the power to make changes, while it imposes costs on those without such power. Second, because the criminal justice system shapes the public's conception of what is dangerous, it creates the impression that the harms it is fighting are *the real threats* to society—thus, even when people see that the system is less than a roaring success, they only demand more of the same: more police, more prisons, longer prison sentences, and so on.

Consider first the benefits that the system provides for those with wealth and power. I have argued that the triple failure of criminal justice policy diverts attention from the harmful noncriminal acts of the well-off and confronts us in our homes and on our streets with a real, substantial threat of crime and in the courts and prisons with a large and visible population of poor criminals. This in turn conveys a vivid image to the American people, namely, that *there is a real threat to our lives and limbs, and it is a threat from the poor.* This image provides benefits to the rich and powerful in America. It carries an *ideological message* that serves to protect their wealth and privilege. Speaking generally, the message is this:

- The threat to law-abiding Middle America comes from below them on the economic ladder, not above them.
- The poor are morally defective, and thus their poverty is their own fault, not a symptom of social or economic injustice.

The effect of this message is to create (or reinforce) in Americans fear of, and hostility toward, the poor. It leads Americans to ignore the ways in which they are injured and robbed by the acts of the affluent (as catalogued in Chapter 2) and leads them to demand harsher doses of "law and order" aimed mainly at the lower classes. Most important, it nudges Americans toward a *conservative* defense of American society with its large disparities of wealth, power, and opportunity—and nudges them away from a progressive demand for equality and a more equitable distribution of wealth and power.

On the other hand, but equally important, is that those who are mainly victimized by the failure to reduce our high crime rates are by and large the poor themselves. The people who are hurt the most by the failure of the criminal justice system are those with the least power to change it. In 2003, households with an annual income of less than $7,500 were victims of violent crimes at a rate nearly three times that of households earning $75,000 and above. Indeed, as Table 4.1 shows, rates of victimization by crimes in all categories are substantially higher for the poorest segment of the population, and drop dramatically as we ascend the economic ladder.

The difference in the rates of property crime victimization between rich and poor understates the difference in the harms that result. The poor are far less likely than the affluent to have insurance against theft, and because they have little to start with, what they lose to theft takes a much deeper bite out of their ability to meet their basic needs. Needless to add, the various noncriminal harms documented in Chapter 2 (occupational hazards, pollution, poverty, and so on) also fall more harshly on workers and those at the bottom of society than on those at the top.

To summarize: Those who suffer most from the failure to reduce crime (and the failure to treat noncriminal harms as crimes) are not in a position to change criminal justice policy. Those who are in a position to change the policy are not seriously harmed by its failure—indeed, there are actual benefits to them from that failure. Note that I have not said that criminal justice policy is created to achieve this distribution of benefits and burdens. Instead, my

TABLE 4.1   Criminal Victimization by Family Income, 2003 (Estimated Rate of Personal Victimization per 1,000 Persons Age 12 and Older)

TYPE OF VICTIMIZATION	Family Income			
	LESS THAN $7,500	$7,500 TO 14,999	$25,000 TO $34,999	$75,000 OR MORE
Crimes of violence	49.9	30.8	24.9	17.5
Robbery with injury	2.5*	1.1*	0.8*	0.2*
Rape/sexual assault	1.6*	1.8*	0.9*	0.5*
Aggravated assault	10.8	7.9	5.0	2.7
Household burglary	58.0	42.2	35.3	20.8

*Based on 10 or fewer cases.

Source: BJS, *Criminal Victimization in the United States: Statistical Tables,* July, NCJ 207811 (2005), Tables 14 and 20, *http://www.ojp.usdoj.gov/bjs/pub/pdf/cvus0301.pdf.*

claim is that the criminal justice policy that has emerged piecemeal over time and usually with the best of intentions happens to produce this distribution of benefits and burdens. And because criminal justice policy happens to produce this distribution, there is no inclination to change the criminal justice system among people with the power to do so. Moreover, because the criminal justice system shapes the public's conception of what is dangerous, it effectively limits the public's conception of how to protect itself to demanding more of the same. Thus, though it fails, it persists.

Before proceeding, a new component of the explanation of the failure of criminal justice now deserves mention: the growing trend toward the privatization of prisons. The rapid and enormous increase in the U.S. prison population over the past 30 years or so has placed strains on state budgets. New policy initiatives, such as mandatory minimum sentences and the "three strikes and you're out" statutes enacted in numerous states, are likely only to continue the increase and the budgetary strains. This has given states an incentive to hire out their prison facilities to private contractors, who claim to be able to run prisons at 10 to 20 percent less cost than state governments (though this claim has proven to be exaggerated).[3] Already, 25 states plus Puerto Rico and the District of Columbia have passed laws allowing private contractors to run correctional facilities. The result has been a dramatic increase in the number of prisoners under private control. In the ten years from 1985 to 1995, the number of prison beds under private management grew from 935 to 63,595, an increase of nearly 7,000 percent! Since then, the rate of growth has slowed. Nonetheless, there were 98,901 inmates in private prisons in 2004, and private prison contractors are expanding their operations into various aspects of community corrections.[4]

Wall Street has not failed to notice this trend, and many stock analysts are urging their clients to invest in the major corporations in the field, such as Corrections Corporation of America (CCC) and Wackenhut Corrections. An article in *The Wall Street Journal* carries the headline: "Shares of Wackenhut Break Out as Prisons Become a Hot Industry." An article on private prisons in *Forbes* is titled "A Surefire Growth Industry."[5] Writes Paulette Thomas, in a *Wall Street Journal* article titled "Making Crime Pay,"

> The gritty work of criminal justice has become the kind of big-ticket commerce to attract the loftiest names in finance. Goldman Sachs & Co., Prudential Insurance Co. of America, Smith Barney Shearson Inc., and Merrill Lynch & Co. Inc. are among those competing to underwrite prison construction with private tax-exempt bonds—no voter approval required.[6]

Ms. Thomas likens the new development to that of the old "military-industrial complex," of which President Eisenhower warned in his farewell address. The comparison is appropriate because many firms in the "defense establishment" got into the private prison business when military spending was cut back due to the ending of the Cold War.[7]

Eric Schlosser takes up this analogy in an article in *The Atlantic Monthly* titled "The Prison-Industrial Complex." He writes,

> The prison-industrial complex is not a conspiracy. . . . It is a confluence of interests that has given prison construction in the United States a seemingly unstoppable momentum. It is composed of politicians . . . who have used the fear of crime to gain votes; impoverished rural areas where prisons have become a cornerstone of economic development; [and] private companies that regard the roughly $35 billion spent each year on corrections not as a burden on American taxpayers but as a lucrative market.[8]

What is most troubling about these developments is that, as Paul Leighton has pointed out, "they create large numbers of people who have a vested financial interest in having a large and increasing incarceration rate."[9] The American Legislative Exchange Council (ALEC), an organization that lobbies state legislators and that receives substantial contributions from CCC, says proudly that lawmakers on its crime task force have been actively leading in the drive for more incarceration in the states.[10] The National Institute on Money in State Politics reports, "Private prison companies gave more than $1.1 million in campaign contributions to state-level candidates in 14 Southern states during the 2000 elections."[11] In short, thus far in this book I have been pointing out how *the rich get richer* WHILE *the poor get prison,* but the privatization movement points to a new phase in which *the rich get richer* BECAUSE *the poor get prison!*

My argument in the remainder of this chapter takes the following form. In the section titled "The Poverty of Criminals and the Crime of Poverty,"

I spell in detail out the content of the ideological message broadcast by the failure of the criminal justice system. In the section titled "Ideology, or How to Fool Enough of the People Enough of the Time," I discuss the *nature* of ideology in general and the *need* for it in America. For those who doubt that our legal system could function in such questionable ways, I also present evidence on how the criminal justice system has been used in the past to protect the rich and powerful against those who would challenge their privileges or their policies. These sections, then, flesh out the historical inertia explanation of the failure of criminal justice by showing the ideological benefits that that failure yields and to whom.

Ultimately, the test of the argument in this chapter is whether it provides a plausible explanation of the failure of criminal justice and draws the arguments of the previous chapters together into a coherent theory of contemporary criminal justice policy and practice.

THE POVERTY OF CRIMINALS
AND THE CRIME OF POVERTY

Criminal justice is a very visible part of the American scene. As fact and fiction, countless images of crime and the struggle against it assail our senses daily, even hourly. In every newspaper, in every TV or radio newscast, there is at least one criminal justice story and often more. It is as if we live in an embattled city, besieged by the forces of crime and bravely defended by the forces of the law, and as we go about our daily tasks, we are always conscious of the war raging not very far away. Newspapers bring us daily, and newscasts bring us hourly, reports from the "front." Between reports, we are vividly reminded of the stakes and the desperateness of the battle by fictionalized portrayals of the struggle between the forces of the law and the breakers of the law. There is scarcely an hour on television without some dramatization of the struggle against crime. ("Before the average American child leaves elementary school, researchers estimate that he or she will have witnessed more than 8,000 murders on television." Although a few of these are killed by science fiction monsters, the figure still suggests that the extent of the impact of the televised portrayal of crime and the struggle against it on the imaginations of Americans are nothing short of astounding—particularly on children. And, in a joint statement on the impact of entertainment violence on children, issued on July 26, 2000, the American Academy of Pediatrics, American Medical Association, American Academy of Child and Adolescent Psychiatry, and American Psychological Association stated that "the average American child spends as much as 28 hours a week watching television," and "well over 1000 studies—including reports from the Surgeon General's office, the National Institute of Mental Health, and numerous studies conducted by leading figures within our medical and public health organizations—our own members—point overwhelmingly to a causal connection between media violence and aggressive behavior in some children.")[12] In the mid-1980s, it was estimated that "detective, police, and other criminal justice–related programs accounted for some eighty percent of prime-time TV viewing."[13] A quick look at the television section of the newspaper suggests that, if anything, this has only increased in recent years, with certain cable channels largely devoted to crime and justice programming. If we add to this the news accounts, the panel discussions, the movies, the novels, the video games, the comic books, and the TV cartoon shows that imitate the comics, as well as the political speeches about crime, there can be no doubt that as fact or fantasy or both, criminal justice is vividly present in the imaginations of most Americans.

This is no accident. Everyone can relate to criminal justice in personal and emotional terms. Everyone has some fear of crime, and as we saw in Chapter 3, just about everyone has committed some. Everyone knows the primitive satisfaction of seeing justice done and the evildoers served up their just deserts. Furthermore, in reality or in fiction, criminal justice is naturally dramatic. It contains the acts of courage and cunning, the high risks and high stakes, and the life-and-death struggle between good and evil missing from the routine lives so many of us lead. To identify with the struggle against crime is to expand one's experience vicariously to include the danger, the suspense, the triumphs, and the meaningfulness—in a word, the drama—often missing in ordinary life. How else can we explain the seemingly bottomless appetite Americans have for the endless repetition, in only slightly altered form, of the same theme: the struggle of the forces of law against the forces of crime? Criminal justice has a firm grip on the imaginations of Americans and is thus in a unique position to convey a message to Americans and to convey it with drama and with conviction.

Let us now look at this message in detail. Our task falls naturally into two parts. There is an ideological message supportive of the status quo, built into *any* criminal justice system by its very nature. Even if the criminal justice system were not failing, even if it were not biased against the poor, it would still—by its very nature—broadcast a message supportive of established institutions. This is the *implicit ideology of criminal justice*. Beyond this, there is an additional ideological message conveyed by the *failure* of the system and by its *biased* concentration on the poor. I call this the *bonus of bias*.

The Implicit Ideology of Criminal Justice

Any criminal justice system like ours conveys a subtle yet powerful message in support of established institutions. It does this for two interconnected reasons. First, it concentrates on *individual* wrongdoers. This means that *it diverts our attention away from our institutions, away from consideration of whether our institutions themselves are wrong or unjust or indeed "criminal."*

Second, the criminal law is put forth as the *minimum neutral ground rules* for any social living. We are taught that no society can exist without rules against theft and violence, and thus the criminal law seems to be politically neutral: the minimum requirements for *any* society, the minimum obligations that any individual owes his or her fellows to make social life of any decent sort possible. Thus, the criminal law not only diverts our attention away from the possible injustice of our social institutions, but also bestows upon those institutions the mantle of its own neutrality.

Because the criminal law protects the established institutions (the prevailing economic arrangements are protected by laws against theft, and so on), attacks on those established institutions become equivalent to violations of the minimum requirements for any social life at all. In effect, the criminal law enshrines the established institutions as equivalent to the minimum requirements for *any* decent social existence—and it brands the individual who attacks those institutions as one who has declared war on *all* organized society and who must therefore be met with the weapons of war.

This is the powerful magic of criminal justice. By virtue of its focus on *individual* criminals, it diverts us from the evils of the social order. By virtue of its presumed neutrality, it transforms the established social (and economic) order from being merely *one* form of society open to critical comparison with others into *the* conditions of *any* social order and thus immune from criticism. Let us look more closely at this process.

What is the effect of focusing on individual guilt? Not only does this divert our attention from the possible evils in our institutions, but it also puts forth half the problem of justice as if it were the *whole* problem. To focus on individual guilt is to ask whether the individual citizen has fulfilled his or her obligations to his or her fellow citizens. *It is to look away from the issue of whether the fellow citizens have fulfilled their obligations to him or her.* To look only at individual responsibility is to look away from social responsibility. Writing about her stint as a "story analyst" for a prime-time TV "real crime" show based on videotapes of actual police busts, Debra Seagal describes the way focus on individual criminals deflects attention away from the social context of crime and how television reproduces this effect in millions of homes daily:

> By the time our 9 million viewers flip on their tubes, we've reduced fifty or sixty hours of mundane and compromising video into short, action-packed segments of tantalizing, crack-filled, dope-dealing, junkie-busting cop culture. How easily we downplay the pathos of the suspect; how cleverly we breeze past the complexities that cast doubt on the very system that has produced the criminal activity in the first place.[14]

Seagal's description illustrates as well how a television program that shows nothing but videos of actual events, that uses no reenactments whatsoever, can distort reality by selecting and recombining pieces of real events.

A study of 69 TV law and crime dramas finds that fictional presentations of homicide focus on individual motivations and ignore social conditions:

> Television crime dramas portray these events as specific psychological episodes in the characters' lives and little, if any, effort is made to connect them to basic social institutions or the nature of society within which they occur.[15]

To look only at individual criminality is to close one's eyes to social injustice and to close one's ears to the question of whether our social institutions have exploited or violated the individual. *Justice is a two-way street—but criminal justice is a one-way street.* Individuals owe obligations to their fellow citizens because their fellow citizens owe obligations to them. Criminal justice focuses on the first and looks away from the second. *Thus, by focusing on individual responsibility for crime, the criminal justice system effectively acquits the existing social order of any charge of injustice!*

This is an extremely important bit of ideological alchemy. It stems from the fact that the same act can be criminal or not, unjust or just, depending on the circumstances in which it takes place. Killing someone is ordinarily a crime, but if it is in self-defense or to stop a deadly crime, it is not. Taking property by force is usually a crime, but if the taking is retrieving what has been stolen, then no crime has been committed. Acts of violence are ordinarily crimes, but if the violence is provoked by the threat of violence or by oppressive conditions, then, like the Boston Tea Party, what might ordinarily be called criminal is celebrated as just. This means that when we call an act a crime, *we are also making an implicit judgment about the conditions in response to which it takes place.* When we call an act a crime, we are saying that the conditions in which it occurs are not themselves criminal or deadly or oppressive or so unjust as to make an extreme response reasonable or justified or noncriminal. This means that when the system holds an individual responsible for a crime, *it implicitly conveys the message that the social conditions in which the crime occurred are not responsible for the crime,* that they are not so unjust as to make a violent response to them excusable.

Judges are prone to hold that an individual's responsibility for a violent crime is diminished if it was provoked by something that might lead a "reasonable man" to respond violently and that criminal responsibility is eliminated if the act was in response to conditions so intolerable that any "reasonable man" would have been likely to respond in the same way. In this vein, the law acquits those who kill or injure in self-defense and treats leniently those who commit a crime when confronted with extreme provocation. The law treats understandingly the man who kills his wife's lover, and the woman who kills her brutal husband even when she has not acted directly in self-defense. By this logic, when we hold an individual completely responsible for a crime, we are saying that the conditions in which it occurred are such that a "reasonable man" should find them tolerable. In other words, by focusing on individual responsibility for crimes, *the criminal justice system broadcasts the message that the social order itself is reasonable and not intolerably unjust.*

Thus, the criminal justice system focuses moral condemnation on individuals and deflects it away from the social order that may have either violated the individual's rights or dignity or pushed him or her to the brink of the crime. This not only serves to carry the message that our social institutions are not in need of fundamental questioning, but further suggests that the justice of our institutions is obvious, not to be doubted. Indeed, because it is deviations from these institutions that are crimes, the established institutions become the implicit standard of justice from which criminal deviations are measured.

This leads to the second way in which a criminal justice system always conveys an implicit ideology. It arises from the presumption that the criminal law is nothing but the politically neutral minimum requirements of any decent social life. What is the consequence of this? As already suggested, this presumption transforms the prevailing social order into justice incarnate and all violations of the prevailing order into injustice incarnate. This process is so obvious that it may be easily missed.

Consider, for example, the law against theft. It does seem to be one of the minimum requirements of social living. As long as there is scarcity, any society—capitalist or socialist—will need rules to deter individuals from taking what does not belong to them. The law against theft, however, is more: It is a law against stealing what individuals *presently own*. Such a law has the effect of making the present distribution of property a part of the criminal law.

Because stealing is a violation of the law, this means that the present distribution of property becomes the implicit standard of justice against which criminal deviations are measured. Because criminal law is thought of as the minimum requirements of any social life, this means that the present distribution of property is treated as the equivalent of the minimum requirements of *any* social life. The criminal who would alter the present distribution of property becomes someone who is declaring war on all organized society. The question of whether this "war" is provoked by the injustice or brutality of the society is swept aside. Indeed, this suggests yet another way in which the criminal justice system conveys an ideological message in support of the established society.

Not only does the criminal justice system acquit the social order of any charge of injustice; it also specifically cloaks the society's own crime-producing tendencies. I have already observed that by blaming the individual for a crime, the society is acquitted of the charge of injustice. I would like to go further now and argue that by blaming the individual for a crime, the society is acquitted of the charge of *complicity* in that crime. This is a point worth developing, because many observers have maintained that modern competitive societies such as our own have structural features that tend to generate crime. Thus, holding the individual responsible for his or her crime serves the function of taking the rest of society off the hook for their role in sustaining and benefiting from social arrangements that produce crime. Let us take a brief detour to look more closely at this process.

Cloward and Ohlin argued in their book, *Delinquency and Opportunity*,[16] that much crime is the result of the discrepancy between social goals and the legitimate opportunities available for achieving them. The same point is basic to "strain theory," including recent variations like Messner and Rosenfeld's *Crime and the American Dream*.[17] Simply put, in our society everyone is encouraged to be a success, but the avenues to success are open only to some. The conventional wisdom of our free-enterprise democracy is that anyone can be a success if he or she has the talent and the ambition. Thus, if one is not a success, it is because of one's own shortcomings: laziness, lack of ability, or both. On the other hand, opportunities to achieve success are not equally open to all. Access to the best schools and the best jobs is effectively closed to all but a few of the poor and becomes more available only as one goes up the economic ladder. The result is that many are called but few are chosen. Many who have taken the bait and accepted the belief in the importance of success and the belief that achieving success is a result of individual ability must cope with feelings of frustration and failure that result when they find the avenues to success closed. Cloward and Ohlin argue that one method of coping with these stresses is to develop alternative avenues to success. Crime is such an alternative avenue.

Crime is a means by which people who believe in the American dream pursue it when they find the traditional routes barred. Indeed, it is plain to see that the goals pursued by most criminals are as American as apple pie. One of the reasons that American moviegoers enjoy gangster films—movies in which gangsters such as Al Capone, Bonnie and Clyde, or Butch Cassidy and the Sundance Kid are the heroes, as distinct from police and detective films, whose heroes are defenders of the law—is that even when we deplore the hero's methods, we identify with his or her notion of success, because it is ours as well, and we admire the courage and cunning displayed in achieving that success.

It is important to note that the discrepancy between success goals and legitimate opportunities in America is not an aberration. It is a structural feature of modern competitive industrialized society, a feature from which many benefits flow. Cloward and Ohlin write that

> a crucial problem in the industrial world is to locate and train the most talented persons in every generation, irrespective of the vicissitudes of birth, to occupy technical work roles. Since we cannot know in advance who can best fulfill the requirements of the various occupational roles, the matter is presumably settled through the process of competition. But how can men throughout the social order be motivated to participate in this competition?

One of the ways in which the industrial society attempts to solve this problem is by defining success-goals as potentially accessible to all, regardless of race, creed, or socioeconomic position.[18]

Because these universal goals are urged to encourage a competition to select the best, there are necessarily fewer openings than seekers. Also, because those who achieve success are in a particularly good position to exploit their success to make access for their own children easier, the competition is rigged to work in favor of the middle and upper classes. As a result, "many lower-class persons are the victims of a contradiction between the goals toward which they have been led to orient themselves and socially structured means of striving for these goals."[19]

[The poor] experience desperation born of the certainty that their position in the economic structure is relatively fixed and immutable—a desperation made all the more poignant by their exposure to a cultural ideology in which failure to orient oneself upward is regarded as a moral defect and failure to become mobile as a proof of it.[20]

The outcome is predictable. "Under these conditions, there is an acute pressure to depart from institutional norms and to adopt illegitimate alternatives."[21]

This means that the very way in which our society is structured to draw out the talents and energies that go into producing our high standard of living has a costly side effect: It produces crime. By holding individuals responsible for this crime, those who enjoy that high standard of living can have their cake and eat it too. They can reap the benefits of the competition for success and escape the responsibility of paying for the costs of the competition. By holding the poor crook legally and morally guilty, the rest of society not only passes the costs of competition on to the poor, but also effectively denies that it (meaning primarily the affluent part of society) is the beneficiary of an economic system that exacts such a high toll in frustration and suffering.

William Bonger, the Dutch Marxist criminologist, maintained that competitive capitalism produces egotistic motives and undermines compassion for the misfortunes of others, and thus makes human beings literally *more capable of crime*—more capable of preying on their fellows without moral inhibition or remorse—than earlier cultures that emphasized cooperation rather than competition.[22] Here again, the criminal justice system relieves those who benefit from the American economic system of the costs of that system. By holding criminals morally and individually responsible for their crimes, we can forget that the motives that lead to crime—the drive for success, linked with the beliefs that success means outdoing others and that violence is an acceptable way of achieving one's goals—are the *same motives* that powered the drive across the American continent and that continue to fuel the engine of America's prosperity.

David Gordon, a contemporary political economist, maintains "that nearly all crimes in capitalist societies represent perfectly *rational* responses to the structure of institutions upon which capitalist societies are based."[23] Like Bonger, Gordon believes that capitalism tends to provoke crime in all economic strata. This is so because most crime is motivated by a desire for property or money and is an understandable way of coping with the pressures of inequality, competition, and insecurity, all of which are essential ingredients of capitalism. Capitalism depends, Gordon writes,

> on basically competitive forms of social and economic interaction and upon substantial inequalities in the allocation of social resources. Without inequalities, it would be much more difficult to induce workers to work in alienating environments. Without competition and a competitive ideology, workers might not be inclined to struggle to improve their relative income and status in society by working harder. Finally, although rights of property are protected, capitalist societies do not guarantee economic security to most of their individual members. Individuals must fend for themselves, finding the best available opportunities to provide for themselves and their families. Driven by the fear of economic insecurity and by a competitive desire to gain some of the goods unequally distributed throughout the society, many individuals will eventually become "criminals."[24]

To the extent that a society makes crime a reasonable alternative for a large number of its members from all classes, that society is itself not very reasonably or humanely organized and bears some degree of responsibility for the crime it encourages. Because the criminal law is put forth as the minimum requirements that can be expected of any "reasonable man," its enforcement amounts to a denial of the real nature of the social order to which Gordon and the others point. Here again, by blaming the individual criminal, the criminal justice system serves implicitly but dramatically to acquit the society of its criminality.

The Bonus of Bias

We now consider the additional ideological bonus derived from the criminal justice system's bias against the poor. This bonus is a product of the association of crime and poverty in the popular mind. This association, the merging of the "criminal classes" and the "lower classes" into the "dangerous classes," was not invented in America. The word *villain* is derived from the Latin *villanus*, which means a farm servant. The term *villein* was used in feudal England to refer to a serf who farmed the land of a great lord and who was wholly subject to that lord.[25] In this respect, our present criminal justice system is heir to a long tradition.

The value of this association was already seen when we explored the average citizen's concept of the Typical Criminal and the Typical Crime. It is quite obvious that throughout the great mass of Middle America, far more fear and hostility are directed toward the predatory acts of the poor than toward the acts of the rich. Compare the fate of politicians in recent history who call for tax reform, income redistribution, prosecution of corporate crime, and any sort of regulation of business that would make it better serve American social goals with that of politicians who erect their platform on a call for "law and order," more police, fewer limits on police power, and stiffer prison sentences for criminals—and consider this in light of what we have already seen about the real dangers posed by corporate crime and "business as usual."

It seems clear that Americans have been effectively deceived as to what are the greatest dangers to their lives, limbs, and possessions. The very persistence with which the system functions to apprehend and punish poor crooks and ignore or slap on the wrist equally or more dangerous individuals is testimony to the sticking power of this deception. That Americans continue to tolerate the comparatively gentle treatment meted out to white-collar criminals, corporate price fixers, industrial polluters, and political-influence peddlers while voting in droves to lock up more poor people faster and for longer sentences indicates the degree to which they harbor illusions as to who most threatens them. It is perhaps also part of the explanation for the continued dismal failure of class-based politics in America. American workers rarely seem able to forget their differences and unite to defend their shared interests against the rich whose wealth they produce. Ethnic divisions serve this divisive function well, but undoubtedly the vivid portrayal of the poor—and, of course, blacks—as hovering birds of prey waiting for the opportunity to snatch away the workers' meager gains serves also to deflect opposition away from the upper classes. A politician who promises to keep working-class communities free of blacks and the prisons full of them can get votes even if the major portion of his or her policies amount to continuation of the favored treatment of the rich at their expense. The sensationalistic use, in the 1988 presidential election, of photos of Willie Horton (a convicted black criminal who committed a brutal rape while out of prison on a furlough) suggests that such tactics are effective politics. Recent studies suggest that the identification of race and violent crime continues, albeit in subtler form.[26]

The most important "bonus" derived from the identification of crime and poverty is that it paints the picture that the threat to decent Middle Americans comes from those below them on the economic ladder, not from those above. For this to happen, the system must not only identify crime and poverty, *but also fail enough in the fight to reduce crime that crime remains a real threat*. By doing this, it deflects the fear and discontent of Middle Americans, and their possible opposition, away from the wealthy.

There are other bonuses as well. For instance, if the criminal justice system sends out a message that bestows legitimacy on the present distribution of property, the dramatic impact is greatly enhanced if the violator of the present arrangements is without property. In other words, the crimes of the well-to-do "redistribute" property among the haves. In that sense, they do not pose a symbolic challenge to the larger system in which some have much and many have little or nothing. If the criminal threat can be portrayed as coming from the poor, then the punishment of the poor criminal becomes a morality play in which the sanctity and legitimacy of the system in which some have plenty and others have little or nothing are dramatically affirmed. It matters little whom the poor criminals really victimize. What counts is that Middle Americans come to fear that those poor criminals are out to steal what they own.

There is yet another bonus for the powerful in America, produced by the identification of crime and poverty. It might be thought that the identification of crime and poverty would produce sympathy for the criminals. My suspicion is that it produces or at least reinforces the reverse: *hostility toward the poor.*

There is little evidence that Americans are very sympathetic to poor criminals. Very few Americans believe poverty to be a cause of crime (6 percent of those questioned in a 1981 survey, although 21 percent thought unemployment was a cause—in keeping with our general blindness to class, these questions are not even to be found in recent surveys). Other surveys find that most Americans believe that courts do not deal harshly enough with criminals (67 percent of those questioned in 2002), and that the death penalty should be used for convicted murderers (66 percent of those questioned in 2002).[27]

Indeed, the experience with white-collar crime discussed in Chapter 3 suggests that sympathy for criminals begins to flower only when we approach the higher reaches of the ladder of wealth and power. For some poor ghetto youth who robs a liquor store, five years in a penitentiary is our idea of tempering justice with mercy. When corporate crooks rob millions, incarceration is rare. A fine is usually thought sufficient punishment.

My view is that, because the criminal justice system, in fact and fiction, deals with *individual legal and moral guilt*, the association of crime with poverty does not mitigate the image of individual moral responsibility for crime, the image that crime is the result of an individual's poor character. It does the reverse: It generates the association of poverty and individual moral failing and thus *the belief that poverty itself is a sign of poor or weak character.* The clearest evidence that Americans hold this belief is to be found in the fact that attempts to aid the poor are regarded as acts of charity rather than as acts of justice. Our welfare system has all the demeaning attributes of an institution designed to give handouts to the undeserving and none of the dignity of an institution designed to make good on our responsibilities to our fellow human beings. If we acknowledged the degree to which our economic and social institutions themselves breed poverty, we would have to recognize our own responsibilities toward the poor. If we can convince ourselves that the poor are poor because of their own shortcomings, particularly moral shortcomings such as incontinence and indolence, then we need acknowledge no such responsibility to the poor. Indeed, we can go further and pat ourselves on the back for our generosity in handing out the little that we do, and, of course, we can make our recipients go through all the indignities that mark them as the undeserving objects of our benevolence. By and large, this has been the way in which Americans have dealt with their poor.[28] It is a way that enables us to avoid asking the question of why the richest nation in the world continues to produce massive poverty. It is my view that this conception of the poor is subtly conveyed by how our criminal justice system functions.

Obviously, no ideological message could be more supportive of the present social and economic order than this. It suggests that poverty is a sign of individual failing, not a symptom of social or economic injustice. It tells us loud and clear that massive poverty in the midst of abundance is not a sign pointing toward the need for fundamental changes in our social and economic institutions. It suggests that the poor are poor because they deserve to be poor or at least because they lack the strength of character to overcome poverty. When the poor are seen to be poor in character, then economic poverty coincides with moral poverty and the economic order coincides with the moral order. As if a divine hand guided its workings, capitalism leads to everyone getting what he or she morally deserves!

If this association takes root, then when the poor individual is found guilty of a crime, the criminal justice system acquits the society of its responsibility not only for crime *but for poverty as well.*

With this, the ideological message of criminal justice is complete. The poor rather than the rich are seen as the enemies of the majority of decent Americans. Our social and economic institutions are held to be responsible for neither crime nor poverty, and thus are in need of no fundamental questioning or reform. The poor are poor because they are poor of character. The economic order and the moral order are one. To the extent that this message sinks in, the wealthy can rest easily—even if they cannot sleep the sleep of the just.

We can understand why the criminal justice system is allowed to create the image of crime as the work of the poor and fails to reduce it so that the threat of crime remains real and credible. The result is ideological alchemy of the highest order. The poor are seen as the real threat to decent society. The ultimate sanctions of criminal justice dramatically sanctify the present social and economic order, and *the poverty of criminals makes poverty itself an individual moral crime!*

Such are the ideological fruits of a losing war against crime whose distorted image is reflected in the criminal justice carnival mirror and widely broadcast to reach the minds and imaginations of America.

IDEOLOGY, OR HOW TO FOOL ENOUGH OF THE PEOPLE ENOUGH OF THE TIME

What Is Ideology?

The view that the laws of a state or nation are made to serve the interests of those with power, rather than to promote the well-being of the whole society, is not a new discovery. It is a doctrine with a pedigree even older than Christianity. Writing during the fourth century B.C., virtually at the dawn of Western thought, Plato expressed this view through the lips of Thrasymachus.[29] A more contemporary and more systematic formulation of the idea is found in the works of Karl Marx, written during the nineteenth century, not long after the dawn of Western industrialism. Marx wrote in *The Communist Manifesto* that the bourgeoisie—the class of owners of businesses and factories, the class of capitalists—has

> conquered for itself, in the modern representative State, exclusive political sway. The executive of the modern State is but a committee for managing the common affairs of the whole bourgeoisie.[30]

Anyone who thinks this is a ridiculous idea ought to look at the backgrounds of our political leaders. The vast majority of the president's cabinet, the administrators of the federal regulatory agencies, and the members of the two houses of Congress come from the ranks of business or are lawyers who serve business. Many still maintain their business ties or law practices, with no sense of a conflict of interest with their political role.[31] Even those who start from humble beginnings are usually quite rich by the time they finally make it into office. If either Thrasymachus or Marx is right, there *is* no conflict with their political role because that role is to protect and promote the interests of business.

It is clear that the most powerful criminal justice policy makers come from the have-plenties, not from the have-littles. It is no surprise that legislators and judges—those who make the laws that define criminality and those who interpret those laws—are predominantly members of the upper classes, if not at birth then surely by the time they take office. One study of justices appointed to the U.S. Supreme Court between 1933 and 1957 found that 81 percent were sons of fathers with high-social-status occupations and that 61 percent had been educated in schools of high standing. Richard Quinney compiled background data on key members of criminal justice policy-making and policy-advising committees and agencies, such as the President's Commission on Law Enforcement and Administration of Justice, the National Advisory Commission on Civil Disorders, the National Commission on the Causes and Prevention of Violence, the Senate Judiciary Committee's Subcommittee on Criminal Laws and Procedures (the subcommittee had a strong hand in shaping the Omnibus Crime Control and

Safe Streets Act of 1968), the Law Enforcement Assistance Administration, the Federal Bureau of Investigation, and, last but not least, the U.S. Department of Justice. With few exceptions, Quinney's report reads like a *Who's Who* of the business, legal, and political elite. For instance, 63 percent of the members of the President's Crime Commission had business and corporate connections.[32]

Further, there is considerable evidence that the American criminal justice system has been used throughout its history in rather unsubtle ways to protect the interests of the powerful against the lower classes and political dissenters. The use of the FBI and local police forces to repress dissent by discrediting, harassing, and undermining dissident individuals and groups has been abundantly revealed. The FBI, often with active cooperation or tacit consent of local police, has engaged in literally hundreds of illegal burglaries of the offices of law-abiding left-wing political parties,[33] and in political sabotage against the Black Panthers (e.g., "a Catholic priest, the Rev. Frank Curran, became the target of FBI operations because he permitted the Black Panthers to use his church for serving breakfasts to ghetto children").[34] It conducted a campaign to discredit the late Martin Luther King Jr. ("the FBI secretly categorized King as a 'Communist' months before it ever started investigating him").[35] Directors of the FBI have said that the bureau is "truly sorry" for these past abuses and that they are over. Later reports indicate that abuses continue.[36]

These acts of repression are only the latest in a long tradition. The first organized uniformed police force in the English-speaking world was established in London in 1829. They came to be called "bobbies" because of the role played by Sir Robert Peel in securing passage of the London Metropolitan Police Act, which established the force. The first full-time uniformed police force in the United States was set up in New York City in 1845.[37] It was also in the period from the 1820s to the 1840s that the movement to build penitentiaries to house and reform criminals began in New York and Pennsylvania and spread rapidly through the states of the young nation.[38] That these are also the years that saw the beginnings of a large industrial working class in the cities of England and America is a coincidence too striking to ignore.

The police were repeatedly used to break strikes and harass strikers.[39] The penitentiaries were used mainly to house the laborers and foreigners (often one and the same) whom the middle and upper classes perceived as a threat.[40] Throughout the formative years of the American labor movement, public police forces, private police such as the Pinkertons, regular army troops, and the National Guard were used repeatedly to protect the interests of capital against the attempts of labor to organize in defense of its interests. The result was that "the United States has had the bloodiest and most violent labor history of any industrialized nation in the world"—with most of the casualties on the side of labor.[41]

Marx, of course, went further. Not only are the laws of a society made to protect the interests of the most powerful economic class, but also, Marx argued, the prevailing ways of thinking about the world—from economic theory to religion to conventional moral ideas about good and evil, guilt and responsibility—are shaped in ways that promote the belief that the existing society is the best of all possible worlds. Marx wrote that

> the ideas of the ruling class are in every epoch the ruling ideas: i.e. the class which is the ruling material force of society, is at the same time its ruling intellectual force. The class which has the means of material production at its disposal, has control at the same time over the means of mental production.[42]

Because those who have economic power own the newspapers, endow the universities, finance the publication of books and journals, and (in our own time) control the television and radio industries, they have a prevailing say in what is heard, thought, and believed by the millions who get their ideas—their picture of reality—from these sources. This does not mean that the controllers of the "means of mental production" consciously deceive or manipulate those who receive their message. What it means is that the picture of reality held by these controllers—believed by them, no doubt sincerely, to be an accurate representation of reality—will be largely the picture of reality that fills the heads of the readers and viewers of the mass media. Recognizing this involves no disrespect of the so-called common person. It is simply a matter of facing reality. The average man or woman is almost wholly occupied with the personal tasks of earning a living, piloting a family, and the like. He or she lacks the time (and usually the training) necessary to seek out and evaluate alternative sources of information. Most people are lucky when they have the time to catch a bit of news on television or in the papers. Moreover, except when there is division of opinion among those who control the media, the average person is so surrounded by unbroken "consensus" that he or she takes it simply as the way things are, with no particular reason even to consider the possibility that there are other sides of the issue to be considered, much less to seek these out.

Consequently, the vast majority of people will accept, as a true picture of reality, the picture held by those who control the media. This is likely to be a distorted picture, even if those who create it act with the best of intentions and sincerity. The point is that, for a wide variety of reasons, people will tend to view the world in ways that make their own role in it (particularly the advantages and privileges they have in it) seem morally just, indeed, part of the best of all possible worlds. Thus, without any intention to deceive at all, those who control the content of the mass media are virtually certain to convey a picture of reality that supports the existing social order.

As a result, even in a society such as ours, where freedom of expression has reached a level unparalleled in history, there is almost never any fundamental questioning of our political-economic institutions in the mass media, that is, television and radio, the major newspapers, or the news weeklies such as *Time* or *Newsweek*. There is much criticism of individuals and of individual policies. How often, though, does one find the mass media questioning whether the free-enterprise system is really the best choice for America, or whether our political and legal arrangements systematically promote the domination of society by the owners of big business? These issues are rarely, if ever, raised. Instead, it is taken for granted that, although they need some reform tinkering from time to time, our economic institutions are the most productive, our political institutions the freest, and our legal institutions the most just that there can be.

In other words, even in a society as free as ours, the ideas that fill the heads of most Americans and shape their picture of reality either explicitly or implicitly convey the message that our leaders are pursuing the common good (with only occasional lapses into personal venality—note how we congratulate ourselves on how "the system is working" when we expose these "aberrations" and then return to business as usual). Thus, we are told that the interests of the powerful coincide with the common interests of us all,[43] that "what's good for General Motors is good for the country." Where this picture of reality shows up some blemishes, they will always be portrayed as localized problems that can be remedied without fundamental overhaul of the entire social order, aberrations in an otherwise well-functioning social system. Indeed, the very willingness to publicize these blemishes "proves" there is nothing fundamentally wrong with the social system, because if the media are free, willing, and able to portray the blemishes, they would surely portray fundamental problems with the social system if there were any—and because they do not, there must not be any! When ideas, however unintentionally, distort reality in a way that justifies the prevailing distribution of power and wealth, hides society's injustices, and thus secures uncritical allegiance to the existing social order, we have what Marx called *ideology*.[44]

Ideology is not conscious deception. People may spout ideology simply because it is all they know or all they have been taught or because they do not see beyond the "conventional wisdom" that surrounds them. This can be just as true of scholars who fail to see beyond the conventional assumptions of their disciplines as it is of laypersons who fail to see beyond the oversimplifications of what is commonly called "common sense." Such individuals do not mouth an ideology out of a willful desire to deceive and manipulate their fellows, but rather because their own view of reality is distorted by untruths and half-truths—and criminal justice is one source of such distortion. One way in which this works without conscious lying is that we have become so used to the criminal justice carnival mirror (described in Chapter 2) that we don't notice its curves. It looks flat, and thus we take it as an accurate picture of who threatens us in society.

It should be noted in passing that not everyone uses the term "ideology" as I have, to point to what is necessarily deceptive. Some writers speak of ideology as if it meant any individual or group's "belief system" or "value system" or *Weltanschauung*, that is, "worldview."[45] I do not intend to quibble about semantics. However, such a moral neutralization of the concept of "ideology" strikes me as dulling an instrument that thinkers such as Marx and others have sharpened into an effective tool for cutting through the illusions that dog our political life. Such tools are few and hard to find. Once found, they should be carefully preserved, especially when concepts such as "belief system" and "worldview" are available to perform the more neutral function.

The Need for Ideology

A simple and persuasive argument can be made for the claim that the rich and powerful in America have an interest in conveying an ideological message to the rest of the nation. The have-nots and have-littles far outnumber the have-plenties. This means, to put it rather crudely, that the have-nots and the have-littles could have more if they decided to take it from the have-plenties. This, in turn, means that the have-plenties need the cooperation of the have-nots and the have-littles. Because the have-plenties are such a small minority that they could never *force* this cooperation on the have-nots and have-littles, this cooperation must be voluntary. For the cooperation to be voluntary, the have-nots and the have-littles must believe it would not be right or reasonable to take away what the have-plenties have. In other words, they must believe that for all its problems, the present social, political, and economic order, with its disparities of wealth and power and privilege, is about the best that human beings can create. More specifically, the have-nots and have-littles must believe that they are not being exploited or being treated unfairly by the have-plenties, and these beliefs must be in some considerable degree false, because the distribution of wealth and power in the United States is so evidently arbitrary and unjust. Ergo, the need for ideology.

A disquisition on the inequitable distribution of wealth and income in the United States is beyond the scope and purpose of this book. This subject, as well as the existence of a "dominant" or "ruling" class in America, has been documented extensively by others.[46] I will make only two points here. First, there are indeed wide disparities in the distribution of wealth and income in the United States. Second, these disparities are so obviously unjust that it is reasonable to assume that the vast majority of people who must struggle to make ends meet put up with them only because they have been sold a bill of goods, that is, an ideology.

In 2004, the richest 20 percent of American households were expected to receive 50.1 percent of the income received by all families, whereas the poorest 60 percent of American households will receive 26.8 percent of the total income. In crude terms, this means that while the wealthiest 23 million American households will have more than half the money pie to themselves, the least wealthy 67 million American households will share about a quarter of that pie among them. At the outer edges the figures are more extreme: For 2003, the richest 5 percent of families are expected to receive 20.5 percent of total income, substantially more than the poorest 40 percent of families, who will receive 13.7 percent. This means that the richest 5 percent— less than 4 million families—have more money to divide among themselves than the 30.4 million families who make up the bottom 40 percent.[47]

The distribution of *wealth* (property such as stocks, as well as owner-ship of businesses and land, that generate income and tend to give one a say in major economic decisions) is even worse than the distribution of income.[48] According to an analysis by a senior economist at the Federal Reserve, in 2001 the top 10 percent of households owned 70 percent of the nation's wealth, and the remaining 90 percent shared 30 percent. Worse still, the bot-tom half of the distribution collectively owned 2.8 percent of the nation's wealth and 0.5 percent of stocks.[49] A recent study of long-term trends in wealth inequality shows that the top one-fifth of households has owned three-quarters of the nation's wealth at least over the period from 1962 to 1989. The author writes, "If anything, wealth concentration increased during the 1980s. It is estimated that the top 1 percent of households in 1989 owned 33 percent of household wealth, compared to 30 percent in 1986 and 28 per-cent in 1983." Looking back over the whole period from colonial times to the present, the author concludes that "at no time has the majority of the U.S. adult population or households managed to gain title to any more than about 10 percent of the nation's wealth." And, she adds, "[T]he governmental poli-cies of the past two decades have been hostile to progressive tax rates and economic measures benefiting workers. Real per capita income began declin-ing in the early 1970s, benefits eroded in the 1980s. . . . This situation sug-gests that the lower four quintiles' share of total wealth may well shrink in future years."[50] A recent report by the Federal Reserve confirms this predic-tion. According to *The Washington Post* for January 23, 2003, "The rising eco-nomic tide of the late 1990s lifted the boats of almost all American families but also sharply increased the wealth gap between the rich and the rest of society, according to a survey released yesterday by the Federal Reserve."[51]

I offer no complicated philosophical argument to prove that these dis-parities are unjust, although such arguments abound for those who are inter-ested.[52] It is a scandal that, in a nation as rich as ours, some 37 million people (somewhat less when reckoned with the most generous valuation of in-kind benefits, such as food stamps) live below what the government conserva-tively defines as the poverty level and that many millions more must scram-ble to make ends meet.[53] It is shameful that more than a third of the individuals below the poverty line are children! It is tragic that in our wealthy nation, so many millions cannot afford a proper diet, a college edu-cation, a decent place to live, and good health care. We know too much about the causes of wealth and poverty to believe that the rich become rich simply because of their talent or contribution to society or that the poor are poor because they are lazy or incapable. Because we are nowhere near offering all

Americans a good education and an equal opportunity to get ahead, we have no right to think that the distribution of income reflects what people have truly earned. The distribution of income in America is so fundamentally shaped by factors such as race, educational opportunity, and the economic class of one's parents[54] that few people who are well-off can honestly claim they deserve *all* that they have. Those who think they do should ask themselves where they would be today if they had been born to migrant laborers in California or to a poor black family in the Harlem ghetto.

Enough said. I take it, then, as established that the disparities of wealth and income in America are wide and unjustified. For the vast majority, the many millions struggling hard to satisfy basic needs, to acquiesce to the vast wealth of a small minority, it is necessary that the majority come to believe that these disparities are justified, that the present order is the best that human beings can accomplish, and that they are not being exploited by the have-plenties. In other words, the system requires an effective ideology to fool enough of the people enough of the time.

This account of the nature and need for ideology, coupled with the historical inertia explanation of the persistence of criminal justice in its current form and the analysis of the ideological benefits produced by the criminal justice system, adds up to an explanation of the continued failure of criminal justice in the United States and its persistent bias against the poor.

SUMMARY

This chapter has presented the "historical inertia" explanation of the triple failure of criminal justice in the United States (1) to institute policies likely to reduce the high incidence of crime, (2) to treat as crimes the dangerous acts of the well-off, and (3) to eliminate the bias against the poor in the treatment of those acts labeled "crimes." It was argued that these failures harm most those who lack the power to change things, and benefit those who have that power. They benefit the latter by broadcasting the message that the threat to Americans' well-being comes from below them on the economic ladder, not from above them, and that poverty results not from social causes but from the moral depravity of the poor. It was also argued that, aside from these "bonuses of bias," there is an implicit ideological message of any criminal justice system, insofar as such systems, by focusing on individual guilt, implicitly broadcast the message that the social system itself is a just one.

STUDY QUESTIONS

1. What is a conspiracy theory? What are the shortcomings of such a theory? Is the Pyrrhic defeat theory a conspiracy theory?

2. What is meant by "ideology"? What is the difference between ideology and propaganda? Is ideology needed in the United States?

3. How does any criminal justice system broadcast an ideological message supportive of the prevailing social and economic arrangements?

4. What additional ideological benefits result from the bias against the poor in the definition and treatment of crime?

5. Why are poor people in the United States poor?

6. Now that you have reviewed the historical inertia explanation of criminal justice in the United States, has the Pyrrhic defeat theory been proven?

7. What risks are posed by the privatization of prisons?

A companion website to this book, with a chapter outline and summary, links to additional information, and Internet-based exercises, is available at "Rich Get Richer," *www.paulsjusticepage.com.*

ADDITIONAL READINGS

Baum, Dan. *Smoke and Mirrors: The War on Drugs and the Politics of Failure.* Boston: Little, Brown, 1996.

Box, Steven. *Power, Crime and Mystification.* London: Tavistock, 1983.

Chambliss, William, and Milton Mankoff. *Whose Law and What Order? A Conflict Approach to Criminology.* New York: Wiley, 1976.

Chambliss, William, and Robert Seidman. *Law, Order and Power.* Reading, Mass.: Addison-Wesley, 1982.

Fishman, Mark, and Gray Cavender. *Entertaining Crime.* New York: Aldine de Gruyter, 1998.

Kappeler, Victor, et al. *The Mythology of Crime and Criminal Justice,* 4th ed. Long Grove, Ill.: Waveland, 2004.

Lynch, Michael, Raymond Michalowski, and W. Byron Groves. *The New Primer in Radical Criminology: Critical Perspectives on Crime, Power and Identity.* Monsey, N.Y.: Willow Tree Press, 2000.

Reiman, Jeffrey. "The Rich (Still) Get Richer. . . . Understanding Ideology, Outrage and Economic Bias." *www.paulsjusticepage.com.*

Surette, Ray. *Media, Crime and Criminal Justice: Images and Realities,* 2nd ed. Pacific Grove, Calif.: Brooks/Cole, 1996.

Turk, Austin. *Political Criminality: The Defiance and Defense of Authority.* Beverly Hills, Calif.: Sage, 1982.

NOTES

1. *Challenge,* p. 44.
2. *Sourcebook—2003,* Table 2.35, p. 128.
3. "For example, it was discovered that, rather than the projected 20 percent savings, the average saving from privatization was only about 1 percent, and most of that was achieved through lower labor costs. Nevertheless, there were indications that the mere prospect of

privatization had a positive effect on prison administration, making it more responsive to reform. It is hoped that this monograph will prove enlightening to those involved with the issue of privatized prisons and promote a greater discussion about it." James Austin and Garry Coventry, "Emerging Issues on Privatized Prisons by James Austin and Garry Coventry," U.S. Department of Justice, Office of Justice Programs, Bureau of Justice Assistance, February 2001, NCJ 181249, p. iii.

4. BJS, *Prisoners in 2004,* p. 5.

5. Karen L. Tippett, "Shares of Wackenhut Break Out as Prisons Become a Hot Industry," *The Wall Street Journal,* April 10, 1996, p. F2; and Michael Schuman, "A Sure-fire Growth Industry," *Forbes,* January 16, 1995, p. 81.

6. Paulette Thomas, "Making Crime Pay," *The Wall Street Journal,* May 12, 1994, p. A1.

7. Ibid.

8. Eric Schlosser, "The Prison-Industrial Complex," *Atlantic Monthly,* December 1998, p. 54.

9. Paul Leighton, "Industrialized Social Control," *Peace Review* 7, nos. 3–4 (1995): p. 390.

10. John Biewen, "Corrections, Inc: Corporate-Sponsored Crime Laws," *www .americanradioworks.org/features/corrections/index.html.*

11. National Institute on Money in State Politics, "Prison Companies Give $1.1 Million to Campaigns in Southern States," *www.followthemoney.org/press/prisons/phtml.*

12. "FRONTLINE Examines Impact of Television on Society in 'Does TV Kill?'" *Media Literacy Review,* Media Literacy Online Project of University of Oregon–Eugene, *http://interact .uoregon.edu/medialit/MLR/readings/articles/front.html.* The Frontline program was aired in 1995; the joint statement of the AAP, AMA, AACAP, and APA is available at *www.aap.org/ advocacy/releases/jstmtevc.htm.* Brandon Centerwall, "Television Violence: The Scale of the Problem and Where to Go from Here," *Journal of the American Medical Association* 267, no. 22 (June 10, 1992): pp. 3059, 3062; Jean Tepperman, "TV: The Violence Teacher," *www.4children .org;* report of the American Psychological Association cited in Sisela Bok, *Mayhem: Violence as Pubic Entertainment* (Reading, Mass.: Perseus, 1998), p. 57.

13. Graeme R. Newman, "Popular Culture and Criminal Justice: A Preliminary Analysis," *Journal of Criminal Justice* 18 (1990): p. 261.

14. Debra Seagal, "Tales from the Cutting-Room Floor: The Reality of 'Reality-Based' Television," *Harper's Magazine,* November 1993, p. 52.

15. David Fabianic, "Television Dramas and Homicide Causation," *Journal of Criminal Justice* 25, no. 3: p. 201.

16. Richard A. Cloward and Lloyd E. Ohlin, *Delinquency and Opportunity: A Theory of Delinquent Gangs* (New York: Free Press, 1960), esp. pp. 77–107.

17. Steven Messner and Richard Rosenfeld, *Crime and the American Dream,* 3rd ed. (Belmont, Calif.: Wadsworth), 2000.

18. Ibid., p. 81.

19. Ibid., p. 10.

20. Ibid., p. 107.

21. Ibid., p. 10.

22. Willem Bonger, *Criminality and Economic Conditions,* abridged and with an intro. by Austin T. Turk (Bloomington: Indiana University Press, 1969), pp. 7–12, 40–47. Willem Adriaan Bonger was born in Holland in 1876 and died by his own hand in 1940 rather than submit to the Nazis. His *Criminalité et conditions économiques* first appeared in 1905. It was translated into English and published in the United States in 1916. Ibid., pp. 3–4.

23. David M. Gordon, "Capitalism, Class and Crime in America," *Crime and Delinquency* (April 1973): p. 174.

24. Ibid.

25. William and Mary Morris, *Dictionary of Word and Phrase Origins,* vol. 2 (New York: Harper & Row, 1967), p. 282.

26. See, for example, Jon Hurwitz and Mark Peffley, "Playing the Race Card in the Post–Willie Horton Era: The Impact of Racialized Code Words on Support for Punitive Crime Policy," *Public Opinion Quarterly* 69, no. 1 (2005): pp. 99–113.

27. *Sourcebook—1981*, pp. 192, 205, 210–11; and *Sourcebook—2003*, p. 126, Table 2.27; p. 141, Table 2.47; and p. 145, Table 2.50.

28. Historical documentation of this can be found in David J. Rothman, *The Discovery of the Asylum: Social Order and Disorder in the New Republic* (Boston: Little, Brown, 1971); and in Frances Fox Piven and Richard A. Cloward, *Regulating the Poor: The Functions of Public Welfare* (New York: Pantheon, 1971), which brings the analysis up to recent times.

29. *The Republic of Plato*, trans. F. M. Cornford (New York: Oxford University Press, 1945), p. 18 [I. 338]. Plato was born in Athens in the year 428 B.C. (or 427, depending on the reckoning) and died there in 348 B.C. (or 347). Scholars generally agree that at least Book One of *The Republic* (the section in which Thrasymachus speaks) was written between the death of Socrates in 399 B.C. and Plato's first journey to Sicily, from which he returned in 388 B.C. (or 387). See Frederick Copleston, S. J., *A History of Philosophy, Volume 1: Greece and Rome* (Westminster, Md.: Newman Press, 1946), pp. 127–141.

30. Karl Marx and Friedrich Engels, *Manifesto of the Communist Party*, in *The Marx–Engels Reader*, ed. Robert C. Tucker (New York: Norton, 1972), p. 337. Marx was born in Trier, Prussia (now in Germany), on May 5, 1818, and died on March 14, 1883. *The Manifesto* was first published in London in February 1848—when Marx was nearly 30 years old. Ibid., pp. xi–xiv.

31. An article on congressional ethics in *Newsweek* (June 14, 1976) makes the point so graphically that it is worth quoting at length:

> *Some of the Hill's most powerful veterans have long earned part of their income from outside business interests—and may be tempted to vote with their own bank accounts in mind when legislation affecting those interests has come before Congress. House whip Thomas P. (Tip) O'Neill is active in real estate and insurance in Massachusetts, Minority Leader John Rhodes of Arizona is a director and vice-president of a life insurance company and scores of other senior members are involved with the banking industry, oil and gas companies and farming operations. Do these connections destroy their judgment? Not necessarily, argues Russell Long of Louisiana, chairman of the powerful Senate Finance Committee and a reliable defender of oil interests—who nevertheless refuses to disclose the size of his personal oil and gas holdings, most of them inherited from his father, former Gov. Huey Long. "A long time ago I became convinced that if you have financial interests completely parallel to your state, then you have no problem," says Long. "If I didn't represent the oil and gas industry, I wouldn't represent the state of Louisiana." Even more difficult to trace is the influence of representatives who keep their law practices—and their clients, many of whom do business with the Federal government—when they become members of Congress. (p. 25)*

For recent analyses of the marriage of economic and political power, see William Greider, *Who Will Tell the People? The Betrayal of American Democracy* (New York: Touchstone/Simon & Schuster, 1993); Phillip Stern, *Still the Best Congress Money Can Buy*, rev. and expanded ed. (Washington, D.C.: Regnery Gateway, 1992); John Jackley, *Hill Rat: Blowing the Lid off Congress* (Washington, D.C.: Regnery Gateway, 1992); Donald Axelrod, *Shadow Government: The Hidden World of Public Authorities—and How They Control over $1 Trillion of Your Money* (New York: Wiley, 1992); Michael Useem, *The Inner Circle: Large Corporations and the Rise of Business Political Activity in the US and UK* (New York: Oxford University Press, 1984); and Kim McQuaid, *Big Business and Presidential Power: From FDR to Reagan* (New York: Morrow, 1982).

32. J. A. Schmidhauser, "The Justices of the Supreme Court: A Collective Portrait," *Midwest Journal of Political Science* 3 (1959): pp. 2–37, 40–49, cited in William J. Chambliss and Robert B. Seidman, *Law, Order and Power* (Reading, Mass.: Addison-Wesley, 1971), p. 96; and Richard

Quinney, *Critique of Legal Order: Crime Control in Capitalist Society* (Boston: Little, Brown, 1973), pp. 60–82, 86–92.

33. See Ross Gelbspan, *Break-ins, Death Threats and the FBI: The Covert War against the Central American Movement* (Boston: South End Press, 1991); Margaret Jayko, *FBI on Trial: The Victory in the Socialist Workers Party Suit against Government Spying* (New York: Pathfinder Press, 1988); "F.B.I. Burglarized Leftist Offices Here 92 Times in 1960–66, Official Files Show," *The New York Times,* March 29, 1976, p. A1; and "Burglaries by FBI Listed in Hundreds," *The Washington Post,* July 16, 1975, p. A1. See also Cathy Perkus, ed., *Cointelpro: The FBI's Secret War on Political Freedom,* intro. Noam Chomsky (New York: Monad Press, 1975).

34. "Hill Panel Raps FBI's Anti-Panthers Tactics," *The Washington Post,* May 7, 1976, pp. A1, A22.

35. "FBI Labeled King 'Communist' in '62," *The Washington Post,* May 6, 1976, pp. A1, A26; and Michael Friedly and David Gallen, *Martin Luther King, Jr: The FBI File* (New York: Carroll & Graf, 1993). See also Carson Clayborne and David Gallen, *Malcolm X: The FBI File* (New York: Carroll & Graf, 1991); and Kenneth O'Reilly, *"Racial Matters": The FBI's Secret File on Black America, 1960–1972* (New York: Free Press, 1989).

36. "Kelley Says FBI Is 'Truly Sorry' for Past Abuses," *The Washington Post,* May 9, 1976, pp. A1, A14; and "FBI Break-Ins Still Go on, Panel Reports," *The Washington Post,* May 11, 1976. For more recent accounts, see "FBI Tactics Questioned in Probe of Activists," *The Chicago Tribune,* March 2, 1990, p. 1:5; "Here Come the '60s, with FBI in Tow," *Los Angeles Times,* June 26, 1990, p. A3; Peter Matthiessen, *In the Spirit of Crazy Horse* (New York: Viking, 1983), which discusses the FBI and the American Indian Movement (AIM), and regarding which the FBI sued the author and delayed publication for several years; and Rex Weyler, *Blood of the Land: The Government and Corporate War against First Nations* (Philadelphia: New Society Publishers, 1992), which covers FBI and AIM. For other agencies of the government see, for example, "Military Spied on King, Other Blacks, Paper Says: Army Reportedly Targeted Southern Churches," *The Washington Post,* March 21, 1993, p. A16.

37. James F. Richardson, *Urban Police in the United States* (Port Washington, N.Y.: Kennikat Press, 1974), pp. 8–13, 22. See also Richardson's *The New York Police: Colonial Times to 1901* (New York: Oxford University Press, 1970).

38. Rothman, *The Discovery of the Asylum,* pp. 57–108, especially pp. 79–81. Cf. Michel Foucault, *Discipline and Punish: The Birth of the Prison* (London: Allen Lane, 1977).

39. Richardson, *Urban Police,* pp. 158–61. See also R. Boyer and H. Morais, *Labor's Untold Story* (New York: United Electrical, Radio & Machine Workers of America, 1976).

40. Rothman, *The Discovery of the Asylum,* pp. 253–54.

41. Philip Taft and Philip Ross, "American Labor Violence: Its Causes, Character, and Outcome," in *The History of Violence in America,* ed. H. D. Graham and T. R. Gurr (New York: Bantam, 1969), pp. 281–395, especially pp. 281, 380; and Richard E. Rubenstein, *Rebels in Eden: Mass Political Violence in the United States* (Boston: Little, Brown, 1970), p. 81 inter alia. See also Center for Research in Criminal Justice, *The Iron Fist and the Velvet Glove* (Berkeley: University of California Press, 1975), pp. 16–19.

42. Karl Marx, *The German Ideology,* in *The Marx-Engels Reader,* ed. Tucker, p. 136.

43. Each new ruling class "is compelled, merely in order to carry through its aim, to represent its interest as the common interest of all the members of society." Marx, *The German Ideology,* p. 138.

44. Marx was not the first to use the term "ideology." The term was coined by a Frenchman, Antoine Destutt de Tracy, who was among the intellectuals named in 1795 to direct the researches of the newly founded Institut de France. The *idéologues* of the Institut generally believed that existing ideas were prejudices rooted in individual psychology or in political conditions and that the path to liberation from these prejudices and thus toward a rational society lay in a science of ideas (literally, an "idea-ology"), which made human beings aware of the sources of their ideas. Thomas Jefferson tried (albeit unsuccessfully) to have Destutt de Tracy's theory made part of the original curriculum of the University of Virginia. See

George Lichtheim, "The Concept of Ideology," *History and Theory* 4, no. 2 (1965): pp. 164–95; and Richard H. Cox, ed., *Ideology, Politics, and Political Theory* (Belmont, Calif.: Wadsworth, 1969), pp. 7–8. Needless to say, Marx used the term "ideology" in ways that neither Destutt de Tracy nor Jefferson anticipated.

45. Lichtheim's essay provides a good discussion of the philosophical antecedents of the gradual separation of the notion of ideology from that of false consciousness. Undoubtedly, this separation is of a piece with the current wisdom that insists that all views of the world are conditioned and rendered partial by the limits of the viewer's historical and social vantage point, and thus shrinks from trying to say anything true about the human condition. An illuminating contemporary example of this "current wisdom" applied to the criminal justice system is Walter B. Miller, "Ideology and Criminal Justice Policy: Some Current Issues," *Journal of Criminal Law and Criminology* 64, no. 2 (1973): pp. 141–62. I shall use the concept of ideology in the Marxian sense, that is, to include that of false consciousness.

46. What follows is just a smattering of the literature documenting the wide and abiding disparities of wealth in America or the existence of a very small, not necessarily organized, group of individuals who, in addition to being extremely wealthy, make most of the economic and political decisions that shape America's destiny: Douglas Massey and Nancy Denton, *American Apartheid* (Cambridge, Mass.: Harvard University Press, 1993); Thomas Dye, *Who's Running America: The Bush Era,* 5th ed. (Englewood Cliffs, N.J.: Prentice Hall, 1990); G. William Domhoff, *The Power Elite and the State: How Policy Is Made in America* (New York: de Gruyter, 1990); Michael Parenti, *Democracy for the Few,* 5th ed. (New York: St. Martin's, 1988); William Julius Wilson, *The Truly Disadvantaged: The Inner City, the Underclass, and Public Policy* (Chicago: University of Chicago Press, 1987); J. Quirk, *Industry and Influence in Federal Regulatory Agencies* (Princeton, N.J.: Princeton University Press, 1981); Bertram Gross, *Friendly Fascism: The New Face of Power in America* (Boston: South End Press, 1980); G. William Domhoff, *The Powers That Be: Processes of Ruling Class Domination in America* (New York: Vintage, 1979); Edward S. Greenberg, *Serving the Few: Corporate Capitalism and the Bias of Government Policy* (New York: Wiley, 1974); Joseph Pechman and Benjamin A. Okner, *Who Bears the Tax Burden?* (Washington, D.C.: Brookings Institution, 1974); Philip M. Stern, *The Rape of the Taxpayer* (New York: Vintage, 1974); Richard C. Edwards, Michael Reich, and Thomas E. Weisskopf, *The Capitalist System: A Radical Analysis of American Society* (Englewood Cliffs, N.J.: Prentice Hall, 1972); John Kenneth Galbraith, *The New Industrial State* (New York: Signet, 1968); G. William Domhoff, *Who Rules America?* (Englewood Cliffs, N.J.: Prentice Hall, 1967); Gabriel Kolko, *Wealth and Power in America: An Analysis of Social Class and Income Distribution* (New York: Praeger, 1962); and C. Wright Mills, *The Power Elite* (New York: Oxford University Press, 1956).

47. U.S. Bureau of the Census, *Income, Poverty and Health Insurance Coverage in the U.S.: 2004*, p. 4; *StatAbst—2006*, Table 680, p. 464. Note that "households" and "families" are similar but not identical units of measure.

48. Alan S. Blinder, "The Level and Distribution of Economic Well-Being," in *The American Economy in Transition,* ed. Martin Feldstein (Chicago: University of Chicago Press, 1980), p. 194466.

49. Arthur Kennickell, "A Rolling Tide: Changes in the Distribution of Wealth in the U.S., 1989–2001," Federal Reserve Board, September 2003, *www.federalreserve.gov/pubs/oss/oss2/papers/concentration.2001.10.pdf.*

50. Carole Shammas, "A New Look at Long-Term Trends in Wealth Inequality in the United States," *American Historical Review* 98, no. 2 (April 1993): pp. 420, 421, 429. See Denis Kessler and Edward N. Wolff, "A Comparative Analysis of Household Wealth Patterns in France and the United States," *Review of Income and Wealth* 37 (1991): pp. 249–66, which concludes, "The major finding of this study is that wealth is distributed more unequally in the U.S. than in France. The differences are considerable" (p. 262).

51. Albert Crenshaw, "Gap between Rich and Poor Grows: Fed Report Details Families' Income Situations," *The Washington Post,* January 23, 2003, p. E1.

52. Undoubtedly, the most interesting recent work on this topic is John Rawls's *A Theory of Justice* (Cambridge, Mass.: Harvard University Press, 1971). The noted British philosopher Stuart Hampshire has called it the most important work in moral philosophy since World War II. It has largely dominated theoretical discussions of political, legal, and economic justice for the last three decades. Rawls's approach is essentially "naturalistic"; that is, he takes the "good" to be that which people rationally desire, and the "moral good" to be that which would best serve all people's rational desires. From this, he takes justice to be those social (legal, political, and economic) arrangements that best serve the interests of all. To reach specific principles of justice, he asks for those principles that it would be rational for all people to agree to if each could not use force or influence to tailor the principles to his or her own interest. On the question of the distribution of income or wealth, this way of questioning leads to the principle that economic inequalities are just only if they work to everyone's advantage, for instance, as incentives that work to raise the level of productivity and thus the level of well-being for all. It would be the task of government to rectify inequalities that exceed this point, by means of taxes and transfers. I cannot, of course, do justice here to what Rawls takes 600 pages to explain and defend. However, I offer this short summary to suggest that the disparities of income in the United States are far from just in the light of contemporary moral philosophy. Clearly, those disparities are far greater than anything that could be claimed to be necessary to increase the well-being of all. Indeed, one would have to be blind not to see that they are not increasing the well-being of all. Robert Nozick has replied to Rawls in a book titled *Anarchy, State and Utopia* (New York: Basic Books, 1974), which no doubt represents the free-enterprise system's theory of justice. Nozick holds that no theory (such as Rawls's) that calls for government intervention to rectify income distribution can be just. His argument is that if people acquire their property (including money) legitimately, then they have the right to sell or spend it as they wish. If this leads to disparities in wealth, one cannot alter this outcome without denying that those sellers or spenders had the right to dispose of their property or money as they saw fit. I shall not try to answer Nozick here. It should be noted, however, that his view starts from the assumption that the property or money that is sold or spent was acquired legitimately. In light of the fact that so much U.S. property was stolen at gunpoint from Indians or Mexicans and so much wealth was taken from the hides of black slaves, applying Nozick's theory in the U.S. context would require a massive redistribution of wealth to reach the starting point at which we could say that individuals own what they own legitimately. For an extended discussion of these theories of justice, see Jeffrey Reiman, *Justice and Modern Moral Philosophy* (New Haven, Conn.: Yale University Press, 1990).

53. U.S. Bureau of the Census, *Income, Poverty and Health Insurance Coverage in the U.S.: 2004*, p. 9.

54. One study reports that "among high school graduates with equal academic ability, the proportion going on to college averages nearly 25 percentage points lower for males (and nearly 35 for females) in the bottom socioeconomic quarter of the population than in the top quarter." Another indicates that "the sons of families in the top fifth of the socioeconomic pyramid have average incomes 75 percent higher than those coming from the bottom fifth." Arthur M. Okun, *Equality and Efficiency* (Washington, D.C.: Brookings Institution, 1975), pp. 81, 75.

CONCLUSION
Criminal *Justice* or *Criminal* Justice

Justice being taken away, then, what are kingdoms but great robberies?
—St. Augustine, *The City of God*

*. . . unjust social arrangements are themselves a kind of extortion,
even violence.*
—John Rawls, *A Theory of Justice*

*. . . the policeman moves through Harlem, therefore, like an occupying
soldier in a bitterly hostile country; which is precisely what, and where he
is, and the reason he walks in twos and threes.*
—James Baldwin, *Nobody Knows My Name*

THE CRIME OF JUSTICE

Robbers, extortionists, and *occupying soldiers* are terms used to characterize those who enforce an unjust law and an unjust order. It would be a mistake to think this is merely a matter of rhetoric. There is a very real and very important sense in which those who use force unjustly or who use force to protect an unjust social order are no different from a band of criminals or an occupying army. If this isn't understood, you are likely to think that what has been described in the first three chapters and accounted for in the fourth amounts to no more than another call for reform of the criminal justice system to make it more effective and fairer, when in fact it is much more. A criminal justice system that functions like ours—that imposes its penalties on the poor and not equally on all who threaten society, that does not protect us against threats to our lives and possessions equal to or graver than those presently defined as "crimes," and that fails even to do those things that could better protect us against the crimes of the poor—*is morally no better than the criminality it claims to fight.*

Later in this chapter, I propose some reforms of the system. However, these should not be taken as proposals aimed merely at improving the effectiveness or fairness of American criminal justice. If the argument of this chapter is correct, then these proposals represent the necessary conditions for

197

establishing the moral superiority of criminal justice to criminality. They are the conditions that must be fulfilled if the criminal justice system is to be acquitted of the indictment implicit in the statements above from St. Augustine, Rawls, and Baldwin. Bear in mind that by the "criminal justice system," I do not mean only police, courts, and prisons. I include the entire legal system, from lawmakers to law enforcers.

What is common to the charge implicit in the statements of St. Augustine, Rawls, and Baldwin is the idea that *injustice transforms a legal system into its opposite.* What is common to the robber, the extortionist, and the occupying soldier is that each uses force (or the threat of force) to coerce people to serve the interests of others at the expense of their own. The robber and the extortionist use force to make other people hand over things of value. The occupying soldier uses force to subject one people to domination by another. The injustice that characterizes criminal acts is the forcing of people to serve the interests of others.

A legal system, of course, also uses force. Its defenders, however, maintain that it uses force to protect people's control over the things they value and over their own destinies. They claim that the legal system protects what people possess against robbers and extortionists and protects their autonomy against those who would try to impose their will on them by force. In short, although both a legal system and its opposite, either criminality or military domination, use force, the moral superiority claimed for the legal system lies in the fact that it uses force to protect the interests of all people subject to its force equally, whereas criminals and occupation troops use force to subject some people to the interests of others. The moral legitimacy of a legal system and the lack of legitimacy of crime and military domination hinge, then, on the question of whether coercion is being used in the interests of all equally, or to promote some people's interests at the expense of others.

To say that the criminal justice system uses force to coerce people into serving the interests of others at the expense of their own *is to say the same thing about the criminal justice system that we say of crime!* In the absence of some compelling moral reason, force used to coerce people into serving the interests of others at the expense of their own is *morally no better than criminal force.* Because a legal system purports to do the reverse—to use force to protect *everyone's* interest in freedom and security equally by preventing and rectifying violations of those interests—legal systems call themselves *systems of justice.*

This adds up to something that should be obvious but is not. *A criminal justice system is criminal to the extent that it is not a system of justice.* To call the criminal justice system a "system of justice" is to assert that the force used by the criminal justice system is morally opposite from, and morally superior to, the force used by criminals or conquerors. But then we must ask whether this assertion is true. A criminal justice system is a system of justice to the extent that it protects equally the interests and rights of all and to the extent that it punishes equally all who endanger these interests or who violate these rights. To the extent that it veers from these goals, the criminal justice system is guilty of the same sacrificing of the interests of some for the benefit of others that it exists to combat. It is, therefore, morally speaking, guilty of crime. Which is it?

The experience of the twentieth century has taught us that we should not take for granted that every legal system is a system of justice. Hitler's Germany and Stalin's Soviet Union, as well as South Africa when it practiced apartheid, are testimony to the fact that what is put forth as law may well be outrageously unjust. We have come to recognize the truth implicit in the statements of St. Augustine, Rawls, and Baldwin: What is put forth under color of law may be morally no better than crime or tyranny. Therefore, we can no longer uncritically take for granted that our own legal order is just merely because it is legal. We must subject it to the moral test of whether it serves and protects the interests of all to make sure it is not injustice disguised as justice, criminality wearing the mask of law. (In Appendix II, "Between Philosophy and Criminology," I argue that criminology requires a moral evaluation of crime as part of its identification of its object of study.) It is, of course, not my aim to place the U.S. legal system on par with that of Hitler's Germany or Stalin's Soviet Union. As I have acknowledged, there is much in the system that is legitimate, and many are caught by the system who should be. Stated precisely, my claim is this:

> *To the extent that* the American criminal justice system fails to implement policies that could significantly reduce crime and the suffering it produces (as argued in Chapter 1),
> *To the extent that* the American criminal justice system fails to protect Americans against the gravest dangers to their lives and property (as argued in Chapter 2),
> *To the extent that* the American criminal justice system apprehends and punishes individuals not because they are dangerous but because they are *dangerous and poor* (as argued in Chapter 3),
> *Then, to that same extent,* the American criminal justice system fails to give all Americans either protection or justice, aids and abets those who pose the greatest dangers to Americans, and uses force in ways that do not serve equally the interests of all who are subject to that force, and *thus its use of force is morally no better than crime itself.*

REHABILITATING CRIMINAL JUSTICE IN AMERICA

The criminal justice system in America is morally indistinguishable from criminality insofar as it exercises force and imposes suffering on human beings *while violating its own morally justifying ideals: protection and justice.*

Once this is understood, the requirements for rehabilitating the system follow rather directly. The system must institute policies that make good on its claim to protect society and to do justice. In the remainder of this chapter, I briefly suggest the outlines of a "treatment strategy" for *helping the system go straight*. It cannot be reiterated too frequently that these proposals are not offered as a means of *improving* the system. Nor am I under any illusion that these proposals will be easily adopted or implemented. They are presented as the necessary requirements for establishing the criminal justice system's moral difference from, and moral superiority to, *crime*; and even if not implemented or not likely to be implemented, they stand as a measure against which this moral difference and superiority can be judged. The proposals fall under the headings of the two ideals that justify the existence of a criminal justice system. These ideals are that the criminal justice system protect us against the real dangers that threaten us and that it not be an accomplice to injustice in the larger society. To realize these ideals, it is necessary that the harms and injustices done by the criminal justice system themselves be eliminated.

Protecting Society

First, it must be acknowledged that every day that we refuse to implement those strategies that have a good chance of cutting down on the crimes people fear—the crimes on the FBI Index—the system is an accomplice to those crimes and bears responsibility for the suffering they impose. Thus,

We must put an end to the crime-producing poverty in our midst.

Throughout this book I have documented the striking persistence of large-scale poverty in the United States as well as the link between that poverty and much of the crime people fear the most. The elimination of poverty is the most promising crime-fighting strategy there is, and, in the long run, the most cost-effective. It is sometimes observed that poverty itself doesn't cause crime, because, for example, there was more poverty in earlier times than now and yet less crime. There is an important truth here, but it is easy to miss it. The truth is that it is not poverty as such that breeds crime, but the things that poverty brings with it in a modern, free, and free-enterprise society like ours: lack of good education (because schools are financed primarily out of local property taxes), lack of parental authority (because unemployed parents easily lose their children's respect), lack of cohesive local community (because those who can will escape the poor inner cities as quickly as possible), lack of allegiance to social institutions (due to feeling left out—recall the discussion of John Rawls's views in Chapter 1), and so on.

It is these things, rather than lack of money itself, that lead to crime. Investing in our inner cities and providing high-quality education, job training, and jobs for the unemployed will give us more productive citizens with a stake in playing by the rules. And it will be cheaper than paying for police and prisons to house those who break the rules.

Eliminating the debilitating and crime-producing poverty around us is essential to any serious, long-term effort to protect society from crime. But along with it, we must

Let the crime fit the harm and the punishment fit the crime.

For the criminal justice system to justify its methods, it must make good on its claim to protect society. This requires that the criminal law be redrawn so that the list of crimes reflects the real dangers that individuals pose to society. I am not saying that we should start punishing people for things that are currently not crimes. For all that I have said about the harms of occupational hazards, for example, I do not say that we should simply treat the people responsible for them as if they were criminals, if there are not yet criminal laws against what they have done. The traditional prohibition against ex post facto criminal laws—that is, against punishing people for things they did before those things were crimes—is an important principle of justice. Rather, we must make new and clear laws against imposing certain dangers on workers and citizens generally, and then hold people to those laws no matter what their class standing. Crime in the suites should be prosecuted and punished as vigorously as crime in the streets.

The law must be drawn carefully so that individuals are not punished for harm they could not foresee or could not have avoided, or that others have freely consented to risk. Moreover, this is not a matter of punishing people for anything and everything they do that might lead to harm. The pursuit of security must not swamp the legitimate claims of liberty and progress. Some risks are the inevitable companions of freedom, and some are part of modern life. For every mile of highway we build, we can predict the number of people who will be killed in accidents on it. This does not justify treating the highway engineer as a murderer. Rather, we must have an open and ongoing discussion about risk and decide together which risks are worth taking and what level of risk is reasonable to impose on workers or citizens generally. Within this framework, we must stop treating *indirect* harm as merely a regulatory matter and start *treating all intentional harm-producing acts in proportion to the actual harm they produce. We must enact and implement punishments that fit the harmfulness of the crime without respect to the class of the criminal.* There is, for instance, general agreement that incarceration functions as an effective deterrent to corporate crime when the threat of imprisonment is believed.[1] To be believed, however, it must be used.

Because responsibility for corporate actions tends to be spread or even blurred in large organizations, we need legal requirements that make corporations identify in advance the individuals who are legally responsible for specific acts. Kip Schlegel recommends that a standard of "reckless supervision" be built into sentencing guidelines for corporate offenses, so that individuals with supervisory authority could be held responsible for failure to exercise that authority when there is substantial risk of harm.[2] The Sarbanes-Oxley financial reform legislation takes a step in this direction by requiring executives to certify the accuracy of financial statements, so that they cannot get paid big money to run a company and then claim they had no idea about massive, systemic, billion-dollar frauds. The principle is sound and should be applied more widely in the business world.

But this is only the beginning. There is much more that can and should be done. In his book, *Corporate Crime and Violence,* Russell Mokhiber sets out a "50-Point Law-and-Order Program to Curb Corporate Crime."[3] Mokhiber's suggestions are quite realistic, and many fit well within the framework just outlined. Among them are recommendations for new laws that would require corporate executives to report activities that might cause death or injury, that would make it a criminal offense to willfully or recklessly fail to oversee an assigned activity that results in criminal conduct, that would enable federal prosecutors to bring federal homicide charges against companies that have caused death on a national scale (such as Manville or the tobacco companies), that would hold corporations responsible for how they respond to wrongful acts (do they cover up or take measures to prevent recurrence, etc.?), that would facilitate class action suits against corporations, that would require convicted companies to notify their victims and to make restitution to them, that would better protect whistleblowers from reprisal, that would increase the penalties for convicted corporate executives, that would make it a crime for a corporation to have a faulty system for ensuring compliance with the law, and that would—for serious or repeated offenses—"execute" corporations (by stripping them of their corporate charters). Such laws, duly applied, would begin to make the criminal justice system's response proportionate to the real dangers in our society.

The other side of the coin is the decriminalization of "victimless crimes," acts such as prostitution, homosexual sodomy, gambling, vagrancy, drunkenness, and, of course, drug use. As long as these acts involve only persons who have freely chosen to participate, they are no threat to the liberty of any citizen. This also means that there is generally no complainant for these crimes, no person who is harmed by these acts and who is ready and able to press charges and testify against the wrongdoers. Therefore, police have to use a variety of shady tactics involving deception and actions bordering on entrapment, which undermine the public's respect for the police and the police officers' respect for themselves. In any event, the use of such low-visibility tactics increases the likelihood of corruption and arbitrariness in the enforcement of the law. Beyond this, because these acts produce no tangible harm to others, laws against them make criminals out of people who have no intention to harm or take advantage of others. In short, such laws fill our prisons with people who aren't dangerous, while we leave truly dangerous people on the streets. To make good on its claim to protect society, the criminal justice system must not only treat the dangerous acts of business executives as crimes but also decriminalize those acts that are not clearly dangerous.[4]

More than 100 years ago, John Stuart Mill formulated a guiding principle, still relevant to our time, for the design of legislation in a society committed to personal liberty:

> That principle is, that the sole end for which mankind are warranted, individually or collectively, in interfering with the liberty of action of any of their number, is self-protection. That the only purpose for which power can be rightfully exercised over any [sane adult] member of a civilized community, against his will, is to prevent harm to others.[5]

Although this principle needs to be modified in recognition of some of the ways in which individuals can cause future harm to themselves in a complex modern society where people must deal with machines and chemicals beyond their understanding,[6] the heart of the principle is still widely accepted. This is the notion that a necessary condition of any justifiable legal prohibition is that it prohibit an act that does foreseeable harm to someone other than the actor himself. Because priority should be given to freedom of action, this harm should be *demonstrable* (i.e., verifiable by some widely agreed-upon means, say, those used by science), and it should be of sufficient gravity to outweigh the value of the freedom that is to be legally prohibited.[7]

This principle not only should guide legislators and those engaged in revising and codifying criminal law but also should be raised to the level of an implicit constitutional principle. The U.S. Supreme Court recognizes certain traditional principles of legality as constitutional requirements even though they are not explicitly written into the Constitution. For instance, some laws have been held unconstitutional because of their vagueness[8] and others because they penalized a condition (such as being a drunk or an addict) rather than an action (such as drinking or using drugs).[9] The tenor of the Bill of Rights is to enshrine and protect individual liberty from the encroachment of the state, and thus Mill's principle is arguably already implicitly there.

Whether as a legislative or a judicial criterion, however, applying Mill's principle would undoubtedly rid our law of the residues of our puritan moralism. And it would eliminate the forced induction into criminality of the individuals, mainly those of the lower class, who are arrested for "victimless crimes." It would eliminate the pressure toward secondary crime (the need of the prostitute for a pimp to provide protection, theft by drug addicts to support their habits, violent turf wars between drug gangs, and so on). And it would free up resources for the fight against the really dangerous crimes. Before all, then,

We must legalize the production and sale of "illicit drugs" and treat addiction as a medical problem.

When drug addicts cannot obtain their fix legally, they will obtain it illegally. Because those who sell it illegally have a captive market, they will charge high prices to make their own risks worthwhile. To pay the high prices, addicts must, will, and do resort to crime. Thus, every day in which we keep the acquisition of drugs a crime, we are using the law to protect the high profits of drug black marketeers, *and* we are creating a situation in which large numbers of individuals are virtually physically compelled to commit theft. There can be little doubt that our present "cure" for narcotics use is more criminal (and criminogenic) than the narcotics themselves. Kurt Schmoke, while mayor of Baltimore, said that of 335 homicides committed in Baltimore in 1992, 48 percent were drug-related.[10] Another observer says that it is the drug war—not the drugs—that is shattering our inner cities. One of its effects is that a quarter of all black American men between the ages of 20 and 29 are behind bars, on parole, or on probation—which in turn makes them even less likely to find decent employment, and this locks them further into poverty.[11] And while we lock up so many young black men, we wonder why there are so many single black mothers and we don't notice the connection.

Ethan Nadelmann, of the Woodrow Wilson School of Public and International Affairs, points out that "there is no single legalization option. Legalization can mean a free market, or one closely regulated by the government, or even a government monopoly. . . . Legalization under almost any regime, however, does promise many advantages over the current approach. Government expenditures on drug-law enforcement would drop dramatically. So would organized crime revenues."[12] I will not enter into debate about the various ways in which drugs can be legalized. Many observers seem to agree that the British system in which doctors may prescribe heroin for addicts is superior to our own punitive system. For example, an editorial in the *Montreal Gazette* states, "A Dutch study, reported this month in the British Medical Journal, found prescribing heroin to abusers is not only cost-effective, but provided better quality of life to addicts. Savings to society were estimated at more than $20,000 a year per addict in reduced policing costs and property crime. Without this program, addicts on average were spending $1,500 a month on heroin, and were involved in a crime every three days to get extra money for drugs."[13]

A number of experts have gone even further. Norval Morris and Gordon Hawkins urge that narcotics use be decriminalized and the drugs be sold in pharmacies by prescription. Arnold Trebach urges that doctors be permitted to prescribe heroin for the treatment of addicts and as a powerful painkiller. Kurt Schmoke, former mayor of Baltimore, has called for permitting health professionals to give drugs to addicts as part of a treatment and detoxification plan. Phillip Baridon recommends that pure heroin—clearly labeled as to contents, recommended dosage, and addictive potential—be sold at a low fixed price in pharmacies, without prescription, to anyone aged 18 or over.[14] Jerry Wilson, former Washington, D.C., police chief, has suggested the possibility of selling and taxing marijuana in the way that tobacco is currently sold and taxed, and treating opiates and cocaine derivatives the way alcohol currently is treated, while keeping some psychoactive drugs available only at pharmacies with a doctor's prescription.[15]

Any reasonable plan of legalization will start by decriminalizing marijuana, which is virtually harmless. On the other hand, there may be some drugs that are so addictive or so likely to stimulate people to violence that we must keep them illegal. This may be the case with "crack" and with PCP, also known as "angel dust." If this turns out to be true (and the government has so exaggerated the dangers of illicit drugs over the years that healthy skepticism is warranted about these recent claims), it may be necessary to exclude these from the general program of decriminalization. With less dangerous drugs decriminalized, however, many users of crack or PCP might switch to the less dangerous ones, and, in any event, already overstretched law enforcement resources would be freed up to concentrate on the really dangerous drugs and on the crucial problem of keeping drugs away from youngsters.

Ending poverty, criminalizing the really dangerous acts of the well-off, and decriminalizing victimless crimes will reduce crime, protect society, and free up our police and prisons for the fight against the criminals who really threaten our lives and limbs. For these, however,

We must develop correctional programs that promote rather than undermine personal responsibility, and we must offer ex-offenders real preparation and a real opportunity to succeed as law-abiding citizens.

The scandal of our prisons has been amply documented. Like our drug policy, our prisons seem more calculated to produce than reduce crime. The enforced childhood of imprisonment may be the painful penalty that offenders deserve, but if it undermines their capacity to go straight after release, we are cutting off our noses to spite our faces. People cannot learn to control themselves responsibly if they have spent years having every aspect of their lives—the hour they wake, the number of minutes they wash, the time and content of eating and working and exercising, and the hour at which lights go out—regulated by someone else. Add to this the fact that convicts usually emerge with no marketable skill and little chance of getting a decent job with the stigma of a prison sentence hanging over them. The result is a system in which we never let criminals finish paying their debt to society and instead give them every incentive to return to crime.

Former National Institute of Justice Director Jeremy Travis states that 630,000 people leave prison each year and reenter society. He writes that "reentry is not an option. Reentry reflects the iron law of imprisonment: they all come back."[16] Thus, if we are going to continue to punish people by depriving them of their liberty, we must do it in a way that prepares them for the life they will lead when their liberty is returned. Anything less than this is a violation of the Constitution's Eighth Amendment guarantee against "cruel and unusual punishment." Depriving a person of his or her liberty may be an acceptable punishment, but *depriving people of their dignity and a chance to live a law-abiding life when their punishment is supposed to be over is cruel and* (should be but sadly is not) *unusual!*

If, as I think, depriving people of a chance to live a law-abiding life after prison is cruel and unusual punishment, then pursuant to the guarantee of the Eighth Amendment, every imprisoned person should have a right to training at a marketable skill as well as a right to compete equally with non-ex-convicts for a job once the punishment is over. This might require making it illegal to discriminate against ex-convicts in hiring and illegal to require job applicants to state whether they had ever been arrested, convicted, and/or imprisoned for a crime. This requirement might have to be modified for particularly sensitive occupations, although on the whole I think it would be fairer and more effective in rehabilitating ex-cons to enact it across the board and to have the government finance or subsidize a fund to insure losses incurred as a result of hiring ex-convicts. My hunch is that this would be much less costly than paying to support ex-cons in prison and their families on welfare when they return to crime for lack of a job. Beyond this, prison industries should pay inmates at prevailing wages; this money then could be used for restitution to victims and to purchase privileges and possibly increased privacy or freedom for the prisoners—all of which would give them greater practice at controlling their own lives so that they will be prepared to do so after release.

To release them back into a safer and more peaceful society, however,

We must enact and vigorously enforce stringent gun controls.

Americans are armed to the teeth. The handgun is the most easily concealed, the most effective, and the deadliest weapon there is. Its ubiquity is a constant temptation to would-be crooks who lack the courage or skill to commit crime without weapons or to chance hand-to-hand combat. Its ubiquity also means that any dispute may be transformed into a fatal conflict beyond the desires or expectations of the disputants. And the handgun is only part of the story. In recent years, it has become relatively easy to obtain rapid-firing assault rifles. Trying to fight crime while allowing such easy access to guns is like trying to teach a child to walk and tripping him each time he stands up. In its most charitable light, it is hypocrisy. Less charitably, it is complicity in murder.[17]

If, because of the Second Amendment, we continue to allow private individuals to own guns, we can at least require that gun owners be registered and perhaps certified after completing a course on safe use of guns (safety classes are already commonly required as part of qualifying for gun permits). We can surely ban assault rifles and require all guns to have trigger locks that children and gun thieves cannot open.

These changes, taken together, would be likely to reduce dangerous crime and to bring us a legal order that actually punished (and, it is hoped, deterred) all and only those acts that really threaten our lives, limbs, and possessions and punished them in proportion to the harm they really produce. Such a legal system could be truly said to protect society.

Promoting Justice

The changes recommended above would, in part, make the criminal justice system more just, because people would be punished in proportion to the seriousness of their antisocial acts, and the number of innocent persons victimized by those acts would be reduced. At the same time, however, we have seen that the criminal justice system is biased against the poor, and until poverty is eliminated, much must be done to assure justice for the poor people who get caught up in the criminal justice system.

A criminal justice system should arrest, charge, convict, and sentence individuals with an eye only to their crime, not to their class. Any evidence of more frequent arrests or harsher penalties for poor persons than for others accused of the same crime is a grave injustice that undermines the legitimacy of the criminal justice system. Because many of the decisions that work to the disadvantage of the poor—police decisions to arrest, prosecutors' decisions to charge, and judges' decisions on how long to sentence—are exercises of discretion often out of public view, they are particularly resistant to control. Because, unlike prosecutors' or judges' decisions, the police officer's decision *not* to arrest is *not* a matter of record, it is the least visible exercise of discretion and the most difficult to control. Our best hope to make arrests by police more just lies in increased citizen awareness and education of police officers so that they at least become aware of the operation and impact of their own biases and are held more directly accountable to, and by, the public they serve and sometimes arrest.

As for prosecutorial and judicial discretion, two approaches seem potentially fruitful. First, lawmakers ought to spell out the acceptable criteria that prosecutors may use in deciding whether or what to charge and the criteria that judges may use in deciding whether or what to sentence. The practice of multiple charging (charging an accused burglar with "the lesser included crimes" of breaking and entering, possession of burglar's tools, and so on) should be eliminated. It is used by prosecutors to "coax" accused persons into pleading guilty to one charge by threatening to press *all* charges. Of all the dubious features of our system of bargain justice, this seems most clearly without justification because it works to coerce a plea of guilty that should be uncoerced if it is to be legally valid.[18] The recently developed federal sentencing guidelines (followed by the inception of sentencing guidelines in many states) are an important step toward reducing discretion, and thus discrimination, in the criminal justice system.[19] But they are only a step. They have not eliminated discrimination. D'Alessio and Stolzenberg found that lower-socioeconomic-status (SES) offenders were likely to receive harsher sentences for nonproperty and morals offenses than higher-SES offenders, and that sentencing guidelines did not appear to reduce these disparities.[20] And, as I pointed out in Chapter 3, for similar charges white defendants are more likely to get sentences below the guideline minimums than blacks. It appears that such guidelines have not so much eliminated discretion as shifted it from judges to prosecutors (who decide what to charge), and because prosecutors are less insulated from political pressures than judges, that is a step backwards. Thus, sentencing guidelines must be matched with charging guidelines.[21] Neither sort of guidelines need be so rigid as to leave no room for the expert judgment of judges or prosecutors. Rather, we need rules that hold those officials accountable for their judgments by requiring them to explain and justify their decisions.

Moreover, the sentencing guidelines that we have arose during the Reagan era, with its emphasis on extreme punitiveness. (In 2005, the Supreme Court decided that sentencing guidelines are only advisory and not legally binding on judges; but research by the U.S. Sentencing Commission indicates that sentencing practices in the year following the decision are consistent with earlier sentencing under the guidelines, so all the problems with them remain.)[22] They often either include or are accompanied by draconian mandatory minimum sentences for small crimes, particularly anything to do with drugs. In response to this, an advocacy group was formed called Families against Mandatory Minimums, whose "files bulge with cases of citizens serving drug sentences of 5, 10 and 20 years without parole chances for first and often minor offenses."[23] California recently sentenced a man to 50 years in prison for two shoplifting incidents involving stealing videocassettes from K-Mart, and the Supreme Court upheld the sentence in 2003 as not being unreasonable or disproportionate.[24] Because this very punitive approach has dramatically expanded our prison populations with only small gains in reducing crime, it is time to separate the task of assuring even-handed sentencing from that of hard-fisted sentencing. However we achieve it, it is clear that to make the criminal justice system function justly,

We must narrow the range in which police officers, prosecutors, and judges exercise discretion, and we must develop procedures to hold them accountable to the public for the fairness and reasonableness of their decisions.

All these changes still leave standing what is probably the largest source of injustice to the poor in the system: *unequal access to quality legal counsel.* We know that, by and large, privately retained counsel will have more incentive to put in the time and effort to get their clients off the hook, and we know that this results in a situation in which, *for equal crimes,* those who can retain their own counsel are more likely to be acquitted than those who cannot. The present system of allocating assigned counsel or public defenders to the poor and privately retained lawyers to the affluent is little more than a parody of the constitutional guarantee of *equal protection under the law.*

There are simply no two ways about this. In our system, even though lawyers are assigned to the poor, justice has a price. Those who pay get the choicest cut—those who cannot, get the scraps. Little over a century ago, before there were public police forces in every town and city, people got "police protection" by hiring private police officers or bodyguards if they could afford it. Protection was available for a price, and so those who had more money were better protected under the law. Today, we regard it as every citizen's right to have police protection, and we would find it outrageous if police protection were allocated to citizens on a fee-for-service basis. *This is precisely where we stand with respect to the legal protection provided by lawyers!*

Legal protection is provided not only by the police. Attorneys are necessary to protect individuals from losing their freedom at the hands of the law before they have exhausted the legal defenses that are theirs by right. Both police officers and lawyers are essential to the individual's legal protection. It is sheer hypocrisy to acknowledge everyone's right to equal protection under the law by the police and then to allocate protection under the law by lawyers on the basis of what individuals can pay. As long as this continues, we cannot claim that there is anything like equal treatment before the law in the criminal justice system. Therefore,

We must transform the equal right to counsel into the right to equal counsel as far as it is possible.

Although this would appear to be a clear requirement of the equal protection and due process clauses of the Constitution, the Supreme Court has avoided it, perhaps because it poses massive practical problems—and surely it does. However, the creation of public police forces to protect everyone posed great practical problems in its time as well.

Certainly it would not be appropriate to use the police as a model for resolving the problem of equal counsel. To establish a government legal service for all—in effect, to nationalize the legal profession—might make equal legal representation available to all. It would, however, undermine the adversary system by undercutting the independence of defense attorneys from the state. Some form of national legal insurance to enable all individuals to hire private attorneys of their own choice, however, could bring us closer to equal legal protection without compromising the adversarial relationship.

Such insurance would undoubtedly have to be subsidized by the government, as are the police, courts, and prisons; but it would not necessarily have to be totally paid for out of taxes. People can rightly be expected to pay their legal bills up to some fraction of their income, if they have one. The rest would be paid for by a government subsidy that would pay the difference between what the accused could afford and the going rate for high-quality legal counsel. Nothing in the system need interfere with the freedom of the accused to select the lawyer of his or her choice (an option closer to the hearts of free enterprisers than the present public defender system allows) or interfere with the independence of the lawyer.

Undoubtedly, such a system would be costly. Our commitment to equal justice, however, remains a sham until we are willing to pay this price. Americans have paid dearly to protect the value of liberty enshrined in the Constitution. Is it too much to ask that they pay to realize the ideal of justice enshrined there too?

One final recommendation remains to be made. I have already argued that the criminal justice system, by its very nature, embodies the prevailing economic relations in its laws. This means that it is an error to think of the criminal justice system as an entity that can be reformed in isolation from the larger social order. A criminal justice system is a means to protect that social order, and it can be no more just than the order it protects. A law against theft may be enforced with an even and just hand. But if it protects an unjust distribution of wealth and property, the result is *injustice evenly enforced*. A criminal justice system cannot hold individuals guilty of the injustice of breaking the law if the law itself supports and defends an unjust social order.

Without economic and social justice, the police officer in the ghetto is indeed an occupying soldier with no more legitimacy than his or her gun provides. Without economic and social justice, the criminal justice system is the defender of injustice and is thus morally indistinguishable from the criminal. *A criminal justice system can be no more just than the society its laws protect.* Along with the other recommendations I have made in this chapter, the achievement of economic and social justice is a necessary condition for establishing the criminal justice system's moral superiority to crime.

We must establish a more just distribution of wealth and income and make equal opportunity a reality for all Americans.

This is not merely a matter of throwing money in the direction of poor people. It is a call for investment in our most important resource—people—

and for targeting that investment where it is most urgently needed and morally required: to rebuild our squalid inner cities, to educate our young, and to offer real opportunity to poor people to lift themselves out of poverty without lowering themselves into dependency. This would amount to a redistribution of wealth and income in the direction of greater social and economic justice. Because it would also reduce the temptations to crime produced by poverty, it brings us full circle to the first recommendation that I made for protecting society. *Here the requirements of safety and justice converge.*

SUMMARY

Every step toward reducing poverty and its debilitating effects, toward criminalization of the dangerous acts of the affluent and vigorous prosecution of white-collar crime, toward decriminalization of "illicit drugs" and other "victimless crimes," and toward domestic disarmament; every step toward creating a correctional system that promotes human dignity, toward giving ex-offenders a real opportunity to go straight, toward making the exercise of power by police officers, prosecutors, and judges more reasonable and more just, toward giving all individuals accused of crime equal access to high-quality legal expertise in their defense; and every step toward establishing economic and social justice are steps that move us from a system of *criminal* justice to a system of criminal *justice*. The refusal to take those steps is a move in the opposite direction.

STUDY QUESTIONS

1. What do the three quotations at the beginning of this chapter mean? How do they apply to the American criminal justice system?

2. What are the necessary conditions for establishing the moral superiority of criminal justice to criminality?

3. What is meant by "victimless crimes"? Why does the author feel they should not be kept criminal?

4. Would you be willing to have your taxes go to pay for equal-quality legal counsel for the poor?

5. Is the distribution of wealth and income in America just? How is this related to the justice of the criminal justice system?

6. Are the recommendations made in this chapter likely to be instituted? What does your answer imply about your view of the American legal system?

   A companion website to this book, with a chapter outline and summary, links to additional information, and Internet-based exercises, is available at "Rich Get Richer," *www.paulsjusticepage.com.*

ADDITIONAL READINGS

Currie, Elliott. *Crime and Punishment in America.* New York: Metropolitan Books/Henry Holt, 1998.

Elias, Robert. *Victims Still: The Political Manipulation of Crime Victims.* Newbury Park, Calif.: Sage, 1993.

Kleinig, John, ed. *Handled with Discretion: Ethical Issues in Police Decision Making.* Lanham, Md.: Rowman & Littlefield, 1996.

Korten, David. *When Corporations Rule the World.* West Hartford, Conn.: Kumarian Press, 1995.

Leighton, Paul, and Jeffrey Reiman, eds. *Criminal Justice Ethics.* Upper Saddle River, N.J.: Prentice Hall, 2001.

Miller, Jerome. *Last One over the Wall: The Massachusetts Experiment in Closing Reform Schools.* Columbus: Ohio State University Press, 1992.

Reich, Charles. *Opposing the System.* New York: Crown, 1995.

Schlegel, Kip. *Just Deserts for Corporate Criminals.* Boston: Northeastern University Press, 1990.

Travis, Jeremy. *But They All Come Back: Facing the Challenges of Prisoner Reentry.* Washington, D.C.: Urban Institute Press, 2005.

Trebach, Arnold, and James Inciardi. *Legalize It? Debating American Drug Policy.* Washington, D.C.: American University Press, 1993.

Welch, Michael. *Punishment in America: Social Control and the Ironies of Imprisonment.* Thousand Oaks, Calif.: Sage, 1999.

NOTES

1. These are the words of a former director of the fraud division of the Department of Justice:

> No one in direct contact with the living reality of business conduct in the United States is unaware of the effect the imprisonment of seven high officials in the Electrical Machinery Industry in 1960 had on the conspiratorial price fixing in many areas of our economy; similar sentences in a few cases each decade would almost completely cleanse our economy of the cancer of collusive price fixing and the mere prospect of such sentences is itself the strongest available deterrent to such activities.

Gordon B. Spivak, "Antitrust Enforcement in the United States: A Primer," *Connecticut Bar Journal* 37 (September 1963): p. 382.

2. Kip Schlegel, *Just Deserts for Corporate Criminals* (Boston: Northeastern University Press, 1990), p. 137. This book contains a very extensive and valuable analysis of the jurisprudential and philosophical issues involved in assessing the guilt of both individual corporate officers and corporations themselves.

3. Russell Mokhiber, *Corporate Crime and Violence: Big Business Power and the Abuse of Public Trust* (San Francisco: Sierra Club, 1988), pp. 38–65.

4. See Norval Morris and Gordon Hawkins, *The Honest Politician's Guide to Crime Control* (Chicago: University of Chicago Press, 1970), ch. 1, "The Overreach of the Criminal Law," pp. 1–28; Herbert Packer, *The Limits of the Criminal Sanction* (Stanford, Calif.: Stanford University Press, 1968); and Jeffrey H. Reiman, "Can We Avoid the Legislation of Morality?" in *Legality, Morality and Ethics in Criminal Justice,* ed. Nicholas N. Kittrie and Jackwell Susman (New York: Praeger, 1979), pp. 130–41.

5. John Stuart Mill, *On Liberty* (1859; reprint, New York: Appleton-Century-Crofts, 1973), p. 9.

6. See, for example, Gerald Dworkin, "Paternalism," in *Morality and the Law*, ed. Richard Wasserstrom (Belmont, Calif.: Wadsworth, 1971), pp. 107–26; and Joel Feinberg, "Legal Paternalism," in *Today's Moral Problems*, ed. Richard Wasserstrom (New York: Macmillan, 1975), pp. 33–50.

7. See, for instance, the excellent discussion of the principle in Peter T. Manicas, *The Death of the State* (New York: Putnam, 1974), ch. 5, "The Liberal Moral Ideal," pp. 194–241; and H. L. A. Hart, *Law, Liberty and Morality* (New York: Vintage, 1963).

8. The standard laid down in *Conally v. General Constr. Co*, 269 U.S. 385, 391, 70 L. Ed. 322, 46 S. Ct. 126 (1926), is "whether or not the vagueness is of such a character, 'that men of common intelligence must necessarily guess at its meaning.'" See also *Lanzetta et al. v. State of New Jersey*, 306, U.S. 451, 83 L. Ed. 888, 59 S. Ct. 618 (1939), in which the U.S. Supreme Court struck down a New Jersey statute that made it a felony for anyone not engaged in any lawful occupation to be a member of a gang because the terms of the statute were "vague, indefinite and uncertain" and thus "repugnant to the due process clause of the Fourteenth Amendment." Both cases are cited and discussed in Jerome Hall, *General Principles of Criminal Law*, 2nd ed. (New York: Bobbs-Merrill, 1960), pp. 36–48. For a constitutional and philosophical argument for treating Mills's harm principle as an implied constitutional principle, see David A. J. Richards, *Sex, Drugs, Death, and the Law: An Essay on Human Rights and Overcriminalization* (Totowa, N.J.: Rowman and Littlefield, 1982), pp. 1–34, inter alia.

9. See *Robinson v. California*, 370 U.S. 66 (1962), in which the court held that a state law penalizing a person for a "status" such as addiction constitutes "cruel and unusual punishment" in violation of the Eighth Amendment. Cited and discussed in Nicholas N. Kittrie, *The Right to Be Different: Deviance and Enforced Therapy* (Baltimore: Johns Hopkins University Press, 1971), pp. 35–36, inter alia.

10. Kurt Schmoke, "It's Time to Get Real about Guns and Drugs," *The Washington Post Outlook*, October 3, 1993, p. C4.

11. Jonathan Marshall, "How Our War on Drugs Shattered the Cities," *The Washington Post Outlook*, May 17, 1992, pp. C1, C2.

12. Ethan Nadelmann, "U.S. Drug Policy: A Bad Export," in *Drugs in America*, ed. Robert Lang (New York: Wilson, 1993), p. 232.

13. "Prescription Heroin? It Just Might Work," *Montreal Gazette*, June 8, 2005, p A24.

14. Morris and Hawkins, *The Honest Politician's Guide to Crime Control*, pp. 3, 8–10; Arnold S. Trebach, *The Heroin Solution* (New Haven, Conn.: Yale University Press, 1982), pp. 267–70; Phillip C. Baridon, *Addiction, Crime, and Social Policy* (Lexington, Mass.: Lexington Books, 1976), p. 88; and Schmoke, "It's Time to Get Real about Guns and Drugs," pp. C1, C4.

15. Jerry V. Wilson, "Our Wasteful War on Drugs," *The Washington Post*, January 18, 1994, p. A20.

16. Jeremy Travis, *And They All Come Back* (Washington, D.C.: Urban Institute Press, 2005), p. xxi.

17. See the thoughtful recommendations for gun control and their rationale in Morris and Hawkins, *The Honest Politician's Guide to Crime Control*, pp. 63–71.

18. I have already pointed out that the vast majority of persons convicted of crimes in the United States are not convicted by juries. They plead guilty as the result of a "bargain" with the prosecutor (underwritten by the judge), in which the prosecutor agrees to drop other charges in return for the guilty plea. Kenneth Kipnis argues that the entire system of bargain justice is a violation of the ideal of justice because it amounts to coercing a guilty plea and often to punishing an offender for a crime other than the one he or she has committed. It is an argument worth considering. See Kenneth Kipnis, "Criminal Justice and the Negotiated Plea," *Ethics* 86, no. 2 (January 1976): pp. 93–106.

19. "Justices Uphold Disputed System of U.S. Sentencing," *The New York Times*, January 19, 1989, p. A1.

20. Stewart D'Alessio and Lisa Stolzenberg, "Socioeconomic Status and the Sentencing of the Traditional Offender," *Journal of Criminal Justice* 21 (1993): pp. 71, 73, 74.

21. This proposal is also made in Note, "Developments in the Law: Race and the Criminal Process," *Harvard Law Review* 101 (1988): pp. 1550–1. The authors of this article recommend that charging guidelines be supplemented with an "impact-inference standard." Under this standard, a defendant who believes that he or she has been discriminatorily charged would have to show that (1) he or she is the member of an identifiable class, (2) there is statistical evidence of discriminatory impact of prosecutorial decisions in the jurisdiction, and (3) the prosecutor's office lacked internal guidelines and procedures adequate to prevent abuse. If a defendant succeeded in showing these three elements, the burden of proof would shift to the government to explain its actions. Ibid., pp. 1552–3.

22. See John Council, "Survey Reveals Little Change in Sentencing Habits after 'Booker,'" *www.law.com/jsp/article.jsp?id=1123684510748*. The U.S. Sentencing Commission regularly monitors sentencing practices, and the latest reports are available at U.S. Sentencing Commission, *www.ussc.gov/bf.HTM*.

23. Colman McCarthy, "Justice Mocked: The Farce of Mandatory Minimum Sentences," *The Washington Post*, February 27, 1993, p. A23.

24. *Lockyer V. Andrade*, 538 U.S. 63 (2003). This case is discussed in Jeffrey Reiman and Paul Leighton, *A Tale of Two Criminals: We're Tougher on Corporate Criminals, But They Still Don't Get What They Deserve* (Boston: Allyn & Bacon, 2004), *www.paulsjusticepage.com*.

THE MARXIAN CRITIQUE
OF CRIMINAL JUSTICE

Here in the first appendix,[1] I shall try to present the reader with an overview of Marxian theory that goes from Marxism's theory of capitalism to its theory of law and from there to criminal justice. This addresses some of the same aspects of criminal justice discussed in the main text of this book, but it sets them in a theoretical framework different from (although not incompatible with) the Pyrrhic defeat theory, with its historical inertia explanation of the peculiar failure of criminal justice. I shall close with comments on the ethical implications of the Marxian analysis.

Criminal justice has a concrete reality comprising police, prisons, courts, guns, and the rest. What is most important for our purposes, however, is the particular shape that this concrete reality takes in capitalism. This shape is governed according to certain principles that spell out what shall count as violations, what shall be done to violators, and so on. (For simplicity's sake, I shall use the term *criminal justice* as shorthand for the principles that normally govern criminal justice practices and practitioners in capitalism, and use the term *criminal justice system* as shorthand for the concrete reality of the practices and practitioners so governed.) Marxian analysis is in the first instance directed toward these governing principles. It aims to show that these principles are "economic reflexes," that is, they reflect and thus support the existing economic arrangements—in our case, the capitalist mode of production.

Criminal justice plays an ideological role in support of capitalism because people do not recognize that the principles governing criminal justice are reflections of capitalism. The principles of criminal justice appear instead to be the result of pure reason, and thus a system that supports capitalism is (mistakenly) seen as an expression of rationality itself! Engels—Marx's longtime collaborator—writes that "the jurist imagines he is operating with *a priori* [i.e., purely rational] principles, whereas they are really only economic reflexes; so everything is upside-down. And it seems to me obvious that this inversion . . . so long as it remains unrecognized, forms what we call *ideological conception*."[2] As a consequence of this "inversion," criminal justice embodies and conveys a misleading and partisan view of the reality of the whole capitalist system. Because capitalism requires laws that give individual capitalists the right to own factories and resources, a view of these laws that makes them appear to be purely rational makes capitalism appear purely rational as well.

Before proceeding, a few words about the nature of Marxian theory are in order. First of all, Marx's theory of capitalism is separate from his advocacy of socialism and communism. Marx might be right about how capitalism works or about capitalism's unjust nature, even if socialism or communism would in fact be worse or even if they are merely utopian dreams that cannot be made real. This is important because of the tendency to think that the collapse of communism in eastern Europe and the former Soviet Union (as well as the unpalatable features of that communism before it collapsed) refutes Marxian theory generally. This is quite untrue. What the collapse of eastern European and Soviet communism refutes is, if anything, the theories of Lenin and Stalin about how to establish communism. Marx himself said very little about such things, and what he does say generally favors a much more democratic kind of socialism and communism than what Lenin and Stalin managed to bring about. Accordingly, it is still useful to look at what Marx thought about capitalism, even if one is convinced by recent events of the undesirability of actual communism or the impossibility of ideal communism.

Second, when we turn to Marx's theory of capitalism, we see that Marx portrays capitalism in pure form. He does so not to claim that that is how it actually exists anywhere, but rather to show the shape to which it tends everywhere. Actual systems will be a product of the force of that tendency versus the force of local factors, traditions, talent, innovation, luck, resources, the success or failure of particular human actions, and so on. Likewise, a Marxian analysis of criminal justice will indicate the pure form toward which criminal justice systems tend insofar as they support the functioning of capitalism. Actual criminal justice systems will be approximations of this tendency. Actual criminal justice systems will also clearly be shaped by human actions—often substantially so. No Marxist need deny that the criminal justice system in the capitalist United States is quite a different thing from the criminal justice system in, say, capitalist Chile. What she must claim, rather, is that as capitalism develops in both, their criminal justice systems will increasingly tend to take on the shape that the theory implies.

I shall try to show how Marxism leads to a theory of the structure that criminal justice systems tend to have under capitalism, while at the same time recognizing that any existing criminal justice system is only an approximation of this structure. To give the reader as complete a picture as possible (in this short space) of the whole of Marxian theory—from general theory of capitalism to particular theory of criminal justice, and from there to ethical evaluation—I will have to sacrifice a lot of detail. I shall largely ignore the differences that individual actions may make in determining the shape of actual systems. I hope I have said enough to suggest that this in no way implies that human actions are irrelevant to actual historical outcomes.

I proceed in the following way. In the first section, "Marxism and Capitalism," I sketch out enough of Marx's theory of the capitalist mode of production as is necessary to lay the foundation for a Marxian theory of law. Because law is, for Marxism, a form of ideology, we shall have to see how ideology works in capitalism. I take this up in the next section, "Capitalism and Ideology." In "Ideology and Law," I develop the Marxian theory of law and from it the Marxian theory of criminal justice. Then, in the final section, "Law and Ethics," I consider the characteristic Marxian moral judgments about criminal justice—particularly about guilt and punishment—that are appropriate in light of the Marxian account.

MARXISM AND CAPITALISM

Marx says that capitalism is a system of "forced labour—no matter how much it may seem to result from free contractual agreement."[3] Here is both the truth that Marx asserts about capitalism and the legal ideology that shrouds that truth. To understand precisely how this works, we must consider the nature of the coercion that Marx discovered in capitalism.

For Marx, the value of any commodity is equivalent to the average amount of labor-time necessary to produce it.[4] Under capitalism, the worker's ability to labor—Marx calls this *labor-power*—is sold to the capitalist in return for a wage. Because labor-power is also a commodity, its value is also equivalent to the average amount of labor-time necessary to produce it. *Producing labor-power* means producing the goods needed to maintain a functioning worker. The value of labor-power then is equivalent to the labor-time that on the average goes into producing the goods (food, clothing, shelter, and so on) necessary to maintain a functioning worker at the prevailing standard of living, which Marx understood to differ among countries depending on their respective histories (*Capital*, vol. 1, p. 171). The worker receives this in the form of a wage, that is, in the form of the money necessary to purchase these goods.

The capitalist obtains the money she pays as a wage by selling what the worker produces during the time for which he is employed. If the worker produced an amount of value equivalent only to his wage, there would be nothing left over for the capitalist and no reason for her to hire the worker in the first place. Labor-power, however, has the unique capacity to produce more value than its own value (*Capital*, vol. 1, pp. 193–94). The worker can work longer than the labor-time equivalent of the value of the wage he receives. The amount of labor-time that the worker works to produce value equivalent to his wage Marx calls *necessary labor*. The additional labor-time that the worker works beyond this Marx calls *surplus labor*, and the value it produces he calls *surplus value*. The surplus value, of course, belongs to the capitalist and is the source of her profit (*Capital*, vol. 1, pp. 184–86); that is, when the capitalist sells the product made by the worker, the capitalist gives some of the money she gets back to the worker as a wage (this corresponds to the value that the worker put into the product during his necessary labor-time), and the capitalist keeps the rest as profit (this corresponds to the surplus labor-time that the worker puts in after his necessary labor-time).

Profit, then, rests on the extraction of unpaid surplus labor from the worker. To see this, one need only recall that although all products in the economy are produced by labor, only a portion of those products are wage-goods that the workers get paid with (they get them for the money they receive as wages). The remainder belongs to their bosses and is effectively uncompensated. The wage-goods only compensate necessary labor-time to which they are equivalent in value. What workers produce beyond this goes to the capitalist gratis. Thus, writes Marx, "The secret of the self-expansion of capital [that is, the secret of profit] resolves itself into having the disposal of a definite quantity of other people's unpaid labour" (*Capital*, vol. 1, p. 534).

For Marx, however, capitalism is not only a system in which unpaid labor is extracted from workers, it is also a system in which workers are *forced* to provide this unpaid labor. Workers are not merely shortchanged; they are enslaved. Capitalism is "a coercive relation" (*Capital*, vol. 1, p. 309). The coercion, however, is not of the direct sort that characterized slavery or feudal serfdom. It is, rather, an indirect force built into the very fact that capitalists own the means of production and laborers do not. Means of production are things such as factories and machines and land and resources—things that are necessary for productive labor. Lacking ownership of means of production, workers lack their own access to the means of producing a livelihood. *By this very fact*, workers are compelled to sell their labor to capitalists for a wage because the alternative is (depending on conditions) either painful or fatal: relative pauperization or absolute starvation.

This compulsion is not in conflict with the fact that the terms upon which the worker works for the capitalist are the result of free contractual agreements. Indeed, the compulsion works *through* free agreements. Because the agreements are free, each side must offer the other a reason for agreeing. If workers offered capitalists only as much labor as went into the wage-goods they will get back in return from the capitalists, the capitalists would have no reason to purchase their labor. It follows that, no matter how free the wage contract is, as long as it occurs in a context in which a few own all the means of production, those who do not own means of production will be compelled to give up some of their labor without compensation to those who do. Thus, Marx describes the wage-worker as a "man who is compelled to sell himself of his own free will" (*Capital*, vol. 1, p. 766). The compulsion of the worker operates through the structure of property relations: "The dull compulsion of economic relations completes the subjection of the labourer to the capitalist. Direct force, outside economic conditions, is of course still used, but only exceptionally" (*Capital*, vol. 1, p. 737).

The very existence of the social roles of capitalist and worker—defined by ownership and nonownership of means of production, respectively—is what coerces the worker to work without compensation. It coerces in the same way that a social structure that allotted to one group ownership and thus control of all the available oxygen would coerce. Beyond what was necessary to defend this group against challenges to its ownership of the oxygen, no additional force would be necessary for the coercion to operate. Indeed, it would operate quite effectively by means of bargains freely struck in which the non-oxygen-owners had to offer something to the owners to get the chance to breathe. They, too, would be compelled to sell themselves of their own free will. The same can be said of capitalism. Once its structure of social roles is in place, all that is necessary is that individuals choose, from among the alternatives available to them in their roles, the course of action that best serves their self-interest, and the extraction of unpaid surplus labor is enforced without further need for overt force except in unusual circumstances.

As with the oxygen-owning society, so too with capitalism: Overt force is used or threatened to defend owners against challenges to their ownership. That is just another way of saying that, in capitalism, the state uses overt force to protect private property. And this force is used to protect both the property of the capitalist (her factories and resources) and the property of the worker (his labor-power). This differs crucially from the way in which overt force is exercised in social relations like slavery. In slavery, the use of overt force is part of the normal exercise of the master's power. In capitalism, overt force is used to defend all against forceful interference with their right to dispose of whatever property they happen to own, be it means of production or labor-power. Accordingly, such force is not part of the capitalist's power but is left to a third party that, in this respect, functions neutrally toward all owners—the state.

With both capitalists and workers protected in their capacity to dispose of what they own, the process by which workers are forced to work gratis can proceed apace. This effect can be achieved with the state functioning neutrally. Although the state normally favors the interests of capitalists over workers,[5] it can serve the process of forced extraction of unpaid labor by protecting both capitalists and workers alike in their freedom to dispose of what they happen to own. Thus the state can treat capitalists and workers as having the same or "equal" property rights over what they own. It just turns out that what capitalists happen to own is means of production, and what workers happen to own is the muscles in their arms. Capitalism, then, naturally appears as a system of free exchanges between people with equal rights (over unequal amounts of property). This brings us to the phenomenon of ideology.

CAPITALISM AND IDEOLOGY

Of the study of social revolutions, Marx writes,

> In considering such transformations a distinction should always be made between the material transformation of the economic conditions of production, which can be determined with the precision of natural science, and the legal, political, religious, aesthetic or philosophic—in short, ideological forms in which men become conscious of this conflict and fight it out.[6]

The legal, then, is an ideological form. This is not to say that it is merely mental. It has a material reality in the form of police and prisons and guns and courts and legislators and law books and the rest. What is crucial is how this material reality is shaped, and for that we must understand how ideology is shaped.

As its etymology suggests, *ideology* means the science of ideas, where science can be taken in the ordinary sense as the study of causal connections. (Recall the discussion of ideology in Chapter 4.) In the context of Marxian theory, ideology comes to mean the ideas caused by the mode of production (in our case, the capitalist mode of production), and, equally important for Marxism, the caused ideas are in some important way false. Thus understood, for Marxism, the study of ideology denotes the study of how the mode of production gives rise to people's false beliefs about society. In *The German Ideology*, Marx writes,

> If in all ideology men and their circumstances appear upside down as in a camera obscura, this phenomenon arises just as much from their historical life-process as the inversion of objects on the retina does from their physical life-process. . . .
> The phantoms formed in the human brain are also, necessarily, sublimates of their material life-process, which is empirically verifiable and bound to material premises.[7]

As this statement makes clear, the study of ideology requires that both the existence and the falsity of ideological beliefs be given a *materialist* explanation.

To understand this requirement, consider that Marxian materialism is the conjunction of two distinct claims, an ontological claim and a social scientific one. The *ontological* claim is that what exists is material, that is, physical objects in space. Mind and spirit, in any immaterial sense, are chimera. ("From the start the 'spirit' is afflicted with the curse of being 'burdened' with matter, which here makes its appearance in the form of agitated layers of air, sounds, in short, of language" [*German Ideology*, p. 19].) The *social scientific* claim is that the way in which a society is organized for the production of the material conditions of its existence and reproduction ("the mode of production") plays the chief (though by no means the only) causal role in determining the nature and occurrence of social events. ("The mode of production of material life conditions the social, political and intellectual life process in general.")[8] According to this social scientific claim, the belief that societies are shaped primarily by their members' attitudes, or that history is shaped by the progressive development of knowledge or ideals, is false. Rather, it is primarily the organization of production that shapes people's attitudes, and the progressive development of modes of production that shapes history. ("That is to say, we do not set out from what men say, imagine, conceive, nor from men as narrated, thought of, conceived, in order to arrive at men in the flesh. We set out from real, active men, and on the basis of their real life-process we demonstrate the development of the ideological reflexes and echoes of this life-process" [*German Ideology*, p. 14]; "it is not the consciousness of men that determines their being, but, on the contrary, their social being that determines their consciousness.")[9]

Of these two claims, the social scientific is more restrictive than the ontological. The ontological claim requires only that we attribute ideology to material realities, be they brains or agitated layers of air or modes of production. The social scientific claim requires that among these material realities, priority be given to the mode of production as the primary cause of ideological beliefs. This means that the *main* source of false ideology is to be found not in the perceiving subject but in the perceived objects. It is not a "subjective illusion," the result of erroneous perception by individuals of their material conditions, but an "objective illusion," the result of more or less accurate perception of those conditions.[10] Viewing ideology this way has the added benefit of leaving the door open just wide enough so that the theory of ideology does not exclude the possibility of all true beliefs—and thus of the very science upon which it is based. A materialist theory of ideology, then, must show that false ideology is an *objective illusion* arising primarily from more or less accurate perception of the organization of material production, rather than from some subjective error.[11] Bear in mind that this is a matter of placing primary emphasis on objective factors, not of absolutely excluding subjective ones.

We can fix the idea of an "objective illusion" by considering a very common example of one, namely, the illusion that the sun goes around the earth. Any illusion, any erroneous belief that an individual holds, can be *stated* as a subjective error—but not every erroneous belief arises primarily *because* of a subjective error. A person who believes that the sun rises above a stationary horizon in the morning makes a mistake. However, this sort of mistake differs crucially from, say, the mistake that a color-blind person might make of believing that the light is green when it is red, or the mistake a person balancing her checkbook might make of believing that a number is 4 when it is 2. In these latter cases, the mistaken beliefs are not merely held by the individuals; they arise in the individuals primarily as the result of a defective perceptual faculty or misuse of a sound one. These are subjective illusions. In these cases, correcting the defect in the perceptual faculty (or in its use) should undo the mistake. The mistaken belief that the sun goes around the earth, by contrast, arises as a result of a sound perceptual faculty properly exercised. This is an objective illusion. Neither healthier vision nor looking more carefully is likely to enable an individual to correct this mistake and see that what occurs at dawn is not the sun rising above the horizon, but the horizon tipping down below the sun.

The ideology of capitalism is the illusion that capitalism is noncoercive. This illusion is a mistake of the same type as the illusion that the sun goes around the earth. What corresponds in capitalism to the movement of the sun seen from the earth is the free exchange of wages and labor-power between capitalists and workers. That the sphere of exchange is the objective basis of ideology is recognized in effect by Marx, when he writes that this sphere,

> within whose boundaries the sale and purchase of labour-power goes on, is in fact a very Eden of the innate rights of man. There alone rule Freedom, Equality, Property. Freedom, because both buyer and seller of a commodity, say of labour-power, are constrained only by their free will. (*Capital*, vol. 1, p. 176)

The normal perception of what goes on in exchange gives rise to the ideological illusion that capitalism is uncoercive. This is not because the freedom in exchange is an illusion. The fact is that, for Marx, capitalism works only because the moment of exchange, through which the circuit of capital continually passes, is truly free.

> For the conversion of his money into capital, therefore, the owner of money must meet in the market with the free labourer, free in the double sense, that as a free man he can dispose of his labour-power as his own commodity, and that on the other hand, he has no other commodity for sale, is short of everything necessary for the realization of his labour-power. (*Capital*, vol. 1, p. 169)

That the second of these senses of freedom is the worker's "freedom from" ownership of means of production does not deny the reality of the first sense, without which we would have slavery or serfdom rather than capitalism.

In exchange, the power that capitalists have over workers recedes from view. If we distinguish two sorts of power—the power to withhold one's commodity until offered something preferable, and the power to command obedience and back this up with violent force—then it is clear that, in the sphere of exchange, the latter power is suspended and all that remains is the former power. This former power is a power that all parties to the exchange have equally. Thus, the unequal power of capitalist and worker appears as their equal power to withhold from exchange what they happen to own, and their social inequality appears as the difference between the things that they happen to own. To use the celebrated words of Marx's analysis of the fetishism of commodities, a "social relation between men assumes, in their eyes, the fantastic form of a relation between things" (*Capital*, vol. 1, p. 72).

If this accurate perception of what goes on in exchange is to explain how capitalism appears uncoercive, we need to understand how the sphere of exchange—which is only part of capitalism—should be the source of beliefs about the whole of capitalism. Why should the experience of freedom in exchange, rather than, say, the experience of taking orders on the production line, determine the beliefs that members of capitalist societies come naturally to have? How is the representation of exchange *generalized* into a view of capitalism as a whole?

Marx offers a clue to the answer to this question when he says that the fetishism of commodities results because "the producers do not come into contact with each other until they exchange" (*Capital*, vol. 1, p. 73). Exchange transactions are the salient points of social contact for economic actors in capitalism. They punctuate capitalist social relations. Every social interaction between individuals playing roles in the capitalist mode of production begins with such a transaction (say, the signing of a wage contract exchanging labor-power for money) and can be ended with such a transaction (say, the dissolution of the wage contract). Each of these beginnings and endings is characterized by the absence of either party's having the power to command the other's obedience and use violence to get it. Each party knows that he can enter or withdraw from any capitalist social interaction without being subject to the command or the overt force of the other. What constraint either feels seems to be only a matter of what he happens to own, which naturally appears as a feature of his own good or bad fortune rather than a condition coercively imposed by the other. Thus, *all* capitalist social interactions, *not just the exchanges themselves*, appear as voluntary undertakings between equal people who happen to own different things.

Exchange accurately perceived and then generalized is what leads workers in capitalist societies to believe that they are free, although they take orders most of their waking lives. Thus, ideologically false beliefs about capitalism result from accurate perception of exchange, when the rest of capitalism is, by default, assumed to be more of the same. The law follows suit.

IDEOLOGY AND LAW

"Law," wrote Marx in *The Poverty of Philosophy*, "is only the official recognition of fact."[12] For capitalist law, the fact is exchange. Law in capitalism is the official recognition of the fact of the economic relations in which the exchangers stand to one another. This insight—which will guide the materialist explanation of criminal law that I shall develop in this section—must be credited to the work of the Soviet legal theorist Evgeny Pashukanis, whose *General Theory of Law and Marxism* was published in Russian in 1924.[13] Among the things for which Pashukanis argued was that law was a product of capitalism and consequently had no legitimate place in socialism. As Stalin took firm control of the Soviet Union and saw fit to use the law to shore up that control, Pashukanis came eventually into disfavor. He recanted his views to some extent, but it was too late. By 1937 he had been declared an enemy of the people, and he "disappeared" shortly thereafter. Recently rediscovered by Western Marxists, Pashukanis's work was first the object of lavish praise and subsequently the target of harsh criticism. I do not intend to endorse or defend the whole of Pashukanis's theory. He aimed at a general theory of law and made only a few observations about criminal law, which is my main concern here. I shall try to show that his basic insight about the relation between law and exchange can be developed into an explanation of the content of the criminal law and of the constitutional protections relevant to criminal justice.

Marx writes that parties to an exchange

> must behave in such a way that each does not appropriate the commodity of the other, and part with his own, except by means of an act done by mutual consent. They must, therefore, mutually recognize in each other the rights of private proprietors. This juridical relation, which thus expresses itself in a contract, whether such contract be part of a developed legal system or not, is a relation between two wills, and is but the reflex of the real economic relation between the two. (*Capital*, vol. 1, pp. 88–89)

Exchangers must in fact refrain from forcing those with whom they would trade to part with their goods or services or money. Official recognition of this fact takes the form of granting to exchangers "the rights of private proprietors." Because this recognition is related to the ideological failure to perceive the coerciveness reproduced in exchanges between proprietors of capital and proprietors of labor, exchanges are understood legally as acts of the free will of the parties as long as no overt violence is used or threatened. Consequently, exchangers treat one another as *free subjects* whose freedom is expressed in their *right to dispose of their property without interference from others.*

It is the difference between what capitalists own and what workers own that, for Marx, makes it possible to reproduce a coercive relation through free exchange. If the law follows ideology in representing the relation between exchangers as noncoercive, then the law must abstract from this difference in what is owned and treat each party as having the same right to dispose of his property regardless of what that property is. The law reflects this in its formality. The legal right of property is an empty form to be filled in with different content, depending on what an individual owns. Capitalists and workers have the same right of property; they just happen to own different things. It just happens that what some people own are factories and what others own are their bodies, but their property rights in these things are the same. Their freedom to dispose of their property also is the same.[14] Thus, exchangers treat each other as *equal* free subjects with equal property rights—that is to say, as legal *persons*.[15]

We saw in the previous section that ideology is not to be understood as merely a subjective illusion. Ideology reflects the real way in which capitalism appears to its participants. By the same token, the ideological nature of law reflects the real relations in which exchangers stand to one another. The written law, even the institutions of law (from lawmakers to law enforcers), are not the source of law. They reflect real, objective relations between members of a capitalist society, relations that exist, so to speak, on the ground first and only later on the page or in the courts for that matter. It is here that the "inversion" of which Engels wrote does its ideological work. Although the law is a reflection of the relations of exchangers on the ground, it appears that the law is an expression of rationality itself, with the consequence that the relations among exchangers seem so as well.

Here, however, a problem arises for the Marxian materialist: If law is the reflection of the actual practice of economic exchange, how does law come to function as a norm? A simple reflection would represent whatever occurs and thus could not identify some actions as infractions. How can the materialist account for the normative dimension of law that arises as a reflection of economic relations?

The answer to this is that law is not a simple reflection of economic relations but an *idealized* reflection. Actual exchanges will be characterized by the full range of violations and deviations, from failure to meet agreed-upon deadlines to gross expropriation with the threat or use of violence. All such violations undermine the likelihood of the same parties exchanging again. Because it is generally in people's long-term interest that stable trading relationships be maintained, it will generally be in people's interest to eliminate such violations. Accordingly, over time the vast majority of exchanges, particularly those between people in continuing exchange relationships, will tend to be free of violations. Thus, an average core of exchange, characterized by absence of violence and fraud as well as by dependable fulfillment of agreements, will emerge as the norm. The law in general will represent this norm.

This tendency to go from what happens "on average" to what is normative is a common feature of human social existence. People tend to take what usually happens as what should happen. This tendency of the statistical norm (what people can generally be expected to do) to become the moral norm (what is expected of people) is visible in early civilization (where, for example, natural and moral law are not distinguished from each other) and in advanced civilization (where, for example, existing business practice is often taken by courts as creating legally enforceable obligations).

This brings us to a second question. It would seem that law that reflects (even the idealized "average" core of) exchanges would include not only the criminal law but also what we currently understand as contract or civil law. How can the theory that traces law to exchange account for the nature of the criminal law per se, with its special content and its unique remedies?

To answer this, note first that there is considerable overlap in the content of criminal and civil law; criminal acts, such as theft or battery, also can be causes of civil action. This overlap, however, is largely asymmetrical: Virtually any criminal act can be a cause of civil action, but only some civil causes are subject to criminal prosecution. This suggests that the criminal law is more distinctive in its remedies than in its content. In general, criminal prosecution seeks punishment of the guilty, and civil action seeks recovery of damages from the one responsible for a loss. Now, on the materialist theory, both sorts of law—criminal and civil—represent the "essential core" of normal exchange and aim to rectify violations of or deviations from that core. Thus, to explain the nature of the criminal law per se, we must show why some class of deviations from normal exchange is singled out for the distinctive "criminal" remedy, namely, punishment. Because punishment is generally a graver matter than recovery of damages, we should expect the criminal law to be addressed to the most serious violations of normal exchange, whereas the civil law can be addressed to all violations.

Violations of normal exchange can be distinguished in the following way: Some threaten the very possibility of free exchange by depriving people of the ability to dispose of their property. Other violations threaten not the possibility of free exchange but its success in meeting the wishes of the exchangers. What threatens the very possibility of exchange are acts of violence that overtly block the capacity of individuals to exercise their wills, acts of theft that overtly bypass the capacity of individuals to choose how their property is disposed of, and acts of deception that have the same effect, so to speak, behind the backs of their victims. These are so serious that they must be prevented in advance—and that requires a standing threat of punishment. Accordingly, the criminal law is primarily aimed at acts of violence, theft, and fraud.[16]

Less serious violations are compatible with the existence of exchange but cause exchanges in some way to fall short of the wishes of the exchangers. These violations are mainly failures to live up to the terms of explicit or implied contracts. They can be remedied by requiring performance or payment from the one responsible. These are suitable targets for the civil law, although nothing is lost by allowing the civil law to apply to recovery of losses due to the more serious violations as well.

On the whole, then, although the entire law in capitalism reflects the conditions of normal exchange, the content of the criminal law is composed of those acts that threaten the very possibility of normal exchange. These are the acts that are identified as "crimes." Moreover, because the normal relations of exchange are not only idealized but also (as we saw in the previous section) generalized to the whole of capitalism, they will shape people's normative expectations beyond exchange. Thus, they determine the limits that will be imposed on officials taxed with the job of finding and prosecuting criminals, the shape of court proceedings, the relation of punishment to offense, and the emphasis on the free will of the offender. Accordingly, by tracing law to its source in exchange, we can account for at least the general content of criminal law and the general shape of the criminal justice system and of the constitutional limits within which that system operates. Here, briefly sketched and numbered for ease of identification, are the main ways in which this works.

1. Normal exchange presupposes that people are treated as having property rights in whatever they are to trade, and that must mean not only goods but their bodies as well, because bodily actions are what workers trade with capitalists for their wage. Crime, then, is any violation by one individual of the property rights of another in whatever he owns, including his body. This explains why the criminal law is directed primarily against acts of violence, theft, and fraud. Moreover, because criminal law protects an individual's body because he owns it (and not, say, because it is the earthly vessel of his immortal soul), the law will be concerned primarily with injuries done to people's bodies against their will—otherwise, such injuries do not violate the individual's ownership of his body. This accounts for the liberal principle *volenti non fit injuria* (no injury to one who has consented) and thus, via generalization, for the tendency in capitalism to decriminalize (or reduce in importance) "victimless crimes" or "morals offenses."

2. This account also tells us what we are not likely to see as crime in capitalist society, namely, exercises of the power inherent in the ownership of property itself. Thus, we will not generally find that death due to preventable dangers in the workplace will be taken as murder because that would assume that the worker was somehow forced into the workplace by the power inherent in his boss's private ownership of the means of production. Because that is just the power that is invisible in capitalism, the worker is taken as freely consenting to his job and thus freely accepting its risks. Accordingly, when the criminal law is used against employers to get them to eliminate occupational hazards, it is never with the understanding that employers who do not eliminate such hazards are violent criminals. If the criminal law is used in these cases at all, it is as a regulatory mechanism applied to employers because this is the most efficient way to reduce the social costs of occupational injury and disease. The treatment of guilty employers is generally light-handed, even though far more people lose their lives due to preventable occupational hazards than as a result of what the law currently treats as murder. In capitalism, subjection to one person is seen as arbitrary and thus unlawful coercion, but subjection to the capitalist class is not seen at all. (Here is how the Marxian theory understands the phenomena discussed in the main text of this book and accounted for with the historical inertia explanation.)

3. The other side of criminal law—the limits placed on legal officials in their pursuit of suspected criminals (for example, in the Bill of Rights)—likewise reflects the generalized conception of people as owners of their bodies and other property. Accordingly, we find protections against official invasions of suspects' property (for example, the Fourth Amendment protections against unreasonable search and seizure) and against penetration of suspects' bodies or minds (for example, the Fifth Amendment protection against self-incrimination). Moreover, this explains why corporal punishment, which was the norm in feudalism and slavery, tends to be eliminated in capitalism. The bodies of slaves are literally owned by their masters, and lords have natural (that is, parentlike) authority over their serfs. In these cases, corporal punishment fits the existing social relations. In capitalism, employer and employee meet as owners of their respective bodies, and thus corporal punishment looks increasingly out of place.

The existence of these various limitations on what can be done to enforce the law is evidence that the Marxian view of law includes recognition of the way law functions not only to control the working class but also as a limit on the behavior of the ruling class. Indeed, the Marxian view can be taken as claiming that it is precisely as a system that protects everyone alike in her property (including the body), by limiting both what citizens and law enforcers can do to the bodies (and other property) of other citizens, that the law most effectively serves the purpose of keeping the working class selling its labor-power to owners of means of production—both classes safe in the knowledge that no one can interfere with their right to dispose of what they happen to own.

4. As crime is a violation of normal exchange, so punishment is thought of on the same model of equivalence as exists in exchange. "Punishment emerges as an equivalent which compensates the damage sustained by the injured party."[17] The commercial model doesn't end here. The adversary system reproduces it in court. "The public prosecutor demands a 'high' price, that is to say a severe sentence. The offender pleads for leniency, a 'discount,' and the court passes sentence in equity."[18] Crime deforms exchange by taking with force rather than payment. Punishment restores exchange by using force to pay back the criminal for his force. This is the *tribute* in retribution. The court is the extraordinary market where this extraordinary exchange is negotiated. The scales in Justice's hands are the same as those used by the merchant.

5. Because exchange normally brings payment to an individual only when she freely chooses to offer up her goods or services for it, so then the payment of punishment comes due only when the offender has freely chosen to commit the offense for which the punishment is payment. Accordingly, liability for punishment is subject to conditions of the same sort as apply to liability to contractual obligations. One is not bound by a contract that she has not signed freely, or that she signed while insane or in ignorance of its contents, and so on. Likewise, the offender is liable to punishment, and thus is truly a criminal, only if he has committed his violation freely, sanely, and with knowledge of what he was doing. By the same logic, the law generally prohibits ex post facto attribution of criminal liability because a person cannot choose freely to violate a law before it has been passed.

Here, then, we read off the face of exchange, albeit idealized and generalized, the main contours of criminal justice as it develops in capitalism. As I suggested at the outset, this is no more than a skeleton. It does not aim to account for the full, rich detail of any particular criminal justice system. Actual criminal justice systems exist in societies with other modes of production present alongside capitalism, are affected by the complex interplay of human actions, and so on, so that each actual system—like each actual face—will have a distinct physiognomy while sharing in the basic structure. Some criminal justice systems will be slower in eliminating "morals offenses," some will be stricter on occupational hazards, some will abolish the death penalty while others will retain it, and so on.[19] These specific outcomes will be a function of the strength that various social groupings (such as religious organizations, labor unions, academia, the press, and the like) come to have in the specific history of specific countries, and of all the largely unpredictable features that determine the outcome of particular battles over the content of the law and the funding of the legal apparatus. This notwithstanding, the Marxian claim is that criminal justice (principles and systems) in capitalist countries will tend toward the shape sketched out above.

LAW AND ETHICS

We reach now the question of the moral stance toward capitalist criminal justice that is appropriate if the Marxian account is correct. Marxism describes capitalism as an exploitative system, meaning one in which workers are forced to work for capitalists without compensation. Marxists characteristically regard exploitation, and consequently capitalism, as unjust or immoral. Broadly speaking, they reach this condemnation by one of three routes. One is to view capitalist exploitation as wrong because it promotes antagonistic or alienated relations between human beings.[20] The second way is to view capitalist exploitation as wrong because it is a form of forced servitude or slavery.[21] The third way is to view capitalist exploitation as wrong because it is based on an unjust distribution of wealth, namely, the unjustifiable exclusive ownership by a few of the means of production.[22] I shall call these three views, respectively, the *alienation charge*, the *slavery charge*, and the *maldistribution charge*. Each of these has moral implications for capitalist criminal justice. The task of identifying these implications is simplified by the fact that the second and third charges incorporate each other. The slavery charge accepts that private ownership of means of production is a case of unjust maldistribution (because it is a means of forcing servitude), and the maldistribution charge accepts that private ownership of means of production is a means of enslavement (because it is a power wrongly monopolized by a few). For our purposes, then, the charges against capitalism can be reduced to two: the alienation charge and the slavery–maldistribution charge.

Those who raise the alienation charge point out that capitalism is a system in which each person's well-being is in conflict with that of others. Capitalism pits class against class (competing over the division of the economic product into wages versus profit), worker against worker (competing for jobs), and capitalist against capitalist (competing for market shares). Moreover, proponents of this charge hold that antagonism of interests is neither a necessary feature of human life nor a desirable condition. It is caused by capitalism. It was less marked in feudalism and might be eliminated in the future if a more cooperative arrangement, such as socialism, could be established. Criminal justice as it emerges in capitalism is understood as a means to regulate this antagonism of interests. Because it assumes that this antagonism is inevitable, criminal justice serves to confer permanent validity on capitalism. Moreover, criminal justice promotes this antagonism by teaching people that the rights of each are in conflict with the rights of others rather than mutually supportive, that freedom is *freedom from* invasion by others rather than freedom to develop with others, that what people owe each other is noninterference rather than a helping hand.

Also important is the fact that a society based on antagonism of interests is one in which people earn their daily bread only as long as someone else can profit as a result. When that changes, workers may find themselves in need and with little in the way of help from the rest of society. On this view, then, the high crime rates characteristic of capitalism are due to the fact that people in capitalism are taught to see their interests as in conflict with others' and thus they are trained to have limited altruism and fellow feeling, and to the fact that a society based on antagonism of interests is one in which economic need and insecurity are endemic. When limited fellow feeling meets economic need and insecurity, the result is crime. (Recall the views of

Bonger and Gordon, discussed in Chapter 4.) The same system that calls criminals individually guilty, then, is responsible for the antagonism of interests that breeds crime in the first place. The upshot of this charge is that criminals are not—or at least not wholly—guilty of the crimes they commit. On this charge, criminals are in large measure unjustly punished for actions caused by the very system that punishes them.

On the slavery–maldistribution charge, the emphasis is on the wrongness and coerciveness of private ownership of means of production. Capitalism promotes a system of criminal justice based on protecting the freedom of individuals to dispose of what they rightly own; but the system itself is based on the wrongful appropriation of means of production, and with it the power to coerce others to labor without compensation. On this view, socialism would cure capitalism not so much by replacing antagonism of interests with harmony but by replacing private ownership of means of production by a few with social ownership by everyone.

To understand the moral implications for criminal justice of this charge, imagine for a moment that we see someone take a sheep from a field owned by another. In response, suppose that we make the normal judgment that a theft, an unjust expropriation, has occurred. Now suppose further that we learn that the field owner had himself stolen the sheep from the sheep taker some time before. According to these new facts, we shall change our views about the moral status of the sheep taking. Now we are likely to say that the one we saw take the sheep was not, morally speaking, a criminal but the opposite, a victim responding justifiably to an earlier crime. Likewise, if we come to see ownership of means of production as itself a violation of justice (because it is unjustly maldistributive or unjustifiably coercive), we will see the things that people do in response to it as more just than they appeared when we didn't question the justice of ownership of means of production. Recall the discussion in Chapter 4 of how a judgment that an individual is guilty of a crime presupposes that the social context in which his act occurred was just. By the same logic, judgment that the social context is unjust weakens the judgment that the individual is guilty.

On the slavery–maldistribution view, then, the individuals normally labeled "criminal" are seen as the victims of a prior "crime" to which they are responding.

That criminals may not (and usually do not) see themselves as doing this only reflects the fact that they are taken in by capitalist ideology no less than law-abiding folks are. The "criminal," then, is not a doer of injustice but the reverse. He is a victim of injustice trying to improve his situation by means that have been made necessary by the fact that capitalism leaves him few alternatives. The upshot of this charge is that criminals are not really morally guilty. They are in large measure unjustly punished for *re*acting against crimes perpetrated by the very system that punishes them.

In sum, the Marxist critique of criminal justice does lead to a moral condemnation of criminal justice under capitalism. This moral condemnation comes in two forms, both of which share the claim that capitalist criminal justice wrongly punishes people who do not deserve to be punished. In the first form, the alienation charge, criminals are thought not to deserve punishment because their acts are caused by socially conditioned antagonism to their fellows in conjunction with limited and unstable opportunities to satisfy their needs and desires. In the second form, the slavery–maldistribution charge, criminals are thought not to deserve punishment because their apparent crimes are legitimate reactions against conditions that are themselves, morally speaking, criminal. Needless to say, it is possible for the same person to endorse both forms of condemnation.

Several things that apply to both charges are worth noting. First of all, in both cases, the features of capitalist criminal justice that come in for ethical condemnation reflect the failure to see the way criminal justice reflects the mode of production—mentioned at the outset. In the case of the alienation charge, the failure is that of not seeing that capitalist criminal justice emerges to regulate the antagonistic relations between human beings that capitalism produces. Seeing capitalist criminal justice as the product of independent reason, it sees those antagonistic relations as a natural feature of human life that always must be so regulated. Then, capitalist criminal justice, rather than protecting the interests of capitalists, appears merely to be the necessary condition of any peaceful social coexistence.

In the case of the slavery–maldistribution charge, the failure is of not seeing how property in capitalism is an expression of a particular and morally questionable constellation of social forces. Seeing capitalist criminal justice as the product of independent reason, it sees the property criminal justice protects as a natural feature of human life that is always in need of such protection. Then, capitalist criminal justice, rather than protecting the interests of capitalists, appears merely to be protecting everyone's interest.

What's more, it follows that the continued and heavily publicized activities of criminal justice serve to reinforce ideological blindness: on the first view, blindness to capitalism's role in causing the alienated and antisocial attitudes and conditions that lead to crime; and, on the second view, blindness to the moral dubiousness of capitalist property relations.

It also must be borne in mind that the ethical implications of both charges are general propositions that will fit actual criminal cases in varying degrees. For example, while the alienation charge suggests that criminals are not culpable because they are shaped by an antagonistic society, in actual cases the degree to which individual lawbreakers have been so shaped will vary. There may be some who have largely escaped the deleterious influences and yet, out of selfishness or greed, commit crimes. Marxism naturally claims that the number of criminals of this sort is small compared with the number of criminals all told. Marxism, however, need not deny that there are

some criminals like this and thus that they deserve punishment. Likewise, on the slavery–maldistribution charge, whereas criminals are generally taken to be victims of the prior injustice of private ownership of means of production, actual criminals differ in the degree to which they are so victimized and in the degree to which their actual crimes can be thought of as reactions thereto. Relatively privileged persons, or others whose crimes bear little relation to their class position (some rapists, for example), may well be more culpable than the general run of criminals. It seems to me appropriate for Marxists to view responsibility—and thus guilt—as existing in varying degrees, relative to the actual impact of the social structure on a given individual's criminal act.

Finally, note that on neither of the two views we have discussed does the criminal emerge as any kind of "proto-revolutionary," as is sometimes asserted of Marxism. On the alienation charge, the criminal is at best relieved of responsibility because he has been shaped by the social system to have antisocial attitudes and fated by that system to experience need and insecurity that, together with those attitudes, lead to crime. On the slavery–maldistribution charge, the criminal is at best a victim because he is the object of the unjust coercion or expropriation characteristic of private ownership of means of production. His crime, rather than being a kind of rebellion against what victimizes him, is most often a narrowly self-interested striking out against whatever he can get his hands on. On both charges, Marxism does imply reduced or no blame for (most) criminals; but it does not imply any celebration of their acts. This is particularly so in light of the fact that most victims of crime are other exploited people, members or would-be members of the working class. Crime and criminality must on the whole be placed by Marxism among the costs of capitalism, lined up alongside poverty, unemployment, pollution, and the rest.

NOTES

1. This essay is a revised and shortened version of an article that appeared in *Criminal Justice Ethics* 6, no. 1 (Winter–Spring 1987): pp. 30–50. Peter Darvas assisted me with the research for that article.

2. Frederick Engels, "Letter to Conrad Schmidt (October 27, 1890)," in Karl Marx, *Selected Works*, ed. V. Adoratsky (Moscow: Cooperative Publishing Society of Foreign Workers in the USSR, 1935), vol. 1, p. 386.

3. Karl Marx, *Capital* (New York: International Publishers, 1967), vol. 3, p. 819.

4. Note that Marx does not hold that the value of a commodity is equivalent to the actual amount of labor-time that goes into producing it. On that view, commodities would increase in value the more inefficiently they were produced. Instead, recognizing that a commodity will command a price no higher than that for which commodities like it are selling, Marx takes the commodity's value to be determined by the average or socially necessary labor-time it takes to produce commodities of its kind. See *Capital*, vol. 1, p. 189. Furthermore, although Marx claims that value is equivalent to average labor-time, he assumes that values and

market prices coincide only for the purposes of the argument of volume 1 of *Capital* about the fundamental nature of capitalism. In the subsequent volumes, Marx shows at length the mechanisms in capitalism that lead prices to diverge from values. Even after these common misinterpretations of the theory are eliminated, it must be admitted that Marx's labor theory of value has come in for so much criticism in recent years that many, even many Marxists, have given it up for dead.

5. See, for example, G. William Domhoff, *Who Rules America?* (Englewood Cliffs, NJ: Prentice-Hall, 1967); M. Green, J. Fallows, and D. Zwick, The Ralph Nader Congress Project, *Who Runs Congress?* (New York: Grossman, 1972); Edward S. Greenberg, *Serving the Few: Corporate Capitalism and the Bias of Government Policy* (New York: Wiley, 1974); and Ralph Miliband, *The State in Capitalist Society* (New York: Basic Books, 1969).

6. Karl Marx, "Preface to *A Contribution to a Critique of Political Economy*," in *The Marx-Engels Reader*, 2nd ed., ed. Robert Tucker (New York: Norton, 1978), p. 5.

7. Karl Marx and Friedrich Engels, *The German Ideology*, pts. 1 and 3 (New York: International Publishers, 1947), p. 14.

8. Marx, "Preface to *A Contribution to a Critique of Political Economy*," p. 4.

9. Ibid.

10. "It is not the subject who deceives himself, but reality which deceives him"; Maurice Godelier, "Structure and Contradiction in Capital," in *Ideology in Social Science*, ed. Robin Blackburn (Glasgow: Fontana/Collins, 1977), p. 337.

11. Examples of theories of ideology that trace its distortions to subjective illusions are the attempt by some members of the Frankfurt School to explain the affection of German laborers for fascism by means of a Freudian account of the persistence of irrational authoritarian attitudes and the attempt of some sociologists to trace ideology to an existential need to reify a mythic worldview as protection against the terrors of meaninglessness. For the former, see Martin Jay, *The Dialectical Imagination: A History of the Frankfurt School and the Institute for Social Research, 1923–1950* (Boston: Little, Brown, 1973). For the latter, see Peter Berger and Thomas Luckmann, *The Social Construction of Reality* (New York: Doubleday, 1966).

12. Karl Marx, *The Poverty of Philosophy* (Moscow: Progress Publishers, 1955), p. 75.

13. Evgeny B. Pashukanis, *Law and Marxism: A General Theory*, trans. B. Einhom, ed. C. Arthur (London: Ink Links, 1978).

14. As Frederick Engels wrote,

> The labor contract is to be freely entered into by both parties. But it is considered to have been freely entered into as soon as the law makes both parties equal on paper. The power conferred on the one party by the difference of class position, the pressure thereby brought to bear on the other party—the real economic position of both—that is not the law's business. (Frederick Engels, The Origin of the Family, Private Property, and the State [New York: International Publishers, 1942], p. 64)

15. Pashukanis, *Law and Marxism*, pp. 112–113, inter alia.

16. Pashukanis approvingly attributes to Aristotle "the definition of crime as an involuntarily concluded contract" (ibid., p. 169).

17. Ibid., p. 169; see also Alan Norrie, "Pashukanis and 'the Commodity Form Theory': A Reply to Warrington," *International Journal of the Sociology of Law* 10 (1982): pp. 431–434.

18. Pashukanis, *Law and Marxism*, p. 177.

19. See Georg Rusch and Otto Kirchheimer, *Punishment and Social Structure* (New York: Russell & Russell, 1968), for a classic Marxian-inspired historical study of the relationship between penal policy and the supply and demand for labor.

20. This is the view of, for example, Allen Buchanan in *Marx and Justice* (Totowa, NJ: Rowman & Littlefield, 1982).

21. This is essentially the view argued for by, for example, Allen Wood in "The Marxian Critique of Justice," *Philosophy & Public Affairs* 1, no. 3 (Spring 1972): pp. 244–282.

22. This is the view of, for example, G. A. Cohen in "Freedom, Justice and Capitalism," *New Left Review* 126 (March–April 1981): pp. 3–16. There is, by the way, a substantial literature on the question of whether Marxism holds that capitalism is wrong because it is unjust or that justice is part of what's wrong with capitalism. See articles in M. Cohen, T. Nagel, and T. Scanlon, eds., *Marx, Justice, and History* (Princeton, NJ: Princeton University Press, 1980); K. Nielsen and S. Patten, eds., *Marx and Morality, Canadian Journal of Philosophy* 7 (suppl., 1981); and J. Pennock and J. Chapman, eds., *Nomos XXVI: Marxism* (New York: New York University Press, 1983); as well as Norman Geras's review of the whole discussion, "The Controversy about Marx and Justice," *New Left Review* 150 (March–April 1985): pp. 47–85. My own views are presented in "The Possibility of a Marxian Theory of Justice," in Nielsen and Patten, *Marx and Morality*, pp. 307–22.

BETWEEN PHILOSOPHY AND CRIMINOLOGY

Though *The Rich Get Richer and the Poor Get Prison* is more frequently assigned in criminology courses than in philosophy courses,[1] it raises a philosophical question, perhaps *the* central philosophical question of criminology, namely, "What should be a crime?"; and it aims to use that question to shed a special kind of light on the criminal justice establishment in the United States, but I suspect as well on just about any criminal justice system anywhere.[2]

I say this by way of introduction because my aim here is to explore the relationship between philosophy and criminology. In light of criminology's multidisciplinary nature, however, criminology might be thought already to include philosophy. Thus, to be precise, I should say that I want to explore the relationship between philosophy and the nonphilosophical aspects of criminology, that is, between philosophy and criminology considered as a social science. In general, this is what I shall mean when I speak of *criminology*.

To give you a hint about where I am headed, I shall argue that criminology needs philosophy, and not only in the way that, as I also believe, everything and everyone need philosophy, but also in very special ways. For example, I shall argue that criminology has a special need for philosophy because criminology is in the unusual position of being a mode of social inquiry whose central concept—*crime*—is defined officially, by governments. We hear a lot these days about the politics of knowledge and of research, but this is politics with a vengeance. Politics openly, necessarily, insinuates itself into the heart of criminology. Political systems hand criminology a ready-made research agenda. And so I shall argue that criminology needs philosophical reflection on the concept of crime in order to establish its intellectual independence of the state, which to my mind is equivalent to declaring its status as a social science rather than an agency of social control, as critical rather than servile, as illumination rather than propaganda.

This is not, however, where I shall start. Rather, I will start, so to speak, at the outer ring of a series of concentric circles, by indicating the philosophical assumptions that I think are necessary to all forms of social science. I shall proceed from there to talk about the philosophical assumptions that I think are special to criminology, the ones it especially needs. And then, arriving at the smallest inner circle, I shall say something about my own particular philosophical commitments, the ones that underlie *The Rich Get Richer and the Poor Get Prison*. I hope that somewhere along the line, readers will recognize some of their own philosophical assumptions, and thus be in a better position to reflect on them, to consider what else they entail, and to decide whether in the end they are ready to endorse them explicitly, or want to consider others.

Before starting this, I want to make one thing clear. I shall be talking about "what criminology needs," but this is shorthand for what I think people who practice criminology need in order to do criminology in a coherent and plausible way. Moreover, when I say, for example, that criminology needs a theory of crime, I do not mean that it needs one particular theory. This too is shorthand, in this case for the idea that everyone who practices criminology needs *some* theory of crime, not that all need the same one. I put these all as claims about "what criminology needs" rather than as about what criminologists need, to emphasize that the needs are disciplinary and conceptual, not personal or psychological.

PHILOSOPHICAL ASSUMPTIONS OF SOCIAL SCIENCE GENERALLY

First of all, to engage in social science, you must believe that there is such a thing as society, and that it can become an object of knowledge. That there is such a thing as society means that there are real human beings, in real social relations, in a real world, manipulating real objects, and so on. That there can be knowledge of society means that knowledge is possible, and that we can know when we've got some. In short, a social scientist cannot be a thoroughgoing *ontological* skeptic or agnostic.[3] He or she cannot suppose that society is only an idea or a construct, and all the more so, he or she cannot suppose society to be an illusion. Nor can a social scientist be a thoroughgoing *epistemological* skeptic or agnostic.[4] To seek knowledge of society is to assume that such knowledge is possible for us.

Along the same lines, I believe that social scientists must believe it is important to aim at *scientific objectivity*, and that this aim can be adequately achieved. Some authors writing about the development of modern science in the time of Bacon and Galileo speak of the attempt at scientific objectivity as nothing but following certain conventions aimed at giving science a higher status than, say, religious inspiration.[5] My claim is that, even if the attempt at scientific objectivity is this, it cannot be *only* this.

No one could use conventions of objectivity without believing that they were effective ways of getting at the way things are, anymore than one can use language without believing that one is speaking about things beyond the words one uses. Even those who think of objectivity as just so many conventions think that *that* is the objective truth! They think that they are telling us the way things are, not the way they would like them to be. Notice here that I am not claiming that we always succeed in freeing ourselves of our biases. What a social scientist must believe is that the attempt to represent the world as it is, as opposed to how we wish it were, can succeed generally and does succeed in many particular cases.

In affirming that, as social science, criminology must presuppose that there are real people doing real actions in a real world and that we can have knowledge of them, I do not mean to resurrect some hoary positivistic model of science. I grant that the facts we study may be the product of the interaction of beliefs and language and objects. However, for the study of those facts to be fruitful, the process by which beliefs and language and objects interact must itself be knowable as an objective reality. It is a general philosophical requirement of social theorizing that one's theory leave open the possibility of its own status as knowledge—this is a test that many statements of post-modernist theory, and of relativism generally, seem to me to fail, even as their practitioners produce valuable *objective* knowledge in spite of what they say they are doing.

Before leaving the discussion of the general philosophical requirements of social science, I want to say a word about *value-neutrality*. Value-neutrality is related to objectivity, but it's not the same thing. Later I shall suggest that criminology needs some value commitments, at least to some conception of justice. Thus, I do not think that criminology should be value-neutral all the way down, even though I think it should aim at objective knowledge. There is no contradiction here.

The point is this. I believe that the proper study of crime requires taking some position on the justice of the social system in which certain acts are treated as criminal. Suppose that I make explicit the ideal of justice that I endorse. This doesn't mean I am no longer objective. First of all, I believe, and I may try to show, that my ideal of justice is appropriate, not merely what I want or what serves my interests. Second and equally important is that, once I have stated my ideal of justice, I want to know objectively whether or to what extent that ideal is realized. If I misperceive or bend the facts because I want to show that the criminal justice system is unjust, I fool myself as much as anyone else. I am not honestly committed to my ideal of justice unless I am willing to apply it as objectively as I can.

I turn now to consider the special philosophical needs of criminology.

THE SPECIAL PHILOSOPHICAL NEEDS OF CRIMINOLOGY

I shall make three arguments aimed at showing that criminology has a special need for philosophical reflection. First, I will contend that criminology has such a need because it is a multidisciplinary study and thus requires an explanation for why crime is worthy of its own organized inquiry. Second, I will make the political argument for criminology's need for philosophy at which I hinted in my opening remarks. And, third, I will argue that the need for philosophy arises from the topic itself, that crime cannot be studied without coming to some judgment about its moral status, which requires philosophical reflection.

Turn first to the fact that criminology is a multidisciplinary mode of inquiry. The traditional disciplines, history or sociology or philosophy, are not defined by their topics. Rather than study *something* in the world, some problem or problem area, they study *everything*, but from a particular angle. Criminology is the reverse. It studies the problem area of crime and criminal justice, from a wide variety of angles. But, then, why *this* problem area?

What makes crime an interesting focus of study? That it is crime, or a violation of a rule, is not enough of an answer. Why not study people who cheat at solitaire, or those who arrive late for dates with friends, or drivers who fail to put on their turn signal before turning left, or folks who have bad manners, or speakers who say *ain't*? They are all rule violators. And these rule violations are all subject to penalties of some sort, but hardly worth devoting a special discipline to their study. What makes crime worthy of its own study?

Since the mere fact that crime is a rule violation does not earn it special treatment, the mere fact that it is a law violation will not do so either. Responding to this need for explanation requires you to say what you think crime is, such that it is an important occurrence in a society. Is crime a breakdown in social order, an alternative career route, a way of coping with acute need or insecurity, a rebellion against injustice, a cry for help, a form of play, a form of self-defense, an exciting walk on the wild side, a symptom of individual or social pathology, a label—and accompanying treatment—applied for political purposes? Choosing among alternatives like these requires you to say what you think a society is, such that crime is important to it. Is society a rational association among individuals, a site of conflict or consensus or of continual negotiation between the two; is it a mechanism of control of labor and resources, a struggle among classes, a pluralistic ragbag of interest groups?

I do not mean to suggest that these ways of thinking about crime and about society exhaust the possibilities. My point is that unless you have some thought like this about crime and society, you don't really have an answer to why crime is worth studying. And, then, you do not have an answer to why there should be a field of social inquiry devoted specially to the study of crime. A thought like this about crime is a theory of crime, and a theory of crime is a part of a theory of society. And a theory of society is a work of philosophizing.

To move now to the political dimension of the issue, consider this question: What's the difference between what criminologists do and what the FBI does in compiling the annual *Uniform Crime Report*? Both seek to amass and disseminate knowledge about crime; both chart trends and correlations. There are numerous differences, but one is, to my mind, of chief importance. The *UCR* simply accepts the legal system's definitions of crimes as well as the legal system's grading of their gravity. It needs no more; in fact, it would exceed its mandate if it varied from this. But criminology cannot simply accept the legal definition of crimes and the legal system's determination of their gravity, because criminology is not a branch of law or of the legal system.

Unless criminologists have their own view of what crime is and of what makes it especially important, if they simply study what the legal system calls crimes in the order of gravity the legal system assigns them, then criminology accepts the research agenda handed to it by the government. Criminology is then an arm of the state. Even if it comes up with some news that the state would rather not hear, it is doing the state's work, which is to amass and disseminate knowledge about law violations.

To affirm its intellectual independence from the state as a social science, criminology must look at crime while staying open to the idea that the legal definitions and, just as crucially, all the righteous beliefs that normally surround the legal enterprise are less than the whole truth, and perhaps even misleading or ideological. That means that criminology must keep its distance from the legal system as such, and that in turn requires that criminology seek its own understanding of what crime is. And I contend again that this requires a theory of crime, and a theory of crime is part of a theory of society, and a theory of society is a work of philosophizing.

You may think that this argument only amounts to showing that criminologists need a bit of social theory, which may be an interesting fact, but not very startling. You may think that social theory is a thing different from social philosophy, something that sociologists do rather than philosophers. I disagree. I think that social theorizing is philosophizing, but that doesn't mean that it can or should only be done by philosophers.

Every discipline has a place where it overlaps with philosophy, where its questions become philosophical questions. When art historians ask what art or beauty is, when psychologists ask what a mind is, when political scientists ask what a state is, and when sociologists or criminologists or anyone else asks what crime or society is, the questions they ask are philosophical ones. One clear reason that they are philosophical questions is that they are distinctively about the *validity* of norms or criteria—what makes the *Mona Lisa* beautiful, what makes a property mental rather than physical, when is a group a state, what should be prohibited by criminal law? To be sure, sociologists and others also study norms and criteria. Their focus is on the existence and consequences of norms and criteria. The questions that are distinctive to philosophy are those about the *justification* of norms and criteria. Philosophy aims to evaluate their credentials and, where those credentials pass muster, to defend the norms and criteria as valid ones.

That said, be clear that I do not think that philosophical questions can *only* be asked or competently answered by people with PhDs in philosophy. I think rather that whoever answers them should recognize that he or she is no longer in the realm of empirical scientific endeavor but is engaged in the conceptual and normative reflection that is properly philosophy's domain.

I do not want to leave the issue here. There is a dimension to the theorizing needed about crime that I think is uncontroversially philosophical. We reach this dimension by recognizing that crime is a *violation*, and not just any old violation. It is not just the sort of rule violation that is involved in saying *ain't* (or pronouncing *nuclear* "nuculer," as President Bush does). It's not the sort of violation that occurs when someone cheats at solitaire.

Because crime affects other people and often in very serious ways, it is a morally consequential act. And, as a result, you cannot say *what crime is* without taking a position on its moral status. That in turn will require a position on the moral obligation to obey the law. I am not saying that you must believe that the criminal does a moral wrong or violates a moral obligation. My point rather is that you must have *some* position on this. You cannot be neutral. If you are neutral, you treat crime as no different from any old rule violation, which is less than what crime is, and thus a distortion of your object of study.

This, then, is my third argument. Crime itself requires moral assessment. To be studied, it must be identified for what it is, and that includes its moral nature. Even if you do not think that criminals violate a moral obligation in committing crimes, you probably do think that many, if not most, crimes would, under normal circumstances, constitute immoral actions. After all, all crimes with victims violate the Golden Rule. The criminal does things to people that he wouldn't want done to him. And this is important. It constitutes, so to speak, the default position on the moral status of crimes. Suppose you think that violating laws against illicit drug use or prostitution involves no violation of a moral obligation. Then, you probably think that those acts should not be crimes. This implies that you assume that the sorts of things that should be crimes are the sorts of things the doing of which do violate moral obligations.

Or, suppose you think something rather radical, say, that inner-city violence against the police is not immoral because it is a kind of legitimate self-defense or even retribution. Even here, you are taking a position on the moral status of criminal acts. Most importantly, calling an act *self-defense* or *retribution* is a way of saying that an act that is normally immoral is morally permissible in light of what it is a response to. You are assuming that the same acts, if not done in self-defense or as retribution, would be immoral.

That is what I mean by saying that the view that crime is a moral violation is the default position. Crime is prima facie a moral violation; that is, it is a moral violation, unless reasons to the contrary can be given. To hold that crime is a moral violation is to affirm part, not just of a social theory of crime, but of a moral theory about what human beings owe to their fellows in the way of conduct. And, insofar as you affirm such a moral theory, not blindly, but after reflecting on its validity, you are squarely in philosophy's jurisdiction.

There's another way to make this argument. Many criminologists believe—as I do—that the legal catalogue of crimes is biased in certain ways; for example, it focuses on the acts of poor people, and ignores much of the antisocial behavior of the well-off. Those criminologists may also believe—as I do—that this bias weakens in some measure the obligations of the poor to obey the law. Other criminologists disagree on both the claim of bias and on the weakening of obligation, or they might accept one of these and not the other. What is this disagreement about?

Well, certainly, it is a disagreement about what should be crime. This is clearly a normative disagreement. In disagreeing about what should be crime, we are disagreeing more generally about what kind of conduct individual human beings owe to each other. This is a disagreement about the requirements of *interpersonal justice.* In disagreeing about how bias in the legal determination of crime affects the moral obligations of the victims of that bias, we are disagreeing about what society as a whole owes its members. This is a disagreement about the requirements of *social justice.* Both are philosophical disagreements that arise from trying to say what crime really is in the society that we are studying. And since all criminologists must believe that the definitions of crime are biased or that they aren't or that some are and some aren't, and they must believe as well that this does or does not weaken obligation, it follows that all criminologists must hold philosophical views that fill out their notions of what crime is. And the reflection that leads them to believe that these philosophical views are valid is philosophical reflection.

I turn now to the specific philosophic commitments that underlie *The Rich Get Richer and the Poor Get Prison.*

THE RICH GET RICHER AND THE POOR GET PHILOSOPHY

I got the idea for *The Rich Get Richer* while reading Richard Quinney's seminal work, *The Social Reality of Crime.*[6] That provocative book contended that crime was not some real, objective event in the world, but the creation of a labeling process, the crucial step in which was the definition of crimes by lawmakers. In short, crime has a social rather than a physical reality. What's more, Quinney held that this social reality was created in a politically biased way. Quinney contended that the labeling of some acts as crimes by lawmakers reflected the interests of the wealthy and powerful in the society at the expense of the rest. I found this conclusion very believable, but I was dissatisfied with the argument by which Quinney arrived at it. In effect, he contended that lawmakers were from the wealthy and powerful groups in society; that they tended to act in their own self-interest; and consequently, that the criminal laws they wrote must reflect their interests, which is to say, the interests of the wealthy and powerful and not the interests of the rest of society.[7]

This argument has the advantage of being neat and economical, but the disadvantage of being inconclusive. It assumes that, because people *tend* to act in their self-interest, then we can conclude of anything they do that it is in their self-interest. But, sometimes people act contrary to their self-interest. They may occasionally act to do their duty, or to do what they think is right. Think, for example, of people who risked their own lives and the lives of their families to hide Jews from the Nazis during the Second World War—it can happen that people are motivated to do the morally right thing! And it's just possible that lawmakers were doing this at the moment that they were writing criminal laws, even if in general they tend to act in their own interest.

Moreover, that something is in the interest of the wealthy and powerful doesn't entail that it is *not* in the interests of others. It might be that what is in one person's interest is also in that of others, such that when the one acts in his own self-interest, he serves the interests of the others in spite of himself. And this is arguably the case regarding the criminal law, since both wealthy people and poor ones have an interest in, say, not being robbed or murdered. Then, even if the wealthy and powerful draw up laws against robbery and murder to serve their own interests, they would be serving the interests of the rest of society at the same time.

To get to the politically critical conclusion that Quinney wanted to reach, a different sort of argument was needed. What sort? First of all, as I have been suggesting all along in this essay, it was necessary to take some distance from the legal system's list of crimes. That required establishing some normative standard of what *should* be crime, against which the actual legal definitions could be assessed as fair or biased. The normative standard with which I started in *The Rich Get Richer* was simple and uncontroversial. I contended that a criminal justice system ought to be protecting the lives and limbs and possessions of the citizenry, and thus that the legal list of crimes ought to follow this imperative. The most serious crimes should be the gravest threats to life, limb, or property; and the gravest threats to life, limb, or property should be the most serious crimes.

With this notion in mind, I looked at the most serious threats to life, limb, and property in society and compared them to the law's list of crimes. What I found was that, while the criminal law did label some of the greatest threats as crimes, many equally or even more dangerous acts were not treated as crimes: Either they were not labeled crimes, or they were not labeled serious crimes in proportion to the danger they threatened, or, if they were labeled serious crimes, they were rarely treated as such in practice. I noted as well that some acts labeled crimes did not seem to be threatening or dangerous to society at all—here I have in mind the so-called "victimless crimes" of voluntary recreational drug use by adults, consensual commercial sex, and so on.

This, in turn, led me to ask what the acts labeled crimes had in common and what the dangerous acts not labeled crimes had in common. And my conclusion was that the acts labeled crimes, instead of being all dangerous acts, were predominantly acts of the poor in society. And the dangerous acts not labeled crime were predominantly acts of the well-off. With these conclusions, I could show that Quinney's conclusion was indeed largely correct: The law's definitions of crimes serve the interests of the wealthy and powerful at the expense of the rest of society. I say *largely correct* because there are crimes in the law's list that are acts that threaten the poor (the FBI's Index crimes certainly do), and there are dangerous acts of the well-off that are occasionally treated as serious crimes (as Enron's Andrew Fastow and WorldCom's Bernard Ebbers are currently learning). But *largely correct* is correct enough to support the critical conclusion.

My point here is that reaching this conclusion required a reflection on what crime is that could not rest satisfied with legal or conventional understandings. It had to be a normative, and thus philosophical, reflection on what crime should be in order to compare reality to this and find it lacking. The route from what acts are and are not crimes to the conclusion that the legal definitions of crime serve the interests of the wealthy and powerful had to pass through a theory of what *should* be crime. In sum, the social inquiry that leads to the view defended in *The Rich Get Richer*, namely, that the criminal justice system is economically biased against the poor, relies on an irreducibly normative and thus philosophical conception of crime.

Moreover, this conception of crime was not simply pulled out of a hat. It was the product of philosophical reflection. This philosophical conception of crime is based on an equally philosophical conception of social and political justice. I contend that the ways in which the coercive apparatus of the law is used must be justified in principle to all citizens. This is so for three reasons.

First, both our tradition and our social order take freedom—the right of sane adults to do what they want—as a paramount value. Freedom is important because people tend to enjoy acting as they wish, and because it is the necessary condition of having a life that can be seen as one's own accomplishment, a life of which one can be proud. Without freedom, we are playing out a script of which we are not the author. Freedom is also important as a source of new ideas and creativity and thus of social progress. For these reasons and others, I start with the idea that freedom is a great value and thus that those who would limit it owe a satisfactory justification to those whose freedom is to be limited.

Second, on the social contract tradition in political and moral philosophy (which is enshrined in the *Declaration of Independence*) and, indeed, on any democratic view, the coercive power of the state—police, prisons, and so on—represents the people's own power, and thus can only legitimately be used for the people's own purposes. Consequently, the exercise of that power must be justifiable to the people in terms of their own purposes.

Third, the legal system appeals to the citizens morally, that is, it implicitly and explicitly asserts that the citizens are morally obligated to comply with it. But, on the contract model, obligation is a matter of owing fair compensation for benefits one receives. And, thus, only laws that benefit people can obligate people. Ultimately, this has to be cashed out individually, because it is as individuals that we are obligated or not. The law must benefit me, protect me against something that really threatens me, for me to be morally obligated to obey it. The law must serve people's interests to be morally binding on them. And thus the claim of the law to morally obligate citizens requires that it be justifiable to them in light of their interests.

This is not the whole story. I am, for example, also benefited by the fact that the law is the product of a democratic process, whose benefits are only available on the assumption that laws will be binding even on those who do not approve of them or find them in their interest. And, I am benefited by order itself, by the predictability and regularity of my fellow citizens' conduct that come of their obeying the law even if they are unhappy with it. Consequently, the argument as to whether I am or am not obligated to a particular law starts with consideration of whether it serves an interest I have, but it doesn't end there. Even if a particular law doesn't benefit me, some weight must be given to the fact that democratic lawmaking systems are beneficial generally, and order is as well, and that both democracy and order require people to accept laws which they don't think serve their interests. Nonetheless, if a law or a whole legal system significantly veers from serving all citizens' interests and toward serving the interests of some segment of society at the expense of the rest, the weight of democracy and order will not be enough to preserve the obligatory nature of the law. That veering away from serving all citizens' interests will weaken, if not eliminate, the obligations of those whose interests are served less or not at all.

This is the philosophical reflection that underlies the simpler claim that the criminal law should be protecting citizens' life and limb and possessions generally. Because it must serve all citizens' interests, a just legal order must criminalize behavior that threatens the interests of all citizens, and it must do so in proportion to the gravity of the threat posed. It must not be protecting citizens only or even mainly against threats posed by the poor, while leaving the threats posed by the wealthy either untouched or only lightly grazed. This philosophical argument also creates a presumption against the legitimacy of laws against victimless crimes because laws that criminalize actions that do not clearly have victims—actions that some people detest but others accept—will surely appear to many in society as nothing more than the majority building its moral preferences into the law with no more justification than that they are the majority. Large numbers of citizens will tend not to view themselves as obligated by such laws and, in my view, they will often be correct. Thus, not only does my argument pass through a normative theory of crime, but also that theory is itself based on a theory of social justice.

Moreover, since a theory of crime is part of a theory of society, this conception of crime reflects a conception of how society works that is, to my mind, equally a matter of philosophical reflection. Basically, my view of U.S. society is that it works roughly the way Marx supposed it would. It is dominated by the capitalist mode of production, which brings with it a crucial class divide between those who own means of production and those who don't. This has the consequence that, in a certain significant sense, the nonowners are forced to work for the owners. The divide between owners and nonowners amounts to an inequality in power between the two classes, which goes far toward explaining what is and what is not treated as crime in capitalist societies.

However, the Marxian view has even richer resources for explaining this bias. It holds that the capitalist mode of production is accompanied by an ideology, the core of which is blindness to the coerciveness of ownership of means of production vis-à-vis nonowners.[8] I believe, by the way, that, within these coercive relations, a capitalist economy works pretty much the way neoclassical economists—such as Milton Friedman—think it does (and Marx generally believed this as well). This accounts for the general success of neoclassical economics, while its blindness to the coerciveness explains how neoclassical economics can be ideological even as it accurately describes market tendencies.

Blindness to the coerciveness of private ownership of means of production is not primarily due to active deception by those in power. It is rather the way in which capitalism normally looks to its participants who view it, so to speak, up close. The illusion that capitalist transactions are fully free is similar to the illusion that the sun goes around the earth—it's just what you'd expect people to see from where they are standing. Up close, the fact that capitalists, unlike feudal lords or slave owners, cannot use violence to get people to work for them makes the transactions between owners and nonowners of means of production appear free. They are, of course, free in important ways, but not as free as they seem. Workers are free to choose among capitalists, but not free to avoid working for one of them after all (leaving aside the marginal alternatives, working for the church or the government, stealing, or begging—and, for the few who have the initiative and willingness to sacrifice as well as plenty of luck, the possibility of going into business on one's own).

Since most of the ways that the wealthy pose dangers to the rest of society are as threats either to employees (subjecting them to preventable occupational hazards) or to consumers (subjecting them to shoddy products or to higher prices due to corporate skullduggery), blindness to the coerciveness of capitalism makes it appear as if employees and consumers—who are, of course, the same people—have signed on freely to the risks involved. Consequently, those responsible for these threats don't seem like criminals, because criminals characteristically force dangers on their victims. In light of the coerciveness of capitalism, however, this difference is largely illusory: For all intents and purposes, occupational harms are forced on workers (they must choose among the jobs that are available), and product risks as well as corporate financial shenanigans are forced on consumers (they must choose among the products that are available, and they must pay for the losses due to corporate misdeeds when they are passed on in the form of higher prices). Nonetheless, the law in capitalism continues the illusion by focusing mainly on one-on-one theft and violence, while deadlier preventable occupational hazards as well as consumer risks and costlier financial misdeeds are usually treated as regulatory matters. Consequently, the Marxian view will lead us to expect just the bias in the legal definition of crimes that *The Rich Get Richer* documents.

I should add that my Marxism is tempered by recognition of two interconnected failings in Marxian analysis. One is the failure to see how dangerous to human freedom socialism could be, even though there is a good Marxian reason for expecting socialism to be dangerous. If ownership of the means of production is the main instrument of coercion in a society, one must have a very idealistic view of human beings to be willing to place that instrument of coercion, whole and entire, into the hands of a single institution, the government. Socialism only has a chance of being a truly liberating social form for a society in which democracy is already very well developed, and in which citizens are already extremely sophisticated about the exercise of their democratic power. This leads me to believe that the likelihood of a truly liberating socialism is way off in the future. For the foreseeable future, the future in which we are all likely to live and die, I can see no truly liberating alternative to capitalism. And, sad to say, the current and recent examples of socialism—China, North Korea, and the former Soviet Union—confirm this bleak conclusion.

On the other hand, there is a good Marxian reason to expect capitalism to maintain individual freedom. As a system of multiple competing owners of means of production, capitalism distributes the main instrument of social coercion among a multiplicity of separate agents. Thus, capitalism maintains a space for individual freedom that results, not from an enlightened citizenry or officialdom, but rather from the material conditions of capitalist production itself. In a kind of Madisonian fashion, the multiple competing owners each have an interest in resisting the control of the economy by other firms and thus in keeping the market generally open and the government in a wide variety of hands. Moreover, capitalism does, as Marx very explicitly noted, create enormous technological progress that reduces unwanted toil and increases the material income of the workers. The impoverishment to which Marx thought capitalism led is a matter of workers' decreasing relative share of the product of their labor—but, since this is caused by the fact that labor under capitalism becomes increasingly productive, this share buys more and more goods.

To be sure, capitalism is also a system that generates large (and, recently, growing) inequalities, which in turn give some people great power to determine the way others live. That is, capitalism not only makes some people richer than others, but also makes some people freer than others. Moreover, capitalism subjects all of us, but the poor most of all, to forces and developments beyond our control, making life uncertain for most and painful for many. These facts, taken together with the dangerousness of socialism and the freedom-maintaining tendency of capitalism, mean that Marxism implies of capitalism roughly what Winston Churchill said of democracy, namely, that it is the worst form of economic system, except for all the others.

The second failing in Marxian analysis offers some compensation for this conclusion, which some readers may find too dismal. The second failing is that of not seeing how progressive capitalism is culturally, that is, in the dimension that Marx called the *relations of production*. Marx and Marxists saw clearly that capitalism is progressive with respect to the *means of production*, that is, the development and implementation of labor-saving technology. But, Marx and Marxists did not (though Marx did more so than Marxists) see that capitalism is also progressive with respect to the relations of production, that is, *the growth and spread of liberal values and institutions*.

Under these, I include the preference for greater personal freedom (tending toward the requirement of harm as a justification for restricting freedom, and against victimless crimes or other restraints based on faith or tradition or custom), the inclination toward using rational criteria for evaluating people (tending toward use of merit and conduct to judge people rather than race or gender or creed or age), and the insistence on more effective and responsive government (demanding freedom to vote and the progressive extension of eligibility to vote, freedom to assemble, and the rest). These progressive tendencies are, of course, very imperfectly realized. Nonetheless, that does not mean that they are unimportant or without effect. I think that Jürgen Habermas has gone some distance toward integrating this progressive dimension of capitalism's liberal culture into Marxian theory.[9]

The second failing is connected to the first in several ways. One way of explaining why existing or recent socialist societies have been as unattractive as they have is that they embraced capitalist technology without embracing capitalist liberalism. Socialists failed to realize that socialism itself is sure to be oppressive unless it is staffed by officials who are deeply imbued with liberal values, and held democratically accountable by a populace that is equally so imbued.

But the second failing has a bright side as well. In recognizing the progressiveness of capitalism with regard to the relations of production, we can see a way in which the fact that we are probably stuck with capitalism for our lives and beyond presents a special opportunity. Capitalism produces the cultural tools needed to push it to become fairer. The struggle to make people freer and more equal is a struggle to make capitalism live up to its own liberal ideals. And, there is reason to hope that this struggle can succeed, since the values that guide it are the very ones affirmed by cultural institutions within capitalism.

This, to my mind, locates *The Rich Get Richer and the Poor Get Prison* in philosophical space. *It is a radical critique of criminal justice in capitalism that works by confronting capitalist criminal justice with capitalism's own liberal moral philosophy.*

NOTES

1. This paper is a revised version of my article of the same title appearing in the *Journal of Law* 1 (2004): pp. 42–58, which in turn was a revised version of my keynote address to the second annual conference of the Canadian Society of Criminology, Toronto, April 1, 2004.

2. For its relevance to Canadian criminal justice, see, for example, Stuart Henry, "Law Commission of Canada's Discussion Paper 'What Is a Crime?' A Commentary on the Issue of Power," paper presented at the annual meeting of the American Society of Criminology, Denver, November, 19–22, 2003.

3. *Ontology* is the philosophical study of what is real. An ontological skeptic about society doubts that society exists, and an ontological agnostic about society believes we cannot know if society exists.

4. *Epistemology* is the philosophical study of what knowledge is and how or if it is possible. An epistemological skeptic about social science doubts that social science provides knowledge; an epistemological agnostic about social science believes that we cannot know whether social science provides knowledge.

5. See, for example, Julie R. Solomon, *Objectivity in the Making: Francis Bacon and the Politics of Inquiry* (Baltimore: Johns Hopkins University Press, 1998).

6. Richard Quinney, *The Social Reality of Crime* (Boston: Little, Brown, 1970).

7. Quinney, *Social Reality*, p. 15 inter alia; and see the section entitled "Criminal Justice as Creative Art" in Chapter 2 of the present book.

8. This analysis of Marxian theory and its relationship to the issue of what is and what is not treated as crime in capitalist societies is developed in Appendix I to this book, "The Marxian Critique of Criminal Justice." That appendix is a shorter version of an article that was originally published in *Criminal Justice Ethics* 6, no. 1 (Winter–Spring 1987): pp. 30–50.

9. See, for example, Jürgen Habermas, *Communication and the Evolution of Society* (Boston: Beacon Press, 1979), esp. chs. 4 and 5.

INDEX